Intellectuals in Politics

What has been the role of intellectuals in the twentieth-century and what, if any, will be their role in the future? Frequently scorned and reviled, intellectuals have nevertheless played a vital part in shaping our century. From their original intervention in the Dreyfus affair to the case of Salman Rushdie, intellectuals have aroused controversy.

Jeremy Jennings and Anthony Kemp-Welch edit a collection of essays from leading academics in the fields of political theory, philosophy, history and sociology. After their introduction on the major issues confronting intellectuals the book explores the various different aspects of the intellectual's role including:

- how to define the role and function of the intellectual
- how intellectuals have assumed the status of the conscience of the nation and the voice of the oppressed
- the interaction of intellectuals with Marxism
- the place of the intellectual in American society

Covering countries as diverse as Israel, Algeria, Britain, Ireland, France, Germany, Poland, Russia and America, this collection considers the question of whether the intellectual can still lay claim to the language of truth. In addressing this question *Intellectuals in Politics* tells us much about the modern world in which we live.

Jeremy Jennings is Reader in Political Theory at the University of Birmingham.

Anthony Kemp-Welch is the Dean of the School of Economic and Social Studies at the University of East Anglia.

Intellectuals in Politics

From the Dreyfus Affair to Salman Rushdie

Edited by Jeremy Jennings and Anthony Kemp-Welch

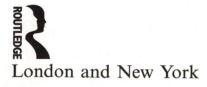

London and New York

First published 1997
by Routledge
11 New Fetter Lane, London EC4P 4EE

Simultaneously published in the USA and Canada
by Routledge
29 West 35th Street, New York, NY 10001

Typeset in Times by Routledge
Printed and bound in Great Britain by Biddles Ltd, Guildford and King's Lynn

British Library Cataloguing in Publication Data
A catalogue record for this book is available from the British Library

Library of Congress Cataloguing in Publication Data
Intellectuals in politics: from the Dreyfus Affair to Salman Rushdie/edited
by Jeremy Jennings and Anthony Kemp-Welch.
1. Intellectuals – Political activity – History – 20th century. I. Jennings, Jeremy,
1952– . II. Kemp-Welch, A., 1949– .
HM213.I5474 1997
305.5'52-dc21

96–47160
CIP

ISBN 0–415–14995–9 (hbk)
ISBN 0–415–14996–7 (pbk)

Contents

Part III Slavonic jesters

Part IV American agnostics

Epilogue

Contributors

Edward Acton is Professor of Modern European History at the University of East Anglia. He is the author of *Alexander Herzen and the Role of the Intellectual Revolutionary* (1979), *Russia: The Present and the Past* (1986) and *Rethinking the Russian Revolution* (1990). A revised and expanded edition of his history of Russia has been published as *Russia: the Tsarist and Soviet legacy* (1995).

Lahouari Addi is Professor of Politics at the Université de Lyon II. He is the author of *État et Pouvoir* (1990), *L'impasse du populisme* (1991) and *L'Algérie et la démocratie* (1994). He is a regular contributor to *Le Monde* on Algerian affairs.

Richard Bellamy is Professor of Politics at the University of Reading. His many publications include: *Modern Italian Social Theory* (1987), *Liberalism and Modern Society* (1992) and *Gramsci and the Italian State* (1993).

Steven Biel teaches at Harvard University. He is the author of *Independent Intellectuals in the United States, 1910–1945* (1992) and *Down with the Old Canoe: A Cultural History of the Titanic Disaster* (1996).

George Boyce is Professor of Politics at the University of Wales, Swansea. He is the author of *The Irish Question and British Politics* (1988), *Nineteenth-Century Ireland: The Search for Stability* (1990), *Nationalism in Ireland* (1991), *Ireland, 1828–1923: From Ascendancy to Democracy* (1992) and co-editor of *Political Thought in Ireland since the Seventeenth Century* (1993).

George Cotkin is Professor of History at Cal Poly State University, San Luis Obispo. He is the author of *William James, Public Philosopher* (1990) and *Reluctant Modernism: American Thought and Culture, 1880–1900* (1992). He is currently working on an intellectual and cultural history of existentialism in America.

Neil Harding is Professor of Politics at the University of Wales, Swansea. He is the author of *Lenin's Political Thought* (1983), winner of the Isaac Deutscher Memorial Prize, and editor of *Marxism in Russia* (1983) and *The State in Socialist Society* (1984).

Martin Hollis is Professor of Philosophy at the University of East Anglia and a Fellow of the British Academy. He is the author of many books, amongst the most recent of which are *The Cunning of Reason* (1989) and *The Philosophy of the Social Sciences* (1994).

Jeremy Jennings is Reader in Political Theory at the University of Birmingham. He is the author of *Georges Sorel* (1985) and *Syndicalism in France: A History of Ideas* (1990), and editor of *Intellectuals in Twentieth-Century France: Mandarins and Samurais* (1993).

Tony Kemp-Welch is Senior Lecturer in Politics and International Relations at the University of East Anglia. He is the author of *The Birth of Solidarity* (1991), *Stalin and the Literary Intelligentsia* (1994) and *editor of The Ideas of Nikolai Bukharin* (1992).

Shlomo Sand is Professor in the Department of History at the University of Tel Aviv and Associate Professor at the Ecole des Hautes Etudes en Sciences Sociales, Paris. He is the author of *L'Illusion du politique* (1985) and (with Jacques Julliard) of *Georges Sorel en son temps* (1985). He is the editor of a recently published collection of the writings of Bernard Lazare.

David Schalk is Professor of History at Vassar College and Visiting Professor at the University of Columbia and the Institute of French Studies at NYU. He is the author of *Roger Martin du Gard: The Novelist and History* (1967), *The Spectrum of Political Engagement* (1979) and *War and the Ivory Tower: Algeria and Vietnam* (1991).

Alan Scott is Senior Lecturer in Sociology at the University of East Anglia. He is the author of *Ideology and New Social Movements* (1990), co-author of *The Uncertain Science* (1992) and editor of *The Limits of Globalization* (1997).

1   The century of the intellectual
From the Dreyfus Affair to Salman Rushdie

Jeremy Jennings and Tony Kemp-Welch

Every year the BBC organizes a series of lectures in London. Dating from 1948, when they were first given by Bertrand Russell, the Reith Lectures are a major event in British cultural life and generally lead to wider public discussion. In 1993 the person chosen to present these lectures was Edward Said: his subject was the role of the intellectual.

Said is a fascinating figure. A Palestinian Christian, educated in Cairo, he is now Professor of English and Comparative Literature at Columbia University. When his lectures referred to the intellectual in exile there was a clear element of autobiography. Moreover, Professor Said's academic interest in intellectuals is of long-standing. Ten years earlier he had described them as a 'class badly in need today of moral rehabilitation and social redefinition'[1] and he vigorously restated this view in his widely read *Culture and Imperialism*.[2] There, the argument was directed against the American intellectual cocooned in the 'munificence' and 'Utopian sanctuary' of the American university campus. The professionalization of intellectual life, Said contended, was such that the 'true' intellectual had all but disappeared, leaving the landscape to be dominated by 'policy-oriented intellectuals' who had internalized the norms of the state. This was most obviously the case in foreign policy where the necessity of American use of force and the ultimate justice of its cause was never to be questioned. Wider social and economic issues, such as racism, poverty, ecological disaster and disease were now thought to be none of the intellectual's concern. Intellectuals had been 'defanged' and their task had been reduced to that of the 'manufacturing of consent'.

Not surprisingly, therefore, Said's lectures were, in part, a contemporary restatement of Julien Benda's classic definition of the intellectual: the guardian and possessor of independent judgement owing loyalty to truth alone.[3] This 'compelling and attractive' portrait, Said told his audience, reveals:

> the figure of the intellectual as a being set apart, someone able to speak the truth, a...courageous and angry individual for whom no worldly power is too big and imposing to be criticised and pointedly taken to task.

The real or 'true' intellectual is therefore always an outsider, living in self-imposed exile and on the margins of society. He or she speaks to, as well as for, a public, necessarily in public, and is properly on the side of the dispossessed, the unrepresented and the forgotten.

In support of his argument, Said referred to an impressive body of literature on the role of the intellectual. While Benda received pride of place, he also cited Régis Debray, Antonio Gramsci, C. Wright Mills, Frantz Fanon, Theodor Adorno, Noam Chomsky, and many more. All are marshalled to justify Said's central contention that the intellectual must above all avoid an unquestioning subservience to the state. Yet, if the nature and character of Said's polemic merits our attention (and will be explored later), first we enquire why such a subject arose at all. For Said himself, an exiled academic born into a community that has suffered years of oppression, a preoccupation with the responsibility and commitment of the intellectual is not unduly difficult to understand. But why should the BBC be prepared to broadcast seven lectures on the subject, week by week, in a country that has traditionally conceived the intellectual to be someone foreign and alien? Whence came the interest and why?

A typical retort to the lectures came from the historian Norman Stone. 'The multi-purpose intellectual', he commented, 'is one of the great pains in the neck of the modern age. If ever you had a class of people who got things badly wrong, it was the writers.'[4] Such a strident contempt for the intellectual as one doomed to error and to stupidity has its roots deep in a British empirical tradition stretching back at least two centuries and which stipulates that it is experience rather than abstract ideas, the supposed currency of the intellectual, that offers the surer guide to social and political practice. Thus, Edmund Burke berated the French Revolutionaries for their willingness to follow the precepts of the *philosophes*, with 'civil and military anarchy made the constitution of France'. Two hundred years later, Mrs Thatcher said much the same thing when in her memoirs she described the French Revolution as 'a Utopian attempt to overthrow a traditional order...in the name of abstract ideas, formulated by vain intellectuals'.[5]

Faced with such disdain at home, the British intellectual has often resorted to a dignified but disenchanted cultural despair, a deep antipathy to what has been seen as the selfish and mercantile civilization of the age. Matthew Arnold, always an admirer of French intellectuality and a fierce critic of English philistinism, is one example.[6] A more extreme case would be Oscar Wilde. A second strategy, in which the contrast with the French model of the critical intellectual is most marked, has been one of taming and domestication. Intellectuals have been integrated into the political establishment, often by common educational backgrounds and shared social contexts, frequently cemented by membership of that quintessentially British institution, the gentleman's club. In the nineteenth century this meant that many intellectuals played the role of 'public moralists'. As Stefan Collini writes:

Well-connected Victorian intellectuals persuaded themselves they had a special duty to remind their more self-interested contemporaries of the strenuous commitments entailed by the moral values embedded in the public discourse of their society.[7]

A variant of this model is that delineated by Julia Stapleton in her excellent study of the British political scientist, Sir Ernest Barker.[8] Described is the 'national intellectual' whose self-appointed task was to spread the literary culture of the educated minority to a wider popular audience, with the aim of strengthening social unity. In addition to Barker himself, cited as examples are R. G. Collingwood, A. D. Lindsay and William Beveridge. The pattern of integration also impinged directly upon political practice. Many intellectuals of standing – R. H. Tawney, G. D. H. Cole, Sidney and Beatrice Webb, Leonard Woolf, Harold Laski and Dick Crossman – exercised their influence primarily through and within the Labour Party and its satellites such as the Fabian Society. The oppositional and independent stance of a Bertrand Russell or George Orwell was always less typical.

It is the second strategy, working from within existing institutions rather than adopting a confrontational approach, which gave rise to the idea that behind Britain's long-standing (and once much-admired) political consensus lay what came to be described as a left-conspiracy of social-democratic, liberal and socialist intellectuals. Here, it was argued with increasing frequency and vehemence, was one of the major sources of Britain's post-war decline.

Elected to power in 1979, Mrs Thatcher, in her headlong pursuit of the conservative revolution and the reform of Britain's ancient institutions, could not resist the possibility of disinheriting those she and her acolytes came increasingly to regard as the 'chattering classes', an intellectual establishment that, in their view, dominated Britain's universities, arts world, civil service, higher journalism, the BBC, and even the Church of England. Except for the significant minority that rallied to her cause and who were prepared to fight the battle of ideas on her behalf, most intellectuals responded with ill-disguised loathing, viewing her as philistine, suburban, vulgar, middle-brow and, at bottom, simply uncultured. Indeed, one of the few electoral defeats Mrs Thatcher suffered came in 1985 when the University of Oxford ungraciously voted *not* to award her an honorary doctorate as past practice and tradition dictated.[9] Here is not the place to review Mrs Thatcher's (nor her government's) complicated relationship with the world of ideas, nor to assess the impact of her policies upon Britain's intellectual life in general, but two consequences of her refusal to worship the dethroned intellectual are worthy of mention.

Faced with a government that, its critics claimed, was prepared to use every means at its disposal to defeat its opponents – including the 'enemy within' – and which in so doing showed scant regard for the rights of individual citizens, intellectuals in Britain – arguably for the first time since the 'Auden generation' of the 1930s – came in significant numbers to adopt a self-consciously political and public stance. While still more reticent than their French counterparts to appear in the media (and especially on the television screen), intellectuals such as the playwrights Harold Pinter and Tom Stoppard nevertheless found themselves orchestrating campaigns for institutional reform and articulating political agendas. Pinter's Charter 88 group called (and continues to call) for the reform of Britain's constitution and the introduction of a written Bill of Rights. Stoppard became intimately involved in the defence of Salman Rushdie.

It is the latter case that has been most symbolic of the changed role of the intellectual in Britain over the last decade or more.[10] Unsure of support from a government where both Mrs Thatcher and her Foreign Secretary, Sir Geoffrey Howe, showed themselves prepared to utter words of apology and regret for the 'offence' caused by the publication of *The Satanic Verses* and in an atmosphere where, in his own country, there were those willing to argue that Rushdie was 'arrogant', 'a dangerous opportunist', and 'a multiple renegade',[11] the author had little alternative but to turn to his fellow writers and intellectuals for aid and moral support. Some, though by no means all, were prepared to give it. It is this that provides the context for and interest in Edward Said's lectures.

But the tardiness of the British response to the threats made on Rushdie's life derived not just from a misplaced self-interest of the government of the day but also from the fact that in Britain there has been no widespread acceptance of the legitimacy of the central political role of the writer/ intellectual in society. This brings us to the second consequence of the anti-intellectualism associated with Mrs Thatcher and her government.

Ironically, few modern British prime ministers have been so conscious of the importance of ideas and have so surrounded themselves by academics as Mrs Thatcher. Yet her coterie of admirers and enthusiasts – for the most part drawn from the London School of Economics and Peterhouse, Cambridge, or from such journals as *The Spectator* and the *Sunday Telegraph* – have steadfastly regarded the intellectual as both un-British and anti-British. Thus, in parallel to the Conservative government's political assault upon the bastions of intellectual power and privilege, took place a sustained re-examination of the role of the intellectual viewed from the perspective of the ideologues of the Right. Two examples merit our attention.

The first is Paul Johnson's *Intellectuals*, published originally in 1988 (and now available in French as *Le grand mensonge des intellectuels: vices privés et vertus publiques*).[12] The French title alone is sufficient to indicate the force of Johnson's argument. 'I think I detect today', Johnson writes in his conclusion:

> a certain public scepticism when intellectuals stand up to preach to us, a growing tendency among ordinary people to dispute the right of

academics, writers and philosophers, eminent though they may be, to tell us how to behave and conduct our affairs. The belief seems to be spreading that intellectuals are no wiser as mentors, or worthier as exemplars, than the witch doctors or priests of old.

It is unclear upon what evidence this assessment is based but the argument is easy to follow: judge intellectuals not upon what they write but upon what they do. Thus, in turn, are dissected the private lives and personal foibles of Rousseau, Shelley, Marx, Ibsen, Tolstoy, Hemingway, Brecht, Russell, and later lesser figures such as Edmund Wilson, Lillian Hellman, Norman Mailer, James Baldwin, Frantz Fanon and Rainer Werner Fassbinder. The attention almost always falls upon their sex lives. So we are invited to dismiss whatever Rousseau might have said about education on the grounds of his treatment of his own children. Marx's writings are without value because he appears to have fathered an illegitimate child. But, in fact, the argument goes deeper.

Intellectuals are seen as being as unreasonable, illogical, selfish and superstitious as anyone else. In their passion for radical, absolutist solutions they are – despite their profession of the importance of the word – also drawn ineluctably towards an endorsement of violence. This, Johnson contends, is 'the great crux of the intellectual life'. Echoing (presumably unwittingly) Ferdinand Brunetière's original remarks about the inability of a professor of Tibetan to instruct his fellow citizens about politics, Johnson disputes the right of the intellectual to move out of his or her own subject and into the realm of public affairs. This, he concedes, we have been too ready to accept, and with dire consequences. 'One of the principal lessons of our tragic century', Johnson remarks, 'which has seen so many millions of innocent lives sacrificed in schemes to improve the lot of humanity is – beware intellectuals!'

The intellectual then stands accused not just of hypocrisy but of perpetrating a despotism and tyranny of ideas. The faults in the logic of Johnson's argument are too numerous to mention: rather what matters is that his views are broadly representative of a wider anti-intellectualism in contemporary Britain.

Our second example is of much greater sophistication: *The Intellectuals and the Masses*,[13] by John Carey, Professor of English in the University of Oxford and principal book reviewer for the conservative *The Sunday Times*. An immediate best-seller when first published in July 1992, the book itself is a full-blooded assault upon the prejudices, pretensions and elitism of the British intelligentsia in the period after 1880 when, it is argued, intellectuals first became troubled by the accession of the masses to complete social power. In truth, Carey often hits his target: the likes of Virginia Woolf, George Bernard Shaw, H. G. Wells, D. H. Lawrence and E. M. Forster. Enthusiastically detailed is their loathing for the suburbs, for such lowly figures as the office clerk, for the popular press and for the people as an inert, uncultured dead mass. Modernist literary culture (of the type associated with T. S. Eliot and Virginia Woolf's Bloomsbury set) was self-consciously obscure, Carey argues, so as to exclude the masses. The proclaimed hero of the book is the novelist Arnold Bennett, plebeian, populist, always drawing sustenance from the people and their innocent pleasures. 'What Bennett seeks', Carey remarks, 'are the depths that lie within ordinary, not-particularly-intelligent people'.

Not surprisingly, therefore, Carey makes reference to Virginia Woolf's famous essay *Mr Bennett and Mrs Brown* and her contention that Arnold Bennett was only capable of describing the external detail of conventional characters. The implicit snobbery of Woolf's position, Carey points out, is evident when the socialist and feminist Virginia Woolf 'distinguishes the modern from the Victorian age by reference to the changes observable in the character of "one's cook" '. Thereafter, Carey, in a series of easy steps, manages to take the reader from the liberal E. M. Forster to the cult of the Nietzschean Superman, and from the futurist, anti-democratic Wyndham Lewis (described as the 'intellectual's intellectual') and to the 'intellectual' Hitler whose 'cultural ideals', it is stated, were those of Europe's avant-garde intellectuals. Having told us that dreaming of the extermination and sterilization of the masses or denying that the masses were real people was a typical response of the early twentieth-century intellectual, the way is then clear to state that 'the tragedy of *Mein Kampf* is that it was not, in many respects, a deviant work but one firmly rooted in European intellectual orthodoxy'. The conclusion is simple: it is the intellectuals who are ultimately responsible for the Holocaust.[14] Reviewed in the *Observer*, Peter Conrad commented: 'Belatedly, and perhaps unwittingly, *The Intellectual and the Masses* is an apology for the vendetta conducted against our culture during the 1980s by the Baroness from Finchley'.[15]

To resume: when we address our subject in the British context, it is one in which we have been invited to be frightened and scornful of intellectuals. But the contours of anti-intellectualism are readily found elsewhere. At times it can be rather amusing, as when one of the characters in Woody Allen's *Stardust Memories* remarks: 'Intellectuals are like the mafia. They only kill their own.' It can also take a surprisingly familiar form. Irving Kristol's neo-conservative diatribes against the 'intellectuals and artists' of America and how they subvert bourgeois society with their discontents and fantasies sits easily alongside the rhetoric of Johnson, Carey and other British conservatives.[16] Elsewhere, as Umberto Eco has commented, distrust of the intellectual 'has always been a symptom of Ur-Fascism', be it in statements by Goebbels or references to 'degenerate intellectuals', 'eggheads' and so on.[17] On an altogether different scale is the systematic imprisonment and murder of intellectuals that invariably accompanies the birth and subsequent existence of tyrannical regimes. Today this is given dramatic and bloody illustration in Algeria where the mass of the population are indifferent to their fate.

QUESTIONS OF ORIGIN

What are the origins of this intellectual who provokes so much hatred and dislike? By common consent, the word *intellectual*, used as a noun to describe a particular kind of person, enters into Western European usage at the end of the nineteenth century with the Dreyfus Affair in France. Earlier references can be found, even in Britain. Raymond Williams, for example, cites the poet Byron in 1813 saying: 'I wish I may be well enough to listen to these intellectuals'.[18] But in the late nineteenth-century European sense, the word took on a more specific connotation. This arose from the fact that intellectuals – in this case writers such as Emile Zola, André Gide, Marcel Proust and Anatole France – were prepared to intervene in the public sphere of politics and to protest in the name of Justice in order to secure the release of the innocent Captain Alfred Dreyfus.[19] It was therefore the *action* of intervening in politics by intellectuals that was constitutive of the definition of the noun.

It was from the outset deployed as a term of abuse (by, for example, Brunetière and Maurice Barrès) to describe the unwarranted and groundless intrusion by *déracinés* into matters which were none of their business and upon which they had nothing sound to say. Moreover, this identification of the origin of the term with the specific historical event of the Dreyfus Affair also makes it difficult to speak, as frequently occurs, of Enlightenment intellectuals, Victorian intellectuals, and (especially) medieval intellectuals without some caution. That this is so is reflected in the fact that the meaning of the word in the sense described above is itself parasitic upon the broader sociological definition that refers to those who by profession and occupation are engaged in 'intellectual', as opposed to 'manual', labour. While, in the context of this volume, it is not the sociological definition of the intellectual that is normally being referred to, we do recognize that the intellectual's emergence in the limited political sense was not only contingent upon a dramatic extension of the opportunities for intellectual labour in the nineteenth century, but also upon a pattern of development characterized by a progressive extension over a period of at least three centuries of their independence from such established institutions as the Church and the State.

Turning to Eastern Europe, we see a starker picture of intellectuals in opposition to an autocratic state. As Maxim Gorky put it in 1902, 'a Russian writer should never live in friendship with a Russian government'. When the State acted, the writer submitted its policies to critical scrutiny. When, as was more normal, the State did nothing, the writers tried to goad it into activity. But, though in opposition to the political authorities, the Russian intellectuals of the later nineteenth century found themselves increasingly critical of Russian society, and saw in its backwardness, ignorance and violence rich material for literary expression. Caught in a limbo between state and society, such writer-critics began to be regarded as an *intelligentsia*, whose rootlessness was treated as a unique vantage point from which to survey and articulate the 'social interest' as a whole. To the frequent charge that the intelligentsia lacked conviction, it liked to reply that 'on the contrary, only we are free to have intellectual convictions', untrammelled by social or financial position. Despite numerous cases of compromise with the authorities, the notion developed that the intelligentsia occupied a unique position as custodian of cultural and ethical values against the infringements of the State. Although the term cannot be equated solely with 'left-wing' opposition, it was in politics that it had the most vital consequences, the outcome of which, it would scarcely be an exaggeration to say, was the Russian Revolution itself.[20]

The interval between the revolutions of 1905 and 1917 saw much soul-searching amongst the intelligentsia. There emerged a genre of auto-critique. Thus the volume *Vekhi* (1909) condemned the entire tradition of the Russian intelligentsia for absolutizing social justice to the exclusion of other values: legal, religious, even economic.[21] Against such radicalism, *Vekhi* restated the ideas of the Slavophiles and Dostoyevsky – whose *The Devils* is the most devastating critique ever written on political fanaticism. A sequel volume was edited by Solzhenitsyn during the Soviet period.[22] The young Polish radical Stanislaw Brzozowski (1878–1911) wrote 'spiritually the contemporary Polish intelligentsia is a collective nothing *res nullius* (belonging to no one)'. The intelligentsia was a 'biological paradox' or 'biological absurdity' which attempts to make thought self-sufficient, self-nurturing, as though it had no dependency on life.[23] Brzozowski read and understood *Vekhi* but unlike its authors saw a remedy in the working class: a 'collective Prometheus' setting its heroic virtues against the narrow-minded selfishness and weakness of the intellectuals. In *A Legend of Young Poland: Essays on the Structure of the Cultural Soul* (1910), he anticipates Gramsci's notion of 'organic intellectuals', by arguing that the Polish intelligentsia should subordinate itself to and serve the working class. It had no independent mission of its own. The proletariat thus turned out to be 'a solution to the tragedy of the intelligentsia', enabling it to overcome its helplessness and alienation.

But in fact the Bolshevik Revolution enhanced this alienation. Accustomed to consider themselves the most advanced part of the nation, the intelligentsia was perplexed to find itself left behind by a radical revolution which its earlier actions and writings had done much to engender. A crisis of confidence ensued which led in turn to a re-examination of the intelligentsia's own role and to a search for fresh identities and expressions. Only a handful gave the October Revolution an uncritical welcome. As a Soviet historian complained, 'many members of the intelligentsia were gripped by a deep pessimism, taking the collapse of the rule of the bourgeoisie, a class which they considered to be the only bearer of culture, as the death of culture in general'.[24] Some chose exile, and many others were deported after a round-up of intellectuals in 1922.

For those who remained, some measure of accommodation with the new authorities was unavoidable. The new regime needed the services of 'former specialists' and realized they would have to pay for them. As the 1920s continued, an exciting intellectual life emerged in which the Soviet elites became world leaders in many areas of artistic and social scientific endeavour. But the Party's compromise with the 'bourgeois intelligentsia' was soon cancelled. When, at the end of his novel, Pasternak has Dr Zhivago die of suffocation on a Moscow tram in 1929, this is clearly intended to indicate the death of the 'old intelligentsia' as a whole.

In its place, Stalinism recruited a 'new intelligentsia' of tens of thousands to run the Stalinist state. The sociological change, from the 'educated critic of the establishment' into a broad social stratum lumping together all non-manual workers, gave, as it was intended to, the impression of enormous growth. It also required some massive simplifications of doctrine. Soviet Marxism had previously assumed a tension between the ideal and the actual, a tension that suited intellectual life rather well. From the early 1930s, orthodoxy required unconditional support for the official line, and the repudiation of 'Utopian' prospectuses for the future. Stalin explained that these were not socialist objectives but the anarchist, romantic day-dreaming of bookworms and theologians, 'wild talk' without relevance to post-revolutionary reality. Such visions were highly damaging to intellectual activity which should concentrate exclusively upon 'building socialism' – that is, on the economic and social development of the country. The role of intellectuals in the transformation need not be negligible, he added, provided they ceased their indeterminable discussions, gave up their 'rodent-like' activity in archives, and turned their practical skills over to serve 'socialist construction'.[25]

High Stalinism of the 1940s, during which it was transplanted to Eastern Europe, left no space for the independent intellectual. The outcome is described by philosopher Leszek Kolakowski as an 'age of myths' during which truth, drained of its intellectual content, became a purely institutional device, 'its content being in every case supplied by the decrees of the Infallible Institution' with its own priesthood for domestication and interpretation.[26]

Faced with this, the independent intellectual could only become a jester. As Kolakowski argues:

> The priest sustains the cult of the final and the obvious as acknowledged by and contained in tradition. The jester must stand outside good society and observe it from the sidelines in order to unveil the non-obvious behind the obvious, the non-final behind the final.[27]

Yet he must also frequent good society in order to find out what it holds sacred and to have the opportunity to address it impertinently. Kolakowski notes that when Georges Sorel wrote about the jesting role of philosophy in regard to the Encyclopaedists, he did so pejoratively, as playthings of the aristocracy. But the modern jester – unless, as is quite common, transformed into a priest – distrusts all systems. He or she represents the 'movement of imagination', not from perversity but 'to consider all possible reasons for contradictory ideas'. Both jesters and priests can have unbearable traits: the first of adolescence, the second of senility. 'The difference, of course, is that only the former are curable'.[28]

THE SIGNIFICANCE OF AUTONOMY

Underlying this definition of the intellectual lies not just the idea that intellectuals act and intervene in the public realm, but that they do so from a position of relative autonomy. As Karl Mannheim put it:

> From a sociological point of view the decisive fact of modern times, in contrast with the situation during the Middle Ages, is that [the] monopoly of the ecclesiastical interpretation of the world which was held by the priestly caste is broken, and in place of a closed and thoroughly organized stratum of intellectuals, a free intelligentsia has risen.[29]

It was this position of *relative* autonomy that Mannheim drew upon when he described intellectuals as being 'free-floating', 'unanchored' and 'unattached'. Furthermore, Mannheim concluded that there were a variety of possible roles open to the intellectual; but one of them (Mannheim's preferred option) was that they should 'assimilate [the] point of view and conception of the whole'. As such they were able to escape from the 'interest-bound nature of political thought', providing 'political knowledge' as opposed to false 'ideology'. This takes us closer to the contested ground of the intellectual's role and responsibility.

Talk of autonomy, however relative, is inevitably to conjure up the classic image of the independent intellectual, not necessarily locked away in the ivory tower, but certainly enjoying sufficient freedom and authority to speak out on all issues. But integral to it is the view that stipulates that intellectuals, by the very nature of their work and autonomous position, have a responsibility for truthfulness and towards truth. This was a view put forward by Alan Montefiore when he argued: 'By "an intellectual" I mean here to refer to anyone who takes a committed interest in the validity and truth of ideas for their own sake'.[30] Being an intellectual thus becomes defined in terms of a vocation.

The radical element of this argument – forcefully stated by Julien Benda in *La Trahison des clercs*[31] and reworked by Edward Said in his BBC lectures – is that this responsibility to truth can only be exercised if the intellectual stands apart and is detached from the society in which he or she operates. To this end, Benda provides an idealized description of the *clerc* as someone aloof from everyday material concerns and Said speaks of the intellectual's 'lonely condition'. Distance, on this view, almost necessarily entails an adversarial relationship with that society. Benda was of the opinion that the 'true' intellectual should stand opposed to the new irrationalism he associated with the prevailing passions of race, class and nation. Said describes the intellectual as 'the author of a language that tries to speak the truth to power'. Moreover, it is not only from afar but from the vantage point of abstract and universal values that society must be judged. For Benda, this took the form of what he regarded as an unproblematic Platonism whilst Said, less easily, speaks of 'the attempt to hold to a universal and single standard'.

If their views are broadly representative of this normative definition of the intellectual as vocation, we should be aware of the variety of different forms that this can take. Such an intellectual has received an assortment of titles. If Benda preferred a mediaeval appellation, the twentieth century has chosen more often to speak of the 'universal', 'prophetic' or 'public' intellectual. Less charitably it has spoken of 'the mandarins'. Even more multifaceted has been the way the vocation of the intellectual has been interpreted both for and in practice. Benda and the Dreyfus Affair are again reference points. In his *La Jeunesse d'un clerc*,[32] Benda remarks that he had always remained 'terribly faithful' to the 'attitude of the mandarin' but claims also that what had been at stake was greater than the personal sufferings of 'this courageous man'. Passing from what he describes as 'intellectualism to intellectual action', in the course of the Affair he had protested in the name of 'truth and justice, conceived as abstract values and as being superior to the interests of either place or the moment'. This, though, was the extent of his responsibility. The protest made, it was the duty of intellectuals to 'return to their cells, cleaning their spectacles and leaving society to struggle as best it could with the truth'.

Such comments as these led H. Stuart Hughes to remark that 'had they followed to the letter the advice Benda offered, few European intellectuals would have survived the two decades subsequent to the publication of his book'.[33] The criticism retains its relevance when we consider today's systematic murder of Algeria's francophone intellectuals or the execution of Nigerian novelist Ken Saro-Wiwa. Nevertheless, intellectuals have replicated the strategy outlined by Benda and have done so in a variety of different ways and contexts. They have, moreover, deeply felt the dilemmas and pain of this predicament.

DILEMMAS OF THE INTELLECTUAL

The image of the independent intellectual has held a powerful grip upon the twentieth-century imagination. The enormous attention over the decades devoted to Alexander Solzhenitsyn is an emblematic example. But the independent intellectual has also come under detailed scrutiny. At least three questions have to be addressed. The first concerns the proper role of the intellectual: whether the stance of detached independence has either ever been attained or would be desirable. The second asks whether in sociological terms even the *relative* autonomy of the intellectual can still be said to exist and, thus, whether the societal grounds of the intellectual's authority have been irretrievably undermined. The third explicitly challenges the philosophical basis of the independent intellectual's claim to speak in the name of an abstract and timeless truth and thereby raises the difficulty of in whose name and for whom does the intellectual speak. Taken together, they invite the question: Are we witnessing the disappearance of the intellectual?

Discussion of the first line of inquiry inevitably centres upon the responsibility of the intellectual. Timothy Garton Ash recently commented that 'the intellectual's job is to seek truth and then to present it as fully and as clearly and as interestingly as possible'.[34] Taking the argument further, he assigns to the intellectual 'the role of the thinker or writer who engages in public discussion of issues of public policy, in politics in the broadest sense, while deliberately not engaging in the pursuit of political power'. There should therefore be a 'necessarily adversarial...relationship between the independent intellectual and the professional politician', and this, he believes, should be as much the case in a liberal, democratic state as in a dictatorship.[35]

The call to abandon a position of independence is found in Antonio Gramsci's deliberations on the 'organic' intellectual and the relationship of the latter to the Modern Prince, the Communist Party. But it figures elsewhere, informing the relationship of intellectuals to Marxism in general. This, according to Raymond Aron, has been the 'opium of the intellectuals'. Its most famous product is the communist fellow-traveller, drawn into a world of self-deception by such arch-conspirators as Willi Münzenberg.[36] The debate surfaces in France, especially in the writings of Paul Nizan, Sartre and, later, Michel Foucault. Two powerful examples of the abandonment of independence are found in the contrasting status of the intellectual in Algeria and Israel. In Algeria, certain intellectuals have aligned themselves with the Islamic cause, in the process condoning the savagery directed against their francophone colleagues, whilst in Israel the very embodiment of what the West has taken to be the independent intellectual has been transmuted into an organic intellectual of the Israeli state.

It is, however, in Max Weber's writings that an alternative case is addressed. Of crucial importance is the distinction between what Weber terms the 'ethic of principled conviction' and the 'ethic of responsibility'. Described as 'two fundamentally different, irreconcilably opposed maxims, the former pays scant attention to outcomes and feels "responsible" only for ensuring that the flame of pure conviction...is never extinguished'. The latter focuses upon the foreseeable consequences of actions and therefore takes into account the 'everyday shortcomings of people'. When intellectuals have entered into politics they have done so armed with the ethics of conviction and with inevitably disastrous results.

Does all of this mean that the only true intellectual is detached and that, to the extent that intellectuals have adopted other roles, they have become so morally tainted that they have betrayed their vocation? It is very easy to find examples that prove the point. One case, where controversy still rages, is that of philosopher Martin Heidegger and his support for the Nazis.[37] But can the intellectual's predicament be so easily reduced to a choice between distant independence and the fawning adulation of power, complete with the blindness and lack of critical judgement that goes with it? Is there no possibility of a middle-ground position?

Here it is interesting to reflect upon the words of Václav Havel, dissident playwright turned politician and state president.[38] Havel defines the intellectual as 'a person who has devoted his or her life to thinking in general terms about the affairs of this world and the broader context of things'. Other people do this but what marks out intellectuals, Havel contends, is that they do it professionally. This itself has given rise to a 'broader sense of responsibility for the state of the world and its future', an attitude, he acknowledges, that 'has done a great deal of harm' when intellectuals have presumed to 'offer universal solutions' to the world's problems. Such 'Utopian intellectuals' should therefore be resisted in favour of 'the other type of intellectual: those who are mindful of the ties that link everything in this world together, who approach the world with humility, but also with an increased sense of responsibility, who wage a struggle for every good thing'. Such intellectuals, Havel argues, should be listened to 'with the greatest attention, regardless of whether they work as independent critics, holding up a much-needed mirror to politics and power, or are directly involved in politics.' He concludes, 'After all, who is better equipped to decide about the fate of this globally interconnected civilization than people who are most keenly aware of these interconnections, who pay the greatest regard to them, who take the most responsible attitude toward the world as a whole?'

The second challenge to the classic conception of the intellectual as a being set apart and detached from society comes in the form of the charge that, in sociological terms, the intellectual is no longer even *relatively* autonomous. The two principal culprits are taken to be the mass media and (especially in North America) the universities.

Régis Debray is arguably the best-known analyst and critic of the former. In *Teachers, Writers, Celebrities: The Intellectuals of Modern France*,[39] he structures his argument around a simplistic three-fold division of twentieth-century French intellectual life: from 1900 to 1930 the archetypal intellectual was the teacher who rallied to the cause of Dreyfus and the Republic; from 1930 to 1960 it was the independent writer and specifically the circle that gravitated around André Gide's *Nouvelle Revue Française*; from 1960 onwards, it has been the television celebrity. It was the middle 'cycle', Debray comments, that marked 'the golden age of French thought': what followed has been 'a considerable degradation of the intellectual function'. The 'mass media', Debray argues, 'run on personality, not the collective, the sensational, not the intelligible and the singular, not the universal'. Power – the real power to decide who will be heard – lies with the journalists and the media magnates and what they value is 'the ability to speak brilliantly on a subject about which one knows virtually nothing'. To survive therefore the intellectual has to conform and to abandon scholarship in favour of ambition and corruption. As France is not only governed but also thinks from the centre, what matters for the intellectual is no longer independence but that he or she should have their weekly newspaper column, radio programme or TV show. The result, according to Debray, is frightful: 'An Americanized intelligentsia in a Europeanized France puts the emphasis on smiles, good teeth, nice hair and the adolescent stupidity known as petulance'.

Criticism of the damaging impact of universities upon the independence of the intellectual is best illustrated by Russell Jacoby's *The Last Intellectuals: American Culture in the Age of Academe.*[40] Like Debray, Jacoby divides the twentieth century into three generational periods. The generation of 1900 represents 'classical American intellectuals; they lived their lives by way of books, reviews, and journalism; they never or rarely taught in universities'. The generation of 1920 marked a transitional stage: 'they grew up writing for small magazines when universities remained marginal; this experience informed their style – elegant and accessible essays directed towards the wider intellectual community'. It was, however, the generation of 1940 that felt 'the full weight of academization'. For this generation, the identity of intellectual life with the universities was almost complete: 'to be an intellectual meant being a professor'. This, when combined with the destruction of the independent intellectual's urban environment, transformed intellectuals from critics and Bohemians into academics governed by the realities of bureaucratization and tenured employment. 'New Left intellectuals', Jacoby writes, 'became professors who neither looked backwards or sideways; they kept their eyes on professional journals, monographs and conferences'. The result has been conformity and mediocrity. What has thereby been destroyed is not just the 'incorrigibly independent soul answering to no one' but also 'a commitment not simply to a professional or private domain but to a public world – and a public language, the vernacular'. The argument is simple: 'the missing intellectuals are lost in the universities'.

Jacoby's indictment of the academy has received sustained commentary, not least from those who argue that the idealization of the 'free-floating' intellectual is misplaced.[41] Thus, Bruce Robbins suggests that there was little to admire in the New York intellectuals of Jacoby's imagination – 'intellectuals', he writes, 'have never lived the gloriously independent life so often ascribed to them, and thus must always appear, when observed closely, to be on the point of losing it' – and that the very act of 'grounding' might not merit its frequent simple characterization as an unqualified fall. Professionalization, according to Robbins, offers 'an instance of secular vocation: not an unearned sense of self-importance, not an unquestioned or unaccountable authority, but that part of professional discourse which appeals to (and helps refashion) public values in its efforts to justify (and refashion) professional practice'.

Nevertheless, there seems to be an element of truth in the analyses of the changed environment of the intellectual provided by Debray and Jacoby. If nothing else, we have now seen the emergence of a new type of intellectual: one who appears on television rather than writes! But are the consequences as dire as they both suggest? Have we really seen the last intellectuals? In France, not only has the trend towards the 'mediological order' Debray diagnosed continued, but philosopher Bernard-Henri Lévy, complete with designer shirts and good looks, has become its very embodiment.[42] Yet, after much soul-searching, intellectuals in France have succeeded in re-casting their role, providing a variety of alternative strategies that allow them to speak to and engage with a wider public. In the United States also there has been much recent debate about the re-emergence of the 'public' intellectual, and specifically the black public intellectual.[43] The controversy rages, and will no doubt continue to rage, and the dissimilarities with Jacoby's predominantly male, white and Jewish New York intellectuals are profound, but there can be little doubt that in figures such as Cornel West, bell hooks, Toni Morrison and Henry Louis Gates Jr, America is seeing the appearance of what Robert Boynton describes as 'a viable, if radically different, image of what a public intellectual can be'. Cornel West, for example, uses the language of Benda when he speaks of the black intellectual inhabiting 'an isolated and insulated world' and choosing a 'self-imposed marginality' but then goes on to describe the 'insurgency model', with the black intellectual cast as 'critical organic catalyst'. 'The major priority of black intellectuals', he states, 'should be the creation or reactivation of institutional networks that promote high-quality critical habits primarily for the purpose of black insurgency'.[44] Elsewhere, the situation might seem to have less potential for the intellectual – in the Arab world, for example, where the choice is too frequently between service of the Prince or exile;[45] in Japan where, according to Nobel Prize winning novelist Kenzaburo Oe, intellectuals exercise no influence upon a political class that refuses to recognize the errors of the past;[46] in Germany, where the silence of left-wing intellectuals has left space for a re-awakening of nationalism articulated by such writers as Botho Strauss;[47] or, more surprisingly, in Italy where, despite the immense prestige of someone like Norberto Bobbio, a corrupt political system continues much as before[48] – but the American example is sufficient to indicate that intellectuals can still find a role and still are heard.

It is arguably the third line of inquiry that poses the greatest threat to the intellectual. What are the sources of the intellectual's authority and legitimation? Their roots lie deep in the Western philosophical tradition and have, over the past few centuries, been sustained by the Enlightenment project. It is this that has allowed the intellectual to claim some special insight into human affairs and to assert that it is from afar, and from the vantage point of abstract and universal values, that society must be judged. But is this position, with its Kantian foundations, any longer sustainable? In America, for example, it has received sustained challenge.

Specifically arguing against the universal, rights-based theories of John Rawls, Michael Walzer has argued that justice must be seen to be local, historical and contextual, and thus that the radical dualism we associate with Benda's conception of *le vrai intellectuel* must be abandoned. The mark of the intellectual, Walzer argues in *The Company of Critics*,[49] is not distance from real life but that the intellectual is never wholly uncritical. This suggests, he comments:

> what may be the most attractive picture of the true intellectual: not as the inhabitant of a separate world, the knower of esoteric truths, but as a fellow member of this world who devotes himself, but with a passion, to truths we all know.

Benda's standards, in other words, are not too high but are the wrong standards: the task of the intellectual is to expose the 'easy hypocrisies' and injustices of a society but to do so from *within* and whilst remaining faithful to the common sense of ordinary people.

If Walzer wishes to retain, in however a limited form, the critical function of the intellectual, an even stronger assault upon these claims comes from the champions of postmodernism. Richard Rorty, one of America's most important living philosophers, has detailed the implications of this position, most notably in *Contingency, Irony and Solidarity*.[50] Rorty sees himself as the defender of what he describes as 'postmodernist bourgeois liberalism'.[51] On this view, we cannot talk of such things as intrinsic human dignity, intrinsic human rights or make an ahistorical distinction between the demands of morality and those of prudence. Our language, our conscience, our morality, and even our highest hopes, can at best be seen as contingent products with causes no deeper than contingent historical circumstances. Within this framework the intellectual plays the role of the ironist, 'the person who has doubts about his own final vocabulary, her own moral identity, and perhaps his own sanity'. Denied the buttresses of ahistorical backup, he or she cannot be responsible for the woes of humanity and at most should seek to convince 'our society' that it need be responsible only to its own traditions and not to the claims of a supposed universal moral law. As such, Rorty's intellectual cannot see beyond 'the practices of the rich North Atlantic democracies'.

It is within this framework, as Zygmunt Bauman has argued, that the intellectual ceases to be a legislator and becomes an interpreter, the 'authority to arbitrate...legitimized by superior (objective) knowledge' being replaced by the task of 'translating statements, made within one communally based tradition, so that they can be understood within the system of knowledge based on another tradition'.[52] The strong criticism of this stance, especially when it has been articulated by such high-priests of postmodernism as Jean Baudrillard and Jean-François Lyotard, is that it amounts to ideological collusion with capitalism and its political representatives. Only slightly less severe is the charge that it makes impossible any serious and meaningful engagement by the intellectual of a radical nature. Once the claim (or pretension) to universality has been stripped away, the oppositional function of the intellectual becomes difficult to sustain. All disputes are purely local in character and all truth-claims are discredited. We are left with only discourse.[53]

This, of course, could be the character of the postmodern world in which we are now condemned to live. But, if it is, we should be fully aware that it makes not just intellectuals but all of us effectively powerless to act, except in the most limited of contexts.

If this century began with the Dreyfus Affair and the birth of the modern intellectual, it ends not just with the savagery of the Bosnian conflict but with the continued imprisonment of intellectuals throughout the world, and specifically with the persecution of Salman Rushdie. What is under threat in the case of Rushdie, as well as in others, is what Rushdie himself has described as 'the unfettered republic of the tongue'.[54] As he explains:

> The creative spirit is treated as an enemy by those mighty or petty potentates who resent the power of art to build pictures of the world which quarrel with, or undermine, their own simpler and less open-hearted views.

Why else do despotic and tyrannical regimes, whatever their apparent political complexion, invariably undertake the genocide of intellectuals? In the Rushdie case, it is not liberal democracy that is principally under threat – as frequently alleged – but the intellectual's own integrity and very person. The challenge, not just in the United Kingdom but elsewhere throughout the world, is not just if, but also how, this threat be met. As Rushdie comments: 'Please understand, however: I am making no complaint. I am a writer. I do not accept my condition. I will strive to change it: but I inhabit it. I am trying to learn from it.'[55]

The contributions which follow are arranged in four parts. Each illustrates aspects of the intellectual's role and the dilemmas that have been faced in the twentieth century. First, come the more theoretical considerations associated with those philosophers and academics who have sought to define the place and responsibility of the intellectual. Second, comes a set of national portraits that, in different ways, indicate how intellectuals assume the status of the conscience of the nation and articulate the voice of the oppressed. They reveal the tension between the need for detachment and the demand or desire for political engagement and commitment. Our third section, concentrating not just upon Eastern Europe but upon the connection of the intellectual to Marxism, takes us to the heart of the intellectual's ambiguous relationship to those in power and to the need to fashion and shape history. The final part explores the position of the intellectual in a society whose commercial power and mass culture can likewise pose a challenge to autonomy and dictate a status of marginality. The Epilogue re-assesses the themes of the Introduction in the light of these chapters.

Other chapters and other sections would have served our purpose. Intellectuals play out their different roles in different circumstances throughout the world, alternatively listened to and scorned. This volume is a contribution to the debate about their past and their possible future.

NOTES

1   E. Said, 'Opponents, audiences, constituencies and community', in W. J. T. Mitchell (ed.), *The Politics of Interpretation*, Chicago, University of Chicago Press, 1983, p. 9.
2   E. Said, *Culture and Imperialism*, London, Chatto and Windus, 1993.
3   The text of Said's lectures can be found in the *Independent*, 24 June, 1, 8, 15, 22, 29 July 1993. They were reprinted, with an added Introduction, as *Representations of the Intellectual*, London, Vintage, 1994. In his Introduction, Said comments upon the hostility directed against himself as the presenter of the lectures and against the 'un-English' topic.
4   'Mud in your intellectual eye', *Observer*, 27 June 1993.
5   M. Thatcher, *The Downing Street Years*, London, HarperCollins, 1993, p. 753. Examples of British anti-intellectualism are very easy to find but the following extract from Alan Bennett's widely-read diaries captures something of this mentality: '13 May [1987]: Colin Haycroft and I are chatting on the pavement when a man comes past wheeling a basket of shopping. "Out of the way, you so-called intellectuals", he snarls, "blocking the fucking way". It's curious that it's the intellectual that annoys, though it must never be admitted to be the genuine article but always "pseudo" or "so-called". It is, of course, only in England that "intellectual" is an insult anyway'; A. Bennett, *Writing Home*, London, Faber, 1994, p. 157. Religious non-conformity – and especially Methodism (Mrs Thatcher's faith) – undoubtedly plays a major part in the British antipathy to intellectuals. Here is found a hostility to all forms of priestly caste.
6   See S. Collini (ed.), *Arnold: Culture and Anarchy and other writings*, Cambridge, Cambridge University Press, 1993. It is interesting to note that Cornel West gives a very different characterization of Arnold, describing him as 'an organic intellectual of an emergent middle class'; C. West, *Keeping Faith: Philosophy and Race in America*, London and New York, Routledge, 1993, p. 7.
7   S. Collini, *Public Moralists: Political Thought and Intellectual Life in Britain, 1850–1930*, Oxford, Clarendon Press, 1991, p. 58.
8   J. Stapleton, *Englishness and the Study of Politics: the Social and Political Thought of Ernest Barker*, Cambridge, Cambridge UP, 1994.
9   It should be noted that the University of Oxford had no qualms about honouring its former student, the pro-capital punishment president, Bill Clinton.
10 British anti-intellectualism immediately responded by coining the phrase 'Bollinger socialist' to describe Pinter and his friends.

11 All of these quotations are drawn from non-Muslims and from people occupying positions of eminence within British public life. Others, equally representative of British anti-intellectualism, can be easily found.

12 P. Johnson, *Intellectuals*, London, Weidenfeld and Nicolson, 1988; *Le grand mensonge des intellectuels: vices privés et vertus publiques*, Paris, Laffont, 1993. 'A typical Thatcherite intellectual', Johnson was described in the *New York Review of Books* as 'a crass, eccentric, Catholic ex-socialist'; I. Burama, 'Mrs Thatcher's Revenge', *New York Review of Books*, 21 March 1996, p. 24. Johnson spends much of his time attacking the permissive society and, of course, homosexuality.

13 J. Carey, *The Intellectuals and the Masses* London, Faber, 1992.

14 Carey's latest foray into this subject is in the form of his unlikely editorship of the *Faber Book of Science*. His view is now that it is scientists, rather than the literary intelligentsia, that are the new intellectuals, a position which allowed him to be quoted in *The Times Higher Education Supplement* to the effect that: 'Leonardo de Vinci was a left-handed, vegetarian, homosexual bastard'. Carey seems unacquainted with the fact that the history of science is littered with fraud, shameless prejudice, error and careerism. The prestigious journal *Nature*, for example, printed Nazi denunciations of 'Jewish science'; see W. Gratzer (ed.), *A Bedside Nature: Genius and Eccentricity in Science 1869–1953*, Basingstoke, Macmillan, 1995.

15 'No intellectuals please, we're British', *Observer*, 5 July 1992.

16 T. Draper, 'An Anti-Intellectual Intellectual', *New York Review of Books*, 2 November 1995, pp. 29–34.

17 U. Eco, 'Ur-Fascism', *New York Review of Books*, 22 June 1995, pp. 12–15.

18 R. Williams, *Keywords*, Fontana, London, 1988, p. 169.

19 On the Dreyfus Affair readers should consult J-D. Bredin, *The Affair: the case of Alfred Dreyfus*, New York, Braziller, 1986. On how this experience defined the intellectual in France, see P. Ory, 'Qu'est-ce qu'un intellectuel?', in P. Ory (ed.), *Dernières questions aux intellectuels*, Paris, Olivier Orban, 1990, pp. 9–50.

20 I. Berlin, 'The Birth of the Russian Intelligentsia', in *Russian Thinkers*, London, Hogarth Press, 1978, pp. 114–35.

21 It eventually appeared in English: B. Shragin and A. Todds (eds), *Landmarks: A Collection of Essays on the Russian Intelligentsia*, New York, Karz Howard, 1977. See C. Read, *Religion, Revolution and the Russian Intelligentsia, 1900–1912: The 'Vekhi' Debate and its Intellectual Background*, London, Macmillan, 1979.

22 A. Solzhenitsyn *et al.*, *From Under the Rubble*, Boston, Little Brown, 1975.

23 A. Walicki, *Stanislaw Brzozowski and the Polish Beginnings of 'Western Marxism'*, Oxford, Clarendon Press, 1989, pp. 176–98.

24 S. A. Fedyukin, *The Great October Revolution and the Intelligentsia*, Moscow, Progress Publishers, 1975, p. 25.

25 The *locus classicus* is Stalin's speech to the Society of Marxian Agronomists (December, 1929) in J. V. Stalin, *Sochineniya*, XIII, Moscow, 1950, pp. 141–72.

26 'Permanent and Transitory Aspects of Marxism', in L. Kolakowski, *Marxism and Beyond: On Historical Understanding and Individual Responsibility*, London, Pall Mall Press, 1971, pp. 191–205.

27 'The Priest and the Jester', in Kolakowski, *Marxism and Beyond*, pp. 55–6.

28 'The Priest and the Jester', p. 57. For a critique of Kolakowski's position, see A. MacIntyre, 'Preface', *After Virtue: a study in moral theory*, London, Duckworth Press, 1981, vii–viii.

29 K. Mannheim, *Ideology and Utopia*, 8th edition, London, Routledge and Kegan Paul, 1966, p. 10.

30   See A. Montefiore, 'The political responsibility of intellectuals', in I. Maclean (ed.), *The political responsibility of intellectuals*, Cambridge, Cambridge University Press, 1990, p. 201.

31   J. Benda, *La Trahison des clercs*, Paris, Grasset, 1927.

32   J. Benda, *La Jeunesse d'un clerc*, Paris, Gallimard, 1938.

33   H. Stuart Hughes, *Consciousness and Society: The Reorientation of European Social Thought 1890–1930*, St Albans, Paladin, 1974, p. 417. The book referred to is, of course, *La Trahison des clercs*, published in 1927.

34   T. Garton Ash, 'Prague: Intellectuals and Politicians', *New York Review of Books*, 12 January 1995, p. 35.

35   T. Garton Ash, 'Prague: Intellectuals and Politicians'.

36   S. Koch, *Double Lives: Stalin, Willi Münzenberg and the seduction of the Intellectuals*, London, HarperCollins, 1995.

37   As Alan Ryan comments, 'There may be no very quick route from Heidegger's reflections on Being to Nazism, but it is uphill work to make him anything but elitist, irrationalist, nostalgic and contemptuous of the humanist impulses behind most modern political ideas', 'Dangerous Liaison', *New York Review of Books*, 11 January 1996.

38   V. Havel, 'The Responsibility of Intellectuals', *New York Review of Books*, 22 June 1995, pp. 36–7.

39   R. Debray, *Teachers, Writers, Celebrities: The Intellectuals of Modern France*, London, Verso, 1981. Debray's text was originally published as *Le pouvoir intellectuel en France*, Paris, Ramsay, 1979.

40   R. Jacoby, *The Last Intellectuals: American Culture in the Age of Innocence*, New York, Basic Books, 1987.

41   See B. Robbins (ed.), *Intellectuals: Aesthetics, Politics, Academics*, Minneapolis, University of Minnesota Press, 1990, and *Secular Vocations: Intellectuals, Professionalism, Culture*, London and New York, Verso, 1993.

42   On Lévy, see K. Muir, 'Pretentious, Moi?', *The Times Magazine*, 16 December 1995.

43   See, for example, M. Bérubé, 'Public Academy', *The New Yorker*, 9 January 1995 and R. S. Boynton, 'The New Intellectuals', *Atlantic Monthly*, March 1995, pp. 53–70.

44   See C. West, 'The Dilemma of the Black Intellectual', in *Keeping Faith*, New York and London, Routledge, 1993, pp. 67–85 and 'The Crisis of Black Leadership', in *Race Matters*, New York, Vintage Books, 1994, pp. 53–70.

45   See M. Naïm, 'Intellectuels en quête d'identité', *Le Monde*, 20 May, 1994. The case of Palestinian Hana Ashrawi provides a more positive example: see A. Shlaim, 'Woman of the Year', *New York Review of Books*, 8 June 1995, pp. 24–7.

46   See 'Kenzaburo Oe dans les méandres de l'ambiguité japonaise', *Le Monde*, 28 July 1995.

47   See B. Strauss, 'Anschwellender Bocksgesang' in H. Schwilk and U. Schacht, *Die selbstbewusste Nation*, Frankfurt, Ullstein, 1995, pp. 19–40. It is interesting to note that Strauss, while deeply critical of intellectuals of the left, does not hesitate to equate himself with the 'poet-thinker' and 'lonely-seer'.

48   R. Bellamy, 'How not to make Italians', *The Times Literary Supplement*, 22 December 1995.

49   M. Walzer, *The Company of Critics: Social Criticism and Political Commitment in the Twentieth Century*, London, Peter Halban, 1989.

50   R. Rorty, *Contingency, Irony and Solidarity*, Cambridge, Cambridge University Press, 1989.

51 See here the debate that took place between Rorty, Virginia Held and Alasdair MacIntyre on the social responsibility of the intellectual in *Journal of Philosophy*, 1983, pp. 572–91.

52 Z. Bauman, *Legislators and Interpreters: On modernity, post-modernity and intellectuals*, Oxford, Polity Press, 1987. It is important to recognize that Bauman does not believe that the second role should eliminate the first. As he comments: 'It still remains the function of the intellectuals to bring the project of modernity towards its fulfilment' (p. 192).

53 For an unreserved attack on these positions, see C. Norris, *Uncritical theory: Postmodernism, Intellectuals and the Gulf War*, London, Lawrence and Wishart, 1992. Norris's own sympathies lie with Habermas, Chomsky and Derrida. The latter, according to Norris, does not fall 'into that facile strain of postmodernist rhetoric that cheerfully pronounces an end to the regime of reality, truth and enlightenment critique' (p. 18).

54 S. Rushdie, 'A declaration of independence', *Liber*, 17 March 1994 and C. Simon, 'Algérie, la guerre culturelle', *Le Monde*, 19 May 1994.

55 S. Rushdie, *Imaginary Homelands: Essays and Criticism, 1981–1991*, London, Granta, 1991, p. 414.

Part I

Insiders and outsiders

The central issue of the responsibility of the intellectual is inextricably linked to the question of autonomy and, more broadly, the position from which the intellectual chooses to engage in social and political criticism. The introductory essay highlights the contention of writers such as Benda and Said that the responsibility to truth can only be properly exercised if the intellectual, to a greater or lesser extent, stands apart from society, judging it from the outside. This in turn, however, invites the charge of an Olympian detachment that results in either political impotence and collusion with bourgeois dominance or the misplaced censure of practices from a naively universalistic perspective. The 'universal' intellectual or mandarin is contrasted with the 'specific' intellectual engaged in critique from within a movement or from within a particular set of moral values. The three essays in this section explore the dilemmas that arise from this disagreement.

Richard Bellamy's essay examines two influential attempts to address this question by writers of the left: Antonio Gramsci and Michael Walzer. The chapter compares three central aspects of their theories. The first concerns the epistemological basis of Walzer's and Gramsci's conception of the intellectual's engaged form of social action. The next two are concerned with the sociological account they give of the intellectual – namely, with how they conceive of his or her social role and with how the social and political conditions, the character of society and the political system within which the intellectual finds him or herself, affect that role. It is argued that their epistemological conception of immanent critique proves incoherent and their respective models of the 'organic' and 'national popular' intellectual are implausible. Following the ideas of Norberto Bobbio, it is concluded that the intellectual should not be conceived as a cultural politician but as the upholder of the politics of culture. The latter conception involves defending from a transcendent point of view a political and legal framework within which social criticism and cultural expression are possible.

One of the recurrent themes of German intellectual debate has been, and continues to be, the role and responsibility of intellectuals themselves. The sociologist Norbert Elias has argued that the peculiarly self-referential character of German intellectual life reflects the marginal position of intellectuals within the class structure. But this interpretation does not fully capture the ambiguity of their situation: on the one hand, condemned to 'negative critique'; on the other, repeatedly expected and willing to take a stand on specific questions and even loosely held responsible for entire regimes. The debate surrounding not merely Heidegger's position on National Socialism but also that of intellectuals in the broader sense (e.g. artists such as Gustaf Grüngens or Wilhelm Furtwängler) is the clearest example of the weight of responsibility imputed to intellectuals.

Intellectuals in Germany have thus been trapped between two roles: that of private scholar and that of the public intellectual. By concentrating upon Max Weber, the second essay takes us to the heart of this debate. Critical of the phoney leadership of intellectuals who seek to play a public role, Weber draws a picture of the academic or scholar who operates as an outsider or observer bound to the dictates of impartiality. Value freedom, on this view, serves as a professional strategy and personal code designed to enhance autonomy and reduce control by authority. The question addressed is whether this can be regarded as a subversive strategy capable of extension to the role of intellectuals in general.

It is, however, in France, probably more than anywhere else, that controversy about the position of the intellectual has been at its most intense. Voltaire's defence of Calas and Emile Zola's defence of Captain Dreyfus were couched in the universalistic language of justice and this was the theme developed by Julien Benda when, in *The Treason of the Intellectuals*, he condemned his fellow *clercs* for descending to the level of everyday political passions. The response of Paul Nizan was to formulate the doctrine of commitment. All intellectuals, whether they liked it or not, were on the inside. It is the collapse of both these positions that has forced French intellectuals to reconsider their role and to seek ways of intervening in public debate whilst avoiding the errors of the past. But if intellectuals no longer lay claim to speak in the name of universal conscience, in whose name and with what authority do they now speak?

2 The intellectual as social critic
Antonio Gramsci and Michael Walzer

Richard Bellamy

Intellectuals have often been criticized by Left and Right alike for being detached from the everyday concerns of their fellow human beings. The Left usually characterize this detachment as an ivory-towered and unworldly elitism that leads at best to irrelevance and a passive acquiesence in the oppression of their fellow citizens, and at worst to a spurious legitimation of that oppression as part of the way of the world.[1] The Right, not dissimilarly, typically accuse intellectuals of being snobbish and antipopulist. Even the self-styled friends of the people are said to dislike the popular culture of the masses, which they seek to displace through sinister programmes of re-education.[2] Indeed, intellectuals who engage in politics generally attract much greater criticism than those who shun it. They are accused of either betraying their role as independent guardians of the truth by placing their talents in the service of those in power,[3] or of being dangerous utopians, who oppose their own feeble rational constructions to time-honoured commonsense.[4]

Intellectuals, therefore, seem caught in something of a cleft stick. If they remain outside politics, they end up being charged with aloofness and a selective blindness to injustice. If they enter the political arena, they appear condemned either to prostrate themselves before the powerful or illegitimately to impose their ideals on others. On the one hand, they stand accused of a false objectivity obtained via a refusal to dirty their hands by engaging with the often messy affairs of the world; on the other hand, they are warned against covering their hands in blood by seeking to make a necessarily imperfect world conform to their abstract ideals.[5] Even those who make these sorts of criticisms may not be able to escape this dilemma. Intellectuals themselves (George Orwell and Edmund Burke come to mind as examples from Left and Right respectively), they risk falling into self-contradiction or bad faith. Is there, then, an acceptable form of intellectual engagement with politics? Can intellectuals play a distinctive political role without either trimming their ideals in despicable ways, or indulging in the sorts of reprehensible behaviour associated with various kinds of elitism? Or was Ernest Gellner right to argue that, whether one becomes involved or not, it is practically impossible to avoid committing *la trahison des clercs*?[6]

These issues arise to some degree or other for most moral and political philosophers. However, they have been particularly pressing for intellectuals on the left, who have often felt an obligation to speak for the people, without necessarily being of the people, on the grounds that various barriers, both physical and psychological, have inhibited or prevented them speaking for themselves. In this chapter, I want to address two influential attempts to confront this dilemma by the Italian Marxist Antonio Gramsci and the contemporary American social and political theorist Michael Walzer.

Gramsci's writings have long had a special place in the hearts of Western left-wing intellectuals in this regard. Not only does his theory allot an all important role to the intellectual within the revolutionary struggle, particularly in the West, but he also has the added advantage of being, in Walzer's wonderfully apt phrase, 'an innocent communist'[7]; for imprisonment and death in a Fascist jail saved him from becoming tainted with Stalinism. However, Walzer is ambivalent about Gramsci's thought and rightly so. As he notes, Gramsci's writings can be as plausibly interpreted to suggest that Mussolini 'saved him from Stalinist orthodoxy' as that he 'deprived the left of a brave and supremely intelligent opponent of Stalinism'.[8] So, although Walzer includes Gramsci within the pantheon of his Ancient and Honourable Company of Critics, he is there as much as a salutary example of the pitfalls the social critic needs to avoid as a model of social criticism at its best.

Both the merits and the drawbacks of the Gramscian approach are particularly pertinent for Walzer, since he adopts a very similar perspective to the Sardinian. Like Gramsci, he believes that the dangers of Olympian detachment on the one hand, and rule by an intellectual elite on the other, can best be avoided through a form of immanent critique that evolves out of the prevailing views and practices of ordinary people. Unlike Gramsci, though, he does not wish to adopt a teleological view of history to ground this thesis. Gramsci's criticism of 'scientific' Marxism notwithstanding, Walzer is correct to point out that the Marxist account of history remained central to Gramsci's thinking. As a consequence, Walzer contends that elitism and what he regards as a 'false' objectivism enter via the back door, and that Gramsci's view of intellectuals has more in common with Lenin's notion of the 'vanguard party' than is often thought. However, rejecting any kind of teleology is not unproblematic either, since it potentially denies immanent critique of any critical bite with regard to the *status quo*. Although Walzer seeks to escape the charge of conservative traditionalism, it is unclear that he does so. His belief that he can avoid appealing to any universal or transcultural values may be more the result of his living in liberal America, instead of Fascist Italy, than because of any theoretical advance on his part.

The following comparison of the two thinkers focuses on three central and related aspects of their theories. The first section explores the epistemological theory underlying their conception of the intellectual, and questions the coherence of a view of immanent critique that eschews any teleology. The second section develops this criticism by examining the accompanying sociological account they give of the intellectual's social role and his or her relationship to the people. The third section turns to their views on the social and political context of intellectual activity. I shall argue that Gramsci's difficulties stem from the fact that within the Italy of his time he felt the intellectual had to engage in what Norberto Bobbio has called 'cultural politics' – the advocacy of a particular ideological position.[9] However, this leads to all the difficulties described at the start of this chapter. The way to avoid them lies in intellectuals adopting what Bobbio terms the 'politics of culture'. In other words, they must militate for the conditions necessary for social criticism to occur, rather than arguing for a particular substantive view. The former is something the intellectual may do as a citizen acting within a social and political system that allows us all to be to some degree intellectuals; the latter represents a specific intellectual duty.[10] Walzer's problem turns out to be that he assumes the appropriate social and political pre-conditions are always present.

EPISTEMOLOGY

In developing his epistemological position, Gramsci attempted to distance himself from a crude positivism on the one hand, which he thought characterized vulgar 'scientific' Marxism, and idealism on the other, most especially the branch popularized in contemporary Italy by Benedetto Croce. The nub of Gramsci's criticism was that both Marxist economism and the Crocean doctrine of spirit involved a return to theological modes of thought which negated the agent's freedom of choice and action.[11] In vulgar Marxism, matter replaced God as the final cause and the 'assured rationality of history' became a 'substitute for predestination, for Providence', with human beings mere pawns of some cosmic plan.[12] This providentialism was even clearer in Crocean idealism, which had a tendency to reduce history to 'the work of that truly real individual which is spirit eternally individualising itself'.[13]

In Gramsci's opinion, both views led to either political passivity or a pernicious elitism. 'Scientific' Marxism either encouraged people simply to wait until the process of history brought about the revolution, or turned the party cadre into a quasi-priesthood claiming knowledge of the natural laws of an inner reality distinct from the merely derivative experiences of ordinary believers. The masses had only to trust in the scientific prescriptions of their leaders to achieve salvation. Likewise, Crocean historicism either fostered a quietistic resignation to the station and duties assigned one by spirit, or produced an Olympian detachment on the part of those philosophers who claimed a privileged access to the spiritual reality behind the material world of appearance.

Gramsci sought to avoid these faults, stressing instead the need for political action and popular participation to bring about the revolutionary goal. He believed that the respective drawbacks of each of these theories could be removed through their synthesis. Historical materialism needed to incorporate some of the idealist's insights about human consciousness. Idealism had to take into account the historical materialist's concern with the social and economic context within which ideas are formulated and operated. The resulting philosophy of praxis was a form of pragmatism that was, nevertheless, historicist. Truth was not a matter of the coherence of the beliefs concerned, or a general consensus on their validity, or even their correspondence to a given empirical reality, but rather resulted from an idea's practical efficacy. Ideas, as embodied in whole cultural and political traditions, both shaped and were influenced by changing social and economic conditions.[14]

Criticism, from this perspective, is always immanent critique – for there are no higher principles or unmediated brute facts to be appealed to. Reality and consciousness are complexly intertwined. As he remarked in a series of important notes on the 'so-called "reality" of the external world', objective 'always means "humanly objective", that which can correspond exactly to "historically subjective" '.[15] North and south, for example, 'are arbitrary, conventional, that is historical constructions... And yet these references are real, they correspond to real facts, they permit us to travel by land and by sea... to objectivize reality'.[16] Gramsci was no relativist or voluntarist, therefore. Whilst he thought social being did not mechanically determine consciousness, he certainly believed material conditions constrained it, even whilst being in part a product of it. His point was that social and economic circumstances only determined to the extent that they were theoretically known in ways that allowed them to be practically employed.

Gramsci's account of the nature of human knowledge both opened up avenues for social criticism and threatened to prevent it entirely. Its liberating potential can be seen in his account of the Russian revolution. As he famously argued, since it did not result from the development of the forces of production it was to a large degree a 'revolution against *Kapital*'. However, it had not been produced by spirit unfolding itself through human will and consciousness either. It came about because of the ability of the Bolshevik tacticians to mobilize the people in a revolutionary manner consistent with the material circumstances of the time.[17] The pragmatist epistemology underlying this account is brought out clearly in his observation, in the *Notebooks*, that Lenin had thereby 'advanced philosophy as philosophy in so far as he advanced political doctrine and practice'.[18]

The other side of the coin, however, was Gramsci's acknowledgement of the amazing resilience of capitalist countries. Proletarian revolution should have taken place here long ago. It had failed to do so because of what he termed the cultural and political 'hegemony', or ideological ascendancy, of bourgeois capitalist values within the sphere of civil society.[19] However, the practical efficacy of capitalist ideology meant, on Gramsci's analysis, that it possessed an element of truth. Gramsci's difficulty was whether it possessed a monopoly of the truth, given that capitalist values appeared all pervasive and no appeal could be made to challenge them on the basis of either justice or historical reality. Gramsci's response was that no ideology – at least prior to the establishment of a communist society – was likely to be so complete. Until then, the intellectual hegemony of the ruling class could only be achieved to the extent they made certain concessions to the interests of the subordinate classes. As a result, the ruling ideology tended to contain self-contradictory elements.[20] Whilst a mass might, 'for reasons of intellectual subordination', express overt support for a given view of the world, there were often covert signs in their actions of an alternative 'embryonic' conception of their own.

The resources for criticism were always available, then. The social critic's task was to make people see the internal contradictions within the prevailing hegemonic system of ideas as manifested in the differences between their thought and their actions and interests. Intellectuals achieved this result by developing those same bourgeois ideas. For once a contradiction arose between theory and practice, internal incoherences would become apparent in the ideas themselves. In this way, critics were able to initiate 'a process of differentiation and change in the relative weight that the old ideologies used to possess. What was previously secondary and subordinate . . . is now taken to be primary and becomes the nucleus of a new ideological and theoretical complex'.[21] From this perspective, the scientific superiority of Marxism, for example, lay in its having untangled the theoretical inconsistencies found within nineteenth-century German idealism and British political economy as they related to the practices of Western societies and economies, and laid the basis for working-class revolution.[22]

An unacknowledged progressive teleology underlay Gramsci's thesis at this point, whereby the present was somehow 'truer' and more 'developed' than the past. Why did Gramsci fall into this trap? Michael Rosen has shown how the internal logic of immanent critique is vulnerable to what he calls the '*post festum* paradox', namely the paradox of only being able to evaluate the results of immanent critique by depending upon these same results, validity.[23] The only escape from the circularity of this argument is to assume that history involves the progressive unfolding of truth. In order to ground this belief, Gramsci ended up endorsing the very orthodox Marxism he began by seeking to modify. Although Gramsci was no doctrinaire, the standard Marxist theses concerning the gradual unfolding of different modes of production, the eventual crisis of capitalism, and the status of the proletariat as the universal class embodying human emancipation, ultimately ran through almost all his arguments. They provided the basis for his confidence that only a communist society would be able to provide a 'universally subjective' and 'total' vision of the world, that would be '100 per cent homogeneous on the level of ideology' without the need for either brainwashing, coercion or social engineering of the population.[24]

Walzer's arguments are in many ways less well elaborated than Gramsci's, but follow a parallel trajectory. As he explains in the preface to *The Company of Critics*:

> Over a number of years, I have been arguing (most clearly in *Spheres of Justice*) against the claim that moral principles are necessarily external to the world of everyday experience, waiting *out there* to be discovered by detached and dispassionate philosophers. In fact, it seems to me, the everyday world is a moral world, and we would do better to study its internal rules, maxims, conventions and ideals, rather than to detach ourselves from it in search of a universal or transcendent standpoint.[25]

Walzer believes that those critics who claim to discover moral principles, either through divine revelation or by reference to a 'higher' reality beyond the phenemonal world, will be unable to engage with the beliefs of ordinary people. At best, their views will be irrelevant, at worst they will be tempted to reshape societies and their members to fit them.[26] Equally misguided is the attempt to invent or construct a moral system. This exercise proves similarly utopian.[27] The 'path of invention', like that of 'discovery', has the prime defect of ignoring the moral worth and complexity of the values that inform the various social practices of different societies and provide most individuals with their ethical code. In contrast, Walzer advocates the 'path of interpretation', which takes existing morality as its starting point.[28] This form of social criticism is best conducted in what, following Gramsci, he calls ' "national-popular" mode', which Walzer takes to mean 'national in idiom, popular in argument'.[29] Such criticism involves critics conceiving of themselves as 'members speaking in public to other members who join in the speaking',[30] rather than as a class apart employing an abstruse language of their own.

Walzer admits that this thesis has problems of its own, since at face value it appears to make social criticism impossible. As he notes, many reviewers of his earlier works have argued that 'if we are unable to appeal to the outside, critics inside must turn apologist'.[31] Walzer's reply is that all cultures generally contain their own critical principles. Social criticism is reflexive, therefore, like self-criticism. Although societies may not literally criticize themselves, social critics can promote 'a collective reflection upon the conditions of collective life' through their interaction with other members of the community.[32] The intellectual achieves this result by 'holding up a mirror to a society as a whole' that forces its members to confront their 'social idealism', and by enquiring whether the values which give them their self-respect 'are hypocritically held, or ineffectively enforced by the powers that be, or inadequate in their own terms'.[33] Like Gramsci, Walzer notes that there is often a disjunction between social practices and people's beliefs about them. Unlike the Sardinian, he considers the practices more easily controlled by outside economic and political interests than beliefs, so that they frequently fail to live up to the expectations and ideals of participants within them. Part of the critic's task is to point to this gap by giving voice to the often unarticulated popular understanding of how social institutions ought to be.

Walzer contends that 'the ideal critic in this mode is loyal to men and women in trouble – oppressed, exploited, impoverished, forgotten – but he sees these people and their troubles and the possible solution to their troubles within the framework of national history and culture'.[34] It remains unclear why this should always be so, however. First, Walzer gives us no account of either what counts as morality and how we might distinguish moral beliefs from the general range of opinions, cultural practices and the like that people hold and engage in, or how we might arbitrate between differing moral systems. He appears simply to assume that societies are reasonably morally homogeneous, so that intra-societal moral disputes are resolvable in ways that those between societies are not. But a common complaint made by many oppressed groups is that 'national' morality simply reflects the point of view of the state and the hegemonic groups who control it. In this situation, they either appeal to a universal morality, such as human rights, whose standards the dominant morality fails to uphold, or argue that they have a distinct moral position of their own deriving from their religion or ethnic culture or some other particular source. In such cases, argument in 'national-popular' mode will be anything but liberating. Indeed, as Gramsci fully appreciated, it might simply serve as but another dimension of the exercise of power. Walzer's contention that the national should be prioritized on the grounds of its greater 'inclusiveness' simply begs all the important questions. Why must difference stop at national boundaries, or arguments that appeal to human concerns as such not claim to be the most inclusive of all?

Second, it is similarly obscure what constitutes a good interpretation for Walzer. He seems to suggest that as a social practice, the role of the social critic and the nature of interpretation will differ from society to society. In some it will be a matter of priests engaging in debates about sacred texts, in others of politicians discussing the constitution, and so on. The sources of authority and the style of argument are subject to a high degree of variety, with what counts as a successful interpretation in one context being unacceptable in another. Consequently, the only criteria he offers are rather formal ones, such as consistency, coherence, cogency and verisimilitude.[35] The difficulty here is that what will be cogent and coherent in one style of argument is likely to prove unacceptable in another. The Platonist, for example, will look for an idea's consistency with the ideal forms, a Walzerian interpreter for its proximity to established beliefs.[36] Once again, this position suggests that any society containing more than one form of moral argument will be faced with either deadlock or the arbitrary imposition of a particular dominant view. Moreover, it leaves open the possibility that the role of social critic may not always be available, as would be the case in any system where all authority flowed from the pronouncements of a designated leader who was to be unwaveringly obeyed.

Third, to the extent that interpretation differs from mere reproduction, it is also hard to see how it could avoid involving some degree of each of the two supposedly rejected alternatives. Although Walzer is keen to show how they both involve 'interpretation',[37] the converse also holds. In certain cases, such as the scientific interpretation of experimental data, it will shade into the 'discovery' path of inquiry. In other cases, such as a dance based around a certain piece of music, it involves an element of creativity akin to his path of 'invention'. Both these hybrid types of interpretation prove essential if he is to avoid the charge of conservatism. To show that people are misguided, deluded or suffering from 'false consciousness', for example, will involve some attempt to discover what people's real interests might be. To improve a moral tradition, or apply it to unprecedented situations, will entail a certain creative ingenuity. In each case, we will be concerned to offer the best interpretation of our traditions, not in the sense of its being the most authentic, but because it incorporates the most justifiable elements.[38]

A fourth criticism arises here. Walzer wants to deny that social critics could or should perform either of the above-mentioned tasks. Critics, he argues, need only point out people's hypocrisy, bad faith, dishonesty, and the like. The prophet Amos, for example, is held up as a model social critic for the way he identified 'public pronouncements and respectable opinion as hypocritical', employed hypocrisy as a 'clue' to identifying the 'core values' of his society, and used them to attack the leaders and prevailing institutions of his age.[39] At times this may be enough. But some traditions contain elements of highly dubious moral worth, concerning say the position of women or certain ethnic groups. Walzer acknowledges, for example, that in caste societies social meanings are likely to reinforce hierarchical distributions rather than the egalitarian ones he favours.[40] Here Walzer will be placed in a dilemma. For the critic will be unable to challenge those shared beliefs themselves or seek to alter them in any way.

As Joseph Raz has observed,[41] the thesis that existing morality can be interpreted so as to provide a moral criticism of itself proves incoherent. It implies the paradox that the prevailing morality contains both true and false moral propositions. Yet, if morality is simply the existing morality, it cannot be a source of moral error, only of truth. Likewise, any radical overhaul or even any change of the existing morality would imply that it was, or had somehow become, wrong. This proposition too is logically absurd, since once again the only ground for moral correctness is that self-same morality. The only possible immanent moral critique, therefore, consists of pointing out false deductions from accepted premises, uncovering duplicity and the like – a point that Walzer sometimes appears to concede.

Such reasoning may not produce the radical conclusions Walzer desires, however. As Raz pointedly remarks, neither the protesters in Tienanmen Square nor their foreign supporters, with the apparent exception of Walzer,[42] based their condemnation of the Chinese government on arriving at the correct interpretation of the relevant cultural discourse. It may well be that according to 'national-popular' doctrine the massacre was justified. Critical purchase on this event derives from invoking principles that have a wider and not just a parochial relevance, whereby certain forms of behaviour are condemned as simply wrong, a matter that is likely to involve adopting some aspects of one or other of the rejected paths.

Walzer attempts to answer this criticism by making a distinction between 'thick' and 'thin' moralities. A fifth difficulty surfaces at this point, however. He asserts that we can find a 'thin' universal morality in all (or nearly all) cultures, involving prohibitions against murder, deception and gross cruelty. 'Thick' morality, by contrast, involves notions such as treachery, cowardice, and virtue that are more culturally specific.[43] Note that this claim is descriptive. On Walzer's reasoning, one can only legitimately invoke moral universalism to the extent it actually exists. Nevertheless, this argument offers a hostage to fortune that issues in a thicker universalism and a thinner particularism than Walzer desires. To do any work, universalism has to be more than purely formal – otherwise, Walzer risks the slide into relativism, the avoidance of which motivates this new twist to his thesis. However, if local cultures are to remain consistent with a more substantive universalism, they are likely to simply offer a particular 'thin' elaboration of 'thick' universal concepts, rather than differing totally from them in the way Walzer supposes.[44] Britain, France and Italy, for example, all have recognizably liberal democratic political systems that are informed by certain common 'universal' principles, such as a respect for human rights. Yet there are considerable differences in the political and legal procedures they adopt for realizing them that reflect important local historical differences. Thus, Walzer is undeniably correct to say the Chinese should seek to construct a democratic system suited to China rather than simply importing American institutions. But this need not involve studying Confucian or Mandarin traditions, let alone Maoist–Leninist vanguard doctrines, for an elusive Chinese conception of democracy, as Walzer proposes.[45] To the extent that democracy possesses certain intrinsic merits, it can be justified independently of the existence of any indigenous form. Its introduction merely entails adapting the democratic ideal and its associated rights to Chinese circumstances. That this task will be probably better performed by the Chinese than others, no matter how well-intentioned, is in most cases no doubt also true. Walzer suggests that such regard for the self-determination of peoples only proves consistent for an 'interpretative' approach that respects the 'thick' local moral views of others.[46] But 'thick' universalists need not be paternalistic imperialists, as Walzer fears.[47] They can believe that China will have to embrace democratic practices of its own accord for largely pragmatic reasons, such as that it will probably be more enduring and successful in that case, or because they value autonomy as an inherent aspect of democracy.

The only ways Walzer can consistently adopt an interpretative morality based on a purely immanent critique is for him either, like Gramsci, to adopt some form of progressive immanent teleology, whereby existing morality is seen as the evolution of some inherent principle that must gradually work through various stages with all their contradictions, or he has to argue that existing 'thick' moral systems involve far more 'thin' universal elements than he usually wants to admit, but that these are shockingly poorly observed by many of those who claim to profess them.[48] On occasion, he appears to adopt the former course, as when he argues that the modern view of human equality 'grew out of the critique of a failed hierarchy' during the feudal era, and that progressive interpretations will culminate in the acceptance of egalitarianism.[49] This view, however, is hopelessly optimistic. For example, far from adopting the radical welfare and democratic socialist measures that Walzer contends are at the heart of Western liberal values,[50] the general trend is towards the ever greater extension of the market – a development for which libertarian thinkers can provide a perfectly coherent rationale. This fact does not mean that radical views cannot be defended or libertarian ones criticized, merely that appeals to contemporary mores are unlikely to prove the best ground for conducting a debate between these positions. In contrast, Walzer's frequent complaint that many philosophers fail to recognize the degree to which ordinary people's beliefs are moral points in the direction of the second course. However, this strategy fits ill with his assertions about the variety of moralities. Either way, he cannot avoid offering some criteria for sorting out the wheat from the chaff in any tradition. Nevertheless, this process need not entail either discovering morality on another plane to that inhabited by the rest of us, or of inventing one *de novo*, but merely of combining the tools of investigation and construction with the interpretation of existing views in the manner suggested above.

SOCIAL ROLE OF THE CRITIC

The social role each thinker assigns to the critic follows on pretty straightforwardly from their respective epistemological positions and suffers from parallel incoherencies that reinforce the criticisms of the last section. Gramsci's famous distinction between 'traditional' and 'organic' intellectuals essentially turned on the difference he drew between those who adopt what he variously characterized as a 'transcendent', 'speculative' or 'metaphysical' point of view, and those who reason historically in the sense of immanent critique.[51] Whilst the social stance of the traditional intellectual is detachment, the organic intellectual is engaged. The former 'put themselves forward as autonomous and independent of the dominant social group',[52] as operating in an eternal realm of truth that is somehow separated from the rest of the world. The latter discover the truth through examining the thoughts of common people. Whereas traditional intellectuals aspire to be a caste apart, a latter day priesthood, organic intellectuals form no special *cadre*. They can be found amongst all social groups, and seek to give them 'homogeneity' and an awareness of their 'function' in the social and economic system.[53]

Gramsci believed that the detachment of 'traditional' intellectuals ultimately proved untenable. Either they implicitly and perhaps unwittingly collude with the dominant regime by preaching political passivity – heaven being in the next world – or they seek to impose their version of heaven upon people in the here and now. He thought the Catholic Church provided the best examples of both these positions, though he also accused Croce of having fallen into the first and the Fascist philosopher Giovanni Gentile of adopting the second.[54] Organic intellectuals, in contrast, expressly acknowledged their social connections. In many cases, this stance involved their directly supporting the dominant class. This is true of the various pundits, experts and professionals that the capitalist class creates to further and support its various activities.[55] However, Gramsci also believed that it was possible for a certain kind of organic intellectual to represent the interests of oppressed groups and encourage them to liberate themselves by developing a critical consciousness of their situation from within their own current forms of thinking and acting. It was in this manner that social revolutions came about.

Gramsci maintained that to some degree 'all men are intellectuals',[56] since any practical activity presupposed a certain conceptual schema through which people orientated themselves in the world. This consciousness generally consisted of a 'composite' of often 'disjointed' elements that had been 'deposited' by history in a rather haphazard manner, forming 'an infinity of traces... without an inventory'.[57] Folklore and superstitions offered good examples of this level of thought, often providing what he called the 'spontaneous philosophy' of ordinary people. As a result, the masses were frequently 'intellectually subordinate' to the ruling elites, who monopolized 'high' culture. The function of the 'professional' intellectual lay in helping the masses to go beyond its own 'common sense' understanding of its activities. In Walzerian fashion, the first stage of this process entailed providing the missing 'inventory' by bringing a certain coherence and logical rigour into what might be somewhat loosely connected and badly thought through notions. If one was to avoid the possibility of simply producing well-versed as opposed to inarticulate bigots, however, it was also necessary to get workers and peasants to develop a 'critical' consciousness. This stage involved them attempting to universalize their interests and opinions in ways that addressed the concerns of others as well. Consequently, the opinions of the masses often had to be 'broadened' so as to go beyond mere parochialism or narrow self-interest. A successful hegemony was 'national-popular' rather than provincial-elitist.[58] Walzer and Gramsci begin to part company here.[59] Whilst Gramsci accepted we inevitably start out from the local, he maintained one's aim must be to transcend this position and move from 'dialect' towards a language or mode of thought that can be 'a world-wide means of expression'.[60] This enterprise was necessarily socially and historically conditioned rather than a matter of individual philosophic discovery or creation.[61] It did not require intellectuals to simply instruct peasants or workers on what they ought to think. The 'educational relationship' was, he believed, a matter of mutual dialogue, with the popular element providing 'feeling' and the intellectual element 'knowledge' and 'understanding'.[62] Intellectuals, in other words, had to respond to the often unarticulated needs and values of the people in order to identify their 'real' interests, rather than assuming they could be arrived at *a priori*. None the less, the ultimate result of a revolution would be the subversion of the conception of the world underlying current practices and their substitution by a new social order reflecting a quite different view.

As we saw in the last section, Gramsci regarded theory and practice as being intimately linked within a pragmatic epistemology that avoided relativism through being tied to an essentially orthodox Marxist account of history. Immanent critique and historical materialism went hand in hand. What allowed a class or group to universalize its interests was the degree to which they enabled the transformation of economic and social relations on the basis of the available means of production. Thus, the ideological hegemony exercised in the past by first the feudal aristocracy and then the bourgeoisie reflected their dominant functional position in the economic system of the time. To this extent, their hold on subordinate groups and classes could be historically 'real' and hence 'rational', and so based on consent rather than coercion. Only the interests of the working class were truly universal, however, and communism represented the sole form of social and economic organization capable of providing a genuinely 'total' conception of the world, one that could be freely adopted by all.

The scientific understanding of history offered the warrant by which the Party intellectuals were justified in moulding the new collective man. In working towards this revolutionary goal, the Communist Party could legitimately claim to take 'the place of the Divinity or the categorical imperative' within people's consciences.[63] Its role was to create 'cultural-social unity' capable of welding together 'a multiplicity of dispersed wills, with heterogeneous aims' within a 'common conception of the world'.[64] The Party's policy was to be 'totalitarian', so that 'the members... find in it all the satisfactions previously found in a multiplicity of organizations'.[65] Regional dialects and local practices were to be replaced by a common language and unified moral, social and political structure,[66] as 'the whole system of intellectual and moral relations' was 'overturned' in the process of 'adapting "civilization" and the morality of the vast popular masses to the requirements of the continual development of production'.[67] Only Gramsci's largely untested belief that organic intellectuals could persuade the masses to break with their earlier attachments and ways of thinking of their own accord saved him from resorting to the coercive methods eventually employed by the Soviet state. It seems that the organic intellectual, no less than his traditional colleague, is destined to either support the *status quo* or drift into totalitarianism.

Walzer starts off from remarkably similar premises to Gramsci, but understandably wishes to avoid his conclusion. 'Some critics', he tells us, 'seek only the acquaintance of other critics. They find their peers only outside the cave, in the blaze of Truth.' In contrast, 'others find peers and sometimes even comrades inside, in the shadow of contingent and uncertain truths'.[68] In a similar manner to Gramsci, he assumes that those philosophers who leave the cave are likely to be unable to connect with the needs and preoccupations of their fellow human beings. If and when they elect to return it will be in the guise of legislators, who seek to impose their vision of the world upon an often recalcitrant populace. In contrast, those critics who remain in the cave are best characterized as interpreters who remain respectful of ordinary people's own way of seeing things. As such, he believes they are natural democrats. Critics may well be marginalized – they say disturbing things and those with power are made uncomfortable by that – but they tend not to become detached or alienated. Rather than getting a critical purchase on their society by appealing to principles external to it, connected critics always argue from within the local culture. They explore the degree to which a society measures up to its own standards, often reinterpreting those shared norms in the process by making use of their internal dynamics. By giving expression to people's 'deepest sense of how they want to live', 'false appearances' are unmasked and reforms proposed.[69]

Walzer attempts to distinguish his approach from Gramsci's by contrasting the Sardinian theorist with his co-national and one time fellow communist, the novelist Ignazio Silone. According to Walzer, 'whereas Gramsci repressed whatever there was of Sardinian in him, Silone preserved and cherished the "traces" left by his native Abruzzi'.[70] 'At no point', he claims, 'did Silone stand free, the way the critic is commonly supposed to stand, look around, choose the best moral principles, design the ideal society, compare party programmes, decide on the strategically appropriate course of action.'[71] Instead of a 'grand theory', Silone is said to be blessed with a 'moral sensitivity' derived from rubbing shoulders with salt of the earth, southern Italian peasants. Rather than writing a treatise on oppression or elaborating a purportedly 'scientific' doctrine of human emancipation, he wrote novels, such as *Fontamara*[72], which voiced the peasants own moral indignation and aspirations. Walzer draws the moral that it was Silone's 'natural' identification with the cause of justice and his empathy and closeness to the views of the peasants that made party discipline and Stalinism unpalatable to him and eventually led to his expulsion and exile.[73]

This contrast between Gramsci and Silone is both theoretically and factually highly questionable. Gramsci had just as much admiration for the noble peasant sentiments portrayed in Silone's novels as his compatriot, and remained deeply attached to his Sardinian roots throughout his life – as his *Prison Letters* amply testify.[74] However, he did not romanticize this culture. His experience as a hunchback had also given him knowledge of its downside – the superstition and hostility towards anyone or thing that was different.[75] Walzer is right to report that Gramsci often felt unloved, that he hated Sardinian backwardness, that he was occasionally suspicious of worker solidarity. What he forgets to mention is that Gramsci had good cause for these feelings. Walzer's advocacy of moral empathy cannot come to terms with the tyranny of a bigoted majority whose moral sensitivity may have been warped by their social experience. Whilst it is true that in such circumstances a bad theory is likely to exacerbate these prejudices even further (as Fascism undoubtedly did, for example), moral exhortation on its own is unlikely to be enough to overcome them. Even if the seeds of humanity manage to survive in the barrenest of soils, they amount to little more than cries in the wilderness for human beings to act better unless aligned to a programme for the reform of social and political institutions. Walzer remarks that Gramsci's essay 'On the Southern Question', in which he sought to address the problem of uniting the struggles of peasants and workers, is 'a peculiarly lifeless document' and implies he ought to have followed Silone and written a novel.[76] But whilst (as Gramsci certainly appreciated) social reform without individual intellectual and moral reform will never be effective, the reverse is also true. Social criticism involves more than advocating changes in personal conduct – important though that is. It necessarily aims at a critique of those social and political practices that constrain and frame our action as well. Gramsci's theory may well have been a bad one, but at least it provided him with challengeable grounds as to why certain practices were to be preferred to others. In comparison, Walzer's argument is thin indeed.

CULTURAL POLITICS AND THE POLITICS OF CULTURE

This last observation notwithstanding, Gramsci did share Walzer's predilection for linking moral with social reform, even if 'in the last analysis' the first was dependent on the second. The resulting advocacy of what Norberto Bobbio has termed 'cultural politics' and the relative neglect of what he calls the 'politics of culture' provides the final similarity between the two thinkers to be examined.

Bobbio's two terms refer respectively to 'the planning of culture by politicians' and 'the politics of men of culture in defence of the conditions necessary for the existence and the development of culture'.[77] Bobbio links the first with what he calls the 'revolutionary intellectual', who fights 'against the established government in the name of a new class and in order to create a new society' – a position clearly adopted by Gramsci.[78] By contrast, the second reflects the attitude of the 'pure intellectual' who opposes 'power as such in the name of absolute values such as truth and justice' – a perspective Bobbio associates with Croce.[79] He contends this second path allows intellectuals to avoid the errors of politicizing culture or treating it as apolitical. Rather, culture can be distinguished from everyday party politics and yet possess a distinct political role as the background preconditions of politics itself.[80] A prime weakness of both Gramsci's, and more especially Walzer's, theory lies in a tendency to take the existence of this cultural framework for granted. Whilst understandable to some extent in the Italian, it is less comprehensible in the case of the American thinker.

As is well known, Gramsci argued that intellectuals had to play such an important role in the revolutionary process in more developed countries because within these societies the coercive power of the state was reinforced by the ideological power or hegemony exercised by the institutions of civil society – schools, churches, the media, and all kinds of private associations. Revolution here would only be achieved if the struggle for hegemony had first been gained and the Party had won the hearts and minds of the masses to the cause.

Rather less remarked on is the degree to which Gramsci's argument for a cultural politics was essentially a Marxist variant of a well-worn theme of modern Italian social and political theorists. Most Italian theorists of the nineteenth and early twentieth century had conceived the unification of Italy in terms of 'making Italians' rather than simply creating a unified Italian state. Institutional and constitutional questions related to the exercise and distribution of political power were largely ignored, with the emphasis being placed instead on the attainment of a degree of national cultural homogeneity capable of breaking down various particularist attachments to region and class. Indeed, success in the latter was generally thought to largely obviate the need to consider the former.[81]

Gramsci's analysis reflected these peculiarities of the Italian tradition. In spite of his emphasis on hegemony, he has been rightly criticized for underestimating the degree to which the liberal democratic state can engineer the active consent of its citizens through its procedures, bureaucratic apparatus and capacity for economic and social regulation.[82] He maintained that a 'war of position' to attain hegemonic control of civil society could be distinguished from and precede a direct assault, or 'war of manoeuvre', on the state.[83] This strategy may have been appropriate to a state of the 'capitalist periphery', such as Italy, where the political class was few in number and relatively isolated, and social, economic and political institutions comparatively weak.[84] Within advanced societies, however, state and society are too complexly intertwined to allow such a neat distinction, and the difficulty of mounting a counter-hegemony commensurately harder. In the absence of an effective state, 'cultural politics' may be effective and even necessary to give expression to popular demands. Within more complex political and social systems it will be hopelessly inadequate. Not only will it be much harder for the social critic to get his or her voice heard, opinions will be far more diverse and difficult to mobilize around a given 'national-popular' programme.

Even if a cultural politics was successful, however, cultural homogeneity would not render the political sphere redundant. The fact that everyone had somehow come to internalize the same set of norms and goals would not remove the need to resolve disputes over how best to realize them or the need to safeguard individuals against unwitting errors in their interpretation or implementation by others. On the far more likely scenario that a wide degree of value and interest pluralism persists, then more radical disagreements will arise. It will be necessary to think in some detail about how to ensure that people can make their case, deliberate with others, reach mutually acceptable collective agreements, and be protected against majority or other forms of tyranny or simple myopia or foolishness. Like other thinkers in the Marxist tradition, Gramsci regarded these standard tasks of a liberal constitutional democracy as destined 'to wither away'.[85]

That Gramsci saw no need for a 'politics of culture' is to some degree comprehensible. That Walzer similarly neglects the institutional and moral framework required for the practice of interpretation to be undertaken is less so. To a large extent, Walzer presents his thesis in the guise of an implicit and at times explicit critique of liberal political philosophy. The emphasis on individual rights and state neutrality, combined with the search for a universal justification for these arguments, comes in for especial criticism.[86] In contrast, he regards his own theory as being linked to collectively defined goods that the state may legitimately act to promote on the basis of reasoning peculiar to the particular community involved. He argues that this bottom-up approach is essentially democratic in that it appeals to popular understandings, elucidates shared values and expresses common complaints.[87]

Walzerian interpretation clearly assumes a public forum, for to be successful it must ultimately persuade people that it offers the best reading of their beliefs.[88] Unfortunately, he is unwilling to explore the preconditions for persuasive as opposed to coercive or manipulative argumentation. True, a prime aspect of his argument for distinctive spheres of justice is to perfect the liberal 'art of separation',[89] particularly with regard to limiting the scope of political and economic influence. His argument, however, goes both too far and not far enough. It is excessive to the extent that it ignores the need for politics and markets to cross over spheres in order to coordinate disparate activities. Like Gramsci, he places the burden for this task on the national community possessing a shared set of goals and values that provide an overarching moral framework for the plurality of different spheres. Pluralism, however, frequently undermines such agreement, or at least renders it deeply problematic – as recent debates about multi-culturalism illustrate.

Walzer also overlooks the degree to which social criticism is a political activity. In this respect his views are underdeveloped in not saying anything about the principles and mechanisms, such as rights and democracy, required for a 'collective reflection' on social traditions and goods, and to mediate between rival interpretations and cultures. As an American, he tells us, he does espouse a liberalism 'committed in the strongest possible way to individual rights and...to a rigorously neutral state', because it is 'the official doctrine of immigrant societies like the United States'.[90] However, the Chinese, as we saw, do things differently. Walzer implies that to deprecate this fact is to engage in a form of egregious Podsnappery. We are informed somewhat hesitantly that certain 'thin' conditions may be universal to all cultures and *for that reason* ought to be met, but these are not related to the practice of criticism itself. To do so might well entail conceding the 'thick'–'thin' divide, as Walzer observes.[91] Yet, as we noted earlier, the consequences of not doing so seem theoretically and practically far worse. Thus Walzer, too, albeit in a slightly different way to Gramsci, also divides state and civil society too sharply and indulges in cultural politics whilst neglecting the politics of culture. Somewhat optimistically, the social activity of interpretation is seen as largely autonomous from the state, and in certain circumstances as even capable of toppling it. Once again, Tienanmen Square gives the lie to Walzer's thesis in a somewhat brutal manner.

CONCLUSION

The immanent critique aimed at by Gramsci and Walzer is incoherent. Both thinkers find themselves caught between viewing history as an inherently rational process, on the one hand, and cultural relativism, on the other.[92] Whilst Gramsci ultimately impales himself on the first horn of the dilemma, Walzer tends to fall onto the second. Moreover, this approach issues in a cultural politics that suffers from the very two difficulties they wished to avoid. Either it leads to social conservatism or it turns intellectuals into political servants of the Modern Prince, seeking to engineer human souls in order to achieve a total cultural reform. By contrast, the more traditional view of the intellectual, as the upholder of universal values, proves consistent with the politics of culture. This form of political commitment requires intellectuals to enquire into the presuppositions of the critical enterprise, and hence on occasion to distance themselves from cultures or practices that stifle such activity. They must sometimes act as legislators, but in the classical sense of being concerned with the legal framework that makes both politics and culture possible, rather than actually ruling as Walzer suggests this approach decrees. Only then can a collective reflection upon, and critique of, social norms take place, with intellectuals playing their part alongside their fellow citizens.

NOTES

1 These criticisms are levelled by Gramsci at what he calls 'traditional' intellectuals, for example. See A. Gramsci, *Quaderni del carcere*, V. Gerratana (ed.), Turin, Einaudi, 1975, pp. 1514–6.

2   For a recent example of this type of criticism, see John Carey, *The Intellectuals and the Masses: Pride and Prejudice among the Literary Intelligentsia 1880–1939*, London, Faber and Faber, 1992. Of course, many on the right endorse such views.

3   The classic statement of this view is Julien Benda, *The Betrayal of the Intellectuals*, trans. R. Aldington, Boston, Beacon Press, 1955.

4   A view propounded to the point of caricature by P. Johnson, *Intellectuals*, London, Weidenfeld and Nicholson, 1988. Although these two criticisms are standardly levelled by conservatives against intellectuals on the Left, they have been expressed with equal vigour against right-wing thinkers. With regard to the first argument, Benda's main target was nationalists, whilst the second is as telling against Fascist apologists, such as Giovanni Gentile, as against communist theorists. George Orwell's *1984*, New York, Signet, 1950, for example, represents a socialist's condemnation of totalitarianism as such.

5   Norberto Bobbio regards these as the dangers confronting what he calls the 'pure' and the 'revolutionary' intellectual respectively. See N. Bobbio, *Il dubbio e la scelta: Intellectuali e potere nella società contemporanea*, Rome, La Nuova Italia Scientifica, 1993, p. 165.

6   E. Gellner, 'La trahison de la trahison des clercs', in I. Maclean, A. Montefiore and P. Winch (eds), *The Political Responsibility of Intellectuals*, Cambridge, Cambridge University Press, 1990, p. 27. As Edward Said points out, even this statement constitutes a form of betrayal, since inaction may end up as culpable of some great wrong as positive actions. See E. W. Said, *Representations of the Intellectual: the 1993 Reith Lectures*, London, Vintage, 1994, p. xiii.

7   M. Walzer, *The Company of Critics: Social Criticism and Political Commitment in the Twentieth Century*, London, Peter Halban, 1989, p. 81.

8   Walzer, *Company of Critics*, p. 80.

9   N. Bobbio, *Politica e cultura*, Turin, Einaudi, 1955, Ch. 2.

10 For a more detailed argument to this effect than I can offer here, but with which I basically agree, see A. Montefiore, 'The Political Responsibility of Intellectuals', in Maclean et al. (eds), *The Political Responsibility of Intellectuals*, Ch. 11.

11 For a full discussion of Gramsci's criticisms of historical materialism and Crocean historicism see R. Bellamy and D. Schecter, *Gramsci and the Italian State*, Manchester, Manchester University Press, 1993, Ch. 4.

12 Gramsci, *Quaderni*, pp. 1580, 1591.

13 B. Croce, *Teoria e storia della storiografia* (1917), Bari, Laterza, 1943, p. 87.

14 For a detailed account of Gramsci's theory, together with supporting evidence from the texts, see Bellamy and Schecter, *Gramsci and the Italian State*, pp. 99–106.

15 Gramsci, *Quaderni*, pp. 1415–16.

16 Gramsci, *Quaderni*, p. 1419.

17 A. Gramsci, 'The Revolution Against *Kapital*' (1917), in A. Gramsci, *Pre-Prison Writings*, Richard Bellamy (ed.), Cambridge, Cambridge University Press, 1994, pp. 39–42.

18 Gramsci, *Quaderni*, p. 1250.

19 Gramsci, *Quaderni*, p. 461.

20 Gramsci, *Quaderni*, pp. 1302–3.

21 Gramsci, *Quaderni*, p. 1058.

22 Gramsci, *Quaderni*, p. 1860.

23 M. Rosen, *Hegel's Dialectic and its Criticism*, Cambridge, Cambridge University Press, 1982, Ch. 2.

24 Gramsci, *Quaderni*, pp. 1051–2.

25 Walzer, *Company of Critics*, p. ix.

26 M. Walzer, *Interpretation and Social Criticism*, Cambridge MA, Harvard University Press, 1985, pp. 3–8.
27 Walzer, *Interpretation*, pp. 8–15.
28 Walzer, *Interpretation*, pp. 18–32.
29 Walzer, *Company of Critics*, p. 233.
30 Walzer, *Interpretation*, p. 35.
31 Walzer, *Company of Critics*, p. ix.
32 Walzer, *Interpretation*, p. 35.
33 M. Walzer, 'Maximalism and the Social Critic', in *Thick and Thin: Moral Argument at Home and Abroad*, Notre Dame, University of Notre Dame Press, 1994, pp. 42–3.
34 Walzer, *Company of Critics*, pp. 233–4.
35 Walzer, *Company of Critics*, p. x.
36 B. Barry, 'Social Criticism and Political Philosophy', *Philosophy and Public Affairs*, 19 (1990), p. 365.
37 'A simple maxim: every discovery and invention...requires interpretation.' Walzer, *Interpretation*, p. 26.
38 See Barry, 'Social Criticism', op. cit., p. 369, for a parallel criticism.
39 Walzer, *Interpretation*, pp. 87, 89.
40 M. Walzer, *Spheres of Justice: A Defence of Pluralism and Equality*, Oxford, Martin Robertson, 1983, pp. 26–7.
41 J. Raz, 'Morality as interpretation', *Ethics*, 101, (1991), 392–405.
42 Walzer, 'Maximalism', pp. 59–60.
43 Walzer, *Interpretation*, p. 24.
44 Walzer, 'Moral minimalism', in *Thick and Thin*, Ch. 1, pp. 1–19.
45 Walzer, 'Maximalism', pp. 59–61.
46 A similar argument has recently been put forward at some length by David Miller in his *On Nationality*, Oxford, Oxford University Press, 1995, Ch. 4. I have criticized this position in a review of Miller's book entitled 'National Socialism: A Liberal Defence' in *Radical Philosophy*, 80, 1996, pp. 37–40.
47 Which is not to deny that they have been, usually (though not always) with disastrous results.
48 In a recent critique of Charles Taylor, Ronald Beiner has noted how he, too, oscillates between these two positions: see his 'Hermeneutical Generosity and Social Criticism', *Critical Review*, 9 (1995), 447–64.
49 Walzer, 'Maximalism', p. 45.
50 Walzer, *Spheres of Justice*, p. 318.
51 Gramsci, *Quaderni*, pp. 1550–1.
52 Gramsci, *Quaderni*, p. 1515.
53 Gramsci, *Quaderni*, p. 1513.
54 Gramsci, *Quaderni*, p. 1515.
55 Gramsci, *Quaderni*, pp. 1513–4.
56 Gramsci, *Quaderni*, p. 1516.
57 Gramsci, *Quaderni*, p. 1376.
58 Gramsci, *Quaderni*, pp. 1376–8.
59 See Walzer, *Company of Critics*, pp. 84–8.
60 Gramsci, *Quaderni*, p. 1377. See, too, the letter to his sister in which he urges her to let his nephew learn dialect, whilst at the same time stressing that, unlike Italian, Sardinian was not a 'national' language with a 'great' literature (A. Gramsci, *Lettere dal carcere*, Turin, Einaudi, 1965, n. 23, p. 64). Walzer, in contrast, finds either a linguistic or a moral Esperanto highly improbable (Walzer, 'Moral Minimalism', pp. 7–9).
61 Gramsci, *Quaderni*, pp. 1377–8.
62 Gramsci, *Quaderni*, p. 1505.

63   Gramsci, *Quaderni*, p. 1561.
64   Gramsci, *Quaderni*, p. 1331.
65   Gramsci, *Quaderni*, p. 800.
66   Gramsci, *Quaderni*, pp. 1377–8, 2314.
67   Gramsci, *Quaderni*, pp. 1561, 1565–6.
68   Walzer, *Company of Critics*, pp. ix–x.
69   Walzer, *Company of Critics*, p. 232.
70   Walzer, *Company of Critics*, p. 102.
71   Walzer, *Company of Critics*, p. 106.
72   I. Silone, *Fontamara*, Milan, Mondadori, 1949.
73   Walzer, *Company of Critics*, p. 106.
74   His letters to his family are particularly eloquent in this respect. See, for example, his letter to his mother of 5 March 1928, in which he affirms his keen interest for every kind of news from his native village of Ghilarza (Gramsci, *Lettere dal carcere*, n. 85, p. 184), or his encomium to Sardinian yoghurt in a letter to his sister-in-law of 7 April 1931 (Gramsci, *Lettere dal carcere*, n. 186, p. 425).
75   See, for example, his letter to his sister-in-law of 30 January 1933, recounting a family's cruel treatment of a retarded boy (Gramsci, *Lettere dal carcere*, n. 326, pp. 736–7).
76   Walzer, *Company of Critics*, p. 108.
77   Bobbio, *Politica e cultura*, p. 37.
78   Bobbio, *Il dubbio e la scelta*, p. 164.
79   Bobbio, *Il dubbio e la scelta*, pp. 164, 165–6.
80   Bobbio, *Politica e cultura*, pp. 34–46.
81   For details, see R. Bellamy, *Modern Italian Social Theory: Ideology and Politics from Pareto to the Present*, Cambridge, Polity Press, 1987. Gramsci is aligned to this tradition in Ch. 6.
82   See P. Anderson, 'The antinomies of Antonio Gramsci', *New Left Review*, 100 (1976–7), 5–80, for this critique.
83   Gramsci, *Quaderni*, pp. 1566–7.
84   Gramsci's analysis of Italy as a country of the 'capitalist periphery' is contained in 'A Study of the Italian Situation' (1926), in *Pre-Prison Writings*, especially pp. 297–8.
85   For a critique of the Marxist aspiration to go beyond both justice and the state, see S. Lukes, *Marxism and Morality*, Oxford, Oxford University Press, 1985.
86   Rawls is singled out for especial criticism in both *Spheres of Justice*, e.g. pp. 79–82, and *Interpretation*, e.g. pp. 11–12, 14, 16.
87   Walzer, *Interpretation*, op. cit., pp. 38–9, 64–5, 'Philosophy and Democracy', *Political Theory*, 9 (1981), 379–99.
88   Walzer, *Interpretation*, p. 28.
89   M. Walzer, 'Liberalism and the Art of Separation', *Political Theory*, 12 (1984), 315–30.
90   M. Walzer, 'Comment' in C. Taylor, *Multiculturalism*, Princeton NJ, Princeton University Press, 1994, pp. 99, 101.
91   Walzer, 'Moral Minimalism', pp. 11–15.
92   As Hilary Putnam has noted, this problem is likely to bedevil all attempts to historicize or immanentize morality. See his 'Beyond Historicism' in *Realism and Reason: Philosophical Papers*, Vol. 3, Cambridge, Cambridge University Press, 1983, pp. 287–8.

3 Between autonomy and responsibility

Max Weber on scholars, academics and intellectuals

Alan Scott

INTRODUCTION

In his very elegant essay 'Heinrich Heine and the role of the intellectual in Germany', Jürgen Habermas identifies four views within the German intelligentsia on the public role of the intellectual[1]. Adherents to the first view, held by those such as Hermann Hesse, Thomas Mann and Karl Jaspers whom Habermas characterizes as 'the unpolitical among the writers, and the mandarins among the scholars',[2] assumed a clear separation between 'the sphere of the mind and the sphere of power'.[3] The second view, that of 'theoreticians oriented to *Realpolitik*',[4] mirrors the first by defending this separation of spheres on the grounds that intellectuals are not competent in public matters. The third group consisted of independent but politically engaged intellectuals, for example Ernst Bloch. Finally, there were those, such as Georg Lukács, who put their intellectual work at the disposal of a political party; who 'actually crossed the line to become professional politicians or revolutionaries'.[5]

The best known representative of the 'theoreticians oriented to *Realpolitik*' is Max Weber, in particular in the two classical essays 'Politik als Beruf' ('Politics as a vocation')[6] and 'Wissenschaft als Beruf' ('Science as a vocation').[7] These two essays propose complementary arguments. In the first, Weber argues that the vocation of politics demands a particular form of personal responsibility. In the second, he agrees that scholars, whose role neither demands nor facilitates such responsibility, are therefore bound to a different ethic, namely, that of the observer who, if not exactly impartial, is nevertheless obliged to maintain as high a degree of impartiality as possible. These arguments, as has been commonly recognized, rest upon two pillars: first, upon the distinction between an 'ethic of conviction' (*Gesinnungsethik*) – which is appropriate to neither the professional politician nor the scholar – and an 'ethic of responsibility' (*Verantwortungsethik*); second, upon the claim that 'value freedom' is both a desirable and obtainable aim for the scholar.

In this chapter I want to focus on the second of these pillars; the concept of 'value freedom'. I shall treat Weber's defence of value freedom as a strategic argument rather than, as is more usually the case, a methodological one. This is because I believe that it is in the strategic rather than methodological arguments that Weber's analysis retains a degree of plausibility and contemporary relevance. In the final section I shall try to assess the adequacy of this defence and the implications of its weaknesses for the claim that a clear-cut distinction can be maintained between intellectual and public life. The focus of the discussion will be less on Weber as a representative of a specifically German intellectual tradition than on Weber as a sociologist; as someone attempting to develop a model which has a putative validity beyond the immediate context and concerns of its author.[8] The focus of Weber's analysis is the academic or scholar, rather than the intellectual *per se*, and even within the category 'academic and scholar' his prime concern is with the *Geisteswissenschaftler* (social scientists, but also historians and philosophers). Nevertheless, I want to suggest that his analysis does throw light on the social location of the intellectual and on the possible responsibilities which are associated with social roles within the modern division of labour. But I shall also suggest that the intellectual posed a challenge to Weber's style of sociological analysis.

VALUE FREEDOM: SOME METHODOLOGICAL ISSUES

'Value freedom' has been the object of fierce criticism to the point where the notion appears largely discredited at least as a methodological doctrine. The standard objections raised in the critique of positivism seem unanswerable. Indeed our post-positivist political and ethical sensibilities rob us of any motivation to defend 'value freedom'. It is an idea objectionable on politico–ethical, as well as methodological, grounds. Yet I shall argue that some of the arguments Weber advances in its defence are still interesting because, first, they address questions about politics and ethics in a way which goes beyond the universalism–particularism divide which still today characterizes social scientific debate about matters which are not of a purely 'technical' nature and, second, they raise a series of uncomfortable questions about the position from which social science (or indeed science generally) can intervene in public debate and the effectiveness of that intervention. With regard to both aspects, the power of Weber's argument rests not upon the methodological defence of value freedom, which remains ambiguous and open to objection, but upon the fact that he pays closer attention to 'material' and institutional conditions of intellectual production than is customary. I suggest that reading Weber in this way at least enables us to see why 'value freedom' is in some ways a more interesting and challenging notion than is generally assumed.

The general force of Weber's argument may be understood as follows: social science can make only an *indirect* contribution to public ethical and political debates by addressing a series of questions which are not addressed by other 'voices': politicians, philosophers, moralists, etc. Paradoxically, as a precondition for making any contribution at all we have to start from the recognition of the limits of science and critical reflection in general *and* of the relative weakness of the power base from which the specialist operates.

To search in the already well-trodden and much criticized grounds of Weber's methodological essays for anything still relevant to the issue of social sciences' role in public debate needs some further justification. This is especially so as I do not mean to dispute that the critique of positivism has shown that a literal 'freedom' from values is unattainable, nor that it can be itself used to disguise partiality (cf. Habermas's early essays).

In the first place there is a well-established methodological critique of the notion of value freedom (*Wertfreiheit*). The term itself is, to put it mildly, unfortunate. Difficulties in sustaining clear distinctions between means and ends, technical and substantive claims, etc. were noted early by critics of Weber's philosophy of science. Thus, Erich Wittenberg, who characterizes Weber as 'the last great representative of a European rationalism which is grounded on radical scepticism',[9] notes that he remained 'totally blind to the intimate connection which bound his conception of science to the spirit of the age'.[10] And Heinrich Rickert asks 'the abrupt separation of knowledge and action...has to raise doubts and invite the question: can we *only* separate here? Will we not finally seek a unity that reunites contemplation and activity?'[11]

The difficulty of sustaining a clear conceptual distinction and confining science strictly to the sphere of facts and means becomes clear when we ask 'How limiting are the limits Weber seeks to impose?' In 'Science as a vocation', Weber does claim that science can teach us 'the meaning of our actions' – hardly a modest claim. In ' "Objectivity" in social science and social policy' the meaning of 'meaning' is spelt out in greater detail. We typically act under the influence of ideas or ideals (Weber shifts back and forth between the two terms). Actions, as Peter Winch argues, are 'expressions of ideas'. Social scientific analysis can both identify and judge the ideas under which we act. It can offer us 'knowledge of the meaning of the desired [objective] itself'[12] and, while it cannot judge the ideal in terms of its intrinsic worth, it can do so 'didactically' by offering 'an examination of the ideal according to the postulate of internal consistency of the desired [objective]'.[13]

These abstract formulations of the tasks of the social sciences within their limits are never very satisfying. They tend to be either rather Delphic (What does the 'meaning of the desired [objective] itself' mean?), or very generalized and instrumentalist (internal consistency, etc.). There may simply not be an adequate *methodological* answer in Weber to the questions of the utility of scientific knowledge.

One partial methodological defence is to weaken the sense of 'value freedom' suggesting that Weber is not describing literally value freedom at all, but rather an orientation – even an ethic of responsibility – towards values. It is part of our 'duty' to adopt an attitude of self-criticism and to distance ourselves even from that which we hold to be true. On such a view, open-mindedness rather than strict value freedom may be the duty of the scientist. This interpretation might link the methodological standpoint to the materialist analysis of the conditions of knowledge production discussed below, and specifically to the argument that lack of consensus within scientific discourse demands such self-restraint.[14] 'Objectivity' (a term around which Weber puts scare quotes) would then mean no more, but also no less, than attention to the details rather than the principles, and an attitude of squarely facing the 'facts', particularly the uncomfortable ones. Thus we might take 'objectivity' (*Objektivität*) to mean *Sachlichkeit* in the sense of 'matter-of-factness'. Rene König has argued for such an interpretation by claiming that 'freedom from making judgement on values' (*Werturteilsfreiheit*) rather than value freedom (*Wertfreiheit*) captures Weber's intentions.[15] This reading gives us a important clue to our later discussion: *Werturteilsfreiheit* may be understood as a refusal by the responsible scientist to submit to authority, either the authority of an institution or that of an ideology.

If 'value freedom' can be defended at all then surely only in this weakened sense. But the question still has to be addressed: 'Why should the scientist want to refuse to make judgements of value based upon scientific research?' To understand Weber's views here we have to go beyond methodological reflection. The central claim would then be that even though it is difficult (perhaps impossible) to offer an adequate methodo-logical or philosophical defence of a strong version of the argument for value freedom, there is a set of implicit and explicit non-methodological arguments to which we also need to pay attention. These arguments imply that even if strict value freedom is impossible there are nevertheless both strategic and 'ethical' grounds for us to act as if something like it were possible. Expressed differently, I shall argue that it is Weber's view that we are duty-bound to act as if value freedom were possible even if this may amount to no more than a mixture of self-restraint and dissemblance. I shall thus offer a non-methodological interpretation – and, to a degree, defence – of Weber's methodological pronouncements, claiming that his views on freedom from value judgements have to be understood in the context of, first, his general theory of 'modernity'[16] and power within 'modern' rationally administered societies and, second, his analysis of the position of the teacher–scientist within those structures.[17]

VALUE FREEDOM, MODERNITY AND INSTITUTIONAL POLITICS

Modernity and the lack of consensus

Weber's methodological position cannot be divorced from his general sociological diagnosis of modernity. Since it is this aspect of Weber's analysis which has drawn most attention and appears most attractive to contemporary social theorists, it is not necessary to go over the rationalization thesis once again here. I shall just mention the essential points briefly.

First, with respect to scientific discourse in particular, Weber's defence of value freedom rests on a suspicion of single-order accounts of social life. Scientific research must proceed from the recognition that there is no consensus within the actual scientific community (or even potential consensus within a posited 'community of critical investigators')[18] on questions of ends or upon substantive values. Given this lack of consensus, we must address the question 'How do we as cultural scientists continue to talk when we do not, in fact or theory, agree on fundamental matters?' Only, the implied answer goes, by suspending debate on those areas in which there is not even a potential for agreement. Any attempt to contribute substantively to discussions of the good life, or even to promote a specific value system, mendaciously disguises the absence of agreement on ends and on substantive values within the scientific community, or alternatively halts communication by thematizing fundamental differences. Thus Weber speaks of:

> the senselessness of the thought which occasionally overpowers even historians within our discipline that it could yet be a distant aim of the cultural sciences to create a closed system of concepts in which reality in some sense is fixed once and for all, and from which it could then be deduced. The tide of immeasurable events rolls ceaselessly towards eternity.[19]

It seems to be Weber's view that it is only through recognition of the limits of science and a distancing from our own values that we can go on arguing at all. This relieves the scientist of any responsibility to act as a cultural arbiter.

Second, with respect to the general diagnosis of modernity, lack of consensus characterizes not merely the scientific community, it is also part of the constitution of the modern subject. Not just science, but also disenchanted 'modernity' is characterized by this lack of agreement about the substance of the good life. Thus, not to recognize the limits of critical argument and reflection is not merely 'irresponsible', it is also sociologically naive. And naivety is irresponsible because it denies difference, or disguises it either behind dogma or a never-to-be-attained regulative principle. How does this lack of consensus within the scientific community and society as a whole fit into the defence of value neutrality?

It is unfortunate that Weber's understanding of the limits of science in guiding ethical and political debate is buried under its positivist reception. Re-reading 'Science as a vocation', it is clear that the argument is not being made in the name of objectivism, but rather that an attempt is being made to draw out the practical–ethical implication of the general lack of consensus, and science's necessary failure to amend that state of affairs. Weber is thus using ethical and political, not positivist and merely methodological, arguments to justify the scientist's refusal to address directly Tolstoy's question: 'What shall we do and how shall we live?' To answer the question directly – to offer a Utopia – would be bad faith in that it would be to offer 'leadership' without warrant: '[they seek] a leader and not a teacher. But we are placed upon the platform solely as teachers'.[20] Weber is contemptuous of intellectuals who do not recognize the limits of their calling but feign to offer such phoney leadership. It is not that we have no values, but rather the honest recognition of the fact that science gives those values no warrant which imposes a duty of self-restraint; a duty as teachers or scientists to distance ourselves from our own values. Not to exercise such a responsibility places us in the undignified position of claiming a moral authority to which we have no right. In matters of values we are all dilettantes. To respond to these demands for meaning and leadership can only undermine the authority of the scholar: '[Weber] simply warned of the disappointments that are bound to arise when... people turn to science with excessive expectations during a period of extreme spiritual difficulty'.[21]

It is in this spirit that Weber, famously, confines the role of the social scientist in matters of value to: (i) contributing to the 'knowledge of the technique by which one through calculation controls life in external things just as in the actions of humans'; (ii) developing 'methods of thinking, the tools and training [for such calculation]';[22] (iii) clarity.

The distinction drawn to support this view of science as 'limited' to questions of 'is' (*das Seiende*) is recognized by Weber as being linked to the ethical orientation of an actor seeking scientific guidance. Specifically, it is linked to the ethic of responsibility. I want the 'technical' knowledge science provides me with about the costs of my actions or inaction only in so far as I feel myself to be responsible for the outcomes of these actions. Were I governed by an ethic of conviction alone, I would not have this concern, and scientific knowledge would be irrelevant to my considerations as to how I should act:

> Since, in the vast majority of cases, every striven for goal does 'cost' or can cost something in this sense, the weighing up of the objective and consequence of action cannot be avoided in the self-reflection of a responsibly acting person, and one of the essential functions of the *technical criticism* which we have been discussing is to facilitate this.[23]

So, *contra* the critics of the means–ends disjunction, this distinction is drawn explicitly in the name of self-reflection, but it is a self-reflection which recognizes the limits of the kinds of reflection science facilitates. This provides one response to Critical Theory's accusation of positivism and instrumentalism against the means–ends distinction. Paradoxically, by criticizing the type of argument advanced here by Weber we may over-estimate the cognitive and emancipatory capacities of theoretical reflection in such a way as to fetishize or, better, mystify 'critique', turning it into an uncritical and dogmatic value in itself.[24] We might thus turn the accusation of positivism against Critical Theory and suggest that it is no coincidence that 'critique' and 'self-reflection' can be used to defend highly entrenched political stances.[25]

But the general diagnosis of modernity has a more specific relevance to Weber's methodological reflections when we focus down onto his analysis of the *institutional* contexts of intellectual production and dissemination.

Institutional politics and ethics

In even a casual reading of either 'Politics as a vocation' or 'Science as a vocation' the reader is struck by Weber's peculiar starting point. Before Wittgenstein, it was not the fashion to analyse moral issues through concrete cases, but this is precisely what Weber does. He starts, not from an abstract question of principle, but from the situation of a 'young man'[26] who decides on an academic career in the particular, not to say peculiar, institutional context of the German university system.

Weber pays close attention to the way in which a career is shaped by the structure of power, patronage and reward built into the institutional context in which it is pursued. He notes, for example, that the German and American university systems create different forms of subordination of the young to the old. The German system of *Habilitation* (post-doctoral thesis as condition for a fixed – at that time still normally professorial – post) creates quasi-feudal forms of subordination and mutual obligation between the *Universitätsassistent* and 'his' professor. It represents a kind of superior *Lehrverhältnis* (contract between master and pupil within a feudal apprenticeship system). In contrast, for the young assistant in the 'state–capitalist' universities of the United States:

> there arises here the same condition as wherever the capitalist enterprise starts up: 'the separation of worker from the means of production'. The worker, that is the assistant, is dependent upon the means of production provided by the state. As a result of this, he is just as dependent upon the director of the institute as any employee in a factory.[27]

Weber's comparison of the German and American university systems is a highly materialist account of how institutional arrangements set up complex power relations, and how these in turn create distinct systems of obligation as well as potential for advancement and autonomy for the actors within them. Thus, the market both trapped the American academic and provided him with a strategy for career advancement, while the German system created a client–patron relation which both subordinated the young to the old and provided the young with a sense of their moral claim on a fixed post in return for their services to the professor.

By starting with concrete cases, Weber is implying – *contra* Habermas – that ethical questions appear *only* where there are inequalities of power. Except where power is exercised arbitrarily it creates not only dependency on the part of the subordinates, but also responsibility and obligation on the part of the powerful. There is nothing sentimental about this conception of obligation. Fulfilling obligations is a condition of exercising power over another actor or, in the case of a dominant class, fulfilling obligations is a condition of class rule. Nevertheless, unequal power, for Weber, normally sets up a nexus of dependency, obligation and autonomy for *all* actors in the power relation, and it is because power is a social relation, indeed because it *creates* social relations, that ethical issues and dilemmas arise in the first place. It is this triadic relationship between dependency, obligation, and autonomy which makes social negotiation both necessary and possible. There is no obligation without dependency, but, more radically, there is no autonomy without dependency either. Social life is largely this negotiation of dependency, obligation and autonomy.

We can see this more clearly by examining the relationship between the academic, the state and the student. Weber's 'realist' (or 'materialist') analysis suggests that no discussion of the rights of academics to express opinion can ignore two simple facts about their situation: (i) that they have power over students; (ii) they are state employees (in the German case they were – and remain – civil servants). To ignore this would be to slip into an absolutizing discourse which is prone to self-deception and idealism, not to say hypocrisy. The *practical* ethical question then becomes what kind of 'contract' between teacher and student, and teacher and the state can both protect (relative) academic freedom *and* identify its legitimate limits. Weber's notion of 'value freedom' is intended to resolve both issues at once.

With respect to the state, the central dilemma is how can an academic be a civil servant without being the tool of the state? His essential answer is this: only by being value free. To claim an *absolute right* to the freedom to expound, promulgate and disseminate particular beliefs is to tacitly accept the right of the state to employ the academy as a tool of state propaganda. On the basis of this analysis, we might reconstruct a Weberian's critique of so-called 'radical sociology' as follows: only by leaving their dependency upon the state unacknowledged could radical sociologists claim an absolute right to criticize those institutions upon which they were dependents and whose indulgence, it now turns out, was a condition of the possibility of that critique. A similar mistake was made by those radical sociologists of the Right who generally were converted to new Right ideology at about the time as the new Right's political project had stalled. While dramatically changing the content of radical sociology's values, sociological representatives of the new Right retained their opponent's orientation to political values and its analysis of the relationship between political stance and scientific research. By making an absolute claim to the right to criticize or defend the *status quo*, radical sociology of both the Left and the Right correspond to Schluchter's neat characterization of an ethic of conviction:

The true believer is a rationalist in terms of a cosmic ethic. He [*sic*] seeks to base his value position on an objectively given or intelligible principle that makes possible a permanent hierarchical order of values and at the same time ethically neutralizes the paradox of consequences vis-à-vis the act's intention. He tends towards principled action which is in the nature of a monologue, and either flees from the world or tries to revolutionize it. He sanctifies either the retreat into inwardness or the charismatic new beginning. His political maxim is 'all or nothing'.[28]

The 'paradox of consequences' ignored in this case stems from the fact that value freedom is part of the contract between the academic and the state in which the autonomy of the former is recognized and respected by the latter, and in which the scholar accepts that politics provides the appropriate public space for ideological dispute. It is only this contract which demarcates state from academy where the state is paymaster[29]. Since the line of demarcation is vulnerable, to break the contract by laying claim to an absolute right to employ the lecture theatre as a platform for expounding a substantive *Weltanschauung* is to enter into a Faustian pact. We are here confronted with an uncomfortable and disquieting possibility: for the state-employed scholar self-censorship in certain spheres may be a precondition for freedom to talk at all from any position of 'authority'.

Weber's defence of this argument is similarly attentive to the material conditions under which academic life is practised. Academic freedom of speech is distinguished from other free expression of opinion because it is not (or should not be) the subject of (non-academic) supervision, surveillance, or even criticism. The lecture theatre is thus a privileged space, and this places an obligation upon the teacher. With respect to the students, obligation arises because of the power the teacher has vis-à-vis the student. Here again it is the privileged space of the lecture theatre which is crucial:

> To the prophet and the demagogue it is said 'go forth into the streets and speak openly'; that is to say, where criticism is possible. In the lecture theatre where one stands in front of the listeners, it is theirs to be silent and the teacher's to speak. Where students must follow a teacher's course for the sake of their advancement and where there is no one present to meet the teacher with criticism, I hold it to be irresponsible to use the opportunity not, as it is his task, to be useful to the listeners through his knowledge and scientific experience, but to imprint upon them his own personal political point of view.[30]

The lecturer, unlike the demagogue or prophet, does not have to seek an audience; the audience is captive, sent by the state and the market, and Weber insists that we do not forget this.[31]

Weber's arguments often sound old-fashioned and moralistic. They tend to be cast in terms of self-discipline, self-restraint, responsibility, duty, etc. These are values not inappropriate to one who was not merely an academic in the German university system but also a bourgeois liberal. But to understand Weber's standpoint further, we must turn to the 'ethical theory' which underpins it. But I want to repeat the point made above: Weber does not have an *ethical* theory which can be clearly demarcated from his political (strategic) and sociological (diagnostic) analysis. Weber's concerns are both ethical and political, and it is thus perhaps less surprising that he should dress an argument for value freedom in a highly moralistic and politicized rhetoric.

Politics and ethics

As Wolfgang Schluchter[32] has shown, the ethical view implicit in Weber's emphasis on the limits of technical criticism and scientific knowledge turns on the distinction between an 'ethic of conviction' (*Gesinnungsethik*) and an 'ethic of responsibility' (*Verantwortungsethik* – literally, an ethic of answerability), and upon his argument that it is the latter which is appropriate to the scientist (as it is to the modern politician).

The moral concept with which an ethic of responsibility is most closely linked is 'duty',[33] and the scientist is above all a *Pflichtmensch* (a duty-bound person). The concept of duty as the ethical basis of an action has particular characteristics which distinguish it from the other ethical arguments which are common when social scientists discuss their discipline. In the first place, 'duty' is role specific. One cannot say 'my duty' without implying 'my duty as...'. Thus duty is an ethical part of the constitution of an empirical subject and is not universalizable; it is not open to 'rational reconstruction'. But neither is it an arbitrary expression of that individual's will. Duty is binding ('Here I am I can do no other') in two senses: first, it is bound by roles which are located in a network of complex social relations and practices from which an actor cannot simply escape; second, it is bound by the intrinsic characteristics of the tasks at hand in that role. It is my duty to recognize the implications and limitation of the tasks I, as a scientist, politician, etc., undertake:

> With every professional task the matter as such demands its due and wants to be tackled according to its inherent laws. With every professional task he to whom it has been assigned has to restrict himself and eliminate everything that is not strictly proper to the task – particularly his own loves and hates. [34]

Habermas is thus wrong to criticize Weber's ethical views as 'decisionistic'.[35] It is not that we make ethical decisions in isolation as an expression of individual will or predilection, but rather that all our decisions – including practical, e.g. career ones – commit us to a web of interrelated obligations and duties of which we may at first be only dimly aware, but which are nevertheless constraining and binding.

Weber's account of action is an attempt to overcome the idealistic polarization of communication–action and power by arguing that *all* acts are 'always already' *both* the 'expression of an idea' *and* an exercise of power. It is this characteristic of action as power–action which makes an ethic of responsibility both necessary and possible. Acts which are solely the imposition of the will of one actor upon another without raising questions of responsibility and obligation for the powerful or are meaningful for those accepting that another's will cannot be taken as a paradigm of social action in general. Thus in Habermas's ideal speech situation where unequal power relations are excluded *a priori*, there would, on Weber's view, simply be no ethical matters to discuss. Ethical questions arise only in the process of the negotiation and legitimation of power relations; including its obligations and limitations. This is not to deny that actors are unequal, nor that exploitation is taking place, but does assume that in all but the most grotesque and arbitrary acts there is a negotiation of meaning between the actors in which appeals to responsibility, fairness and consistency do have some form of purchase and are not merely ideological smokescreens.

The central point I am making about the ethical basis of Weber's defence of the means–ends distinction is this: the notion of an ethic of responsibility provides us with a language for discussing ethical matters in science which is neither universalist and formal nor implies an arbitrary act of will or merely the exercise of naked power. Another, and I think more accurate, way of making this point would be to argue that Weber does not have a *theory* of ethics at all, but a theory of social action in which 'ethical' and 'practical' questions cannot be separated. Such a reading would make Weber's views seem paradoxical, contradictory even. We appear to have a defence of a distinction between means and ends which itself presupposes its opposite – i.e. the entanglement of the practical and the ethical; of *Zweck* and *Wert*.

VALUE FREEDOM AS STRATEGY AND PERSONAL CODE

The above discussion raises the question: if value freedom is not a strict methodological principle, then what is it? The answer I shall suggest here is that it must be understood in terms of the two interrelated practices: first, as the professional strategy of the scholar; second, and more conventionally, as his/her ethic or code of conduct.

Value freedom as a professional strategy

For those excluded from the means of production there remain several spheres of activity and institutions monopoly over which secures advantage. Among these are forms of non-productive property (e.g. residential property), the administrative apparatus, knowledge, the right to withdraw labour, credentials (or the right to bestow credentials), etc. The dilemma of the German scholar to which Weber refers is that 'his' access to the means of production was being primitively accumulated by the state–capitalist

university system as the quasi-independent intellectual producer – the
Privatdozent – was being converted into an employee. We can understand the
precarious nature of this situation if we compare the academic with other
civil servants.

Civil servants in the narrower (English) sense are said by Weber to have
two chief sources of power: (i) knowledge of the rules and procedures of
decision-making and implementation (*Dienstwissen*); (ii) specialized expertise (*Fachwissen*).[36] The power of civil servants' *Dienstwissen* derives from
their location with the bureaucratic institutions of the state. Being outside
powerful decision-making bureaucracies, the academic's *Dienstwissen*
cannot be a major source of power. Where academics are excluded from
internal university decision-making their *Dienstwissen* is not a source of
power even *within* the institutions in which they work. We could almost offer
a Weberian definition of academics as 'civil servants without *Dienstwissen*'.
They are thus forced to make do with that form of knowledge over which
they, even more than the civil servants, can lay a legitimate claim (i.e.
Fachwissen). But in the human sciences their grasp on even this tenuous
source of power is weak. They, more than the natural sciences who have long
since won decisive victories over common-sense naturalistic knowledge, have
the constant task of differentiating their knowledge from that of the lay
person. The problem here is one of *authority* and *legitimacy* (i.e. of the
recognition of the knowledge we claim as legitimate). Since the only other
source of power within the academy is the monopoly right to bestow
legitimate credentials, it is particularly important that the authoritative
status of specialized knowledge within the universities is maintained.

Thus Weber's analysis of the duties and responsibilities of the scholar
links methodological issues not merely to a professional ethic but also to
status group strategy: i.e. the academic's dilemma must be understood also
in terms of his/her class position and the types of strategy which may be
deployed to defend or improve that position. The situation to be 'defended'
has been neatly summarized by Gostä Esping-Andersen speaking of
professionals more generally:

> the professional will usually stand outside the lines of command, possess
> a great deal of autonomy but probably little authority over subordinates;
> professionals' approach to work is task-orientated and their authority,
> legitimacy and collective identity are more likely to derive from the
> scientific standards of their chosen discipline, and not from bureaucratic
> office.[37]

He goes on to add, 'the professional is, indeed, the antithesis to hierarchy
and a Fordist system of regulation'.[38] My argument here is that the chief
strategic function of value freedom is to maintain this distance from 'lines of
command' and autonomy from 'Fordist systems of regulation'.

If this pragmatic reconstruction of Weber's politics of institutions is valid,
then it becomes clear why he should insist on the technical character of

social scientific knowledge *even if he does not have sufficiently strong philosophical or methodological arguments to defend the view*. Since there is no expert knowledge about values, a sphere in which we are all equally specialists or dilettantes, to admit too overt value judgements into academic debate is not merely to abuse the right to speak in the privileged space of the lecture theatre, it is also to undermine the conditions which maintain and perpetuate that privilege.[39]

To present Weber's views on value judgements as a form of concealment, or dissemblance, and as strategy of a status group whose hold over even that weak source of power which they do have is tenuous and vulnerable to erosion is to open it to the accusation of duplicity. Here the objection would be that value freedom is no more than a self-serving strategy; that by withdrawing from public debate academic dignity is protected. But this would be too hasty. The question is also one of the *effectiveness* of possible interventions. If Weber is right to argue that a monopoly of specialized knowledge is the sole source of academic authority, then it would follow, first, that authority must be secured and defended *before* effective intervention in public debate is possible and, second, effective intervention is limited. To enter the public arena on the same (value) territory as the politician is to compete directly from a position of strategic weakness. The issue here is not then merely one of the 'dignity' of professionals, but also of their effectiveness as actors in a public and political arena, and effectiveness cannot be separated from legitimate authority.

There is a second, and somewhat more enticing, possibility here. It may be possible to view 'value freedom' not merely as professional dissemblance, but also as a subversive strategy. From a position of political weakness the scholar cannot set the immediate agenda on questions of politics, ethics, etc. But one option which remains open is to constantly question the implicit logical and empirical assumptions which necessarily underlie the arguments of those who can and do set such agendas.[40] The disadvantage of such a strategy is that it, in turn, lets politics set the academic agenda. The alternative is to assume that sooner or later politics is itself an expression of an idea and to view academic work as a means of indirectly influencing non-academic agendas, albeit with a time lag. This latter strategy would attempt to maximize the advantage that can be drawn from the fact of political weakness by grasping the liberating opportunity this offers to those who are not responsible on a day-to-day basis. It takes advantage of the fact that because what we say is in a certain sense of no consequence we can in particular spheres at least say anything we want.[41]

It may be a bit fanciful to present Weber's 'value freedom' as some kind of precursor to Adorno's 'negative dialectics', but as a strategy for effective intervention fighting on that ground on which one is relatively secure may be more 'efficient' than endangering that limited authority which does flow from the position one occupies by over-extending the claims which can legitimately be made. If the power-base of the scholar is as weak as Weber's analysis of *Fachwissen* suggests, then to intervene directly in the substance of public debate would entail seeking some additional source of authority, and this, in turn, would mean subordinating oneself to some external discipline, for example the discipline of a party. We may succeed in having influence, but at the cost of a change of identity – at the cost of becoming a spokesperson. This is clearly also a valid strategy in its own right and a perfectly legitimate personal choice, but it is strategy and choice of a different kind. Value freedom, in the minimalist interpretation suggested here, may be understood as a refusal of such authority and resistance to its consequence: the reformation of an internal academic agenda by an external one.

I think that these strategic concerns constitute half the sociological story about value freedom. But I have also suggested that Weber makes only a loose distinction between ethical and practical concerns. The intellectual has to live this strategy as a personal ethic. It has to be part of what Weber calls the 'personality' of the scientist. Duty and self-interest are thus bound together; not 'merely a duty but also a pleasure', as it were.

Value freedom as ethic and 'personality'

But what does such a code entail? We have to act as though value freedom were possible, and to do so we have not only to refrain from making judgements – or appearing to do so – we must also adopt an attitude of cold *Sachlichkeit* (objectivity, matter-of-factness). Again the comparison with the civil servant is appropriate. *Sachlichkeit* is their code too. But for the civil servant it consists in the emotionless implementation of orders (no matter how absurd one may believe them to be) and in appearing as if one believed things which one may not. *Sachlichkeit* for the intellectual is something else: the cold and emotionless chronicling and interpretation of events and development of which one may either approve or disapprove; and, as Weber repeatedly emphasizes, the 'courage' to face facts which may be uncomfortable and inconvenient.

Social scientists have, on this view, again only an indirect contribution to make to normative debate by raising a series of questions about the material conditions and implications of the various substantive positions available. While we cannot but reflect contemporary values, debates and concerns in our choice of subjects and in the way in which we treat them, it is better that we adumbrate those substantive concerns and leave to others (to non-specialists) the task of drawing the conclusions. It is only by recognizing the limits of what the specialists can contribute that the distinctiveness of their contribution can be identified. And it is only by abstention from the substantive issues in question that they can avoid parochialism. As Habermas points out, for Weber there are only two kinds of modern subject: the specialist and the dilettante.[42] While the attractions of dilettantism are many, it is the sad fate of the specialist to resist them.

'Value freedom' then becomes not a doctrine but the specialist's code of conduct and argumentative tactic.

ACADEMICS, SCHOLARS AND INTELLECTUALS

I have been arguing that Weber's defence of value freedom is grounded at least as much in a sociological analysis of the social location of the academic/scholar as it is in a philosophy of social science. But most academics are not intellectuals, and most intellectuals are not academics. How might such an analysis be applied to the role of the intellectual and what are its limitations in this context?

By identifying the social location of the academic/scholar in terms of (i) their dependence upon an employer (usually but not necessarily the state) and (ii) the specific source of their power and autonomy from that employer (their *Fachwissen*), we have a kind of negative sociological definition of the intellectual as one who has broken free of the chains of dependency by successfully appealing to an audience far beyond the lecture theatre and on the basis of an authority which is relatively independent of any specific institutional context. In this sense at least, Karl Mannheim's much criticized characterization of intelligentsia as *Freischwebend* (free floating) may not be so far wrong when applied to intellectuals. The intellectual may be an employee (even of a university) out of the irksome necessity of earning a crust, but has succeeded in transcending the limitations (and also what Weber considers the duties) of the employee's position. Furthermore, as Zygmunt Bauman's sociological definition of the intellectual as one who can 'legislate' as well as 'interpret'[43] suggests, the mental property to which the intellectual lays claim cannot be restricted to mere *Fachwissen*. One might go further and argue that the claim to know must be focused precisely upon that which Weber says we cannot know in the modern and disenchanted world (and Bauman says we cannot know in the 'postmodern' and fragmented world), namely the answer to Tolstoy's question 'What shall we do and how shall we live?' This is the very question which Weber forbids the scholar even to address.

This breaking free from the kinds of constraints through which Weber analysed the position of the scholar suggests a weakness in his sociological analysis, but also throws light on the dilemma of the intellectuals in addressing the question of their responsibility. I shall address both points briefly.

Weber's strictures on the scholar are too narrow and too strict. They are most appropriate to the specific context of the lecture theatre (where the audience is not there out of their own volition and the possibility of free criticism is weak). But the lines between the academic and the intellectual which Weber clearly wants to defend are not as clear-cut outside the lecture theatre in contexts where there is, at least theoretically, equal and free criticism, and they are even less clear-cut when we remember that in research and writing the academic is not (always) in the normal sense of the term an 'employee' (i.e. one who performs tasks ascribed by superordinates). The ambiguity of the academic's role which hovers between employment and self-employment is a sociological fact Weber chooses to ignore. In a sense, any intellectual work exists both in the lecture theatre and (as for the prophet) on the streets. This problem is a symptom of a more general weakness in Weber's analysis, namely, the tendency to reduce the functionary to the function.[44] In so far as all intellectual work is open to scrutiny in a public sphere in which the appeal to *Fachwissen* cannot protect the author from criticism, academics might be said to have no less right, and perhaps a great deal more opportunity than most, to try their hand at claiming (however bogusly) intellectual authority. Weber's strictures are therefore most likely to appeal to those who least fancy their chances on the wider stage and/or adhere to something like a civil service ethic. It is ironic that Weber was well aware of the inappropriateness of the civil service model for creating leading political figures, but did not draw the same conclusion in the case of intellectual 'leadership'. Indeed, the negative definition of the intellectual as one not fully constrained by institutional conditions parallels Weber's view of the effective politician as one not fully restrained by the procedural and institutional context of political life – i.e. as rule breaker.

But more interesting than the light the peculiarities of social location of the intellectual throws on the weaknesses of Weber's analysis is what it tells us about the dilemma facing intellectuals themselves. It is relatively easy to deduce duties and responsibilities from institutionally-bound social roles. But to whom and in what respects are we answerable if we have succeeded in throwing off those institutional shackles? To our conscience? (But against what should one check this?) To 'society' or 'the public'? (But what is it and who are they?) To the truth? (But what is it and whose?) To our work? (But is it worthy?) To no one? For those for whom the price of such freedom is too high – its associated dilemmas too painful – or who no longer value such autonomy (perhaps out of conviction) there remains the option of voluntarily giving up that autonomy and placing themselves at the service of some chosen institution, for example a party.

In extending the analysis of the scholar to the intellectual, the arts of sociological method as practised by Weber are up against their limitations. Sociological analysis is faced with the challenge of analysing a 'social location' which is relatively unfettered by institutional constraints. The intellectual is a sub-category of the entrepreneur and Weber's analysis is so focused upon those who are, in essence, servants (civil or otherwise) that it is of limited use in understanding the nature of those who – like economic entrepreneurs, politicians and intellectuals – are not, or refuse to be subordinated to a higher authority, who to a degree break free of institutional constraints and who employ social institutions to their own ends.[45] We need, but do not have, a sociological analysis of the entrepreneur – of those who manipulate institutions – which is as convincing as the account Weber offers of the constraints acting upon those who are manipulated by such institutions.

ACKNOWLEDGEMENT

This is an extended version of an article 'Value Freedom and Intellectual Autonomy' which appeared in *History of the Human Sciences*, 8 (3), 1995, pp. 69–88. I would like to thank the journal's editors for permission to republish material from that article here.

NOTES

1 J. Habermas, 'Heinrich Heine and the intellectual in Germany' in *The New Conservatism*, Cambridge: Polity Press, 1989. Following D. Bering, *Die Intellektuellen: Geschichte eines Schimpfwortes*, Stuttgart: Klett-Cotta Verlag, 1978, Habermas also points out that *Intellektuelle* retained pejorative connotations and such terms as *Geistigen*, *Geistesmenschen* and *Geistesadel* – variations on 'those concerned with mental life' which still have a respectful almost deferential ring – were generally preferred.

2 Ibid. pp. 77–8.

3 Ibid, p. 78.

4 Ibid, p. 78.

5 Ibid, p. 78. M. Stark (ed.), *Deutsche Intellektuelle 1910–1933*, Heidelberg, Verlag Lambert Schneider, 1984, contains statements of all these views from a wide range of intellectuals writing between 1910 and 1933. Further discussion of the position of intellectuals in Germany is contained in F. K. Ringer, *The Decline of the German Mandarins: The German Academic Community, 1890–1933*, Cambridge, MA, Harvard University Press, 1969, and Bering, *Die Intellectuellen*, 1978. On the post-war period, see H. Glasser, *Kulturgeschichte der Bundesrepublik Deutschland*, Vol. 1, Munich and Vienna, Carl Hanser Verlag, 1986, Part 3. A well-known sociological analysis of the role and social position of intellectuals in Germany can be found in Norbert Elias's *Civilizing Process*, Oxford, Blackwell, 1994 (1939) along with a useful discussion of terms such as *Kulture* with which, Elias argues, German intellectuals sought to distinguish themselves from the aristocratic circles from which they were in any case excluded. For a conservative critique of German intellectuals, see A. Gehlen, *Einblicke*, Frankfurt am Main, Vittorio Klostermann, 1978, Part 4.

6 M. Weber, 'Politik als Beruf' [1919] in M. Weber, *Gesammelte politische Schriften*, edited by J. Winckelmann, Tübingen, J. C. B. Mohr, 1988. Translated in H. H. Girth and C. Wright Mills (eds): *From Max Weber*, London, Routledge, 1948 and in P. Lassman and R. Speirs (eds), *Weber: Political Writings*, Cambridge, Cambridge University Press, 1994.

7 M. Weber, 'Wissenschaft als Beruf' [1919] in M. Weber, *Gesammelte Aufsätze zur Wissenschaftslehre*, 3rd edition, edited by J. Winckelmann, Tübingen, J. C. B. Mohr, 1968. Translated in H. H. Girth and C. Wright Mills (eds): *From Max Weber* and in P. Lassman. and I. Velody (eds) *Max Weber's 'Science as a Vocation'*, London, Unwin Hyman, 1989. In subsequent notes, I have given both the standard German source and, in square brackets, the standard English translation. (In the case of 'Science as a Vocation', English language references are to the Girth and Mills collection.)

8   This discussion is not primarily intended as a contribution to Weber scholarship, though it will entail an interpretation of his arguments; rather, I want to use some selective aspects of his views on science to throw light on current debates and on the role of the 'intellectual'. There are already a number of excellent non-positivist readings of Weber's views on value freedom which place them in the context of his general sociology, the debates which informed them and the conditions under which they came to be written. See R. König, 'Einige Überlegungen zur Frage der "Werturteilsfreiheit" bei Max Weber', *Kölner Zeitschrift für Soziologie*, 15, 1964, pp. 1–27; W. Schluchter, *Wertfreiheit und Verantwortungsethik*, Tübingen, J. C. B. Mohr, 1971 (translated and revised as Schluchter, 'Value Freedom and the Ethic of Responsibility' in G. Roth and W. Schluchter *Max Weber's Vision of History: Ethics and Method*, Berkeley, University of California Press, 1979); the Afterword to W. J. Mommsen, *Max Weber and German Politics, 1890–1920*, 2nd edition, Chicago, Chicago University Press, 1981; and Part III of P. Lassman and I. Velody (eds), *Max Weber's 'Science as a Vocation'*, 1989. For a sophisticated attempt to develop an ideal typical account of intellectuals on the basis of Weber's general sociology, and particularly on his sociology of religion, see A. Sadri, *Max Weber's Sociology of Intellectuals*, New York and Oxford, Oxford University Press, 1992.

9   E. Wittenberg, 'The crisis of science in Germany in 1919', [1938] in Lassman and Velody (eds), *Max Weber's Science as a Vocation*, p. 114.

10 Ibid, p. 118.

11 H. Rickert, 'Max Weber's view of science' [1926] in Lassman and Velody (eds), *Max Weber's 'Science as a Vocation'*, 1989, p. 85.

12 'Die "Objektivität" sozialwissenschaftlicher und sozialpolitischer Erkenntnis' [1904] in *Wissenschaftslehre*, 1968, p. 150. Translated in M. Weber, *The Methodology of the Social Sciences*, E. A. Shils and H. A. Finch (eds), New York, Free Press, 1949, p. 53.

13 Ibid, p. 151 [*The Methodology*, 1949, p. 54].

14 'After the disintegration of the Christian illusion we must face the inescapability of value conflict and the permanent ethical problem of how to act upon values', Schluchter, 'Value-Neutrality', in Roth and Schluchter, *Max Weber's Vision of History*, op. cit., p. 89.

15 R. König, 'Einige Überlegungen zur Frage der "Werturteilsfreiheit" bei Max Weber', op. cit. 1964.

16 Cf. D. Sayer, *Capitalism and Modernity: an excursus in Marx and Weber*, London, Routledge, 1991, pp. 149–50.

17 Pragmatic and political interpretations of Weber's methodology have been offered before, for example by W. J. Mommsen, *The Political and Social Theory of Max Weber*, Cambridge, Polity Press, 1989 and Schluchter, 'Value-Neutrality', 1979. These have focused on the political conditions in Germany at the time in which Weber was writing. Without wanting to deny the importance of these factors, here we shall focus on the general institutional politics of 'value freedom'.

18 See K-O. Apel, *Towards the Transformation of Philosophy*, London, Routledge, 1980.

19 'Die "Objektivität" ', 1904, p. 184; [*The Methodology*, 1949, p. 84].

20 Weber 'Wissenschaft als Beruf', 1968, p. 605 [Girth and Mills (eds), 1948, p. 149].

21 A. Salz, 'For science against the intellectuals among its despisers' [1921] in Lassman and Velody, *Max Weber's Science as a Vocation*, 1989, p. 49.

22 Weber, 'Wissenschaft als Beruf', p. 607 [Girth and Mills (eds), 1948: 150].

23 'Die "Objektivität" ', 1904, p. 151 [*The Methodology*, 1949, p. 53].

24 Habermas makes a similar criticism of Adorno's and Horkheimer's *Dialectic of Enlightenment*. See J. Habermas, *The Philosophical Discourse of Modernity*, Cambridge, Polity Press, 1987, Ch. 5.

25 Mommsen, *Political and Social Theory*, 1989, notes the oddity of the fact that Weber should argue for value freedom as a scientist while being through and through a political person. It may have been Weber's view that for the scientist the former was a condition for the latter.

26 Since it is so clear that Weber is talking about the position of men in the university system, and since I am arguing that the starting point of the analysis is the location of subjects with empirical identities, I shall use the masculine pronoun when referring to analysis of a turn-of-the-century university career.

27 Weber 'Wissenschaft als Beruf', 1968, p. 584 [Girth and Mills (eds), 1948, p. 131].

28 Schluchter, 'Value-neutrality', 1979, p. 89.

29 Weber was defending the autonomy of the university not only against the state, but against any other potential patron. Thus, for example, he joined Max Planck and Theodor Mommsen in objecting to plans to found a Catholic university in Salzburg. See, W. Weiss, and E. Hanisch (eds) *Vermittlungen: Texte und Kontexte österreichischer Literatur und Geschichte im 20. Jahrhundert* , Salzburg, Residenz Verlag, 1990, p. 39.

30 Weber, 'Wissenschaft als Beruf', 1968, p. 602 [Girth and Mills (eds), 1948, p. 146].

31 To this it may be objected that the 'audiences' towards whom Weber considers us to have a responsibility constitute a highly selective list: merely students and (state) employers. Is there no 'duty' towards a wider social or human community? Is this not the powerful thought which lies behind the kind of radical sociology? This is an important criticism to which the issue of effectiveness is a partial response.

32 'Value-Neutrality', 1979.

33 Beetham has recently argued that 'obedience' on the part of those subject to the power of others has a moral dimension and cannot be understood exclusively as a 'rational choice'; as a pragmatic adjustment to the realities of unequal power. Weber's discussions of 'duty' suggest that it mirrors obedience as the 'moral' dimension of the exercise of power over others. See D. Beetham *The Legitimation of Power*, London, Macmillan, 1991.

34 M. Weber, 'Der Sinn der "Wertfreiheit" ', in *Wissenschaftslehre*, 1968, p. 494 [*The Methodology*, 1949, p. 4.].

35 J. Habermas, *Towards a Rational Society*, London, Heinemann, 1970, Ch.5.

36 Weber, 'Parlament und Regierung im neugeordneten Deutschland' [1918] in Weber 1988, translated in Lassman and Speirs (eds) *Weber: Political Writings*, 1994.

37 'Post-Industrial Class Structures' in G. Esping-Andersen (ed.) *Changing Classes: Stratification and Mobility in Post-Industrial Societies*, London, Sage, 1993, p. 13.

38 Ibid, p. 13.

39 This discussion has a bearing on Zygmunt Bauman's analysis of the intellectual as 'legislator' and 'interpreter', but it suggests the opposite conclusion to that drawn by him. For Bauman, the loss of the right to legislate is a sign of the growing weakness of the intellectual in 'post-modernity'. In contrast, I am suggesting that the refusal to legislate is one of his/her few sources of real power and authority. It might be further possible to argue that the right to legislate was always a sign of weakness rather than strength – i.e. that legislative authority derived from the intellectual's status as spokesperson for some other higher authority (e.g. church or state) and therefore was an index of dependence rather than autonomy. See Z. Bauman, *Legislators and Interpreters*, Cambridge, Polity Press, 1985.

40   This case has been advanced by the German historian Detlev Peukert in *Max Weber's Diagnose der Moderne*, Göttingen, Vandenhoeck and Ruprecht, 1989 (especially Chapter 5). Peukert shows how Weber mobilized the concept of value freedom against the kinds of racialist theories which were current in Germany at the time and which later provided a 'scientific' underpinning for National Socialism. He argues that value freedom has a critical potential: '[Weber's] objections to the social and racial biology of an Alfred Ploetz at the Frankfurt Sociology Conference in 1910 illuminate for us today the critical potential of an insistence on freedom from value judgement' (p. 94).

41   Weber's own frequent and influential interventions in political questions – for example in his proposal for a 'plebiscitary president' during the debate on the Weimar constitution – provide a striking example of the difficulty of sustaining this posture particularly where the individual in question is both an academic and a National Liberal politician. There is marked inconsistency between Weber's methodological posture ('posturing'?) and personality.

42   J. Habermas, *The Theory of Communicative Action*, Vol.2, Cambridge, Polity Press, 1987.

43   Bauman, *Legislators*, 1985.

44   Maurice Halbwachs, a student of Durkheim, offers a powerful critique of Weber on this point. See, Halbwachs, 'Social classes and their traditions' in *On Collective Memory*, edited and translated by Lewis Coser, Chicago, University of Chicago Press, 1992.

45   But for a contrary view, see A. Sadri, *Max Weber's Sociology of Intellectuals*. For example, 'Neither his epistemological views regarding separation of facts and values that undermine those intellectual ideologies that link scholastic knowledge and public good, nor his critique of the irresponsibility and public good, nor his critique of the irresponsibility and naivety of intellectuals dabbling in politics, inhibited Weber's endorsement of intellectuals as champions of individuality' (p. 74).

4 Of treason, blindness and silence

Dilemmas of the intellectual in modern France

Jeremy Jennings

Proof of the concern on the Right to displace the intellectual from what is taken to be an undue and dangerous pre-eminence is not difficult to find. One recent example comes in a volume entitled *Thinkers of the Left*, published in 1985 by one of the most articulate spokesmen of contemporary British conservatism, Roger Scruton.[1] The list of intellectuals under attack diverges only slightly from the standard right-wing demonology, the emphasis falling here upon twentieth-century Marxists, with amongst the culprits E. P. Thompson, Foucault, Althusser, Habermas, Perry Anderson, Lukács, Galbraith and, of course, Sartre. The argument, however, is broadly familiar. In the twentieth century, we are asked to believe, a 'minority consensus' emerged amongst intellectuals that meant it 'ceased to be respectable to defend the customs, institutions and policy of Western States'. Intellectuals, in other words, went soft on communism. To this is then added the usual list of complaints about the self-deception of the intellectual. The Left-intellectual is typically a Jacobin, convinced of his own right to rule and that the world itself is deficient in wisdom: drawn towards a 'totalitarian outlook', he insists on forcing the messy reality of actual human society into the geometrical mould of an abstract idea (with predictable disaster). Personal abuse is also not lacking. Lukács, for example, is described as 'a representative monster of the Habsburg bourgeoisie'. Yet Scruton gives the argument about intellectuals a new, more theological dimension. No one, Scruton argues, gives better witness than Jean-Paul Sartre to the collective consciousness of the post-war intelligentsia: and this is 'a consciousness of Hell'! What the reader is fully to make of this only becomes apparent when we consider Scruton's later remarks about Jacques Derrida and structuralism in general (amongst the guilty are held to be Bourdieu, Baudrillard, Deleuze, Guattari, Kristeva and, of course, Foucault).[2] All are cast as the destroyers of 'bourgeois reality', a reality that Scruton ardently wishes to preserve as 'the gift of human freedom'. The world of deconstruction, challenging the legitimacy of all authority, is therefore characterized as a world not of presence but of absence, not of people but of vacant idols, not of creation but of uncreation. It is, above all, 'a world in which negation has been endowed with the supreme instruments – power and intellect'. As such, Scruton concludes, it is 'the world of the Devil'.

Scruton now teaches in the United States and it is clear that his decision to turn his fire specifically against the *French* intellectual derives much from his experience of the American university campus. There, he believes, the 'academic citadel' is under threat from 'radical feminists, "gay" activists and "multiculturalists"' armed with the theories of French deconstruction.[3]

This, of late, has been a common theme in the English-speaking world. It surfaces, for example, in Robert Hughes's highly-esteemed *Culture of Complaint: The Fraying of America*.[4] Hughes's concern is what he sees as the fragmentation and tribalization of American cultural life, typified by both the political demagogy of the Reaganite Right as well as the passion for political correctness now sweeping the American Left. In the latter, he believes, French writers such as Foucault and Derrida bear a heavy responsibility. It would be difficult, Hughes writes, 'to find a worse – or more authoritarian – dead end than this'. It is, he goes on, little more than a rationalization of failure in which 'the intellectual...is thought to be as helpless against power and control as a salmon in a polluted stream, the only difference being that we, unlike the fish, *know* the water is polluted'. More controversially, it figures in Camille Paglia's polemical remarks deriding what she terms 'the Parisian paper matchbox', with Lacan, Derrida and Foucault cast as 'the perfect prophets for the weak, anxious academic personality, trapped in verbal formulas and perennially defeated by circumstance'.[5] In more sober fashion, Gertrude Himmelfarb has characterized the 'siren call of liberation and creativity' associated with French postmodernism as 'an invitation to intellectual and moral suicide'.[6] Likewise, someone as eminent as the late Ernest Gellner could describe Paris as 'the world capital of obscurity' and then go on to account for the worldwide influence of the likes of Barthes, Foucault and Derrida in terms of 'a demand for obscurity'.[7]

Tony Judt, to considerable controversy (especially in France), has recently said much the same thing in his *Past Imperfect: French Intellectuals, 1944–1956*, a work first published in French.[8] 'The French intellectual', he writes, 'is alive and well everywhere...except in Paris'. In an exercise of uncritical self-denial characterized by the abnegation of their own culture, academics and students from London to Los Angeles, Judt tells us, have turned to such French imports as deconstruction, postmodernity and poststructuralism. 'The prospect of Jacques Derrida', he comments, 'selling his wares on the sun-dappled streets of California is not quite right'. Why this should be so is not exactly clear. Would the sight of the British liberal Sir Isaiah Berlin doing the same thing be thought to be equally incongruous? But the substance of the charge is that the aggressively subjectivist reading of authors such as Foucault and Derrida typical of the United States campus has left us with nothing but 'a post-modern Cheshire cat, with a Ph.D., grinning'.

Judt's own intellectual trajectory itself would merit attention but an early glimpse of the argument that he came to put forward in his latest volume can be found in *The Times Literary Supplement* in 1991.[9] In that piece, the person and project that most evoked Judt's anger was none other than Bernard-Henri Lévy and his *Les Aventures de la liberté*.[10] Rightly observing that the subject of the latter was not the history of French intellectuals in the twentieth century but the author himself, Judt dryly remarks that in his own person, B-HL, however unwittingly, provided evidence of the very problem he was analysing.[11] Specifically – and as proof of the contemporary decline of the intellectual in France – what Judt disputed was Lévy's claim that his group of *nouveaux philosophes* had been the first to grasp the horrible truth about totalitarianism.[12] They said nothing, Judt commented, that had 'not been said earlier, and better, by Camus, Aron and scores of Italians, Poles and Czechs'. That the claim should even have been made, he remarks, is testimony to the insularity and selective amnesia characteristic not just of Lévy's generation, but of generations of intellectuals in France that had preceded it. The only difference between Sartre and his heirs, Judt stated (reworking Marx's old joke), was that the first appeared as tragedy, the second as farce.[13]

Ostensibly Judt's subject in *Past Imperfect* is what he describes as a collective myopia in the face of Stalinism displayed by French intellectuals in the post-war years. The targets of the attack are not surprising: for the most part, Sartre and his various friends plus Emmanuel Mounier's *Esprit* and its editor between 1957–76, Jean-Marie Domenach. It is a reasonably well-known story of what Judt chooses to see as double standards and bad faith in which there is no shortage of material to display what he regards as the naivety and self-delusion of those concerned.

But Judt's subject is in reality much wider than the things said by the likes of Simone de Beauvoir about the Soviet Union. The errors and idiocies of this period, he wants to argue, are rooted in patterns of thought that characterize French political thought as a whole and where are missing 'the central premises and building blocks of a liberal political vision'. That culture, he argues, favours holism and is drawn inevitably towards moral and political absolutes. When combined with a genius for abstraction and generalization the result is a form of intellectual totalitarianism that willingly disregards the individual in the name of some higher level of coherence and logic. Liberals, Judt concedes, have always existed in France but they have, he argues, been a disregarded minority, troublesome and unwanted visitors. 'It is not therefore an accident', Judt remarks, 'if, in France, the literature of political liberalism remains largely imported'. The charge then is that the political culture of French intellectuals is ill at ease with what Judt describes as the 'disorder', 'openness' and 'untidy compromise' that lies at the heart of liberal politics. However, Judt goes even further than this, claiming that 'rare is the thinker who in France has properly addressed the problem of totalitarianism: that it is the logical and historical derivative of this universalist vision of republican democracy that still bedazzles so many French thinkers'. On this view, it is the whole republican tradition that is implicated in the endorsement of Stalinism.

Even this does not capture the sheer venom that informs so much of Judt's text. The book, he declares, is 'an essay on intellectual irresponsibility' and what makes this irresponsibility particularly damnable was the sense of superiority and confidence typical of the French intellectual. Those in France, as Judt acknowledges when he tells us that idiocy is universal, were not alone in their reverence for the Soviet Union but what they said carried extra weight, they more than any others were listened to. Judt's point here is that the indifference of French intellectuals to the values of pluralism and indeterminacy made them incapable of comprehending and sympathizing with those others (most notably intellectuals in Eastern Europe) who sought to defend such a political culture. This was the great betrayal. It cost French intellectuals nothing to endorse revolution in the abstract in an attempt to overcome their 'provincial irrelevance' but in doing so they abandoned those who suffered directly from the Stalinism they glorified.

A range of questions arise either directly or indirectly from Judt's polemic. Most obviously, is Judt's picture an accurate portrayal of French intellectuals as a whole or just one particular group of *left* intellectuals?[14] Beyond this, did French intellectuals exercise greater power or operate in different ways from, for example, their British, American or Russian counterparts, as Judt clearly believes? What real impact, if any, have intellectuals had upon events in France? Have they had the influence that they, as well as the broader public and governments, have sometimes imagined?[15] These questions, in turn, only serve to open the way up for a wider discussion. Can one write and equally can one be silent without consequences? This most clearly has a bearing upon the pivotal relationship in Judt's period of the intellectual to the PCF and, in particular, upon the phenomenon of the fellow traveller. How had it been possible for intellectuals to submit themselves to the authority of a Stalinist party? What sacrifices had been involved? How had the PCF used and exercised its control over a group that it viewed with undisguised suspicion? To get somewhere near to understanding the nature of this phenomenon we would have to make reference to the prevailing idealization of the Soviet Union, the PCF's role in the Resistance, the prestige of the working class and a corresponding sense of bourgeois guilt, the legacy of the 1930s, and anti-Americanism: all these factors and many more explain the attraction of Communism in the post-1945 period and all are powerfully evoked in François Furet's recent exercise in self-exculpation, *La passé d'une illusion: essai sur l'idée communiste au XXe siècle*.[16] According to Furet, the intellectual's love of the Soviet Union was, at bottom, a form of self-hatred.

But similar questions can be asked of all forms of collaboration, on the Right as well as the Left, with Fascism as well as Communism. Where, for example, does collaboration begin and end? What different forms did it take? Should – as, indeed, did happen after the Second World War for the first time since the French Revolution – a writer, a publisher, a literary critic, pay for his life because of the views he had espoused and the company he had kept? Was there even – as some tried to suggest during the post-war *purge* – a 'right to error' which placed the intellectual in a special category beyond judgement? Or was there a continuous chain that tied literary collaboration with responsibility for Auschwitz? Was an intellectual any more responsible for what had occurred during the Second World War than a bricklayer who had built fortifications for the German army?[17] More mundanely, had intellectuals the right like everybody else to earn a living in difficult circumstances, as, for example, Simone de Beauvoir and Sartre clearly did.[18] These have not been idle questions and go right to the heart of the French literary establishment, even touching André Gide's *La Nouvelle Revue Française*.[19]

More generally, Judt's comments invite reflection upon the diverse, and often forgotten, sources of anti-intellectualism in France. Was it exclusively a bourgeois phenomenon, a right-wing fear of a dangerous sect which would betray the nation and its people in the name of pacifism and internationalism (as Simone de Beauvoir's father apparently believed) or did it have more varied roots and deeper implications. Here, a key figure is undoubtedly Drieu la Rochelle, a writer whose wartime journals have only just been published.[20] With Drieu la Rochelle we enter the realm of anti-intellectualism as self-disgust and self-loathing, as a form of shame at physical and sexual weakness and impotence. Here, too, we see anti-intellectualism as anti-semitism (the two are never far apart in France). And, even in an age when there are apparently no intellectuals left, such anti-intellectualism continues to exist. Gérard Depardieu, for example, has explained his preference for performing Macbeth and Othello rather than Hamlet on the grounds that the latter was such a little intellectual![21]

Yet, at the heart of the matter, as Judt acknowledges, is the question of the responsibility of the intellectual. On Judt's account, French intellectuals failed in their responsibility to tell the truth about Soviet totalitarianism and this, in his view, can be explained in terms of 'a network of French intellectual practices' hostile to liberalism. What I wish to address is whether this still remains the case and whether, in an environment where these practices have been abandoned, there still remain grounds for political engagement and commitment on the part of the intellectual. Moreover, these questions are posed in the context of two decades where French intellectuals as a group have suffered from inner decay and decomposition, and where they have been obliged to undergo a painful process of self-examination and re-appraisal. Jean-François Sirinelli, for example, has recently spoken of 'a veritable Copernican revolution at the heart of the intellectual *milieu*'.[22]

Here is the place to say something in general about our subject. The word 'intellectual' as a description of a distinct group of people enters the French language in the latter half of the 1890s. With the Dreyfus Affair it achieved common currency, being used immediately as a term of abuse by the Right.

Significant also was the fact that the eruption of the intellectual before the public gaze gave the word itself a distinctive meaning: the intellectual was the writer, the scientist, the philosopher, the actor, and so on, who chose to enter into that area of public life defined as the world of politics. The emphasis from the outset, in other words, fell upon action, but also action in the name of a humanitarian, and preferably universal, cause. In this case, it was the release of Captain Dreyfus, but in later years it surfaced as, amongst other things, anti-Fascism and anti-colonialism. Whether it be opposition to Franco, American involvement in Korea, or the use of torture in Algeria, the language deployed was that of Truth, Justice, Reason and Universality.[23] Of equal interest was how these new intellectuals chose to demonstrate their capacity to voice an opinion about the act of injustice being perpetrated upon Dreyfus. When signing the first of what later became many manifestos of the intellectuals, they appended their status and qualifications to their names. What we were seeing here, as Christophe Charle has shown,[24] was the cashing in by intellectuals of the public esteem accorded to their professional status and expertise. Drawing sustenance from the nineteenth-century figure of the *savant* and from the prestige of science, the intellectual – most frequently, in this case, a university professor – spoke in the name of objective knowledge and as the enemy of ignorance. It was this that gave them the right to speak on issues that were beyond their technical competence and which guaranteed that they would be listened to.

Yet the figure of the intellectual in France arguably pre-dates the use of the word itself and has its origin not in the *savant* but in the eighteenth-century man of letters. 'Without being fully conscious of it', writes Pierre Lepape, 'they formed a new social group characterized by their unfettered use of knowledge and by their demand for complete liberty of expression, a dispersed community united at the level of ideas by the same creed of the search for truth by means of reason and experimentation'.[25] At its centre was Voltaire and it was he, in his famous defence of Calas, that defined the contours of intellectual action for the future. Having no power but in his words and no competence but in his capacity to move opinion, in the name of humanity he attacked arbitrary political power with all the weapons at his disposal. Not the least of these, as Richard Holmes has commented, was his grin, 'the skull-like smile that sneered at everything sacred'.[26] As writer–philosopher he was omnipresent, ready to express an opinion on all subjects, waging a battle of ideas designed ultimately to secure the triumph of justice. Here was the very model of the 'engaged' and the 'universal' intellectual.

Voltaire also illustrates a further feature of the French intellectual's existence: banished from Paris, his career can be read as a sustained attempt to return to the capital. The stage was, and still is, Paris, producing a geographical concentration of intellectual life that still bedazzles the foreign observer. Here, too, is to be found an educational system that focuses its efforts not upon, as traditionally in Britain, an elitist education but upon the production of an elite. That elite, most famously, was characterized by

Simone de Beauvoir as *Les Mandarins* and it is a characterization of 'a race apart' that makes much sense. To state the obvious: it has also been a predominantly male race.

But so, too, the intellectual in France has been shrouded in controversy. From the very outset there were those prepared to challenge the right and capacity of the intellectual to intervene in public affairs, and then in the 1920s came former Dreyfusard Julien Benda's famous characterization of their *treason*.[27] Dated from 'about 1890' onwards, the nature of that treason was that the 'clercs' had subordinated their mission 'to the service of their political passions', abasing the values of knowledge before the values of action. Doing nothing to resist the passions of race, class and nationality, Benda argued, 'the modern intellectuals have proclaimed that the intellectual function is respectable only to the extent that it is connected to the pursuit of concrete advantage and that the intelligence which is disinterested in these ends is to be scorned'.[28]

In response came what is arguably the first coherent formulation of the doctrine of 'commitment', Paul Nizan's *Les Chiens de garde*.[29] According to Nizan, all philosophies had a bearing upon the world. 'Every philosopher', he argued, 'though he may consider he does not, participates in the impure reality of his age'. Therefore, the decision of the intellectual to sit in an ivory tower was itself a choice. As he put it: 'impartiality and indifference to practical matters are decidedly partisan attitudes... To abstain is to make a choice, to express a preference'. Thus Benda's talk of the abstract and eternal verities of Truth and Justice denoted a refusal to talk about the things that really mattered, 'war, colonialism, the speed-up of industry, love, the varieties of death, unemployment, politics... all of the things that occupy the minds of this planet's inhabitants'. More than this, it was an attempt 'to obscure the miseries of contemporary reality'. Thus, for Nizan, the choice facing the intellectual was a simple one: to be either for the oppressed or the oppressors, for humanity or against humanity. What then was the function of the intellectual? First of all, to form 'the closest possible ties with the class that is the bearer of revolution' and then 'to denounce all the conditions which prevent men from being human'. As such, the intellectual had to become a 'technician of revolutionary philosophy'. Turning the argument against Benda, he concluded: 'If we betray the bourgeoisie for the sake of mankind, let us not be ashamed to admit that we are traitors'.

Not that long afterwards, in the first issue of *Les Temps modernes*, Sartre gave a further characterization of the intellectuals' treason when Flaubert was said to be responsible for the repression of the Paris Commune because he said not one word to prevent it. Putting aside the question of whether Sartre's near-total silence on political issues during the Occupation merited a similar charge, he thereby established a role for the intellectual that married the positions of both Benda and Nizan. Using a term that recalls that of his former friend and fellow student at the *École Normale Supérieure*, Paul Nizan, Sartre defined the intellectual as a 'technician of practical knowledge' and was likewise vituperative in his criticism of those 'false intellectuals' who 'universalize too fast'.[30] 'All those', Sartre proclaimed, 'who adopt a universalist perspective *here and now* are *reassuring* to the established order'. And yet, according to Sartre, the 'true intellectual' speaks in the name of a universalism that is 'yet to come'. He becomes '*a guardian of fundamental ends* (the emancipation, universalization and hence humanization of man)'. On this account, the writer is not an intellectual '*accidentally*... but *essentially*'. This is so because at the heart of the intellectual's status as a technician of practical knowledge there lies a 'fundamental contradiction' that surfaces as soon as 'his universal technique', the search for truth, comes face to face with 'the dominant ideology', bourgeois hegemony. 'It is', Sartre argued, 'by grasping the particular in the demands of the universal and reducing the universal to the movement of a singularity towards universalization, that the intellectual – defined as a man who has *achieved consciousness of his own constituent contradiction* – can help the proletariat to achieve its self-consciousness'.

From the vantage point of this post-war cult of *engagement* the intellectual was under the definite responsibility to acquire dirty hands. The 'true intellectual', Sartre argued, could be 'neither a moralist nor an idealist', but had to recognize that all conflicts – be they 'class, national, [or] racial' – were struggles between particular groups for the 'statute of universality'. The intellectual was thus obliged to take sides, 'to commit himself in every one of the conflicts of our time'. This arguably remained the dominant view until the sea-change effected during the 1970s and early 1980s.

Born out of the twin experiences of the Popular Front and the Second World War, a commitment to Marxism – with all the deep psychological and emotional needs that it satisfied – operated at the level of intellectual orthodoxy, being transmuted first, by Sartre, into *existentialo-marxisme* during the 1960s and then *tiers-mondisme* as intellectuals rushed to endorse, and to visit, the communist regimes of China, Cuba and Vietnam – an experience that has left many a French intellectual with a past, as Julia Kristeva revealed in her novel *Les Samourais*, that invites ridicule. The whole edifice, it seems, came crashing to the ground in 1974, with the publication in French of *The Gulag Archipelago*. This is not the place to discuss in detail the decline of the French Communist Party (PCF) nor to analyse the causes of a more widespread waning of Marxism, but viewed from outside France this episode is something of a mystery. Were not the facts about the Soviet labour camps well-known and widely available long before? Perhaps it was only the self-imposed blindness of the French intellectual, as Judt has argued, that allowed the truth about the Soviet Union to go unnoticed and for Solzhenitsyn's tale to appear shocking and new? Whatever the explanation, the impact of *The Gulag Archipelago* was to jolt France almost overnight into the era of post-Marxism. But towards what? And where did it leave the intellectual?

Most obviously, the past errors, follies and doctrinal rigidities of the now-defunct '*intellectuel de gauche*' became the subject of detailed exposure. Sartre himself was the most illustrious casualty, his life now described by his critics as one long catalogue of political misjudgements and, at a personal level, hypocrisy.[31] Others, only marginally less eminent, suffered a similar fate. The teacher of a whole generation of French philosophers, Louis Althusser, murdered his wife, spent the remainder of his days in and out of mental institutions, and only did further damage to his reputation by leaving behind two autobiographical memoirs that, if nothing else, gave ample ammunition to those who wished to portray him as a charlatan.[32] Michel Foucault could not escape criticism for his initial endorsement of the Iranian Revolution. The controversy later, and more maliciously, turned to his sexual practices and the rumour that he had visited San Francisco's gay bath houses knowing himself to be HIV positive.[33]

But such personalized invective did not exhaust the opprobrium heaped upon the fallen idol of the intellectual. If these years saw the appearance of the first serious academic studies of the intellectual in France – most notably in the work of Christophe Charle, Jean-François Sirinelli and Pascal Ory[34] – they also saw the publication of a series of polemical essays, of variable quality and seriousness, that broadly continued the treason and blindness themes. Alain Finkielkraut's *La Défaite de la pensée*,[35] Bernard-Henri Lévy's *Eloge des intellectuels*,[36] Régis Debray's *Le Pouvoir intellectuel en France*,[37] Hervé Hamon's and Patrick Rotman's *Les Intellocrates: expédition en haute intelligentsia*,[38] all painted a picture of French intellectual life and behaviour that was increasingly conformist and careerist, dominated by the seductive charms of the mass media. In this, the intellectual was cast as a willing accomplice, the summit of the intellectual's ambitions now being, not to publish in such prestigious journals as *Annales* or *Les Temps modernes*, but to appear on television or radio. Fearful of the accusation of elitism, Finkielkraut argued, the intellectual remained mute before the cultural infantilism of modern society, thereby committing a new form of treason.

Of arguably even more import has been the sociological unmasking of the intellectual performed by Pierre Bourdieu. By the early 1970s, Bourdieu was beginning to turn his investigation of the 'intellectual field' on to intellectuals themselves, not only reducing the so-called 'free-floating intellectual' to membership of a 'dominated fraction of the dominant class' but also – in such provocative interviews as 'Les intellectuels sonts-ils hors de jeu?'[39] – challenging their claims to inhabit 'the universe of pure disinterestedness'. Worse still, he denied their pretention to objective knowledge, accused them of 'a propensity to terrorism', mocked their 'desperate' attempts to respond to 'changing fashions', and contested their usurpation of the 'right to legislate in all matters in the name of a social competence that is often quite independent of the technical competence that it seems to guarantee'.

And these are lines of analysis that continue to be heard. In 1993, Rémy

Rieffel published his 're-reading of French intellectual life', *La Tribu des clercs*,[40] a vast sociological compendium that details the habits and habitats of the French intellectual. Yet, beneath the facts about bars, schools, publishing houses and reviews, lies the thesis that the hierarchy of intellectual legitimation has been radically revised, the new dominance of the mass media entailing the emergence of new journalistic elites. 'In place of a clerisy that was formerly relatively drawn in upon itself', Rieffel concludes, 'corresponds a clerisy that is now dispersed; in place of a hierarchy of excellence based upon a scale of prestige has been substituted a form of classification that rests more and more upon levels of notoriety; in place of the model of the prophetic intellectual has sprung up that of the media intellectual'. Less reverential, and undoubtedly more polemical, is Daniel Salvatore Schiffer's *Les intellos ou la dérive d'une caste*, published at the end of 1995.[41] A self-proclaimed work of 'demystification', the slang term 'intello' is used precisely to identify those intellectuals, the great majority, who bear a responsibility for 'the moral and cultural decay of the contemporary world'. Not content with pillorying the usual twentieth-century culprits, Salvatore Schiffer ends his account with a biting invective directed against those intellectuals – with Bernard-Henri Lévy at the forefront – responsible for what he sees as the 'demonization' of the Bosnian Serbs.[42]

In short, what all this has meant is that the 'universal' or 'prophetic' intellectual on the model of Sartre has all but disappeared, swept away from the political scene with a past authority lying in tatters, their former power and influence lost in the evidence of their own fallibility.[43] And what has replaced these earlier *maîtres à penser*? Nothing less, according to their critics, than the media superstars, the *petits marquis*, who in their capacity as 'intellectual–journalist' daily presume to voice their ill-informed opinions on French television screens. Two events can be cited to exemplify these twin developments. The first, most famously, is the 'silence of the intellectuals' that became the subject of much debate in the late summer of 1983.[44] As France's socialist-led government ran into severe economic problems and saw its public support evaporate, government spokesman Max Gallo, drawing an explicit parallel with the earlier Popular Front experience, was led to ask: where 'are the Gide, Malraux, Alain and Langevin of today?' The charitable answer was that they were not prepared to play the role of 'organic intellectuals of the state'; more plausibly, they had retired from the fray in ideological confusion, content with a more modest and humble role, and were certainly unwilling to lend support to a government that included ministers drawn from the communists. Silence seemed the preferable alternative to another bout of commitment and ridicule.[45]

The second is the media event that became the proposed launch of a 'liste "Sarajevo" ' by Bernard-Henri Lévy and others such as André Glucksman in the 1994 European elections.[46] Opinions vary on the merits of this initiative (which, after a public meeting in the famous stomping ground of

Parisian intellectuals, the *salle de la Mutualité*, ultimately saw a withdrawal from the elections), with Jacques Julliard seeing a return to the 'tradition of independence' associated with Voltaire, Hugo and Zola after the 'black parenthesis' of the years of 'commitment' and Jean Daniel, the editor of *Le nouvel Observateur*, not hesitating to compare Lévy with André Malraux. Yet, for critics such as Régis Debray, the whole thing was an exercise in naivety and simplification by publicity-seeking intellectuals whose very criticisms of politicians displayed a Manichaean logic that debased the activity of politics itself. It was nothing else than a triumph of the mass media performed by professional seducers.[47]

And yet it would be a mistake to believe that after the apparent blindness of the years of commitment, the only alternatives have been silence and a new form of treason. What I hope to show in the remainder of this chapter is that the last two decades have seen a series of sophisticated and thoughtful attempts to redefine the relationship of the intellectual to society and to refashion the intellectual's role. Indeed, I would want to argue that the years of 'black parenthesis' themselves provided in embryo two models of the intellectual that have been much in evidence in recent years. It was necessary, however, for the 'network of... intellectual practices' analysed by Judt to be dislodged before they could come to the fore.

The first of these models is that provided by Raymond Aron: the committed observer. As Jean-François Sirinelli has shown, the origins of this notion can be traced back to Aron's experiences in Germany during the 1930s, but it was given much clearer articulation after the publication of *L'Opium des intellectuels* in 1955 and then, much later, in the series of interviews published as *Le Spectateur engagé*.[48] At its heart lies the Weberian distinction between an ethics of commitment and an ethics of responsibility and Aron's belief that very few are those occasions that have the moral simplicity and purity of the Dreyfus Affair. Aron asks of the intellectual, therefore, not indifference and the pose of *l'observateur glacé* but modesty, moderation, lucidity and moral clarity. Above all, they are invited to *penser la politique*, to reflect not upon the attractions of a 'perfect society' but upon the difficult choices and decisions faced by those in power. 'The great proportion of struggles', Aron told an audience at the Weizmann Institute in Jerusalem, 'are of an ambiguous character and the intellectuals who wish to be exclusively at the service of the universal ought not to participate'.[49]

The second model is that provided by Michel Foucault: the 'specific' intellectual. Formulated as early as 1972, this concept received its fullest formulation in an interview given by Foucault in 1977 and was cited by him on many subsequent occasions.[50] Here, too, there is passing reference to 'the great treason of the intellectuals' (in this case, the inculcation amongst the proletariat of the values of 'bourgeois justice') and derogatory comments directed against those Foucault dismisses as *les intellectuels professionnels parisiens*, but centrally, on this view, the intellectual could not claim to be 'a giver of lessons' nor to act as a 'moral legislator'. The 'work of the intellectual', Foucault comments, 'is not to mould the political will of others'. This is so for a variety of reasons. The events of May 1968, Foucault argued, showed that the masses did not need intellectuals to teach them how to think and, moreover, that the intellectual's knowledge of what the workers did could at best only be 'partial'. It therefore no longer made any sense to regard the intellectual as 'the clear, individual figure of a universality whose obscure, collective form is embodied in the proletariat'. Rather the role of the intellectual was 'to make visible the mechanisms of repressive power which operate in a hidden manner'. This was done by providing 'the instruments of analysis' drawn from the intellectual's own work 'within specific sectors'. It was as 'specialists' rather than as 'universal prophets' that they should operate. And with this the point of reference changes from the eighteenth-century man of letters and writer (with Voltaire cast as the prototype) to the nineteenth- and twentieth-century *savant* or expert. Yet Foucault acknowledged that in one respect at least the work of the intellectual could take on a 'general significance' and have implications 'which are not simply professional or sectoral'. Situating the intellectual within his broader discourse on the 'political economy' of truth, Foucault argued that 'the intellectual can operate and struggle at the general level of the regime of truth which is so essential to the structure and functioning of our society'. It was in this sense that Foucault could write: 'I dream of the intellectual who destroys evidence and generalities'.

In Foucault's own particular case (and contrary to the view which suggests that Foucault's own philosophy reduced him to the occasional anarchical gesture) this involved more than the setting up of *Groupe d'information sur les prisons* in 1971 and included numerous acts of support in defence of disadvantaged immigrants, helping Bernard Kouchner establish the now famous *Médecins sans frontières*, aiding the Vietnamese boat people and active support for Poland's *Solidarity* movement in conjunction with the French trade union organization, the CFDT. All of this was done without presuming to speak in the name of other people and with the intention of giving those without a voice the possibility of being heard.[51]

The retreat from the 'intellectual practices' cited by Judt has been a long and painful one. It has also arguably been a humiliating one. Most importantly, the very philosophical foundations that underpinned the Sartrean model of the universal intellectual have been dismantled. Along with its phenomenological bases, his Marxist humanism was jettisoned in a philosophical revolution that, via structuralism, led ultimately to Derrida and deconstruction. Philosophy simply ceased to be an activity engaged in the construction of general theories. And thus writers like Philippe Sollers, the influential editor of the literary review *Tel Quel*,[52] could break with Sartre's definition of committed literature and argue that a writer's commitment was displayed not in any message but in the activity of writing itself. Later, Julia Kristeva, defining the intellectual as 'dissident', reduced the philosophical project to an attempt to destabilize the 'master discourses' that constitute the existing symbolic order.[53] Jean-François Lyotard, the high-priest of post-modernism, could likewise argue that : 'There ought no longer to be "intellectuals", and if there are any, it is because they are blind to this new fact in Western history since the eighteenth century: there is no universal subject-victim'.[54]

From the mid-1970s onwards, however, it has not just been the personnel of French intellectual life and its philosophical preoccupations that have changed, but also its ideological climate and atmosphere.[55] At its most obvious level – as Sunil Khilnani has recently argued[56] – the faith in revolution had to be exorcised. This done, it opened the way up not just for another historical orthodoxy – that associated with François Furet and his friends – but a more general critique of revolutionary politics and the Jacobin state. The gradual emergence of what came increasingly to look like a new political consensus built around the idea of a 'Republic of the Centre' and the end of French 'exceptionalism' rested not only upon a broader reconsideration and reassessment of the rights of the individual, but also saw the search for the theoretical grounding of what it was hoped would be a distinctively French version of liberalism that would avoid the supposed atomizing tendencies of its Anglo-American counterpart.[57] Foucault's former student, Blandine Kriegel, spearheaded a revival of interest in the concept of an *état de droit* that received institutional expression in the appearance of the *Conseil constitutionnel* as a virtual third chamber of government and reflected a growing confidence in the benefits of pluralism and the market.[58] Much of the labour in this enterprise was carried out by journals such as *Le Débat* and *Esprit* (in an earlier period the subject of much of Judt's scorn) and, in popular form, by *Le nouvel Observateur*. Certain publishing houses (for example, *Le Seuil*) also played their part, as did organizations such as the *Fondation Saint-Simon*. Raymond Aron's journal *Commentaire*, established in 1978 to oppose the twin perils of 'the inarticulate cry, pure revolt on the one side, absolute knowledge, total ideology on the other', came to occupy a central place in the struggle against totalitarianism, now frequently redescribed as 'barbarism'.[59] Attention also turned to rediscovering France's long-neglected liberal past, thus producing a detailed rereading of such major figures as Constant, Guizot and Tocqueville.[60] The consequent reappraisal of the importance of *civil society* as a vehicle for individual liberty entailed nothing less than the jettisoning of the formerly hallowed principles, so dear to the Jacobin tradition, of the sovereignty of the nation and of the general will. Simultaneously, and just as importantly, there began a concerted attempt to absorb the lessons of pluralism and distributive justice to be found in the writings of liberal thinkers from abroad. Heidegger, whose Nazi sympathies were the subject of renewed debate in the mid-1980s, found himself dislodged from his former hegemonic position and replaced as the fashionable reading of the Parisian intelligentsia by Hannah Arendt, Isaiah Berlin, Karl Popper, Friedrich von

Hayek, and later John Rawls, Charles Taylor, Richard Rorty and Michael Walzer, all of whom found their work the subject of translation and commentary.[61]

What this meant for the role of the intellectual is excellently illustrated in an inquiry into 'Itinéraires intellectuels des années 1970', published in 1995 by the *Revue Française d'Histoire des Idées Politiques.*[62] The personal testimonies of Pierre Rosanvallon, Rony Brauman and Alain Touraine point not just to the end of 'the ideological imperialism of Marxism' in France but, as Touraine comments, to 'the beginning of the total dissociation of the intelligentsia from society'. Less emphatic is Jean Baudrillard's comment that 'a kind of detachment took place'.[63] The overall conclusion appeared to be that if intellectuals were to survive in what Pierre Nora described in the first issue of *Le Débat* as an era of intellectual democracy then they could no longer claim to be the legislators of the world.[64] The fall of the Berlin Wall in 1989, it could be argued, only added to the intellectual's self-doubt and uncertainty.

It might be wrong to over-exaggerate both the nature of this crisis of self-confidence and the scale of the changes that have occurred – it is interesting to note, for example, that what has recently been said about the damaging impact of the mass media upon the status of the intellectual is on the point of being said about the Internet and was earlier said about even the appearance of bookshops – but the impression has been of a community of intellectuals in disarray, unsure of itself and of how it should act, feeling threatened on all sides by a world in which it no longer enjoyed automatic respect.

Thus challenged, intellectuals have been obliged to rethink and to refashion their role and the relationship that exists between themselves and the society in which they live.[65] The key idea – frequently repeated – when talking about the intervention of the intellectual in public affairs now appears to be that intervention should be on specific issues that are relatively devoid of ideological content and which bear immediately upon the present. It is this project, for example, that Pierre Nora had in mind when in 1980 he launched *Le Débat* and which he reaffirmed at the time of its tenth anniversary issue.[66] 'We wish to propose', Nora commented, 'a form of intervention by intellectuals in social life which is radically different from that practised until now'. The intellectual was no longer to speak in the name of those who could not speak but was rather to utilize his or her critical capacities and judgement to enlighten and to inform. As such, the intellectual becomes what is defined as 'un éclaireur compétent'. 'To be an intellectual today', Nora comments, 'has no other sense'. The point is that the intellectual is no longer entitled to play the role of prophet or hero or (worse) despot. The intellectual is there to demystify and not to preach. Even more recently, Olivier Mongin, the current editor of *Esprit*, has pursued a similar line through his articulation of the concept of 'l'intellectuel démocratique'.[67] Weaving his way between Kantian universalism and

Nietzschean deconstruction, 'l'intellectuel du troisième type' is neither a 'nomade' scorning the reason of Western imperialism nor a 'universaliste' dreaming of the 'République universelle', but is to function as a 'médiateur–critique' actively engaging in democratic debate. Distanced from the 'romantic canonization' of the intellectual, on this view – as with Nora – the purpose of 'intellectual action' is the attempt to 'clarify'. Another slant to this argument has been provided by Pierre Rosanvallon. Rooted in a 'new political culture' that sought a definition of the Left as 'radically anti-totalitarian', as historian Rosanvallon has developed the outlines of a 'conceptual history of politics' that, in his view, reinterprets the nature of the intellectual's commitment. The writing of that history has 'a civic dimension' and as such it is not the 'posture' of the intellectual that defines commitment but rather 'the very content of intellectual work'.[68]

Each of these three accounts falls broadly into the category of Aron's *spectateur engagé* and it is therefore interesting to note that traces of Foucault's concept of the 'specific' intellectual can also be found. Here we need to return to Bourdieu. Unlike many of his contemporaries, Bourdieu had never passed through the Communist Party nor had he participated in the *gauchisme* of the May '68 generation, but it was Bourdieu who, in December 1981, telephoned Michel Foucault to solicit his support for a petition in defence of Poland's *Solidarity* movement. It was when Bourdieu reflected upon this experience after Foucault's death that he not only spoke of the intellectual's need for 'the most complete autonomy vis-à-vis all other powers' but also recognized that if 'they are not the spokesmen of the universal, even less of a "universal class" ' they often have 'an interest in the universal'. This theme was continued by Bourdieu in a lecture he gave in 1989. There he outlined the need for intellectuals 'to establish their autonomy... and to reinforce the positions of the most autonomous producers in each field' and, just as importantly, 'the need to keep the most autonomous cultural producers from the temptation of the ivory tower by creating appropriate institutions to enable them to intervene collectively under their own specific authority'. That autonomy, Bourdieu argued, was under threat from the state, the world of finance, 'the tendency to strip intellectuals of their prerogatives to evaluate themselves', and the growth of technocratic control: to preserve their autonomy, Bourdieu called for an 'International of Intellectuals', 'a large collective of intellectuals, combining the talents of the ensemble of specific intellectuals'. And in this, Bourdieu commented, they should feel no shame: 'by defending themselves as a whole, they defend the universal'.[69] This project was itself given flesh in 1993 with the creation, by Bourdieu and others, of a *Parlement international des écrivains*. Modelled upon the Encyclopaedists and as described by Bourdieu, it was to act as a 'critical countervailing power' rather than as an 'incarnation of the universal conscience'.[70] Where this could lead, and how such an organization could intervene, was demonstrated the same year when Bourdieu also participated in the creation of the *Comité international de soutien aux intellectuels algériens.* Treading carefully through the Algerian quagmire, and refusing the route of easy condemnation, this was done in the name of 'creative liberty'.[71] The following year Bourdieu, along with Jacques Derrida, called for a campaign of 'civil resistance' to defend the right of Algerians to political asylum in France.[72]

All of this raises several questions of great importance. If intellectuals are to have the modest and humble tasks of clarification and demystification, as Nora, Mongin and Rosanvallon believe, and if, contrary to Benda's belief, they no longer have the right to lay claim to the universal conscience, then to what extent are they capable of meaningful social criticism of a radical nature? If the intellectual is to speak out in defiance of the established powers, as Zola demonstrated when he came to the defence of Dreyfus, then in whose name is it to be done? To quote Lyotard: 'The responsibility of "intellectuals" is inseparable from the (shared) idea of a universal subject. It alone can give Voltaire, Zola, Péguy, Sartre (to stay within the confines of France) the authority that has been accorded to them'.[73] Is the autonomy of creative producers grounds enough to secure a new authority for action? In an age where intellectuals are increasingly under attack, where their right to constitute Bourdieu's 'critical countervailing power' is frequently challenged and where (in a situation described as one of 'terrorisme intellectocide')[74] Algerian intellectuals are murdered almost daily, is this sufficient to lay claim to a broader loyalty and to retain or reclaim a place within the public space? Is this relative impotence the price that has had to be paid for the abandonment of the 'intellectual practices' of the past and the classic posture of the intellectual from Voltaire to Sartre?

And yet a casual observer reading the French press in November and December 1995 might have concluded that relatively little had changed and that the old battles which had divided French intellectuals in the past were being fought anew. As France's public sector workers brought the country to a standstill in protest against planned reforms in social security provision, the newspapers again carried the petitions and names of those intellectuals taking rival sides. For reform were Olivier Mongin, Alain Touraine, Pierre Rosanvallon, Rony Brauman, Alain Finkielkraut, Hervé Hamon, Jacques Julliard and the house philosophers of *Esprit*, Claude Lefort and Paul Ricoeur. Expressing 'solidarity' with the strikers were to be found Pierre Bourdieu and Jacques Derrida, as well as the philosopher Etienne Balibar and leading historians Pierre Vidal-Naquet and Michel Vovelle.[75] Viewed simplistically, it was a clash between the 'old' and the 'new' Left. What had quite definitely changed, however, was that few of the many prepared to append their names to the lengthy lists would have presumed to direct events and even fewer would have been under the illusion that what mattered most was the outcome of this skirmish between Parisian intellectuals.

NOTES

1   R. Scruton, *Thinkers of the New Left*, London, Longman, 1985.
2   R. Scruton, *Upon Nothing*, Swansea, University College of Swansea, 1993.
3   For a reading of this from a French angle, see E. Fassin, ' "Political Correctness" en version originale et en version française', *Vingtième siècle*, 43, 1994, pp. 30–42.
4   R. Hughes, *Culture of Complaint: The Fraying of America*, New York and Oxford, Oxford University Press, 1993.
5   C. Paglia, *Sex, Art and American Culture*, New York, Vintage, 1992, p. 211. See especially the chapter entitled 'Junk bonds and corporate raiders: academe in the hour of the wolf'.
6   G. Himmelfarb, *On Looking into the Abyss*, New York, Alfred. A. Knopf, 1994, p. 160.
7   These remarks were originally made on the BBC but also appeared in the *Observer*, 18 October 1992. Likewise the now famous pronouncement by Jean Baudrillard that the Gulf War did not take place gave ample ammunition to those wishing to denounce the irresponsibility of the 'critical critics' living comfortably in their Parisian apartments; see J. Baudrillard, 'La guerre de Golfe n'a pas eu lieu', *Libération*, 29 March 1991.
8   T. Judt, *Past Imperfect: French Intellectuals 1944–56*, Berkeley and Oxford, University of California Press, 1992; *Passé imparfait: Les intellectuels en France 1944–56*, Paris, Fayard, 1992.
9   T. Judt, 'The judgements of Paris', *The Times Literary Supplement*, 28 June 1991.
10 The four-part television series that accompanied *Les Aventures de la liberté* was shown on British television, producing a wonderful piece of satire in the shape of an article entitled 'Dead and Bereted', published in *The Times*, 2 March 1991. Presented is the fictitious portrait of the 'identikit intellectual', Jean-Pierre Lévy, who, the reader is told, 'sprang from that grand tradition of French thinkers who could think of three new reasons to commit suicide or sign a petition before breakfast'. The text has now been published in English as *Adventures on the Freedom Road*, Harvill, London, 1995. It evoked a similar response in *The Times Magazine*, 16 December 1995, with an interview with Lévy headlined 'Pretentious, Moi?' and a cautious review by Roger Scruton, *The Times*, 16 October 1995, allowing the latter to state that it had been his experience of French intellectuals that persuaded him to side with the bourgeoisie.
11 Judt's judgement can only be confirmed by Lévy's publication (with Françoise Giroud) of the truly appalling *Les hommes et les femmes*, Paris, Olivier Orban, 1993.
12 See, for example, Lévy's text *La Barbarie à visage humaine*, Paris, Grasset, 1977.
13 For a recent statement of Judt's views on the 'shame' of French intellectuals see 'French War Stories', *New York Times*, 19 July 1995.
14 For some of the responses to Judt's polemic see M. Zuber, 'Present debates on the past: interview with Pierre Grémion', *French Politics and Society*, Summer 1993, pp. 34–46; D. Lindenberg, 'Les intellectuels français vus d'outre-Atlantique (A propos d'*Un passé imparfait* de Tony Judt)' *Esprit*, 191, 1993, pp. 167–70; and especially the acrimonious debate between Jean-Marie Domenach and Judt in *Commentaire*, 62, 1993, pp. 403–12.
15 On this see 'The political roles of intellectuals', in S. Hazareesingh, *Political Traditions in Modern France*, Oxford, Oxford University Press, 1994, pp. 33–64. Hazareesingh's opinion is that 'intellectuals were never really able to lead opinion in France, and even less to determine the direction of political events'.
16 F. Furet, *Le Passé d'une illusion: essai sur l'idée communiste au XXe siècle*, Paris, Robert Laffont/Calmann Lévy, 1995. See also S. Hazareesingh, *Intellectuals and*

the French Communist Party: Disillusion and Decline, Oxford, Clarendon Press, 1991, and R. Kuisel, *Seducing the French: The Dilemma of Americanization*, Berkeley and Los Angeles, University of California Press, 1993.

17   These, and related, issues are addressed in P. Assouline, *L'Epuration des intellectuels*, Brussels, Editions Complexe, 1985.

18   Accounts of this fascinating period of their lives can be found in D. Bair, *Simone de Beauvoir*, London, Jonathan Cape, 1990 and A. Cohen-Solal, *Sartre: A Life*, London, Heinemann, 1987. For a more controversial assessment see G. Joseph, *Une si douce Occupation... Simone de Beauvoir et Jean-Paul Sartre, 1940–1944*, Paris, Albin Michel, 1991.

19   See, for example, P. Hebey, *La Nouvelle Revue Française des Années Sombres 1940–1941*, Paris, Gallimard, 1992.

20   P. Drieu la Rochelle, *Journal 1939–1945*, Paris, Gallimard, 1992.

21   See P. Balmand, 'Anti-intellectualism in French Political Culture', in J. Jennings (ed.), *Intellectuals in Twentieth-Century France: Mandarins and Samurais*, Basingstoke, Macmillan, 1993, pp. 157–76.

22   J-F. Sirinelli, *Deux intellectuels dans le siècle, Aron et Sartre*, Paris, Fayard, 1995, p. 13.

23   See J-F. Sirinelli, *Intellectuels et passions françaises*, Paris, Fayard, 1990.

24   C. Charle, *Naissance des 'intellectuels', 1880–1900*, Paris, Les Editions de Minuit, 1990.

25   P. Lepape, *Voltaire Le Conquérant: Naissance des intellectuels au siècle des Lumières*, Paris, Seuil, 1994, p. 269. There is, of course, the argument that the origins of the intellectual are first found in the Middle Ages. See here J. Le Goff, *Les Intellectuels au Moyen Age*, Paris, Seuil, 1985. For a review of Lepape's book by Le Goff, see 'Voltaire, le premier des modernes', *Le Monde*, 16 September 1994. Despite stressing the parallels between the two periods, Le Goff accepts that 'the absolute novelty' of the eighteenth century lies in 'the battle for truth, political-moral commitment'.

26   R. Holmes, 'Voltaire's Grin', *New York Review of Books*, 30 November 1995, pp. 49–55.

27   J. Benda, *La Trahison des clercs*, Paris, Bernard Grasset, 1927. Benda's text is available in English as *The Betrayal of the Intellectuals*, Boston, Beacon Press, 1955.

28   For a more general discussion of this issue see D. L. Schalk, *The Spectrum of Political Engagement*, Princeton, Princeton University Press, 1979.

29   P. Nizan, *Les Chiens de garde*, Paris, Maspero, 1976. Nizan's text is available in English as *The Watchdogs*, New York and London, Monthly Review Press, 1971.

30   See especially J-P. Sartre, *Plaidoyer pour les intellectuels*, Paris, Gallimard, 1972. This has been translated as 'A plea for intellectuals', in J-P. Sartre, *Between Existentialism and Marxism*, London, Verso, 1983. See also J-P. Sartre, *Qu'est-ce que la littérature?*, Paris, Gallimard, 1948.

31   Two different examples of this genre are M-A. Burnier, *Le Testament de Sartre*, Paris, Olivier Orban, 1982, and J. Verdès-Leroux, *La Lune et le Caudillo: le rêve des intellectuels et le régime cubain*, Paris, Gallimard, 1989.

32   See L. Althusser, *L'Avenir dure longtemps*, Paris, Stock/IMEC, 1992. This has been translated as *The Future Lasts A Long Time*, London, Chatto, 1993. The most startling of Althusser's admissions is that he knew, and had read little, of Marx's writings. For a controversial assessment see M. Lilla, 'Marx and Murder', *The Times Literary Supplement*, 25 September 1992.

33   The literature on this is extensive but see in particular J. Miller, *The Passion of Michel Foucault*, London, HarperCollins, 1993; D. Eribon, *Michel Foucault*, Paris, Flammarion, 1989 and *Michel Foucault et ses contemporains*, Paris,

Fayard, 1994; D. Halperin, *Saint Foucault: Two Essays in Gay Hagiography*, New York, Oxford University Press, 1995.

34 In addition to those works already cited by these authors see P. Ory and J-F. Sirinelli, *Les Intellectuels en France, de l'Affaire Dreyfus à nos jours*, Paris, Armand Colin, 1986; J-F. Sirinelli, *Génération intellectuelle: Khâgneux et Normaliens dans l'entre-deux-guerres*, Paris, Fayard, 1988; and C. Charle, *Les Elites de la République, 1880–1900*, Paris, Fayard, 1987.

35 A. Finkielkraut, *La Défaite de la pensée*, Paris, Gallimard, 1987. Finkielkraut's text has been translated as *The Undoing of Thought*, London, Claridge Press, 1988.

36 B-H. Lévy, *Eloge des intellectuels*, Paris, Grasset, 1987.

37 R. Debray, *Le Pouvoir intellectuel en France*, Paris, Editions Ramsay, 1979. Debray's text has been translated as *Teachers, Writers and Celebrities*, London, Verso, 1981.

38 H. Hamon and P. Rotman, *Les Intellocrates: expédition en haute intelligentsia*, Paris, Editions Ramsay, 1981.

39 P. Bourdieu, *Questions de sociologie*, Paris, Editions de Minuit, 1984. In translation see *Sociology in Question*, London, Sage, 1993. This interview dates from 1978. Much of Bourdieu's writings explore these themes, but see especially *Le Sens pratique*, Paris, Minuit, 1980; translated as *The Logic of Practice*, Oxford, Polity, 1990.

40 R. Rieffel, *La Tribu des clercs: Les intellectuels sous la Ve République*, Paris, Calmann-Lévy, 1993.

41 D. Salvatore Schiffer, *Les intellos ou la dérive d'une caste*, Lausanne, L'Age d'Homme, 1995.

42 Salvatore Schiffer makes his own contribution to the debate about the role of the intellectual by outlining the contours of what he describes as the *prismatique* intellectual; pp. 287–99.

43 Less noticed, but equally interesting, has been the relative disappearance of the Catholic intellectual: see H. Tincq, 'Le silence des intellectuels catholiques', *Le Monde*, 15 March 1995. This is a subject that merits detailed analysis.

44 See especially the columns of *Le Monde* after 24 July 1983.

45 There have subsequently been many discussions of this so-called 'silence' and frequent claims that intellectuals are returning to the political stage but evidence that the mood continues and that the nature of action by intellectuals has been substantially modified was, for example, provided by the hesitant and prudent pose struck by many intellectuals in the run-up to the 1995 Presidential elections: see 'Les intellectuels saisis par le doute à l'approche de l'élection', *Le Monde*, 20 April 1995.

46 See *Le Monde* from 17 May 1994 onwards.

47 See R. Debray, 'Les frères ennemis', *Le Monde*, 25 May 1994 and the special issue of *Globe-Hebdo*, 68, 25–31 May 1994. For Lévy's response see 'Huits réponses à Régis Debray', *Le Monde*, 27 May 1994.

48 See Sirinelli, *Deux intellectuels dans le siècle, Sartre et Aron*, pp. 115–16; R. Aron, *L'Opium des intellectuels*, Paris, Calmann-Lévy, 1955; translated as *The Opium of the Intellectuals*, Westport CT, Greenwood Press, 1977; R. Aron, *Le Spectateur engagé: entretiens avec Jean-Louis Missika et Dominique Wolton*, Paris, Julliard, 1981; translated as *The Committed Observer*, Chicago, Regnery, 1983; see also R. Aron, *Mémoires: 50 ans de réflexion politique*, Paris, Julliard, 1983 and N. Bavarez, *Raymond Aron*, Paris, Flammarion, 1993.

49 R. Aron, 'Les intellectuels et la politique', *Commentaire*, 22, Summer 1983, pp. 259–63.

50 See, for example, 'Les intellectuels et le pouvoir', in M. Foucault, *Dits et écrits, 1954–1988*, Paris, Gallimard, 1994, II, pp. 306–15; 'Entretien avec Michel

Foucault', ibid., III, pp. 140–60; 'L'intellectuel et les pouvoirs', ibid., IV, pp. 747–52. The second piece appears in English translation in P. Rabinow, *The Foucault Reader*, London, Penguin, 1991, pp. 51–75. The quotations and references that follow are drawn from a wide range of sources in the four volumes of *Dits et écrits*.

51   *Michel Foucault: Une histoire de la vérité*, Paris, Syros, 1985; C. Delacampagne, 'L'intellectuel contre les abus de pouvoir', *Le Monde*, 13 October 1989; D. Eribon, *Michel Foucault*, pp. 314–28.

52   See P. Forest, *Histoire de Tel Quel, 1960–1982*, Paris, Seuil, 1995.

53   See J. Kristeva, 'A new type of intellectual: the dissident', in T. Moi (ed.), *The Kristeva Reader*, Oxford, Basil Blackwell, 1986, pp. 292–300. Kristeva's text was first published in *Tel Quel*, 74, 1977, pp. 3–8.

54   J-F. Lyotard, *Tombeau de l'intellectuel et autres papiers*, Paris, Editions Galilée, 1984; see J-F. Lyotard, *Political Writings*, London, UCL Press, 1993, p. 6.

55   See especially M. Lilla, *New French Thought: Political Philosophy*, Princeton, Princeton University Press, 1994.

56   S. Khilnani, *Arguing Revolution: The Intellectual Left in Postwar France*, New Haven and London, Yale University Press, 1993.

57   See the special issue of *Ratio Juris*, 7 December 1994, devoted to 'A debate about John Rawls, political liberalism and the idea of the common good'. Contained are papers drawn from an Anglo-French conference on 'Consensus and Democracy' held in Oxford during February 1993. Formulating a 'communitarian' critique of John Rawls, Jean-Marc Ferry comments: 'we do not want an atomized society in which all individuals would be alone, cut off from the shared values and references that make concerted action possible' (p. 295).

58   Blandine Kriegel has published extensively but in English see *The State and the Rule of Law*, Princeton, Princeton University Press, 1995. See also my 'From "imperial state" to "l'état de droit": Benjamin Constant, Blandine Kriegel and the reform of the French Constitution', *Political Studies*, 44 , 1996, pp.488–504.

59   See A. Glucksman, *La Cuisinière et le mangeur d'hommes*, Paris, Le Seuil, 1975 and B-H. Lévy, *La Barbarie à visage humain*, Paris, Grasset, 1977.

60   See, for example, P. Rosanvallon, *Le Moment Guizot*, Paris, Gallimard, 1985; P. Manent, *Histoire intellectuelle du libéralisme: dix leçons*, Paris, Calmann-Lévy, 1986; and F. Mélanio, *Tocqueville et les Français*, Paris, Aubier, 1993. The text by Manent has now been translated as *An Intellectual History of Liberalism*, Princeton, Princeton University Press, 1994.

61   It is interesting to note in the context of this chapter the recent translation of Walzer's *The Company of Critics: Social Criticism and Political Commitment in the Twentieth Century* by the publishers Métaillé.

62   *Revue Française d'Histoire des Idées Politiques*, 2, 1995, pp. 353–410.

63   'Intellectuals, Commitment and Political Power', in M. Gane (ed.), *Baudrillard Live: Selected Interviews*, London and New York, Routledge, 1993, p. 74.

64   P. Nora. 'Que peuvent les intellectuels?', *Le Débat*, 1, 1980, pp. 1–19. A shorter version of this article is available in English as 'About Intellectuals', in J. Jennings (ed.), *Intellectuals in Twentieth-Century France*, pp. 187–99.

65   See J. Daniel, 'L'Heure des intellectuels', *Le Débat*, 27, 1983, pp. 168–91 and O. Mongin and P. Thibaud, 'La passion des idées', *Esprit*, 117–118, 1986, pp. 1–8.

66   P. Nora, 'Dix Ans de Débat', *Le Débat*, 60, 1990, pp. 3–11 and 'Un entretien avec Pierre Nora', *Le Monde*, 1 June 1990.

67   O. Mongin, *Face au scepticisme: les mutations du paysage intellectuel ou l'invention de l'intellectuel démocratique* (Paris, 1994).

68   'Faire de l'histoire: Entretien avec Pierre Rosanvallon', *Esprit*, 209, 1995, pp. 25–42.

69 See P. Bourdieu, 'Les intellectuels et les pouvoirs', in *Michel Foucault: Une histoire de la vérité*, pp. 93–4 and 'The corporatism of the universal: the role of intellectuals in the modern world', *Telos*, 81, Fall 1989, pp. 99–110. I owe both of these references to Shlomo Sand.

70 See 'L'intellectuel dans la cité: un entretien avec Pierre Bourdieu', *Le Monde*, 5 November 1993 and 'Un entretien avec Pierre Bourdieu', *Le Monde*, 7 December 1993.

71 'Avec les intellectuels Algériens', *Le Monde*, 7 October 1993.

72 'Non-assistance à personne en danger', *Le Monde*, 20 December 1994. It is interesting to note that Bourdieu taught in Algeria and did much of his earlier fieldwork there whilst Derrida was born there in 1930 and did not arrive in France until 1959. Bourdieu repeated the call for 'civil disobedience' on 29 March 1996, whilst at the beginning of the same month his name appeared, alongside those of Jacques Derrida, Didier Eribon, Michelle Perrot, Paul Veyne and Pierre Vidal-Naquet, calling for the legal recognition of the homosexual couple: see 'Pour une reconnaissance légale du couple homosexuel', *Le Monde*, 1 March 1996.

73 Lyotard, *Political Writings*, p. 3.

74 A. Sayad, 'Intellectuels à titre posthume', *Liber*, 17 March 1994.

75 See 'Pour une réforme de fond de la Sécurité sociale', *Le Monde*, 30 November 1995 and 'Appel des intellectuels en soutien des grévistes', *Le Monde*, 15 December 1995. The activities of the latter group included a public meeting held with the strikers where Bourdieu characterized the strikes as an 'historic opportunity for France and for all those who reject the new alternative of either liberalism or barbarism'.

Part II
Priestly interventions

Intellectuals have been called to and have taken up a variety of roles. One of these has been that of the priest who, in Leszek Kolakowski's words, 'sustains the cult of the final and the obvious as acknowledged by and contained in tradition'. As such, the intellectual acts as the conscience and voice of the nation. But in what capacity? Prophet? Saviour? Philosopher king? Representative of the State? And how does this impinge upon their function? As organic intellectuals of the people-nation, the radicalism of the resistance fighter can easily be replaced by a conservative traditionalism. Drawn into politics, independence can be corrupted and limited by the possession of power. The once revered priest can be either forgotten or reduced to impotence. The capacity to disturb or unsettle can be lost.

The most murderous situation presently facing intellectuals is to be found in Algeria. There hundreds, if not thousands, of intellectuals have been systematically murdered, and yet the vast majority of Algerians have remained indifferent to the fate of a section of the population that played a significant part in securing liberation from colonial rule. In Algeria, however, there are now essentially two types of intellectual, both of whom have played the role of priest. The *francophone* intellectual is organic in the sense that the post-colonial state has been idealized but critical through disapproval and censure of the structure of traditional society. The *arabophone* intellectual, by contrast, is critical with regard to the State but organic in relationship with the values and practices of traditional society. The power of the former has collapsed with economic failure, a loss of legitimacy leaving the way clear for the *arabophone* intellectual to adopt an oppositional position, condemning 'the party of France' for moving Algeria away from its cultural patrimony. Preaching their message from the mosques, they call for solidarity and social peace, denouncing corruption and the liberalization of morals. As the priests of the old system, the *francophone* intellectuals are seen as a legitimate target of attack.

The recent controversy over T. S. Eliot's supposed anti-Semitism centred much upon his remark that 'reasons of race and religion combine to make any large number of free-thinking Jews undesirable'. Clearly such language draws upon Western traditions of anti-Semitic representation, but it also tells us a great deal about our conception of the Jewish intellectual – the 'free-thinker' – as the very embodiment of what an intellectual is taken to be: uprooted, urban and left-wing. It is this that provides the context for the transformation of Jewish intellectuals through the emergence of the Zionist movement and subsequently of the Israeli state. The decline of the status of the rabbi saw Jewish intellectuals cast as organic and secular national intellectuals, harnessed to support the political goals of the new Israeli state. Accentuated with each successive military victory, intellectuals played a key role in the articulation of the cult of the State and, specifically, the cult of the army. Yet Israeli intellectuals were soon to see their priestly role diminish. The victories of Begin's Likud party saw their electoral and cultural marginalization and with that they have, in part, been able to regain both their autonomy and oppositional role.

Nearer home, England and Ireland present contrasting perspectives on the intellectual as priest. The 'national question' in Ireland forced writers to address political questions in the hope of changing 'Mad Ireland'. The poet W. B. Yeats is a paradigmatic case. For Yeats, poets were teachers of their 'race', articulating the values and traditions of the Irish people, reforging the sense of unity and community. At his most romantic he believed that poets were legislators.

Similarly there have been writers in England (for example, Cobbett, H. G. Wells, George Orwell, the 'Pylon' poets of the 1930s) who drew their inspiration from England: its special history, its peculiarities, its decencies, its dislike of grand theories. Hence, intellectuals do matter in England: but not quite in the way in which intellectual influence is usually characterized. These writers were critics of the system – what Cobbett called the 'Thing' – but they all, even the poets of the 1930s who were deeply involved in the Spanish Civil War, still turned inwards, to an ideal of a special kind of England and a special kind of English patriotism, one with a left-wing vision, but a mission rooted in English history and tradition. It was patriotic to attack the 'Thing'. They helped construct a dialogue that stressed the non-internationalism of British political life, and their influence in helping to keep English political discourse insular was quite profound. Their importance lies less in the impact of their ideas on policies than on their contribution to the particularist and localist concept of the English ideology (which they constructed as non-ideological), and on their concept of English intellectuals as addressing the central concerns of their countrymen. In this sense, as E. P. Thompson remarked, they have been jesters to the universal priests.

5   Algeria and the dual image of the intellectual[1]

Lahouari Addi

This article is dedicated to the memory of Tahar Djouat, writer and journalist, murdered in Algiers in June 1993.

The assassination of Algerian intellectuals has shaken public opinion throughout the world. People have asked themselves how is it possible that knowledge and artistic creation can be attacked in the name of a political project, whatever it might be. But in Algeria, beyond the narrow circle of professional colleagues and close friends, these assassinations have not been counter-productive for the Islamists, whose communiqués announce the execution of unbelievers. How is it that Algeria has become indifferent to the murder of its intellectuals? In order to explain this indifference, we need to make reference to the two types of intellectual bequeathed by the colonial experience: the francophone intellectual, separated off from the population, and the Arabic-speaking intellectual, who strongly identifies with that population. But before looking at this in detail, it is useful to consider the diverse contours of the figure of the intellectual, especially in two countries where they have played an important political and ideological role: Russia and France.

THE *ORGANIC* INTELLECTUAL AND THE *CRITICAL* INTELLECTUAL

Each national history produces its own political actors with different goals and different forms of action. This is why, across different countries and different cultures, there does not exist an ideal type of the intellectual. In other words, there is no such thing as the *standard* intellectual. To give several illustrative examples: Russian society, faced with the process of modernization in the second half of the nineteenth century, saw the emergence of the nationalist *organic* intellectual who, along with his illusions and his faith in Utopia, believed that it was sufficient to be heard by – or to replace – the Prince. In this way, from the summit of the State, knowledge and the values of the avant-garde, considered as expressing the aspirations of humanity for justice, equality, and so on, would flow down upon the backward masses. At the end of the nineteenth century the Russian *intelligentsia* became aware of the relative backwardness of their country, and hence embraced Marxism as a simultaneous critique of both state power and society. It was not simply a question of criticizing the absolutism of the Czar but also a matter of seizing power from him in order to modernize society and to create the people's state. The Russian intellectual opposed the existing political power in the name of an ideal contained within a political project. After the revolution of 1917 he entered the service of the new state in order to put this project into concrete form. He was, then, an *organic intellectual* in the sense that his mission was not limited to a simple critique of power, since he chose to share in it.[2] This pattern, established over a hundred years ago, was reproduced once again with the process of *perestroika* in the 1980s.[3]

Very different from the Russian experience, the French situation also presents a paradigmatic example, where the intellectual, perceived as the heir of the Enlightenment and as critic of both state and society, is synonymous with a commitment to universal values. This type of intellectual appeared with great effect at the time of the Dreyfus Affair, but it did not date from this time, even if the word 'intellectual' came into general use with the Dreyfus Affair. The writer hostile to power and the philosopher critical of society certainly predate this event, and Voltaire would be a good example of this. Power in France has always had to deal with the spirit of Voltaire. In general, the intellectual has been on the left, but there have obviously been intellectuals of a right-wing disposition: Raymond Aron, for example, was the same kind of intellectual but he was not on the left.

The debate in France about the intellectual has for long been concerned, and in an obsessional manner, with what Julien Benda had already called by 1927 the *treason of the intellectuals*.[4] As an expression of critical judgement that appeared with the emergence of the social sciences, the intellectual in France has been distrustful of a state that has been suspected of absolutism. By the same token, he has always feared that his actions would be exploited in order to further strengthen the power of the State, perceived as an evil force driven by the temptation to encroach upon individual and public liberties. The worry of a Julien Benda, expressed in similar terms fifty years later by Régis Debray, is that Voltaire will become an organic intellectual, an accomplice to power; and hence the word *treason*. In general, the intellectual in France has been on the side of civil society, always attentive to the absolutist tendencies of power and ready to denounce them. The uneasiness of left-wing intellectuals during the 1980s – an unease given expression in the debate originated by then minister Max Gallo[5] – derived from their attitude towards the socialists in power. The intellectual in France embodies an anti-state counter-culture, but suddenly there was a state which, in its language, laid claim to the values of justice, equality, and so on. As a result, something previously unseen occurred: intellectuals of a right-wing disposition adopted a critical and oppositional stance towards the State whilst the intellectual of the Left became 'voiceless'.

THE ALGERIAN INTELLECTUAL AND THE COLONIAL SITUATION

What has this to do with Algeria? As the historical situation is different, so the problem is posed in a different way. Indeed, to understand the specific characteristics of the Algerian situation we need to return to that history. Algeria is the contradictory product of a colonization which was a system based upon the complete exclusion of the vast majority of Algerians. This system did not allow the discussion of ideas and could not be influenced by the confrontation of ideas, and from this was derived the political weakness of the intellectual who was incapable of influencing the course of events. The intellectual elite – and by this is meant all those educated people capable of delivering either a written or oral message in which political or social ideas are expressed – was composed of both a French-speaking element and an Arab-speaking element. These two components of the elite, although they had the same social origins, did not convey the same political and social message, did not have the same attitude towards the colonial system and did not therefore have the same image of society to defend. This division within the elite took shape under colonization and did not diminish with independence; on the contrary, it tended to become further accentuated.

In the colonial situation, the person of French education did not have the social prestige of the intellectual in France, someone who is capable of having an impact upon public opinion. He was respected in his local neighbourhood because of his personal success, but at a political level his neighbourhood was wary of him because he was suspected of wishing to reproduce or to defend the colonial system whose culture he knew and from which he personally profited. The French-speaking intellectual was perceived as belonging to the colonial camp, especially as very often he was married to either a *pied-noir* or a French woman he had met while being a student. This impression was not completely false, because, impregnated with French culture, he was fascinated by the ideas of the eighteenth century. However, for him colonization was a personal affront on two counts: it injured Algeria, his homeland, but it also injured the image that he had of France. He condemned the colonial system as being unworthy of the France of 1789 and denied the colonial settler the right to lay claim to Robespierre and Saint-Just. He tried to explain to his fellow countrymen that the colonial system was not France, but he did not succeed in convincing them. He had a 'positivist' (in the nineteenth-century meaning of the word) outlook on his society, deploring its sociological archaisms. He was critical of its patriarchal ideology, the relationship between father and son, and of the position of women, in the latter case regretting their social backwardness and passivity (which gave rise to his choice of a French woman as wife). At a subjective level, he remained attached to his homeland through his mother, for whom he felt deep affection. But politically he was drawn to the French model of social relations. The ambiguity of the francophone intellectual has its origin in this stark division: attracted to France, he remained deeply attached to the cultural sensibilities of his country.

At a political level, he was not well organized but, on becoming a nationalist, he sided with the reformist movement led by Ferhat Abbas. The latter, a pharmacy graduate of the Sorbonne in 1919 and married to a French woman, called for gradual reforms which, in time, would lead to independence, whilst respecting a French cultural heritage that was perceived as an object of value and in a positive light.[6] It is this political position that explains the weak levels of support from amongst the popular classes enjoyed by the party of Ferhat Abbas, the *Union Démocratique pour le Manifeste Algérien* (UDMA). For the greater proportion of Algerians colonization was France and its culture; worse still, modernity itself was assimilated to French colonization. Thus, the manner in which Algeria was colonized determined the attitude of Algerians towards modernity and this attitude would have consequences, especially after independence.

It is from this that derives the importance of the *oulamâ* or Muslim cleric as the principal competitor to the francophone intellectual. His religious discourse stands as a defence of tradition against the cultural aggression of modernity. It is not therefore by chance that nationalist doctrine – which in turn inspired the nationalist movement and later the independent state – was to be the work of these Muslim clerics who utilized the cultural patrimony of the past to block the advance of modernity which, in their view, stood accused of justifying colonialism. Already under colonialism, therefore, there existed two types of Algerian intellectual: one, the francophone, imbued with French culture, critical of both the colonial system and of the social structure of the traditional society from which he originated; the other, the arabophone, concentrating on questions of culture and finding in religion the resources to oppose French ideological influence and colonial domination. The credibility of the language of one or the other amongst the masses was clearly determined by their respective attitudes to the colonial system.

When the insurrection began in 1954, the francophone intellectual finished up by siding with the *Front de Libération Nationale* (FLN), which conferred upon him administrative organizational tasks. No intellectual became part of the leadership of the *Front de Libération Nationale/Armée de Libération Nationale* (FLN/ALN). More telling still, Ait Hamouda, alias Colonel Amirouche, leader of one of the six FLN commands (*wilaya III*), had hundreds of *maquisards* who spoke French executed on the grounds that amongst them would have been traitors who informed the French army about the movements of the ALN. Amirouche was able to proceed with this purge, known under the name of *bleuïte* or protection from double agents, because of the anti-intellectual sentiments found in the FLN in particular and amongst the population in general.

After independence, the two types of intellectual opposed each other on the question of development. The francophone wanted to utilize the

State in order to resolve the country's economic and social problems; the Arabophone wanted to invigorate the country's language and religion in order to revive its Arabic–Islamic cultural heritage. Similarly, by force of circumstances, the francophone intellectual was at one and the same time both *organic*, in the Russian sense that he deified the State, and *critical*, in the French sense that he attacked the forms and structures of traditional society from a perspective of development. Conversely, the arabophone intellectual was hostile towards the State but a defender of a society that he wished to extract from what was frequently described in stereotypical language as 'the cultural and political perversions introduced by the West'.

THE COMPETITION BETWEEN FRANCOPHONES AND ARABOPHONES

As has already been indicated, the situation of the intellectual in Algeria has distinctive features that derive from the history of the country and from the conditions through which its society was drawn into the process of modernization and confronted political modernity. Profoundly destructured by a colonial population settlement that lasted for over a century, in the days following its independence Algeria had to face a series of cultural problems that related to its national identity, as well as social and economic problems whose solution would be found through development. This set of different problems expressed itself through divisions within its elite, the francophone section emphasizing economic development to address social issues like unemployment, illiteracy, population growth and malnutrition, whilst the arabophone section were preoccupied with the consolidation of Arabic–Islamic cultural identity.[7] These two sections of the elite had always coexisted within the nationalist movement under colonialism and were both present in the apparatus of the State at the point of independence, each connected by compromises from which strategic considerations were not absent in either camp. But, paradoxically, whilst it was assumed that independence would bring them together and serve to create a new elite, it pushed them further apart and even set them against each other.[8]

On one side, the arabophones, close to the people at the level of culture, pursued their Utopian dream of reviving the pre-colonial cultural past, whilst on the other, the francophones, attracted by universal values, sought to graft on modernity through the vehicle of the State. Divided culturally and ideologically, the elite was also divided at a political level over the control of posts within the machinery of the State, a struggle that was not without material considerations. The State used the francophones for their technical competence, giving them jobs in economic planning and administrative management, and used the arabophones in matters relating to culture and ideology: in teaching, in the ruling party, and in the media. The linguistic divide ran throughout the state machinery, including the army, but tended to be less strong at the summit of power, probably because of a group solidarity amongst those involved. An illegitimate power depends upon its internal cohesion.

But the arabophone elite, in contrast to the francophones, was not limited in size to those of its members who worked in the highest levels of the state apparatus. It was also strongly represented in society as a whole, where it clothed itself in a religious language which ordinary people could understand. Appearing frequently on television, the arabophone intellectuals there defended social values in terms of religious morality and championed what political language in Algeria calls the national constants (*ettawabit el watania*), the ideological values upon which the nation was founded. These are principally two in number: the Arabic language and Islam. This discourse found its continuation in the mosque where, in time, it drifted, on one hand, towards demands about identity and, on the other, towards opposition against the State from a moral point of view.

With the collapse of the managed economy, thought at the outset to provide legitimacy to those in power, the francophone elite found itself doubly discredited due to the fact that it had for long been identified with the economic policies of the State, providing them with scientific credibility. For example, the university economists, for the most part francophones, organized conferences and wrote articles and theses which showed the scientific basis of what became the dominant economic discourse recommending the 'non-capitalist route to development, of socialism, of the system of controlled prices and of manufacturing industry'.[9] By contrast, the arabophone elite, which had shown itself to be disinterested in the social problems of development, did not feel itself implicated in the economic failure and reaped the rewards for its cultural discourse. This position allowed it to move into opposition and to present itself as the ideological voice of the people in their opposition to the State, now accused of being controlled by francophones characterized as *hizb frança* (the party of France). Put schematically, the francophone was the *organic intellectual* identifying himself with a state which he wished to be the instrument of modernization and of social transformation; the arabophone, drawing upon a religious discourse, was a *dissident* who believed that this state corresponded in neither form nor substance to the cultural heritage of a society whose political expression he presumed to be.

THE *IMAM*-TEACHERS

The arabophone elite grew considerably in size due to the arabization of education and its democratization. Composed largely of teachers, this elite grew close to the population through the religious discussions that took place in the local mosques. After his classes, the teacher would frequent the mosque, lead evening prayers, and often lead discussions on the Koran, making references to current events, challenging the consciences of the believers and the responsibility of the country's leaders. These teachers, having volunteered to take on the role of *imam*, displayed certain specific characteristics: they were young (aged between 25–40), had not followed the traditional form of training in the teachings of the Koran, did not live off the generosity of the inhabitants of their district,[10] and were virulently subversive in their sermons. Their impact and their authority over their local population derived from the religious form of their language and its aggressive stance towards the government and its Western allies who, according to them, sought to weaken Islamic morality through the liberalization of customs, most notably by means of the emancipation of women. What was new about this, therefore, was that in the recent past these moral criticisms had been voiced by old people who had been deeply respectful of tradition. The same moralistic discourse of the earlier Muslim cleric was henceforth to be delivered in a menacing, vigorous and aggressive tone, with a definite political goal, and was conveyed by young men who were by training teachers, doctors, engineers, technicians, and so on. Abbassi Madani, founder and president of the FIS, is a professor of educational psychology at the University of Algiers; Ali Belhadj, his deputy, teaches in an institute of higher education; Abdelkader Hachani, the man who replaced them after they were both arrested in June 1991, is an expert in hydrocarbons. Beyond their professional activities, they lead the evening prayers in their neighbourhood mosques and conduct debates on social themes (the role of women, justice, corruption in civil service, etc.) using a language that has drawn enormous crowds to them. They have built their fame upon an aggressive rhetoric directed against the government and based upon a religious rule of conduct. They have subsequently transcended their status as *clercs* and have become men of politics who, with the help of the crowds that follow them, seek to seize hold of the State in order, they specify, to ensure that it conforms to the dictates of morality.

This part-time *imam*, who attracts the interest of believers who come to listen to him in the evening, is usually a government employee, either a teacher (*ousted*) in a school or university, a doctor (*hakim*) in a hospital, or an engineer (*mouhandess*) working in a state enterprise. He is not therefore a person without social position, with an irregular income and dependent upon the good nature of his neighbourhood, but rather he belongs to the privileged strata of society, possesses a house and car, and enjoys the salary of a government employee paid regularly into the bank. The authority conferred upon him by his function as *imam* is thus reinforced by a social status that identifies him with the francophones who, in the eyes of the faithful, have the pretension of monopolizing the attributes of social modernity.

By the end of the 1970s and the beginning of the 1980s, these *imam*-teachers had become important social phenomena. Invited to funerals and to marriage ceremonies, they preached their message, had it recorded on cassettes, to be listened to again and discussed in the home. Moreover, when this elite, born with independence, first interested itself in public affairs, social matters and the State, it became a political actor that, at the outset, the government underestimated because the latter presumed that it could bring this new phenomenon under control when the need arose.

Entering into opposition towards the end of the 1980s, the *imam*-teachers presented themselves as dissident intellectuals, preaching the divine word, calling for solidarity and social justice, condemning corruption and the liberalization of morals, denouncing attacks on religion. If one can define the intellectual as an individual whose speech relates to social values and who finds an audience amongst a wider public, then these *imam*-teachers are intellectuals. But they are intellectuals in a society where the autonomy of politics has not been established, where religion has not been secularized, where the individual has not been set free from the communal mentality which imprisons him and refuses him his political liberty. The *imam* intellectuals have a public in a society where public opinion does not exist, if one understands by public opinion that political actor which changes parliamentary majorities and governments on a regular basis. The *imam* intellectuals are oppositional but not critical, because the critical analysis of social practices is rejected by the religious ideology of which they are the bearers. This is why, at the level of government, they do not criticize either the idea of a one-party state or the supremacy of the army within its institutions. They oppose only the men who are in charge of those institutions and propose to replace them. Nor do they criticize society with a view to changing its social structure; they are reproachful only of the fact that it has become distanced from God, and propose to reverse the process. The *imam*-teacher is therefore an oppositional intellectual who wants to become an organic intellectual within the movement for which he campaigns. But the religious dynamic is such that there will always be oppositional clerics, even in a state which proclaims itself to be religious, because amongst Sunnite Muslims there exists no hierarchy which is the depository of religious authority.

THE FRANCOPHONES: A SECULARIZED ELITE

But why, beyond his rhetorical skills, did Ali Belhadj, a figure emblematic of the *imam*-teacher, become so popular and not, for example, Said Saadi, a doctor who entered politics, or even Norreddine Boukroh, a bilingual journalist who created a party making an appeal both to Islam and to modernity? There are two reasons which can be given to explain the inability of these two figures to create popular political movements. The first is that they are perceived as having an ideological connection with the State, whose language has been that of Western modernity, and therefore as not having the potential to break with the FLN state. This impression was confirmed by the fact that the parties they created recruited their members essentially from social categories at the margin of the State: civil servants, technical specialists, doctors, lawyers, most of whom were French-speaking. The second reason is that the secular character of their language – despite the fact that it was as critical of the government as that of the Islamists – associated them, in the eyes of ordinary people, as turning their back on religion.

The so-called democratic parties have no support amongst the poorer sections of society because they all come up against the Islamic Utopia which encourages the popular masses to believe that it is possible to organize the State democratically upon the basis of a fear of God. If it is suggested that the fear of God is not sufficient to guarantee equality and social justice nor to prevent corruption and the abuse of power, the reply is that you do not sufficiently believe in God. The secular elite therefore finds itself faced with a conception of social relations according to which religious morality should be at the heart of those relations; it finds itself before a conception of politics where politics, at a formal level, cannot be autonomous from religious conscience. The assassination of francophone intellectuals can be explained in part by this moral conception of politics, a conception which they do not share.

The ideology of democracy arouses suspicion from the moment that it is defended by a secular elite, especially when it is a largely French-speaking elite. This is not to say that the masses who have voted recently in elections for the Islamic Salvation Front (FIS) have voted against democracy.[11] In the FIS vote there is, beyond the desire to sanction those in power, a call for democracy that is formulated both implicitly and in a contradictory manner. The popularity of the FIS rests upon democratic demands that relate to participation in the world of politics from which Algerians are excluded, and that also relate to participation in the world of social modernity through such things as work, housing, the facilities associated with urban life, being treated with dignity by the administrative machinery of the State, and so on. Religion is perceived by the masses as the means of access to this modernity which respects their cultural identity. There is therefore a deep democratic impetus in the protests of the Islamists, but it is a protest which does not express itself in the normal words and language of democracy.

This is why there is disagreement between the francophones and the populace, and this disagreement relates as much to the discourse of the francophones as to its secularized content. The people do not understand the arguments of the francophones, whilst the latter, in turn, do not understand that the people formulate their social hopes in religious terms. This mutual incomprehension is a measure of the distance that exists between an elite which wishes that the social aspirations of the people be formulated in a secularized discourse, and a people who do not understand that the elite – or a part of the elite – does not give an important place to religion in its political discourse. This mutual incomprehension between the two entities will last until the point that it is dispelled by historical experience, that is, up to the point that the FIS exercises power. It is only the defeat of the FIS and its incapacity to keep its promises, and therefore the incapacity of religious discourse to ensure equality and the dignity towards which the people aspire, which will bring about a rejection of religious discourse in political struggles. I have called this process through which the Islamists will lose their popularity one of 'fruitful regression'.[12] The error of the secular elite was not to remain democratic in January 1992, when they should have opposed the annulment of the elections and denounced the torture and arbitrary imprisonment that was being inflicted upon the Islamists. The vote of December 1991 was a vote whose effects would in time have brought the people nearer to the secular elite. The quashing of the elections, by contrast, created an infernal dynamic which has further distanced this elite from the populace for what will be a long period, and to incomprehension has been added hatred and the feelings of revenge.

The violence which broke out brought into stark confrontation the State, supported by the army, and the Islamists, enthused by their electoral victory. Those social groups at the periphery of the State – doctors, journalists, technical specialists, French-speaking teachers: in short, all those that in Algeria are called intellectuals – had to decide what side they were on. Their ambiguity was that, whilst they were hostile to the Islamists, they did not unduly demonstrate their support for the army. It is from this that questions and doubts arise about the authors of the killings each time an intellectual is murdered in Algiers.

THE ISOLATION OF THE FRANCOPHONE INTELLECTUALS

But the killing of francophone intellectuals has been – and is – only possible because there does not exist a university system that can be seen to be autonomous of the State and which, consequently, can gain credibility amongst different publics. It is precisely because the francophone intellectuals are not politically and professionally credible and do not have a public, that they can be killed like rabbits. The systematic policy of the leaders of the newly-independent state to combat any slight desire for autonomy in society – be it economic, religious, in the trade unions, universities or the press – gave the francophone elite no chance of being credible in the eyes of the population. Such an elite, emerging independently of the State, could have provided an alternative to the language of religion, or at least limited its hegemonic influence over a society which, in order to show its distrust of government, took refuge in the politics of Islam.

The assassination of intellectuals has not evoked a disapproval from the population which might have persuaded the murderers not to commit further crimes. This shows the position that intellectuals have in their society. The funerals of the victims, exploited by state television as a weapon of propaganda against the Islamists, confirms the average viewer in the belief that the deceased was a supporter of the government. In a programme devoted to the murder of intellectuals broadcast in May 1994, the arabophone writer Tahar Ouettar replied to a question, addressed to him by a journalist from the *Arté* channel, that the death of Tahar Djaout was a loss for his own children and for France, but not for Algeria.[13] Beyond what this horrible phrase tells us of the hatred which exists between Algerians, the fact that Tahar Ouettar was not rebuked by a wider public for having murdered Tahar Djaout for a second time, says much about the isolation of the francophone intellectual in Algeria.

The origin of this isolation lies in the existence of a political domain that is dominated in a coercive and non-ideological manner by the power of the State, which itself is in the hands of the army. This has prevented the emergence of civil elites, with the exception of those social groups that it employs within its institutions and in the economic sector, where, in any case, it exercises power. Even the university is prevented from producing its own elite, being refused its own administrative autonomy and facing opposition from the government towards its reviews and research groups. The rectors of universities – up to the end of the 1980s recruited from amongst doctors and dentists – and of educational institutes were chosen by the relevant government ministry, after consultation with the army, for their willingness slavishly to serve the administrative hierarchy of the State. The principal concern was that the university system should not be a focus of opposition, having elites with which different levels of the population would self-identify. The universities being blocked off, the oppositional elites emerged from the mosques and in such numbers that they were difficult to control.[14]

But it would be an exaggeration to say that the power of the State alone has prevented the emergence of a secular elite, because, in point of fact, the development of such an elite has faced obstacles of a historical, social and ideological kind. Rather, the State has not sought to encourage the emergence of an elite possessing social recognition. It has not aided this process because it feared that this elite would be a competitor to the army, the only institution conceived as providing members for the ruling elite.

Fundamentally, a politically relevant elite cannot be formed before there appears a public opinion operating in a political space that is occupied by political parties, trade unions, associations and newspapers offering both opinion and information. Certainly, public opinion, in the sense of a homogenous political actor obeying a political rationality and reacting as an individual, has never existed.[15] However, what is commonly called public opinion is that collection of different currents of opinion that cross civil society, united around a minimum consensus concerning the procedures of accession to power and the legitimacy of opposition. Public opinion does not express itself through a single party or movement, nor necessarily through a series of parties. Public opinion does not indicate the degree of cohesion or integration of a society, but only that a consensus exists about the way in which differences in society are addressed. Electoral opinion is an illustration of the existence of public opinion as a determining element in the political sphere and domain.

The force of the intellectual derives from his ability to influence public opinion. If the latter does not formally exist, if it does not intervene on a regular basis so as to change the occupants of power, the intellectual remains the individual respected in his neighbourhood for his social status – doctor, journalist, lawyer, university lecturer, and so on – and not as a political actor who influences public debate in the direction of modernity. It is here that resides the principal difference between the intellectual who is critical of the social structure and its forms of collective representation and the oppositional intellectual. The francophone intellectual is critical in a society obsessed by the defence of its cultural identity; the arabophone intellectual is oppositional in a country where the political regime has been rejected. The isolation of the one and the popularity of the other have the same cause: the majority of the population want to change the personnel of the political regime without putting into question the collective and symbolic forms inherited from the past. It is through this fundamental contradiction that society will modernize itself, unhappily at the price of terrible suffering, because nowhere does the unfolding of history conform to reason and intelligence, which alone are capable of saving suffering.

Article translated by Jeremy Jennings.

NOTES

1 This chapter is a revised version of a paper presented to the annual seminar of *Centre d'Analyse et d'Intervention Sociologique* (CADIS), held between 22–24 September 1994 in Dourban, and first published in *Esprit*, January 1995, pp. 130–8. I thank the participants of this seminar and especially A. Bérolowitch, N. Guénif, Y. Pozo and L. Zhang, for their comments.

2 Antonio Gramsci used this expression to characterize those persons who, because of their skills and knowledge, were recruited by the capitalist state in order to ensure the dominance of bourgeois ideology.

3 'The drama of Russian society and the drama of those who consider themselves as belonging to the intelligentsia lies in the long and painful passage from infantilism to maturity... It is understandable that the confusion of those who call themselves democrats should open the door to the most obscure and dangerous forces. If democracy does not possess its cultural and moral elite it will become an oligarchy, an adventurist political dictatorship that will mobilize the masses and manipulate them.' (J. A. Levada, 'Le problème de l'intelligentsia dans la Russie aujourd'hui'.) I thank A. Bérélowitch for having drawn this unpublished text to my attention.

4 See J. Benda, *La Trahison des clercs*, Paris, Grasset, 1927. See also R. Debray, *Le Pouvoir intellectuel en France*, Paris, Grasset, 1979. Benda's text can be found as *The Betrayal of the Intellectuals*, Boston, Beacon Press, 1955; whilst Debray's text has been translated as *Teachers, Writers, and Celebrities: The Intellectuals of Modern France*, London, Verso, 1981.

5 See M. Gallo, 'Les intellectuals, la politique et la modernité', *Le Monde*, 24 July 1983.

6 See B. Stora and Z. Daoud, *Ferhat Abbas*, Paris, Fayard, 1994.

7 There were arabophones who were sensitive to questions of development, but they were not numerous. For example, the editorial board of the arabophone newspaper *Al-Khabar* was not attracted to the language of the Arabo-Islamists. The Islamists made fun of the paper by calling it the arabophone publication of the francophones.

8 A policy of bilingualism might have overcome this division, but after independence it was shelved as being too problematic.

9 Inspired by the ideas of the French academic G. Destanne de Bernis, it was this strategy that directed Algerian economic policy in the 1970s. The model showed that for a country such as Algeria it was better to begin by developing heavy industry rather than the light industry that would produce consumer goods.

10 Under colonialism, the *imam* of the mosque who lived in urban areas was dependent upon the charity of his neighbourhood.

11 For a more detailed assessment of this situation, see L. Addi, 'Democrats caught in the crossfire', *The Times Higher Educational Supplement*, 10 November 1995; L. Addi, 'Dynamique infernale en Algérie', *Le Monde diplomatique*, October 1995; and L. Addi, 'Dynamique et contradictions du système politique algérien', *Le Monde* 29 November 1995.

12 See L. Addi, *L'Algérie et la démocratie*, Paris, La Découverte, 1994 and 'Political Islam and Democracy', in H. Adenius (ed.), *Democracy's Victory and Crisis*, Cambridge, Cambridge University Press, 1996, forthcoming.

13 Tahar Djouat was a poet and founder of the weekly review *Ruptures* (eds).

14 For an assessment of the attacks of Islamic fundamentalists upon university personnel, see S. Hughes, 'Rector murdered by Islamic hitmen', *The Times Higher Education Supplement*, 10 June 1994 (eds).

15 See P. Bourdieu, 'L'opinion publique n'existe pas', *Les Temps modernes*, 318, January 1973, pp. 1292–1309.

6 Between the word and the land
Intellectuals and the State in Israel

Shlomo Sand

Tsahal, Claude Lanzmann's film about the Israeli army, ends with a freeze frame of a gentle young armoured corps instructor sitting on an enormous tank. This army officer, whose face is meant to radiate intelligence, is wearing the round wire-rimmed glasses associated with intellectuals. The shot, encapsulating the film's visual paean to the new Jewish warriors, is intended to show audiences that, although these soldiers' main business is war, the hereditary intellectuality of the 'progeny' of Marx, Freud and Einstein is discernible even in the young face of an armoured corps soldier. The strong State of Israel has become the last imaginary refuge from the impossibility of universalism. Yet the main accomplishment of Zionist settlement has been to transform part of the 'People of the Book' into a nation in which, after many hardships, the position of 'men of letters' is not very different from that assigned to them in other modern cultures.

Some hundred years before *Tsahal*, Theodor Herzl wrote *The State of the Jews*. Like every other nationalism of the modern age, Zionism arose primarily from intellectual milieux that were typical of the end of the nineteenth century. Herzl, the originator of the idea of Jewish political sovereignty, was a successful journalist and an unsuccessful playwright. Max Nordau, his right-hand man and the Trotsky of the Zionist revolution, was one of the most popular and outrageous cultural critics in turn-of-the-century Europe. The Biluists, the emigration movement which arose in Russia after the 1881 pogroms and which preceded political Zionism, was composed mainly of university and high-school students; and up until the First World War the Zionist movement itself was constituted for the most part by a young intelligentsia. It was not until after that war, with the rise of Nazism and the establishment of the State of Israel, that Jewish nationalism began to attract a more socially diversified population.

That the intellectual was an early agent of national culture should not surprise us. In most nationalist movements of both the nineteenth and twentieth centuries, 'men of ideas' were the first ambassadors of modernization involved in the process of shaping collective identities. Precisely because of the abstract nature of national consciousness, at the outset cohesive intellectual groups were needed to take upon themselves the organization and cultivation of a new national culture. If the formation of a nation – to accept part of Ernest Gellner's thesis[1] – means turning the code of a higher culture into the common heritage of an entire society, then the modern intellectual is undoubtedly the kingpin in the formation of every nationalism.[2]

The decline in the status of rabbis, the original intellectuals of the Jewish community, was one of the factors contributing to the appearance of the 'organic' (to use Gramsci's term)[3] secular national intellectual. The second important factor was, of course, the atmosphere of rejection or hostility that confronted any Jewish intellectual who left the cultural ghetto of his parents. The more self-confident nationalisms of Western Europe gave rise primarily to misgivings about assimilation with the 'other' (accompanied by fierce outbursts of animosity). In Eastern Europe, the cradle of Zionism, open enmity towards Jews constituted a cultural element that was almost essential to the construction of new national identities. This widespread hostility was expressed through many channels, from the 'mild' anti-Semitic sentiments which formed part of the linguistic heritage, to savage riots and pogroms. Moreover, what is perhaps more important for our purposes is that young Jewish intellectuals were usually barred from the new careers opened up by the developing division of labour, a discrimination which was endorsed by decrees and laws in the Russian empire and the Romanian kingdom, but which also existed in a more moderate form even in the German empire.

The new Jewish intellectual who sought his place in the social-cultural modernization of Eastern Europe had three options:

1 To join the wholesale emigration to the West, thereby accepting the destiny of integrating into an unknown and completely foreign national culture, and running the serious risk of losing part of the symbolic capital he had acquired thus far – that is, finding his social class de-intellectualized.

2 To join, as an intellectual, socialist movements which, although using the codes of the different national cultures, extolled a non-national univers-alism that obscured the vestiges of Jewish uniqueness. The socialist Jewish intellectual joined a political cultural camp whose code he had learned well, allowing him – so he thought – to preserve the advantages that his intellectual qualifications gave him.

3 To create a new culture of his own based on the traditional elements of identity that the process of modernization had begun to shatter – that is, to reconstruct and nurture a specific culture distinct from surrounding cultures, but also different from the pre-modern religious culture that had hitherto characterized the Jewish communities. In this way, he was able to maintain a high status within the Jewish community, which, although changing and disintegrating, still retained some of its uniqueness.

Before long this third option was characterized by two main perspectives. One perspective held that it was possible to create and nurture a modern Jewish culture while abandoning the principle of political nationalism. If a nation is a people with a consciousness of itself which aspires to political self-sovereignty, the non-nationalist intellectuals organized within the framework of the Bund party and other autonomists assumed they could plan and maintain a new autonomist culture without the paraphernalia of an independent state. Unfortunately, they were wrong.

The second perspective, which is the focus of this chapter, was initially a minority trend. The Central and Eastern European participants in the first Zionist congresses were intellectuals of various professions and conflicting ideologies. Students and journalists sat next to writers, doctors and teachers. Socialist high-school students rubbed elbows with unconventional rabbis and *yeshiva* graduates. Scattered among them were a few merchants, manufacturers and clerks. Since the social history of the Zionist movement has yet to be written in its entirety, it is difficult to give clear statistics on the socio-occupational status of the first Zionist activists. Up until now, the leaders and activists who rallied to the new nationalism have been grouped and classified according to their political and ideological affiliations. In Zionist historiographical syntheses, the intellectuals joining the movement were usually Jews of no particular social or professional distinction, who, of course, had discovered their unique nationality. Yet, it is difficult to ignore the disturbing fact that, even more than the Bolshevik party, the Zionist movement started out mostly as an intellectual minority movement, with no great army of followers. Zionism – that is, the collective assimilation to political modernity – was created primarily by those intellectuals who had been frustrated in their efforts to achieve personal assimilation, as well as those who preferred to translate the traditional culture they loved to a related modern culture.[4]

It must be realized that the Zionist option was in a sense the hardest and most radical choice offered to the Jewish intellectual, even if it was the most tempting spiritually. The intellectual pioneers of national modernity in other nations were occasionally obliged to establish a language, to design a collective memory, to become political men of action, and even to serve as warriors in the army of the new nation. The young Jewish intellectual who became a nationalist intellectual, however, was forced, in addition to all these burdens, to uproot himself physically – in most cases cutting himself off from part of his family – and, at a crucial point, to emigrate to Palestine. Despite the country's abstract fascination for him, its scenery, physical climate and native population were completely alien to him. What was more, while many intellectuals were the architects (not the builders) of the process of turning peoples into nations, Jewish intellectuals, at least initially, were largely obliged to create a 'people' of their own within themselves. The Jewish people were not eager to emigrate to Palestine. Some of the lower middle classes occasionally showed enthusiasm, but were too deeply enmeshed in the difficult struggle for existence. Peasants, who always constitute the decisive majority in a people that becomes a nation, were almost non-existent among Jews in Europe. Most of the Jewish masses voted with their feet and headed West, turned to the social democratic parties, joined the Jewish Bund, or chose to enclose themselves in their previous religious cultural orthodoxy.

Unfortunately, colonization is not an intellectual enterprise. The intellectual activists of political Zionism sought with all their being to create a new nation, and to that end some of them became professional politicians. This, however, did not represent a great transition as the political profession uses some of the same means of production as those of the typical intellectual occupation: magazines, newspapers, and books served the turn-of-the-century politician just as much as assemblies, committees or diplomatic meetings did; and most political–cultural production was still carried out in the known European languages. In contrast, the intellectual who decided to emigrate for good to the territory that would constitute his national homeland risked a radical change in his social and cultural situation.

The wave of immigration that took place between 1904 and 1914, known in Zionist historiography as the *second aliya*, laid the foundations of Jewish settlement in Palestine. In this case, we do have statistics indicating the socio-cultural stratification of the 35,000 immigrants (some of whom returned to their countries of origin, or continued to migrate further westward). Sixty per cent of them were between the ages of fifteen and thirty, most of them unmarried. Twenty-three per cent were high-school graduates with no trade. Some 15 per cent more were graduates of universities or other educational institutions. Many others were *yeshiva* graduates. About 50 per cent already knew Hebrew to some extent or another.[5] There were apparently no illiterates. The most fascinating aspect of this group of young, educated immigrants, however, is the ideological baggage they brought with them.

If nineteenth-century nationalism was carried on the waves of democratization that rose and flooded Western and Central Europe, the nationalism that appeared outside Europe during the twentieth century was formed through a symbiosis with socialist myths. In this respect, the Zionist emigration movement was one of the first nationalist movements of the new century to achieve some of its success on the strength of the egalitarian future it offered. Unlike the liberal ideology that dominated the Zionist establishment in Europe, many of the young people who chose to emigrate to Palestine had adopted the populist or socialist ideas that percolated through Russia before the revolution and immediately after-wards. Only by means of the social Utopia were the offspring of Jewish middle-class families able to turn their backs on the intellectual career paths typically expected of their class and become labourers or farmers in the new land.

The religion of labour, the return to nature, and cooperative socialism were perceived as the remedy for the social 'anomaly' of Jewish life in Europe, and revolutionary romanticism nourished the needs of colonization. Aharon David Gordon, a prototype of the intellectual-turned-farmer who continued to write, was the cultural hero of the generation. Personally repelled by the intelligentsia and by writers who lived by their pens, he contributed a great deal to the development of the ethos that called for an end to the division of labour into intellectual and physical pursuits.[6] Although most immigrants eventually settled in cities, those young intellectuals who set out to conquer the land quickly achieved ideological hegemony, and produced the generation of leaders who would rule over the new immigrant society until the early 1970s.

Among the immigrants who arrived during the twenty-year period between 1904 and 1924, the formative years of Israeli society, were David Green – who would later be known as David Ben-Gurion, the founder of the State of Israel – but also Joseph Hayim Brenner, the brilliant, tormented Hebrew writer who was murdered in 1921; Yitzhak Ben-Zvi, the second president of Israel, but also Shai Agnon, the future recipient of the Nobel Prize for Literature; Golda Meir, prime minister during the 1970s, and finally Hayim Nachman Bialik, who would come to be considered the greatest poet of the new Hebrew culture. The cultural needs of the small civilian society then beginning to expand led to a new division of labour between the political and the intellectual. Although the developing political establishment actively participated in producing the elements of national consciousness – much more than the political sector participated in planned cultural production in established societies – its organizational and administrative functions forced it to share the production of the new culture's symbols with a more professional category. Accordingly, the constitution of a local political power centre was paralleled by the development of a community of cultural agents, who undertook to supervise the production of the elements of the collective identity and memory.[7] Of course, the relative autonomy that the intellectual sectors achieved vis-à-vis political power in the modernization process in the Western world was not expressed in the same way in a society of immigrant settlers. As we know, there was no strong, independent capital deriving from a developed market economy, nor was there a wide audience of culture-consumers. Furthermore, the continuing colonizing effort organized and administered by political elites who had developed directly from the conquest of the land gave those elites a prestige that was difficult to undermine. Although it did not possess the apparatus of a sovereign state, by the 1930s, the political centre had managed, by means of party and labour-union tools, to attain a high level of control over the economic and social systems, and particularly over the capital flowing in from donations and other revenue. This control also led, ultimately, to a relatively strict supervision of the intellectual sector. The degree of dependence in the pre-state political system of the 'authorized' cultural agents soon became evident and reflected in the nature of the hegemonic ideology that was to reign in Israeli society from the mid-1930s onwards. The few attempts by intellectuals to achieve a legitimate status as independent political critics were doomed to failure, whilst the 'revolts' of lone individuals like the radical poets Uri Zvi Greenberg of the right wing and Alexander Pen of the left wing led to their total marginalization for many years.[8] As we will see further on, only one intellectual nucleus managed to maintain a more prolonged resistance.

The bases for the revival of the Hebrew language in Palestine were laid by Eliezer Ben-Yehuda, who may be considered the first Hebrew intellectual in the country. Not only did he write the first Hebrew dictionary, but he also disseminated the revived language through editing and through extensive writing for the press. This does not mean that Hebrew became the dominant language at the beginning of the century. Few people managed to speak fluent Hebrew at that time, despite the dictates of national fashion.[9] It was not, in fact, until the 1920s that, with many neologisms, the language of the Bible became the principal spoken language of the *Yishuv*.

The most prominent intellectual of the time was Joseph Hayim Brenner, whose personality and literary activity left their stamp on his entire generation. None the less, a nucleus of literary creation that needed to rely solely on a small publishing house, one temporary periodical and a restricted reading public still did not qualify as a literary centre. It took the outbreak of the Russian revolution and the decline of Zionist activity in Jewish centres in Russia to force a wave of distinguished 'Hebrew' intellectuals to emigrate to Palestine (eminent Zionist politicians, in contrast, emigrated to Central and Western Europe). The fact that this group did not arrive until after the young pioneers who came as immigrants before the war indirectly contributed not only to the hegemony of socialist, as opposed to liberal, ideas but also to the shaping of the special relationship between the political and intellectual sectors.

Officially, the Hebrew Writers' Association (*Agudat ha-Sofrim*) was founded in 1921. But it was not until 1924, after the arrival of Hayim Nachman Bialik and his group and the establishment of the Dvir publishing house, that one could speak of a Hebrew literary field in Palestine.[10] The Hebrew Writers' Association – now controlled by Bialik in cooperation with those writers associated with the Zionist Left – was the main framework for attaining literary recognition, and most of the battles to achieve renown and immortality were waged in the periodicals it sponsored. At the same time, the Association saw itself as a spiritual avant-garde and cultural leader of the national revolution that was sweeping the new country. Since many of the young pre-war immigrants were in fact the 'cultural progeny' of those eminent writers who had arrived from Odessa or Warsaw, they viewed the latter's work with appreciation and respect, even if most of it was radically at variance with their own social Utopias.[11] The symbolic capital of poets, writers and critics such as Tchernichowski, Ben-Zion, Kabak, Bialik or Yosef Klausner, capital accumulated before they emigrated, stood them in good stead when they came to build an independent literary system, allowing them at an early stage to prevent the increasingly powerful political avant-garde from using the literary centre as a mobilized and mobilizing medium for blatant party politics. This was conditional upon an acceptance that writers would not sabotage or otherwise interfere with the growing political hegemony of the Zionist left.[12]

Although most of the pioneering immigrants shared a heritage that venerated books, the conquest of land and the conquest of labour (to turn them into Hebrew land and Hebrew labour) came before the conquest of words (that is, the cultivation of Hebrew language, literature and education). Hence, the ineluctable process that eventually harnessed the literary elite to the political aims of the new national establishment and its leaders. The 1930s saw the beginning of a growing tendency to see literature first and foremost as a tool for consolidating party ideology.[13] Although previously it had been accepted that intellectual work should serve the cause of national renewal as broadly as possible, towards the end of the 1930s the majority of those who constituted the republic of Israeli writers turned into a camp mobilized along party lines which tried to produce literature with a socio-national message. The values of socialist Zionism acquired an obligatory hegemonic status and began to push to the sidelines literature concerning individual problems or any debate on problems of form. The myth of the Hebrew labourer and the agricultural pioneer, the man of deeds rather than the producer of words, fed the collective ethos during the 1940s as much as it excited the creative imagination. From the beginning, the Zionist enterprise had been conceived as the transformation of a displaced, super-intellectualist people into a strong productive nation. Now the process of shaping the myth reached its apogee. Original elitist creators of modernist Hebrew poetry such as Nathan Alterman or Avraham Shlonski felt a duty to themselves to rally to the ideological camp of the left-wing Zionist movements, and did not hesitate to become their active spokesmen. We should also not forget that the political parties were in a position to finance the publication of books and other printed matter, and thereby to ensure a stable literary production. Of course, personal literature with universal emphases continued to exist; and every so often intellectuals would express qualms about the 'immoral path' of practical politics. Nevertheless, although the dialogue of such intellectuals might occasionally reflect disapproval, the core of the literary system issued no consistent intellectual criticism condemning the practice of the political elites.

For example, the relationship of the Zionist enterprise with the non-Jewish 'other' – whether this involved terminating his employment by Jewish bosses or pushing him off the land where he was living – could not constitute the subject of a critical intellectual discussion within the literary system, which, it may be said, willingly accepted the decisions of the national leadership without question. The Arab population's strong and violent opposition to the colonization process as early as the 1920s and, in particular, the great revolt and general strike of 1936 reinforced the siege mentality of Jewish society and led local writers to eschew any serious criticism that might hurt the leadership's prestige. It was almost impossible to be part of the new national community while publicly taking issue with the continuation of its settlement. The echoes of the Second World War would merely accentuate this process of politicization, whilst the precarious unsupported existence that producers of culture led in a small poor society, (which at the end of the 1930s was also in the middle of an economic crisis) naturally facilitated the integration of the intellectual with the political. Many writers were in fact never able to make a living from writing, and therefore those who did not write for newspapers worked as schoolteachers – in which capacity they were even more dependent on the political establishment.[14]

The only intellectual institution that managed to sustain a relatively high degree of independence up until the establishment of the state in 1948 was the university. The Hebrew University, founded in Jerusalem in 1925, was the breeding ground of a surprising resistance to the power systems and values of the ruling political nucleus (which, although still without sovereignty, wielded increasing authority). Most of those who first worked in the university, like the writers who came as immigrants in the mid-1920s, arrived in Palestine with a recognized symbolic capital and saw themselves as the spiritual representatives of the entire Jewish people, not merely the academic servants of Hebrew society. Their international academic status and their personal relations with the outside world strengthened their demand for cultural independence, something which by the 1930s had become a rare commodity. Since the greater part of the university's budget was covered by direct donations, mostly from the remote United States, the strong trend towards independent thinking in the university grew, to the point that it created a political challenge to the Zionist establishment.[15]

The most fascinating ideological opposition to the central movement of Zionist colonization crystallized in the lecture halls of the university in Jerusalem. The Brit Shalom society, established in the same year as the university, aimed 'to arrive at an understanding between Jews and Arabs'.[16] It was an eminently intellectual organization that had no intention of becoming a political party. Its members, and the contributors to its publications, included university people such as Akiva Ernest Simon, Georg Landauer, Gershom Scholem, Shmuel Hugo Bergman and the celebrated philosopher Martin Buber, who arrived in the country in 1938. Judah L. Magnes, president of the university from 1925 to 1948, was associated with the group, and often presented its views. Most of the university staff were uncomfortable with these opinions, but they honoured the status of the leading lights of the first academic generation who had tried to preserve a Central-European liberal tradition, even under the difficult conditions of colonization.

All the members of Brit Shalom were faithful Zionists, and some of them even came from the centre of the Zionist establishment abroad.

However, although Zionism's principal aim was to establish a sovereign Jewish state, the members of the Brit were committed to the idea of a binational state. They agreed, for example, to accept Jewish demographic inferiority as the condition for integrating in the region; in fact, the group believed that the continuation of immigration must be subject to Arab consent. This view was, of course, rejected outright by the Zionist consensus.[17] Nevertheless, Brit Shalom and its successor, Ha-Ihud, were the most important organizations to protest against the actual form taken by the process of colonization that were to appear from amongst the intellectual elites of the new Jewish society. The failure of the universal messages of these intellectuals, combined with the outbreak of the 1948 war, put an end to this collective organized unease and, once the machinery of the new state had been set up and the university subordinated to the government's budgetary policy, intellectual protests from the university world had a personal rather than collective character (at least up until the 1960s).

The 1948 war, the hardest war ever suffered by Israeli society, contributed to a further unification of Hebrew intellectuals around the new sovereign power. Although the post-war period was distinguished by the publication of *Khribet Khizah*, S. Yizhar's famous novella, which expressed genuine moral qualms concerning the expulsion of Arab refugees, most cultural creation in the first decade of the life of the state consisted in committed, nationalistic works that revelled in the birth of the state.[18] The intellectual classes quickly completed the process of conformist integration within the new cultural establishment, and thereby contributed greatly to erasing the borders between state and civil society. Indeed, reducing the separation between the state and civil society was necessary for continuing the rapid consolidation of a new national culture.

As masses of immigrants arrived from Europe and the Arab world, much less ideologically motivated than immigrants at the beginning of the century, Israeli intellectuals were led by their own inclinations and state support to develop an elitist Hebrew culture that scorned cultural imports and tried to suppress any identity that was not purely Hebrew. This trend, which was already present before the establishment of the state, reduced still further the contradiction that cultural modernity presented between political power and the thirst for autonomy that lies in every intellectual. The job the intellectuals were given of supervising the revolutionary cultural melting pot demanded of them not only total submission, but also the creation of a messianic cult of the state intended to replace most of the assorted beliefs and traditions that the immigrants had brought with them from their countries of origin. Intellectuals, some of them Holocaust refugees, who arrived from the post-war ruins of Europe, were integrated into this process to varying degrees – starting out, of course, from an inferior position and suffering the painful frustrations caused by the speedy relinquishment of part of their identity. Jewish intellectuals from the Arab world, which itself was just on the point of a nationalist awakening, had an even harder time. They were almost completely removed from legitimate cultural discourse, and in many cases underwent a professional de-intellectualization, or were forced to emigrate to other countries.

In the first decade of the state's existence, the 1948 generation of writers, including Moshe Shamir, Aharon Meged, David Shaham and S. Yizhar, and the second generation of Hebrew University notables, such as the sociologist Shmuel Eisenstadt, the philosopher Nathan Rotenstreich, the historian Ben-Zion Dinur, and many others, accepted the subordination of spiritual values to state and collective ones as a historical imperative. The rational bureaucracy headed by the enlightened ruler was the object of uninhibited intellectual admiration, an admiration that permitted Ben-Gurion, the first prime minister, to establish a monolithic political culture which completely ignored criticism from both the Right and the Left.[19] In the 1960s, Eisenstadt himself would term the cultural elitist attitude to the state as 'Byzantine sycophantism'.[20]

Most of the Israeli intellectuals submissively accepted not only the cult of the state, but also the veneration of members of the army, the high priests of this cult of power. Militaristic defence served as a useful tool for unifying immigrants with many different identities around the government and the party that directed it. The 1956 war, in which Israel conquered all of Sinai in seven days, is a fine example of a political culture being swept away by a wave of messianic militarism (a wave that would rise again, as we shall see, in 1967). On the eve of the war, Nathan Alterman, the ruling party's 'court poet', was recruited to compose a paean to Hebrew weapons. When the fighting began, journalists described the war as a new revelation of Sinai. Encouraged by this atmosphere, Ben-Gurion declared the inception of the 'third kingdom of Israel' when Israel proved victorious. However, just as the war brought to light the messianic undertones concealed within the young Israeli culture, so did the manner of the war's end – complete withdrawal from all the occupied areas – reduce national tension and return the young society to a less 'heroic' path of development. It was less heroic because it began a process of moderating the degree of state influence on different sectors of cultural production and duplication. At the same time, intellectual enthusiasm for this irksome influence declined.

The years following the Sinai campaign were characterized by a decline in military conflicts, an accelerated rise in the standard of living and the beginnings of a welfare state. At the same time, institutions of culture and learning expanded.[21] The second half of the 1950s saw the establishment of the University of Tel Aviv, which would eventually become the country's largest academic institution. The number of students in the two universities combined with the Technion increased by 396 per cent in one decade, reaching a total of 10,000.[22] The republic of writers, which had grown significantly, was also augmented by a new generation of young, sceptical creators, dubbed 'the state generation'. The independent press extended its readership, becoming more popular than the party-affiliated papers. In addition, Ben-Gurion's unrestricted control had made him too many enemies in his own party. In 1961, the great political crisis known as 'the Lavon affair' occurred. This episode constituted, in a way, a kind of mini-Dreyfus affair for the intellectual world. The great majority of the 'men of ideas', who up to then had clustered around the centre of political power, now openly came out against the 'philosopher-king', denouncing him for everything they had previously admired about him. In January 1961, a number of professors from the Hebrew University signed a petition accusing Ben-Gurion of anti-democratic arbitrariness and of exploiting the state apparatus for personal power. The anti-Ben-Gurion wing of the government seized on this intellectual uprising and the atmosphere it created to bring Ben-Gurion down. This was the beginning of a major change in the relations between the political centre and the cultural establishment, for the first time presenting the intellectual sectors with the opportunity to increase their relative autonomy.

By the end of the 1950s, various creators had already begun to show the first signs of suffering from the weight of the public ethos that demanded a national ideational collectivity. In the literary world, new writers appeared who had been too young during the 1948 war to experience the 'miracle' of the birth of the Hebrew kingdom. The existence of the state was beginning to be taken for granted. Poets and writers like Nathan Zach, Amos Oz and A. B. Yehoshua began to explore a literary domain that did not sacrifice the personal to the social, and the social to the state.[23] The cultural Westernization of Israeli society during these years, which itself was reflected in the general way of life, also set its stamp on the style of cultural production, which began to focus on the personal, the more intimate. The previous generation still ruled in the centres of cultural power, and national and military heroism was still fostered in school curricula and the mass media. However, Israel's openness to foreign capital investments brought with it a parallel openness to the importation of more liberal cultural models, which began to exert an attraction from the cultural sidelines. The economic crisis of the mid-1960s only added impetus to the less conformist modernistic trend that saw in the Israeli social experience a point of departure for mental creativity rather than an object of reverence. Intellectuals active in the political arena waged a steady protest campaign during those years to revoke the martial law imposed on the Arab population and to halt the eviction of that population from what was left of its lands. Martin Buber, who in the 1950s had been the most prominent intellectual fighting the Ben-Gurion culture, also took part in these organized protests against the government.

The 1967 war put a brake on the slow process whereby nationalism was 'secularized' and what could be called 'civilian' culture was strengthened. The great tension that preceded the actual fighting and the Israeli army's intoxicating victory restored national messianism – which had been fading since the beginning of the 1960s – to the centre of the public stage. The occupation of Old Jerusalem stirred the hearts of most of the 'authorized' providers of culture, and the cult of the new land that had just been conquered replaced the old cult of the state. In contrast to the ruling political elite, which, surprised by the magnitude of the victory, was prey to doubts and vacillations, many of the producers and disseminators of organized culture did not hesitate to give themselves up to the drug of power, and to demand immediate ownership of all the 'liberated' areas of the country. Prominent intellectuals of every political stripe, including the writers Shai Agnon, Haim Hazaz and Moshe Shamir, the poets Uri Zvi Greenberg, Nathan Alterman and Haim Guri, and the literary critics Dov Sadan and Avraham Kariv, called for the establishment of a Movement for the Greater Land of Israel.[24] Other writers, teachers, journalists and students were swept along in their wake, each contributing to the new annexationist drive in his own field. It was an effective intervention of intellectuals in politics, which not only managed to shape a supportive public opinion quickly, but also ultimately pulled the government towards a policy of renewing settlement in the 'promised' land. The official geographers erased the Green Line – that is, the 1948 cease-fire line – from the old maps.

This time, however, there were no young secular nationalists lacking the perspectives of intellectual specialization in their own homelands to undertake the renewal of colonization, as had been the case with the immigrant generation at the beginning of the century. The secular intellectuals of the 'Greater Israel' movement did not settle in the occupied territories. For that, there was a new breed of pioneers. Young non-Orthodox rabbis, graduates of non-ultra-Orthodox *yeshivas* and national religious high schools, felt their great moment had come. Up to then, they had existed at the margins of the culturally prestigious sectors and had even suffered from a certain form of Sabra anti-Jewishness; modernization in Israeli society had kept them in a subordinate position within the secular field of culture. Now that they had become the national settler avant-garde, their status had improved. Gush Emunim – which was an alliance between power-hungry politicians and dynamic intellectuals, both groups veterans of the religious Zionist movement – set out to conquer the land, in the process trying to re-establish hegemony over Israeli society. Its successes in 1974 were impressive. The Zionist left, which had been in power since the establishment of the state, was trapped in its old colonizing myth, 'one more dunam, one more goat', and was carried along by the momentum – something that would contribute to its losing the government to the right wing in 1977.

Faced with the rising wave of nationalism which burst forth after 1967, some intellectuals tried to moderate the uncritical enthusiasm for 'Greater Israel'. The first of these, and the one who reacted most radically, was

Professor Yeshaiyahu Leibovitch, one of the editors of the *Hebrew Encyclopaedia*, who, as soon as the fighting ended, warned that the victory would turn Israel into an oppressive, militaristic nation and completely destroy the Jewish spiritual tradition. By calling for immediate withdrawal from all the occupied territories, he subjected himself to hatred and vilification, and ended up virtually a lone voice crying in the wilderness. The culture of the radical left, then at its apogee in the Western intellectual world, left almost no trace on the Israeli political map, except for the creation of two tiny student groups on the perimeter of the Israeli left. Although the Greater Israel movement had developed primarily in the living rooms of poets, writers and journalists, it was in the corridors of the universities that the *Movement for Peace and Security* was born in 1968.[25] Under the leadership of the historian Yehoshua Arieli, supported by his more famous colleague, Yaakov Talmon, and with the participation of writers and poets such as Amos Kenan, Amos Oz, Leah Goldberg, and many others, an intellectual peace movement was organized that tried unsuccessfully to balance the political intellectual right. This movement collapsed with the outbreak of the 1973 war.

This war was a painful one for Israeli society, both because of its casualty rate and because victory this time was not as clear and straightforward as it had been in the previous wars. These circumstances, together with structural socio-political factors, helped undermine the traditional left-wing government that had ruled the country for thirty years, and contributed to its replacement by the Zionist right. Although this political change represented a significant turning-point in Israeli history, it was especially critical in the history of the relations between cultural elites and the state. From the 1930s up to 1977, the period of uninterrupted rule by the Zionist left, there had been a strong mental symbiosis between the intellectual sectors and the political elites, occasionally punctuated, as we have seen, by transitory disputes and moderate moral protests. The similar social and cultural backgrounds of these two elites – both composed of the scions of well-established middle-class families of European origin – as well as the conditions in which the new national society was melded, softened any overly harsh conflicts that might have resulted from the state's direct control of the cultural field. Moreover, the central political discourse was always careful to seek universalist, socialist or liberal justifications for national practice, a fact which also heightened the family feeling between politicians and intellectuals. Menachem Begin's rise to power on the strength of the votes of Oriental Jews and the support of the national religious sectors challenged, for the first time, the traditional relationship between a large proportion of the intellectual classes and the state leadership.

Unlike Ben-Gurion, his great rival, Begin did not curry favour with the intellectual elites or seek their company. His target audience was different, and perhaps one of the factors that aided his victory was his disapproval of the ruling cultural establishment. His direct, national-populistic style and manifest scorn for intellectualist scruples increased the alienation felt towards him, not only by the doyens of Israeli intellectual life, but also by the wider public of producers and disseminators of culture. Although Begin was the first prime minister to make peace with an Arab state, he was perceived by the average Israeli intellectual as an anachronistic political leader who represented a shallow, ill-considered culture. Now many intellectuals were able to disapprove of the government uninhibitedly without feeling that they were harming the national interest. Many of them had the impression – which they did not trouble to hide – that the government represented another people. The tribal consciousness, which until then had characterized Israeli nationalism, continued to exist among the popular classes but began to recede among the elites, making way for a more pluralistic political culture. The right-wing Likud government's alienation from the 'high' cultural system made the regime less ideological and more liberal, thereby indirectly increasing the relative autonomy of the different systems of cultural production. At the same time, these systems kept losing prestige. From authors to professors, the public's image of the intellectual lost more and more of the remnants of symbolic capital it retained from Jewish tradition – remnants that were cultivated and preserved for years in instrumental form by the Zionist left.

It was against this backdrop that *Peace Now* appeared at the end of the 1970s. Like others of its kind, this pacifist protest movement began in circles typical of the intellectual. In contrast to its predecessors, however, the group became a broad-based organization that rallied large crowds to its demonstrations. It was helped, of course, by the signing of the peace treaty with Egypt, which went a long way towards eliminating Israel's historical feeling of being under siege. The outbreak of the Lebanon war in 1982 did not reverse this trend but rather intensified it. This was the second war Israel had initiated since 1956; but whereas the Sinai campaign had aroused enthusiasm, the Lebanon war, the first to be conducted by the right wing, aroused immediate disapproval, and various intellectuals began to criticize it even before the guns fell silent. This opposition to a war that was still in progress constituted a new phenomenon in Israel, and marked the beginning of a new era.

The world of intellectual production responded accordingly. First, for a short time, there was a lively and wide artistic opposition, producing sharply politicized works. Stories, plays and poems began to treat issues of political existence from a critical distance. In the pre-eminently ideological state systems, such as the elementary and high school systems and the state electronic media, these changes were not yet obvious. In the universities, however, whose members spent some of their time abroad, and in the network of privately owned newspapers, particularly the local press, political sensitivities began to appear. While respected authors like S. Yizhar, A. B. Yehoshua and Amos Oz continued to provide spiritual succour to the Labour party, so that it would again take part in the government that the

Right had 'stolen' from it (and thereby partially restore, perhaps, the writer's shaky status), another intellectual sector began to create surprising, unconventional images: the film sector.

In fact, the most significant change in cultural morphology can be said to have begun in the film industry. The sphere of cultural production least encumbered by the weight of the written word gave birth to the most interesting innovation, as though the written Hebrew word was one of the effective barriers to the revelation of some collective 'subconscious' memory of the historical past whose vestiges continued to exist and to obstruct. The film director did not have a tested verbal code created by his spiritual forefathers to dominate his images, as did writers. Despite the conformity inherent in the conditions of cinematic production, the 1980s saw the appearance of such Israeli films as Daniel Waxman's *Hamsin*, Uri Barabash's *Beyond the Walls*, Yehuda Ne'eman's *Fellow Travellers*, Nissim Dayan's *A Very Narrow Bridge*, Shimon Dotan's *The Smile of the Lamb*, and Amos Gitai's *Esther*.[26] These films are not anti-Zionist, and some of them show traces of Jewish national supremacy, although in one way or another all the films present the Israeli experience as a situation of conflict with that 'other' whose situation does not permit the continuation of normal existence. That which was repressed to the Zionist subconscious has drifted upward into the consciousness, thereby contributing to the continuing change in the definition of the collective 'I'. At times the young movie-making industry seemed to sense the approach of the Palestinian *intifada* that was to break out at the end of 1987.

This 'Palestinian' wave in Israeli film would soon fade, but the *intifada* that was to lead to the Oslo agreements would, among other things, prepare the ground for the public appearance of the first post-Zionist intellectuals. Although this phenomenon is still marginal in the Israeli intellectual world, its location and the attention focused on it have been significant. The cessation of Jewish settlement and the loss of the territorial expansion option occurred just as channels opened to direct the intellectual imagination towards other dimensions. The fact that national cultures in the West, particularly American culture, began to allow Jewish intellectuals to emphasize their 'other' identity once more also helped the Israeli cultural sector to show more tolerance – for the first time in its history – for non-Zionist viewpoints. In a national culture that is well established but perceived as too narrow (in a world whose horizons shrink with each technological advance), 'rejection of the Diaspora', the main battle cry of the Zionist ethos, has lost some of its historic charm. The 'postmodernist' intellectual avant-garde has begun hesitantly to cherish the myth of the wandering Jewish intellectual who is at home in the cultural salons of the Western world.

This atmosphere of tolerance in the Israeli cultural world – particularly in its upper echelons – clearly reflects the greater relative autonomy that this world has been gradually achieving vis-à-vis political authority. From heavy dependence and almost complete submission, in an immigrant settler society subject to traumatic national conflicts, the power relations between the cultural production systems and the world of political decision-making has developed in the direction of a complex and relatively more liberal relationship. In an individualistic society, more secure in its economic strength and its national identity – even if it has not yet managed to resolve the historic conflict from which it sprang – the 'authorized' producers of culture are able to graze more freely in the spiritual fields where ethos, myth and collective memory are conceptualized and encoded. Nor is there any doubt that the decline of the political need for mobilizing ideologies, and the undermining of the original hierarchy of self-images and national images of the past, has also increased pluralism in the intellectual domain itself.

Although this subject is perhaps the real *raison d'être* for this chapter, it is too closely bound to the malign caprices of a multi-directional present. Accordingly, I shall not expand on it in this short synthesis, which has attempted, though imperfectly, to predict a recent past not yet completed.

1986, the year before the *intifada* began, was the year of *Avanti Popolo*, a successful film by the Israeli director Raffi Bukai. The film's hero, played by an Israeli Palestinian actor, is an Egyptian soldier in the 1967 war who, left behind in the Sinai desert, is caught by the Israeli army. In his civilian life, the Egyptian was a professional actor. In the film's climactic scene, the sensitive, intelligent Arab soldier declaims before the rough Israelis Shylock's famous speech, 'Hath not a Jew eyes?' The ignorant Israeli soldiers do not understand, and laugh at their prisoner. These soldiers do not appear in Claude Lanzmann's documentary film on the Israeli army. They are, after all, fictional characters in the 'wild' imagination of a young intellectual who grew up in Israel, not 'real' Israeli officers in a Jewish–French film. It goes without saying that the Israeli film maker was more successful than the Parisian intellectual in diagnosing the 'normalization' that the Zionist revolution wrought among those of the 'People of the Book' who in historic times of trouble preferred the Land to the Word. This 'normalization', of course, is also what gave rise to the Israeli director's ability to film it.

NOTES

1   Ernest Gellner, *Nations and Nationalism*, Oxford, Basil Blackwell, 1983.
2   See E. Shils, *The Intellectuals and the Powers and Other Essays*, Chicago, University of Chicago Press, 1972.
3   A. Gramsci, *The Modern Prince and Other Writings*, New York, International Publishers, 1972, p. 118.
4   On the development of Hebrew culture in Russia, see D. Miron, *When Loners come Together. A Portrait of Hebrew Literature at the Turn of the Twentieth Century*, Tel Aviv, Am Oved, 1970 [Hebrew].

5   Y. Gorny, 'The changes in the social and the political structure of the "Second Aliyah" in the years 1904–1940', *Zionism*, I, 1970, pp. 205–46 [Hebrew].

6   On this exceptional figure, see E. Schweid, *The World of A. D. Gordon*, Tel Aviv, Am Oved, 1970 [Hebrew].

7   On the social profile of the cultured elites between 1918 and 1948, see M. Lissak, *The Elites of the Jewish Community in Palestine*, Tel Aviv, Am Oved, 1981, pp. 93–6, 156–9, 172–5 [Hebrew].

8   See, for example, A. Cordova, 'Unsolicited intellectuals in politics: The case of "Brit ha-Biryonim" ', in P. Ginossar (ed.), *Hebrew Literature and the Labor Movement*, Beersheva, Ben-Gurion University Press, 1989, pp. 224–42 [Hebrew].

9   On the development of the Hebrew language, see I. Even-Zohar, 'The emergence of a native Hebrew culture in Palestine: 1882–1948', *Studies in Zionism*, 4, 1981, pp. 167–84.

10   Z. Shavit, *The Literary Life in Eretz Israel 1910–1933*, Tel Aviv, Hakibbutz Hameuhad, 1982 [Hebrew].

11   A. Cordova, 'The institutionalization of a cultural center in Palestine: The Writers' Association', *Jewish Social Studies*, XLII, No. 1, Winter, 1980, pp. 37–62.

12   A. Cordova and H. Herzog, 'The cultural endeavor of the Labor Movement in Palestine: a study of the relationship between intelligentsia and intellectuals', *Yivo, Annual of Jewish Social Science*, 17, 1978, pp. 241–2.

13   See N. Gertz, *Literature and Ideology in Eretz Israel during the 1930s*, Tel Aviv, Open University, 1988 [Hebrew].

14   On the relationship between the teachers' organization and the political elite, see M. Rinott, 'The struggle between the Teachers' Union and the Zionist Organization for Hegemony in Hebrew Education in Palestine', *Zionism*, IV, 1975, pp. 114–45 [Hebrew], and also Y. Shapiro, *An Elite without Successors. Generations of Political Leaders in Israel*, Tel Aviv, Sifriat Poalim, 1984, pp. 66–92 [Hebrew].

15   See U. Cohen, *Intellectuals in a National Crystallization Process. The Relationship of the Hebrew University in Jerusalem and the Jewish Settlement in Eretz-Israel, 1925–1948*, unpublished MA thesis, Jerusalem, The Hebrew University, 1996 [Hebrew].

16   P. R. Mendes-Flohr (ed.), *A Land of the Peoples. Martin Buber on Jews and Arabs*, New York, Oxford University Press, 1983, p. 74. See also Aharon Kedar,' "Brit Shalom": Documents and Introduction', *The Jerusalem Quarterly*, 18, Winter, 1981, pp. 55–85.

17   H. Lavsky, 'The puzzle of Brit Shalom's impact on the Zionist Polemic during its time and afterwards', *Zionism*, XIX, 1995, pp. 167–81 [Hebrew].

18   D. Miron, 'From creators and builders to homeless', *Igra, Almanac for Literature and Art*, II, 1985–6, pp. 106–18 [Hebrew].

19   On this subject, see M. Keren's interesting book, *Ben-Gurion and the Intellectuals. Power, Knowledge and Charisma*, Illinois, Northern Illinois University Press, 1983.

20   S. N. Eisenstadt, *Israeli Society, Background, Development and Problems*, Jerusalem, The Magnes Press, 1967, p. 331 [Hebrew].

21   On the growth and development of the universities, see J. Ben David, 'Universities in Israel: dilemmas of growth, diversification, and administration', in E. Krausz (ed.), *Education in a Comparative Context. Studies of Israeli Society*, Vol. IV, New Brunswick, Transaction Publishers, 1989, pp. 148–73.

22   On the number of students at the end of the 1950s, see S. N. Eisenstadt, *The Transformation of Israeli Society*, Jerusalem, Magnes Press, 1989, p. 297 [Hebrew].

23 See M. Keren, *The Pen and the Sword. Israeli Intellectuals and the Making of a Nation-State*, Boulder, Westview Press, 1989.
24 D. Miron, 'Document in Israel', *Politika*, 16 August 1987, pp. 37–45 [Hebrew].
25 T. Herman, *From the 'Peace Covenant' to 'Peace Now': The Pragmatic Pacifism of the Israeli Peace Camp*, unpublished PhD thesis, Tel Aviv University, 1989, pp. 258–97 [Hebrew].
26 On this subject, see E. Shohat's book *Israeli Cinema, East/West and the Politics of Representation*, Austin, University of Texas Press, 1989, pp. 237–73.

7 A product of history, not a cause?
Yeats, the 'Auden generation', and the politics of poetry, 1891–1939

D. George Boyce

In the spring of 1939, W. H. Auden published two pieces of work to mark the death of W. B. Yeats. One was a poem, 'In Memory of W. B. Yeats'; the second was an article entitled 'The Public v. the late Mr. William Butler Yeats'. In these, Auden interrogated the relationship between poetry and politics. Poetry itself had an enduring value but it was not necessarily the value that the poet wished to give his work; for the difficulty lay in the fact that the poet's work was subject to a whole host of different interpretations by subsequent generations:

> ... scattered among a hundred cities
> And wholly given over to unfamiliar affections

> The words of a dead man
> Are modified in the guts of the living.[1]

But the poem was not a simple recantation of Auden's earlier belief that poetry could have a public role; rather was it a complex and honest reconsideration of what it was that poetry could achieve in the world of 'happenings'.[2] And it must be read in the light both of Auden's article and his early revision of the poem.

In his article, Auden elaborated his theme. The article was cast in the form of a mock trial, with the Prosecutor castigating Yeats for having failed to live up to the poet's duty to 'understand his age': 'for the great struggle of our time to create a juster social order, he felt nothing but the hatred which is born of fear'. He embraced superstition in an age of science and rationalism. The Defence argued that the central point was that the Prosecution seemed to be claiming that a 'great poet must give the right answers to the problems which perplex his generation. The deceased gave the wrong answers. Therefore the deceased was not a great poet'. Poetry, in this perspective, was like 'filling up a social quiz'.[3]

Contemporary poetry could not be judged in this way. This was not to say that art existed independent of society; every individual was excited emotionally and intellectually by his social and material environment; and poetic talent was the power to 'make personal excitement socially available'.

The most obvious social fact of the last forty years was the failure of liberal capitalist democracy, which, through its values, 'created the most impersonal and the most unequal civilization the world had ever seen, a civilization in which the only emotion common to all classes is a feeling of individual isolation from everyone else, a civilization torn apart by the opposing emotions born of economic injustice, the just envy of the poor and the selfish terror of the rich'. Yeats, in his work, sought to find an alternative; he looked back to a world of peasants and the aristocracy, with their native virtues, and protested against a world imbued with commercial values. But 'to create a united and just society where the former are fostered and the latter cured is the task of the politician, not the poet'. For:

> Art is a product of history, not a cause. Unlike some other products, technical inventions for example, it does not re-enter history as an effective agent, so that the question whether art should or should not be propaganda is unreal. The case for the prosecution rests on the fallacious belief that art ever makes anything happen, whereas the honest truth, gentlemen, is that, if not a poem had been written, not a picture painted, not a bar of music composed, the history of man would be materially unchanged.

The article and poem are inextricably bound together: shortly after Auden published the first version of his poem, on 8 March, he added a third section, interposed between the first and second parts of the original poem. In this, he hit even harder at the notion that poetry made something happen.

> You were silly like us; your gift survived it all:
> The parish of rich women, physical decay,
> Yourself. Mad Ireland hurt you into poetry.
> Now Ireland has her madness and her weather still,
> For poetry makes nothing happen: it survives
> In the valley of its making where executives
> Would never want to tamper...[4]

Auden made a point of dating this poem on the death of Yeats precisely – 'd. Jan. 1939' and it was clearly meant to mark a historical turning point. The greatest poet of the century was dead; the century itself, now, in 1939, had reached a crisis:

> In the nightmare of the dark
> All the dogs of Europe bark,
> And the living nations wait,
> Each sequestered in its hate;

The poem was the product of what might be described as a recurring feature of modern European history : the moment of crisis, the apocalypse. In that moment, the poet could only fight to assert his art, to write and write well, and in so doing could 'let the healing fountain start':

In the prison of his days
Teach the free man how to praise.

Politics, then, would not be moulded or affected by art; yet art could have a function in time of crisis, and could help people cope with the crisis. This might well be considered a political function, and an important one at that.

But this was not what the young Yeats, and the young Auden, and the people who followed their path in the 1890s and the 1930s originally desired; this was not their first position. Yeats, as Auden remarked, was 'silly like us'; he hoped to change 'Mad Ireland'. The Auden generation certainly hoped to change Mad Europe: to create a new, equal society, to make a contribution to a sense of profound injustice that must be righted; to help the good cause in Spain; to replace an outworn capitalist system by a new, Utopian Marxist social order. Yeats, for his part, strove to create what he called a 'unity of being':[5] to search for a binding force in society founded on a cultural and even racial tradition. Yeats, like the Auden generation, had a powerful sense of the crisis in the Europe of their day. And they developed political agendas. What light does a comparison of their motives, movements and reflections throw on the relationship between the writer and politics?

The crisis of Ireland and Europe was, for Yeats, one of using Irish nationalism to lead Ireland away from her parochialism, and into the mainstream of European civilization. Yeats was what is commonly referred to as an 'Anglo-Irishman', of southern Irish Protestant extraction, and belonging to a tradition that was shaped in Ireland, but modified by England; creating antinomies which Yeats explored, sometimes revolted against, but was always fascinated by : his people, the Anglo-Irish, were the people whose ancestors – Swift, Burke – had shaped modern Ireland, or at least had shaped all that was good in modern Ireland.[6] What was bad was what was also bad in modern England: the rise of the philistine bourgeoisie, the 'middle-class mind', the people who, in the case of England, found their 'religion' in their 'opium' of the writings of H. G. Wells,[7] and who in Ireland were in danger of being seduced by the idea that all literature must conform to the propagandist level set by the (in other respects admirable) Young Ireland movement of the 1830s. Young Ireland's most charismatic figure, Thomas Davis – like Yeats, a southern Protestant – had made the mistake of diluting literature by seeking to give it a popular appeal: 'When he sat down to write he had so great a desire to make the peasantry courageous and powerful that he half believed them already "the finest peasantry upon the earth", and wrote not a few verses as such verses as –

"Lead them to fight for native land
His is no courage cold and wary;
The troops live not that could withstand

The headlong charge of Tipperary" –
And today we are paying the reckoning with much bombast.' [8]

Nevertheless, Yeats had sympathies with Nationalist Ireland; he admired the Fenian, John O'Leary, who had struggled all his life to free Ireland from English rule; he took part in planning and enacting the celebrations to commemorate the Rebellion of 1798. It may be this that inspired Masaru Sekine to write in a preface to a collection of essays on Irish writing and politics that 'The problem of being bullied by England since the Norman conquest [*sic*] – is a fact of life'.[9] It was this, he claimed, that drove Irish writers to write about politics. But this is a massive over-simplification. Yeats was sceptical about England's assumption that she was the predominant partner; but what he disliked was her bourgeois ways, not Milton and Shakespeare; and he disliked equally the bourgeois ways of Ireland. Yeats was concerned to court Irish nationalists because he wished to change and mould Irish nationality; to use poetry, and the arts generally, to lead Ireland away from the 'great hatred, little room' that had 'maimed us at the start'.[10] In that sense, Auden was right; Mad Ireland, rather than Bad England, hurled him into poetry, or at least into the politics of poetry.

Those politics were expressed in his belief that the fall of Parnell had created a vacuum in Irish life, had disgusted the 'race', had caused it to turn away from narrow, self-seeking political machinations, and to become 'like soft wax for years to come'.[11] This soft wax could be shaped into the form that Yeats's vision reserved for it: a revival of Irish history and culture, to make young men 'think of Ireland herself'.[12] This Ireland would transcend the demands of narrow nationalists; it would be the home of a newly-forged nation, one that would encompass all Irishmen, whatever their origins, and help them to warm themselves at the fire of a rediscovery of Ireland's past; but not a past based on 'Irish virtue' as against 'English guilt'. No, Ireland would desert the materialistic, narrow world of philistine nationalism, and her poets would direct her people towards their true destination – an acknowledgement of their European heritage – for Irish history and culture were part of Europe's history and culture. The literary revival would use the English language as its medium, but take Ireland herself as the subject matter for writing.

Yet, Yeats not only believed in nations; he believed in race. The race was a cultural entity, shaped by history, and with a distinctive mission in the world; in the case of Ireland, to recall it to its romantic sensibility, to revive it through the remaking of myths and legends. There had been, there could be again, a community; and in that community the poets could be, as they had been in ancient Ireland, the teachers of the race. Irish poetry, unlike English poetry, had to be spoken or sung, not read, for Ireland's literary tradition was oral, whereas England's was made in the printing presses.[13] In Celtic times the bards had ridden 'Hither and thither gathering up the dim feelings of the time, and making them conscious'. And they had exercised much political power: when a bard asked for a king's eye, was it not plucked out for him?[14] Moreover, the leaders of this community would come from the ranks of Yeats's own people, the Anglo-Irish. In this way, Yeats might be said to echo the words of the Protestant United Irishman William Drennan, who claimed that, while the Catholics may save themselves, it was the Protestants must save the nation.[15]

Save it from materialism, bourgeois values, and also reserve a place in it for the Anglo-Irish Protestant. This was not politics, narrowly defined; and Yeats indeed spoke of the nation turning away from politics after the fall of Parnell.[16] But the rediscovery of a nation or race, the recreation of its values, the infusing of that nation with its culture, properly restored, the creation of a unity of being – all this was highly political, explosively so.

How could the poet bring his people into that sense of unity, of history, of shared cultural values? Yeats hoped to tease out the values which he believed were immanent in the Irish people: values of the spirit, ethical values, and a certain kind of Celtic temperament. To this end Yeats spent much of his time in the 1890s telling the 'Celts' of Ireland what they truly were – a people whose best quality was excess of imagination, and who only needed to be brought to this awareness to give them their lost sense of unity and renew their cultural tradition. But he came to appreciate that there was in Ireland a dangerous development in that the spectre of class warfare might yet overcome the Anglo-Irish. To this Yeats responded by insisting that an alliance could be formed between the Anglo-Irish and, not the 'Irish people', but the ingredient that (with Anglo-Irish leadership) would leaven the lump: the peasants, the repository of folklore, traditions, and wisdom, alive, real, vibrant, would become the allies of the gentry in resisting the tide of democracy and materialism, and send the petty bourgeoisie scurrying back to their towns.[17] Moreover, Yeats hoped to by-pass the equally materialistic tenant farmers, now the rising class in Ireland after the Land Acts of the British government, and appeal to the people below the tenants, those who would follow their chieftains as they had in days of old.[18]

But this was still an oversimplified view of modern and modernizing Ireland. The rise of a Roman Catholic middle class was indeed a danger to Yeats's vision; and it was one that came into direct conflict with him on two grounds in particular: that his literary revival was based on the English language, and could hardly be 'Irish' at all; and that his Protestant prejudices remained in place, as revealed in the kind of plays which he was willing to see performed by the National Literary Theatre – in particular J. M. Synge's *Playboy of the Western World*, which more sensitive members of the middle classes saw as an insult to their (not far removed) agrarian roots, and a betrayal of Ireland to English prejudices, as a nation of bumpkins and wordy fools. Moreover, the complexity of the idea of a national literature in the language of another nation, and a nation which had 'robbed' the Irish people of their language, was hard for the Irish language revivalists' Gaelic League to accept. The League and Yeats had seen eye to eye in the 1890s, and indeed its founder, Douglas Hyde, was himself of Yeats's Anglo-Irish stock; but the League could hardly accept the idea that Ireland could have a literature in any tongue other than her 'own'. The Catholic middle classes had felt that they had found Yeats out; indeed, they had found him out as early as 1897 when his play *The Countess Cathleen* attracted unfavourable attention for portraying a noble landlord, the countess, who was willing to sell her soul for gold, gold which would save her tenants in famine times; this selfless action by a landlord hardly fitted in with the nationalist idea that the landlords were a class who should be hunted even beyond their economic grave.[19]

By 1914, arguably, the Anglo-Irish gentry were being herded into their political graves as well. They enjoyed considerable influence in the British Conservative Party but the Liberal government was pressing ahead with a home rule bill which would give power to the Irish democracy, and place the Roman Catholic in the position of permanent majority – except in north-east Ulster, where some provision, as yet unspecified, must be made for the Protestant minority there. Yeats, for his part, saw that he had failed to create that 'unity of being' to which his whole political efforts had been directed; moreover, the philistinism of the nationalist middle classes had been revealed in the Dublin corporation's refusal in 1913 to build a gallery to house the pictures of Hugh Lane – Lady Gregory's nephew – a condition which Lane placed on his bequest to the city. This disgust was increased by the treatment meted out to striking members of the Irish Transport and General Workers Union in 1913. The strikers were severely handled by the Dublin Metropolitan Police; their strike was directed against William Martin Murphy, a prominent businessman and member of the Irish Nationalist Party. This incident convinced Yeats that 'Romantic Ireland' was 'dead and gone'[20]; that a tight-fisted, bourgeois, shop-keeping Ireland had supplanted it; and that the only role that the poet could play was to turn his thoughts inward, and hope that some new chance might come for the best to lead the rest. This hope was dashed by the Easter Rising of 1916, which was the product, not only of a long held conviction by the Irish Republican Brotherhood that England's difficulty was Ireland's opportunity, but by the desire to restore a Celtic community in which all self-seeking would be laid aside, and men would be made anew: free from greed and selfishness, and wishing only to serve the nation. This idea might be expected to appeal to Yeats's idea of community and race. But he realized that it was somebody else's rising – Patrick Pearse's dream, not his – and that the Rising marked the end, not the beginning of the idea of unity: the Rising was a fact, but it would create a myth of self-sacrifice, duty, violence and freedom, which Yeats and his people could hardly share. Yeats reflected that the Rising had overturned 'all the work of years'.[21] But it would be more accurate to say that Yeats was moved by the Rising, and the subsequent war of independence and civil war of 1919–1923, to reflect yet again on the relationship between culture and politics, as the world moved from the crisis of the 1890s, a crisis of democracy, the masses, and capitalism, to a new and as dangerous crisis: that of a disjointed, volatile and uncertain post-war world, where anarchy might prevail and the 'blood-dimmed tide' wash over all.[22]

It was this post-war mood that induced W. H. Auden to believe that Yeats had overcome the 'silliness' of his youth, his romantic period, and his delusion that art could make things happen in politics. Certainly Yeats ceased to believe that, through art, the alliance between the Anglo-Irish and the peasant could be forged. Worse, the forces released by the 1916 Rising, the violence of the war of independence, the anarchy of the civil war, where a Republican soldier could speak of dying of gunshot 'as if it were the finest play under the sun',[23] did seem to show that poetry stood helpless before the divisive, brutal world of politics. And as Yeats reflected on the new Irish state (in whose public service he worked as a senator), he contrasted the politicians of 1933 with the lonely, solitary nobility of Parnell. Yeats accused himself:

> All that was sung
> All that was said in Ireland is a lie
> Bred out of the contagion of the throng...[24]

It is easy, then, to see Yeats, as he seemed to see himself, as one in whom all political (but not sexual) passion had been spent:

> How can I, that girl standing there,
> My attention fix
> On Roman or on Russian
> Or on Spanish politics?[25]

This would be to underestimate Yeats's concern and interest in politics in a wider sense: in the sense of exploring what it was that made history work and explained the rise and fall of nations.[26] In 1921 he wrote, in 'The Second Coming', of the 'mere anarchy' that is loosed upon the world when 'the falcon cannot hear the falconer'.

> And what rough beast, its hour come round at last,
> Slouches towards Bethlehem to be born?[27]

In this, another great European crisis which was coming and, by the 1930s, was imminent, Yeats was anxious, not only about its outcome, but by the fact that 'no one knows what's yet to come'.[28] Yeats's flirtation with fascism, his admiration of the Irish Fascist movement, the Blueshirts, bore witness to his own testimony of himself as one of 'the last Romantics'; but 'all is changed, that high horse riderless'.[29]

Could that Irish mission in the world, that mission that Yeats sought to create and to realize in the 1890s, be recalled? Could the seminal event of modern Irish history, the 1916 Rising, be worked to save the Irish race from the filthy modern tide? Perhaps, for:

> When Pearse summoned Cuchulain to his side,
> What stalked through the Post Office? What intellect,
> What calculation, number, measurement, replied?
> We Irish, born into that ancient sect
> But thrown upon this filthy modern tide
> And by its formless spawning fury wrecked,
> Climb to our proper place, that we may trace,
> The lineaments of a plummet-measured face.[30]

This poem, 'Statues', was written in, and is dated precisely, 9 April 1938. A poem fixed in time; one that recalled Yeats's political and cultural vision, less than a year before his death, reaffirming his belief that the race, saved from 'spawning fury' (an image of violent, overwhelming mass-reproduction, of mass-society) could yet accomplish a unity of being and a distinctive role in history. But it lacked the power, the insight, the authenticity, the wisdom of the Seven Sages, Yeats's eighteenth-century ancestors, 'we old men massed against the world'.

Old men massed against the world: but while Yeats was in the last decade of his life, English or, more properly, British writers, young men, were also massing against the world that they perceived was emerging by the end of the 1920s. Something new seemed to be happening.

Here, a contrast with the place of the writer in Ireland is instructive. The Irish writer in the nineteenth century could never ignore the fact that he had a bone to pick with history; or, rather, that history had a bone to pick with him. Auden's phrase again comes to mind: Mad Ireland hurt Irish writers into poetry. English (and Scottish) writers of the nineteenth century were not, as is sometimes alleged, apolitical, immersing themselves in an Arnoldian contemplation of culture: Disraeli and Trollope wrote directly political novels; Dickens wrote scathing social criticism; Robert Burns helped lay the foundations of a particularly Scottish form of egalitarianism; Thomas Hardy wrote his long poem, reflecting on the rise and fall of historical epochs and personalities, 'The Dynasts'. There may be much in Tom Paulin's belief that English literary criticism has sought to prise the politics of English and Scottish writers away from their poetry: to dismiss them, or to allege that their politics only hurt the poetry.[31]

But what distinguished the 1930s generation of poets from their predecessors was that a group of writers resolved to draw up and pursue a political agenda; and that they felt a compulsion to do so, and to do so from a particular ideological perspective. It was rare for English writers to act in such a collective fashion, even though they could, individually, respond to, for example, the social distress of the turn of the century with a whole range of 'social' writing. Or, to another problem of the century, the advance of democracy, with a heartfelt cry of protest that might have come from the pen of Yeats himself. Here is D. H. Lawrence writing to Lady Cynthia Asquith:

> Let us have done with this foolish form of government, and this idea of democratic control. Let us submit to the knowledge that there are aristocrats and plebeians born, not made.[32]

The 1930s generation were reacting against several traditions when they took up their pens and set out to 'make things happen'. They were reacting against the tradition that poets, of all kinds of writers, must hold themselves aloof from the world of rutting politicians; must live in what Tom Paulin calls a 'soundproof museum'.[33] They were reacting against the privileges that they themselves enjoyed, and enjoyed in a world where privilege was the prerequisite of the very few. Stephen Spender captured the mood of the time. It was in Germany in 1929 that he encountered Walter, a tramp who, Spender admitted, managed to 'take him in'. Spender allowed himself to be thus fooled because 'I felt that as a member of a more fortunate social class I owed him a debt'. Walter, had he robbed Spender, could never have robbed him sufficiently 'of the advantages which society had given me over him'.[34] At this period of his life, Spender admitted that his attitude was one of 'what Yeats called "passive suffering" ',[35] though, by the mid-1930s, he was more active. On the occasion of his wedding in 1936, Spender was seized with guilt:

> Amongst the wedding presents were a few toast racks, silver trays, and so forth. Seized with a sudden impulse of pity for those amongst my friends who were paupers, I thrust these upon them as they left.[36]

This might be dismissed as an extrapolation of his undergraduate days at Oxford when, in reaction against the snobbery and conservatism of his fellow students, Spender 'became affected, wore a red tie, cultivated friends outside college, was unpatriotic, declared myself a pacifist and a Socialist';[37] but the social, economic and political turmoil into which Europe was plunging after 1929 gave young writers like Spender and Auden, Day Lewis and Louis MacNeice, a sense of urgency: 'There was a feeling through all these years of having to race against time to produce a book or a poem'.[38]

They felt they had to race against time because of the conviction that their age was a profoundly political one. In a discussion with L. A. G. Strong that introduced *Modern Verse, 1920–1940: A New Anthology*, when asked: 'Why do you think that the poets of today are likely to offer special difficulty to their contemporaries?' C. Day Lewis replied:

> It's a question of subject matter, and of tradition. Many of us believe that there is nothing in the world which is not potential subject matter for poetry. The world we live in has increased in complexity more rapidly than the world at any other time of history.

When the question of poetry as propaganda was raised by Strong, Day Lewis replied:

> Any poetry which implies a political faith in anything *can* be called propaganda.[39]

The tentative nature of this reply shows that the political poets were wary of their danger of transgressing, of offending a tradition that held that poetry could only be political at the risk of compromising its art. But Day Lewis argued that such poetry produced stylistic adventure; and, as the poet moved from 'disaffection towards a positive faith' then we have poems which 'often very naively, but always sincerely, look towards a promised land and which partly aim, by creating an imaginative picture of a better world, to inspire men to work for that world'. Some political verse was, and was intended to be, ephemeral; some political poets were 'admittedly propagandist'. But 'any subject which appeals passionately to the poet's imagination is capable of producing a universal and permanent poem'.[40]

The search for a 'promised land' drew the young poets to the ideology of Marxism, or at any rate of Socialism. This was partly due to their revolt against their middle-class values, though Spender, for his part, admitted that he never abandoned those values, values of freedom and truth, as he defined them.[41] But the young poets were inspired to act because of what they saw as the failure of a system. Auden, Spender, MacNeice, Day Lewis were poets who were possessed by 'an overwhelming social bitterness'.[42]

The disgust with the deception of the past drove the young poets towards left-wing ideologies which made them into a radical political intelligentsia. In 'The Magnetic Mountain', Day Lewis called upon his readers to:

> Consider these, for we have condemned them;
> Leaders of no sure land, guides their bearings lost
> Or in league with robbers have reversed the signposts,
> Disrespectful to ancestors, irresponsible to heirs...
>
> Drug nor isolation will cure this cancer:
> It is now or never, the hour of the knife,
> The break with the past, the major operation.[43]

The break with the past, the major operation, was the embracing of Marxism. Governments in the democracies were timid and uninspired; democracy was collapsing; drastic measures were needed otherwise this generation would spend their time, as Auden put it, 'lecturing on navigation while the ship was going down'.[44] Writers, while by no means uncritical of Marxism, and by no means satisfied that the Soviet Union represented its best working example, none the less, were attracted to its utopianism and its ethical values, values not compromised by the kind of people who, as Day Lewis put it, were:

> at bay in villas from blood relations,
> Counters of spoons and content with cushions.[45]

Stephen Spender declared himself, from 1931 onwards, 'hounded by external events. There was ever-increasing unemployment in America, Great Britain, and on the Continent. The old world seemed incapable of solving its problems, and out of the disorder Fascist regimes were rising.'[46]

The young poets of the 1930s were linked together, partly through Auden's influence on their style, and partly because they published a series of anthologies in the early years of the decade: in 1932 Michael Roberts edited *New Signatures*, and then a year later *New Country*. In 1933 Spender's *Poems* and Day Lewis's *Transitional Poems* were published. Spender believed that the difference was also created by their break with what he called the 'cynicism' of the 1920s writers; those writers still considered politics as alien to literature.[47] But what really made the distinction was the events to which the new generation reacted; the problems of the time shaped their writing, and they were conscious of the different circumstances in which writers now addressed their craft – and their audience. In 'A Communist to Others', Auden caught the new mood, though still in a whimsical fashion:

> Unhappy poet, you whose only
> Real emotion is feeling lonely...
>
> You need us more than you suppose
> And you could help us if you chose.[48]

The poets chose to help. In 1935, in an article in the *Left Review*, Stephen Spender warned that:

> 'We can no longer permit life to be shaped by a personified ideal, we must serve with all our faculties some actual thing', Mr. Yeats has written in a recent preface. This seems to me to be true. The 'actual thing' is the true moral or widely political subject that must be realized by contemporary literature, if that literature itself is to be moral and serious. Any other art will tend to become a 'personified ideal'.

Spender singled out D. H. Lawrence for criticism on these grounds. 'He wrote about a kind of life which was serious and real: but whereas he meant to write about people, about the life around him, he tended, as he went on, only to write about himself'. There were two worlds at war: 'Revolution and reaction'. Spender acknowledged that this kind of poetry was open to the charge of propaganda (again, that fear emerges) due to the simplification of the issues. But this was not the real claim of the poem to value. 'The implicit assertion of the poem is that it is about realities: that the struggle between the two worlds is *real*'.

Spender spoke of moral values; and, here again, he caught the spirit of the age. 'We live in an age when we have become conscious of great social injustice, of the oppression of one class by another, of nationalities by other nations. Communism, or socialism in its completed form, offers a just world.' Spender acknowledged that he might be accused of being a 'bourgeois intellectual', that 'I know nothing, or next to nothing, of the proletariat etc., etc.' But, in his desire for social justice, he was 'not primarily concerned' with himself, but with 'bringing into being a world quite external to my own interests, in the same way as when one writes a poem, one is allowing the poem to live its own, impersonal, objective being, one is not shoving oneself into it.'

Art was necessarily a criticism of life, just as good architecture was a criticism of slums, and good poetry was a criticism of language, 'of the way in which we express ourselves, the direction of our thoughts, the words we hand down to our children'. Writers everywhere, including the Soviet Union, had a duty to 'push' against the system.[49]

The battle ground between these worlds was now; the place, as it turned out, was Spain. That a conflict between Republicans and Conservative forces in Spain, between Catholicism and anticlericalism and between centralism and regionalism, should attract not just the attention, but the very being of so many English writers in the late 1930s is now taken for granted: so much, that the question of why this was so seems hardly in need of asking. Spain seemed to be the symbol of the conflict, not only between left and right, but the fight for what Louis MacNeice called 'civilised values', a cause which, if lost, would mean that 'nobody with civilised values may be able to get anything out of anything'.[50] Spain, too, was a call that was made upon the Romantic imagination; the violent phases of Spanish history, her location between Europe and Africa, 'that arid square, that fragment nipped off from the hot Africa, soldered so crudely to inventive Europe'.[51] Then there was the spectacle of men prepared to die for their political cause, to die rather than to surrender. The 1930s poets disapproved of political neutrality; here was a conflict where neutrality was not only undesirable, but impossible. The young, involved poets would not have understood Evelyn Waugh's reply to a circular manifesto published in the *Left Review* in 1937, 'Authors take sides on the Spanish War': 'As an Englishman I am not in the predicament of choosing between two evils'.[52]

'Authors take sides' marked both the high water mark of literary involvement in the Spanish Civil War, and the fragmentation of that political earnestness that had characterized the 1930s poets. Stephen Spender made his journey to Spain. One day he asked a journalist who had previously worked for Franco's side, but now worked for a Liberal journal, what was the difference that he found between the two sides in the civil war:

'None', he answered. 'What do you mean? Is there the same enthusiasm on Franco's side.' 'Yes.' 'But isn't it just the ruling classes who are pleased?' 'There's only one difference which I noticed. There they salute by raising their hands like this' (he imitated the Fascist salute), 'and here they clench their fists like this' (he imitated ours).[53]

Spender felt that he 'could not angrily dismiss this answer as I did when people talked of the atrocities committed by the Reds. But I clung to my Republican faith that our minority of genuine supporters had more justice on their side than the minority of Falangists'.[54] Spender's doubts increased on the occasion of a second visit to Spain in 1937 to attend a Writers' Congress in Madrid; he came to the conclusion that the Congress, 'with all its good qualities, had something about it of a Spoiled Children's Party something which brought out the worst in many delegates'.[55] A significant moment for Spender was when, at the village of Minglanilla, the peasants thought that the writers had come to save them from aircraft machine-gunning their husbands as they worked in the fields: 'Somehow the villagers...thought that the Congress of Intellectuals was a visitation which would save them.'[56] The last straw was the sight of intellectuals 'screaming and banging with their fists' against the side of a train carriage to obtain access to their luxury sleeping cars. 'A deep dissatisfaction was the strongest experience I gained from the Writers' Congress.'[57] After his return to England, he was visited by Auden, who had made a very short trip to Spain. Auden 'stated emphatically that political exigence was never a justification for lies'.[58]

Spain would appear to be the rock against which political poetry was dashed. As John Lehmann remarked in *New Writing in Europe* (1940), quoting William Wordsworth:

> The true sorrow of humanity consists in this; not that the mind of man fails, but that the course and demands of action and life so rarely correspond with the dignity and intensity of human desires.[59]

It was this lack of correspondence between action and desires that Spain, far from obscuring, seemed all the more starkly to reveal. Not every contemporary poet felt this unease. John Cornford was convinced that:

> Freedom is an easily spoken word
> But facts are stubborn things. Here, too, in Spain
> Our fight's not won till the workers of all the world
> Stand by our guard on Huesca's plain
> Swear that our dead fought not in vain,
> Raise the red flag triumphantly
> For Communism and for liberty.[60]

Whereas for Spender, the wait before battle was a tragedy for all the soldiers:

> Finally, they cease to hate: for although hate
> Bursts from the air and whips the earth like hail
> Or pours it up in fountains to marvel at,

And although hundreds fell, who can connect
The inexhaustible anger of the guns
With the dumb patience of these tormented animals?[61]

Spain was important, not for what the poets who became involved in the conflict tried to do and failed, that is, defend the Republic against Franco, but for what it reveals about the relationship between the poet and politics. Because they believed, and then tested their beliefs, the young poets became all the more acutely aware of the conflicting demands of poetry and politics. It was this that inspired Spender to write that the war was one of these occasions when a writer could believe that his actions or his failure to act could lead to the winning or the losing of the war.[62] But when he defended his decision to go to Spain (where he hoped to drive an ambulance, though in fact the Republican government gave him the job of broadcasting propaganda), Auden did so, not on the merits of the Government, but on the implications of a Fascist victory for literature:

I support the Valencia Government in Spain because its defeat by the forces of International Fascism would be a major disaster for Europe. It would make a European War more probable; and the spread of Fascist ideology and practice to countries as yet comparatively free from them, which would inevitably follow upon a Fascist victory in Spain, would create an atmosphere in which the creative artist and all who care for justice, liberty and culture would find it impossible to work or even exist.[63]

Auden's 'Spain' showed the poet, not as a propagandist, nor as an aesthete secluded from the conflict, but as a doubtful believer, one who hesitated between the demands of poetry (with its search for truth) and politics (with all its lies and ambivalences). Spain was a cause worth fighting for; it invited them to accept, in what is one of Auden's most controversial phrases, 'necessary murder'.[64] It is the juxtaposition of the words that exemplify the doubt, rather than obscure it (like Yeats's 'Terrible beauty'); that show how Spain was a complex, tragic and disturbing encounter of the poet with the politics of Spain and the history of Europe.[65]

Which returns us to the question posed at the beginning of the chapter: What is the relationship between the intellectual and politics, between poetry and politics? Was Auden right to confess, in his tribute to Yeats, that poetry makes nothing happen, and in his dialogue between prosecutor and defence that Yeats was right to give up his 'silliness', to withdraw from political involvement (this in itself, of course, was a dubious proposition). Was poetry a product of the historical moment, not a cause? Or is this the wrong question, or a misconception of how to put the question anyway?

When Auden paid his valedictory tribute to Yeats, he also appeared to be paying it to the motives that inspired the young 1930s poets: the endeavour, through their art, to influence and perhaps even shape the minds of their country at a time of great European crisis. The crisis in Yeats's day seems, in retrospect, hardly as momentous as that of the 1930s; but this is not so: for Yeats confronted the rise of democracy and modern capitalist society, and sought to direct it away from the abyss: away from the anarchy and chaos that he believed was about to engulf civilization. Similarly, the young poets of the 1930s spoke of their crisis as a crisis of civilization:

> Soon, soon, through dykes of our content
> The crumpling flood will force a rent,
> And, taller than a tree,
> Hold sudden death before our eyes
> Whose river dreams long hid the size
> And vigours of the sea.[66]

Anxiety drove these poets into politics. Yeats sought to create a sense of unity in a divided Ireland: to ensure that a cultural elite could provide Ireland with the leadership to shape her in the coming times; and to save Ireland and her Protestant Ascendancy from the philistinism of the middle classes through an alliance of elite and peasantry. The Auden generation had a strong sense of guilt about their privileged position. As Auden sat in his garden with friends under a moonlit sky, contemplating the coming crisis, he mused on that 'doubtful act' that:

> allows
> Our freedom in this English house,
> Our picnics in the sun.

Yet he, too, hoped to save what was worthy in his culture.

Yeats and the Auden generation alike were determined that their deployment of art to serve a political vision must not mean the subservience of art to propaganda. Yeats attacked Thomas Davis for this surrender. Auden, in 1939, wrote that 'if the criterion of art were its power to incite to action, Goebbels would be one of the greatest artists of all time'.[67] Yeats declared that art must be the 'disinterested contemplation or expression of life'.[68] But it was only what he called 'practical reform' that Yeats shied away from.

Auden wrote that he so disliked 'everyday political activities that I won't do them', but he long searched for some means to 'make action urgent and its nature clear'.[69] While the Auden generation were exploring the relationship between poetry and politics in that wider sense, Yeats, too, was still searching for the key to the remaking of Ireland and Europe, flitting between Italian Fascism, his beloved eighteenth century, a renewed onslaught upon 'English materialism',[70] and even a last plunge into 'neo-Fenianism', warning the British Empire that:

> The ghost of Roger Casement
> Is beating at the door.[71]

But could poetry achieve its aims? Yeats's influence in Ireland has yet to be properly evaluated; the process of cultural formation is more complex than Yeats (and many of those who have written about him) have supposed. The contemporary Irish poet, Paul Muldoon, satirized Yeats's suggestion that he might have helped inspire the 1916 Rising:

'Did that play of mine
send out certain men (*certain* men?)

the English shot . . . ?'
the answer is 'Certainly not'.

If Yeats had saved his pencil-lead
would certain men have stayed in bed?

For history's a twisted root
with art its small, translucent fruit

and never the other way round.

But Muldoon, when interrogating Auden's political phase, allows him to declare that:

. . . in a sense, I haven't changed my mind;
the forces of Good and Evil were indeed
ranged

against each other, though not unambiguously.

And, when he muses on the fate of the Spanish playwright, Lorca, who was shot by Franco's men, the 'drunken soldiers':

. . . heard him calling through the mist,
'When I die leave the balcony shutters open.'
For poetry *can* make things happen –
not only can, but *must*.[72]

The question for Muldoon then, despite his parody of Yeats, was unresolved: poetry cannot/can 'make things happen'. When Yeats suggested that he may have played his own part in the events of Easter 1916, he was of course trying (characteristically) to write himself into history. Specifically, he was referring to the play *Cathleen ni Houlihan*, which was performed at the St Theresa's Hall, Clarendon Street, Dublin, and of which the Irish constitutional nationalist Stephen Gwynn famously wondered if it was right to perform such plays 'unless one was prepared for people to go out to shoot and be shot'. John S. Kelly points out that most of the play was written, not by Yeats, but by Lady Gregory, and that, since Gwynn himself remained firmly unconverted to violent republicanism, then it was hardly likely to have convinced others.[73] Yet the influence of the call for a heroic Ireland, for an Ireland cast in the mould of the ancient Celtic world, is hard to dismiss; the 1916 rebels took their inspiration from the Cuchulain myth and not, as Gwynn would have done, from the eighteenth-century Irish patriots led by Henry Grattan. Again, it is true that by 1902 Yeats was under attack from other would-be cultural formation organizations like Sinn Fein and the Gaelic League, so much so that Lady Gregory advised him not to send any more books to the Dublin press for review since they had 'evidently an idea they should be a sort of truffle dogs where you are concerned, to scent our heresy however concealed'.[74] But Ireland was – and is – a small and intimate enough country for the poet to achieve some kind of response, whether favourable or not: the fact that the Dublin papers thought it worthwhile to 'scent' heresy – heresy, itself a significant term – suggests that Yeats and his fellow revivalists were at any rate not easily marginalized. They did contribute to the debate about the nature of Irish identity, about the question of what Irish culture was, and how it might shape the life and thought of a nation. It may be, too, that there was something in Yeats's belief that Ireland inherited the Celtic tradition of literature as a central and insistent voice in the making of a nation's self-perception. Certainly, his decision to delay his poem 'Easter 1916' was motivated by his desire to avoid contributing to a dangerous political crisis: 'I am in a movement which is non-political [*sic*] and I am an important figure in it and any statement made by me might create a split and cause intense anger in a movement hitherto free from political passions, and in my opinion the only hope for Ireland.'[75]

But the poem itself was intensely political, and highly influential. Yeats may not have shared the passions of the men of 1916, but he certainly caught the mood of the rebels: a mood of mystical self-sacrifice which would commit future generations to the cause of Irish freedom, at whatever the cost. But, there are deep reservations: 'England may keep faith'

> Hearts with one purpose alone
> Through summer and winter seem
> Enchanted to a stone
> To trouble the living stream.

And

> Too long a sacrifice
> Can make a stone of the heart.

Whatever his doubts, Yeats concludes:

> I write it out in a verse –
> MacDonagh and MacBride
> And Connolly and Pearse
> Now and in time to be,

Wherever green is worn,
All changed, changed utterly:
A terrible beauty is born.[76]

These lines, as John Wilson Foster argues, are 'detachable', they can be 'chanted or sung'; and they have the authority of a poet laureate as well as of popular sentiment enshrined by tradition.[77] Yet the poem also questions the song that is sung. In so doing, the tension of these parts of the poem express the tension, the doubts, that the Easter Rising bequeathed to the nationalist tradition and the Catholic people of Ireland. The poem, then, to adopt Auden's phrase in his tribute to Yeats, itself 'survives/A way of happening, a mouth.'[78]

The Auden generation had perhaps a more difficult task than did Yeats. England – Britain – was not a small, intimate, and highly politicized country like Ireland. Yeats's concern with nationality and identity at least offered him as a target for all classes and groups in Ireland; he would elicit a response, at least. But the ideas of the young left-wing poets troubled even themselves: how could they break out of the confines of their own English privileged class, and reach what they liked to call 'the working-class movement?'. It was these classes that Auden referred to in 'Out on the Lawn' in lines which he later excised from the poem:

The creepered wall stands up to hide
The gathering multitudes outside
Whose grievances hunger worsens;
Concealing from their wretchedness
Our metaphysical distress,
Our kindness to ten persons.[79]

C. Day Lewis was so anxious about the 'bourgeois poet' influencing only a few of his fellow men that he urged the working classes to create their own poets. 'Let him not think of poetry as a mystery whose secret is held only by the educated bourgeois'. Day Lewis disarmingly suggested that 'if the writing of poetry is his [the worker's] natural activity (and he will soon find that out), all he needs is an English dictionary and a thorough soaking in the English poets. After that, it is a matter of compelling an alien tradition into his own service'. To speak for the workers, he concluded 'he does not need, as bourgeois poets do, to learn a new tongue: he has only to make poetry of what is his native language.'[80]

As early as 1937, it was becoming increasingly clear that the Auden generation was losing its coherence as a set of writers with a common political agenda. In 1939, Auden, unable any longer to fulfil his role as 'court poet to the Left', removed himself to America, and sat in:

one of the dives
On Fifty-Second Street
Uncertain and afraid

as the clever hopes expire
Of a low dishonest decade[81]

The outbreak of war occurred when Louis MacNeice was in Ireland. He had just begun work on a book on Yeats's poetry, and he recalled how:

> I had only written a little of this book when Germany invaded Poland. On that day I was in Galway. As soon as I heard on the wireless of the outbreak of war, Galway became unreal. And Yeats and his poetry became unreal also. This was not merely because Galway and Yeats belong in a sense to a past order of things. The unreality which now overtook them was also overtaking in my mind modern London, modernist art, and Left Wing politics. If the war made nonsense of Yeats' poetry and of all the works that are called 'escapist', it also made nonsense of the poetry that professes to be 'realist'. My friends had been writing for years about guns and frontiers and factories, about the 'facts' of psychology, politics, science, economics, but the fact of war made their writing seem as remote as the pleasure dome of Xanadu.[82]

The apparently complete abjuration of political poetry, then, might indicate that the poet in England could hardly hope to achieve anything; that indeed, poetry made nothing happen. It did not end the economic depression of the 1930s (which was over the worst by 1934, anyway); it did not win the Spanish Civil War for the Republicans; it did not prevent the outbreak of the Second World War; it did not find its way into a single piece of government legislation: in this, very restricted, sense, whatever poets were, they were not, as Shelley claimed, 'unacknowledged legislators'.

Spender later admitted that 'the political poetry of Auden, Day Lewis, MacNeice and Spender had a temporary "for the duration" look.... It might be classified as a variety of war poetry'.[83] This, like Auden's recantation, was to push the argument too far: the 1930s produced some fine and enduring poems, not least Auden's own 'Spain'. Moreover, it showed that English poets could break through the great tradition which Spender later realized derived from T. S. Eliot's famous essay 'Tradition and the Individual Talent', where the poet was held to a position of being 'detached, clinical, and never expressing his own opinions or personality'.[84] But there was a deeper significance to the 1930s' achievement. Or, rather, several. Like Yeats, they handed on certain phrases, words, which seemed to catch the spirit of the historical events through which they lived, and which they sought in part to chronicle, in part to influence. Just as Yeats's poem captured the mood of the 1916 Rising, and conveyed its mystery and significance to future generations, so did Auden's description of the 1930s as a 'low dishonest decade' contribute to the popular image of that era despite the more recent historical revisionist writing, which portrays it as a decade of improving living standards, public health, housing and social welfarism. They used their poetry to offer a moral commentary on politics, and they contributed to a sense of guilt about the privileges that they, and those like them, enjoyed, the privileges which Auden contemplated in his 'A Summer Night', in June 1933. In this sense they were, as MacNeice claimed, the nation's 'conscience, its critical faculty, its generous instinct'.[85]

Yeats and the Auden generation, whatever their doubts, and in Yeats's case downright deception, about their political motivation, and the relationship between their art and that motivation, showed that poetry could explore politics in a way perhaps peculiar to the intellectual in public life. Art was at its most vulnerable, most compromised, and, also, more importantly, least effective, when it addressed its audience in a propagandist mode. It was ephemeral. It was almost embarrassingly futile. But, when the poet adopted a less clear-cut, more ambiguous role, as Yeats did in his 'Easter 1916', and Auden in his 'Spain', then the poet showed that literature could be political, in that it could explore politics and history more deeply than could politics and history themselves. As Stephen Spender wrote in July 1937:

> The function of a political poetry is vividly to bring into our consciousness the origins in life from which political theory and political action spring, and at the same time to face, on another plane of reality, the significance and implications of what is being done.[86]

It was for this reason that MacNeice, who, like Auden and Spender returned to Yeats as his inspiration, wrote:

> He can serve us... as an example of zest. Much modern poetry has inevitably a gloomy content; so had much of Yeats' poetry, but whether it is nostalgic, love-lorn, cynical, darkly prophetic, angry over politics, or embittered over old age, there is nearly always a leaping vitality – the vitality of Cleopatra waiting for the asp. The poet kicks against life but that is because his demands from life are high.

It was this vitality, and these demands, from Yeats and the English poets of the 1930s who wrote so much under his influence, that give immediacy to MacNeice's lines in 'Bagpipe Music':

> It's no go my honey love, it's no go my poppet;
> Work your hands from day to day, the winds will blow the profit.
> The glass is falling hour by hour, the glass will fall forever,
> But if you break the bloody glass you won't hold up the weather.

The political work of the Auden generation reveals that, while the writer can no more hold up the weather than can anyone else (including politicians themselves), they can at least 'break the bloody glass'.[87]

The implication of these decades for Irish and English writing may now be considered. When Yeats launched his great enterprise in the 1890s, he hoped to use literature, and especially his own poetry, to create a new Irish mind; and, for all his repetition of the poet's necessity to stand back and contemplate, he engaged closely, and often fractiously, with the pre-dominant political movement and ideology of the day – nationalism. Since Yeats, Irish poets have lived under the gaze of the founder of the Literary Revival; and the quality of poetry, especially in the last few decades, is only equalled by its volume. But Irish poets have also followed Yeats, or perhaps accepted the inevitability of pursuing his path, in that they have engaged deeply with political concerns; a glance at any recent anthology of Irish poetry, for example, Patrick Crotty's *Modern Irish Poetry*,[88] will show how nearly every poet whose work appears there has had something to say about the Irish predicament. A closer reading will also reveal that they say it very well.[89] And while some (notably Seamus Heaney) have adopted a position sympathetic to nationalism, most have adopted Heaney's second thoughts on the subject, and taken what he discerned as James Joyce's advice: 'Keep at a tangent'.[90] As John Wilson Foster put it, most have 'put a welcome brake on any reflex, extreme or ancestral response to a difficult situation'.[91]

English poets have followed a very different line since their engagement with political affairs in the 1930s. The Auden generation engaged with politics with a conscious feeling that they were breaking new ground: *New Country, New Signatures* referred not just to 'new' in the sense of previously unpublished work, but new in that these poets had something original to say, not only about the human predicament, but about how poets could engage with the political predicament. Auden expressed this best in his 'A Summer Night', written in the troubled year of 1933; he valued the culture that enabled him to enjoy his summer night on the lawn with friends; but his advice, 'gentle, do not care to know/Where Poland draws her eastern bow/What violence is done', is tempered by his recognition that these events would, must, invade the poet's content.[92]

This engagement produced work of high, as well as poor, quality; but as early as 1937 the Auden generation began to feel that politics were making too heavy a demand on their art. They feared that political ideology would damage art, in that the criterion of judgement would become purely a political one (as Davis asserted it should in the case of Irish nationalism). Would it or would it not help the cause? And would it damage politics, in that some of the values they had never lost – Spender's individualism, Auden's powerful sense of Englishness – would be demolished? When Auden went to Spain, he was shocked at the spectacle of closed-down churches; and while this is too incomplete an explanation of his re-embracing the Anglican religion, it was symptomatic of his desire to keep what was good about the old system and its cultural legacy.[93]

By 1937, therefore, the Auden generation was on the retreat from its most forward political position. Spain splintered, rather than united, them. Auden left for America, and later on revised his 1930s poems, or omitted them altogether, from his anthologies. He revised 'Spain', substituting 'the conscious acceptance of guilt in the fact of murder' for his controversial words (which George Orwell pilloried) 'necessary murder': though it seems clear that this is to make the same point, express the same feelings, in a less effective way. He regarded his poem '1 September 1939' as 'infected with incurable dishonesty – and must be scrapped'.[94] English poets, it would appear, were warned not to involve themselves so deeply in politics, perhaps not to involve themselves at all; the Auden generation was signalling that it had flown too close to the flame, or (to use Paulin's metaphor) had moved in too closely to the world 'of compromise, cruelty, dead language and junk cars which Manichaeans dismiss as mere politics'.[95] There was, indeed, always something of the Manichaean about Auden as regards politics, which he revealed when he described politics as a 'disease'.[96]

In part, too, this difference is explained by the contrasting circumstances in England and Ireland. Ireland had, and has, a 'national question' which, while its place in Irish society must not be exaggerated, nevertheless existed and has returned to trouble the present generation. The individual is part of that problem both as an individual seeking, perhaps, to accept or reject it, and as a member of a tribe which expects certain things from the writer: Seamus Heaney's *North* is an example, where Heaney felt obliged to consult his personal and group history, and again in his 'Open Letter' when he protested against the inclusion of his work in an anthology of contemporary *British* poetry as a 'colonialist venture'.[97] English writers have no such problem,[98] or, rather, they perceive none, even though their culture might be expected to have to redefine itself in the modern world of national 'decline', loss of power, and multicultural development. Some poets may choose to discuss political issues; most do not; but the point is that theirs is a sense of choice: the Irish poet finds it hard to feel a sense of choice, because, as MacNeice put it in 1934:

> I cannot deny my past to which my self is wed,
> The woven figure cannot undo its thread.[99]

That thread was the history, personal and national, and therefore the politics, personal and national, of Ireland. Yeats, for his part, was convinced that a country could not produce good literature until it ceased to consider history as 'merely a chronicle of facts' and began to consider history 'imaginatively'.[100] As Patrick Crotty remarks, many modern Irish poets 'extend a characteristically Yeatsian and Revivalist practice in so far as they approach the present through a heroising reading of the past', while others, standing on the primacy of the here and now, offer the 'indirect homage of counterstatement to the Literary Revival's premise that only a recovery of the past can effect liberation in the present'.[101] The English poets' experience was quite different. They took up a political role because they felt that they had no alternative, but they could not embrace it with the same confidence and energy that inspired Yeats, with his sense of a great Anglo-Irish tradition behind him. They felt naked in the face of history, because English history, with its Whig tradition of steady, unspectacular progress, offered no encouraging reading of the past. History could not be summoned to help set matters right, for, as Auden wrote in 'Spain':

> The stars are dead; the animals will not look:
> We are left alone with our day, and the time is short and
> History to the defeated
> May say Alas but cannot help or pardon.[102]

The English poets' enterprise in the end weakened an already tenuous belief in the relationship between history, politics and poetry. This, whether for good or ill, constituted the sharply different legacies left by Yeats, and the Auden generation, to their literary successors and to the politics of poetry. For when, in 1939, Auden interrogated Yeats, and, in 1987, Muldoon interrogated both Yeats and Auden, they asked a question to which, perhaps, there is no clear-cut answer; but English poets nowadays do not even ask the question.

NOTES

1 'In memory of W. B. Yeats', in E. Mendelson, *The English Auden*, London, Faber, 1977, pp. 241–3.
2 See M. O'Neill and G. Reeves, *Auden, MacNiece, Spender: The Thirties Poetry*, London, Routledge, 1992.
3 Mendelson, op. cit., pp. 389–93. (Originally published in *Partisan Review*, Spring, 1939).
4 For a discussion of this interpolation see S. Hynes, *The Auden Generation: Literature and Politics in England in the Thirties*, London, Bodley Head, 1976, pp. 349–50.
5 J. S. Kelly, 'The Fifth Bell: race and class in Yeats' political thought', in O. Komesu and M. Sekine (eds), *Irish Writers and Politics* (Irish Literary Studies, No. 36), Gerrards Cross, Colin Smythe, 1989, pp. 109–75, at p. 110.
6 D. Pierce, *Yeats' World: Ireland, England and the Poetic Imagination*, London and New Haven, Yale University Press, 1995, pp. 5–6.
7 Ibid., p. 6.
8 Ibid., pp. 68–9. See also Yeats's correspondence on the New Library of Ireland which he tried, and failed, to prevent falling into the Davisite mould; J. S. Kelly (ed.), *The Collected Letters of W. B. Yeats*, Oxford, Clarendon Press, 1986, pp. 296–317.
9 Komesu and Sekine, op. cit., p. 1.
10 'Remorse for an Intemperate Speech', in A. Norman Jeffares, *W. B. Yeats: Selected Poetry*, London, Macmillan, 1964, p. 159.
11 J. S. Kelly, 'The fall of Parnell and the rise of literature: an investigation', *Anglo-Irish Studies*, II, 1976, pp. 1–23.
12 Pierce, op. cit., p. 69.
13 M. H. Thuente, *W. B. Yeats and Irish Folklore*, Dublin, Gill and Macmillan, 1980, p. 243.
14 D. G. Boyce, ' "One Last Burial": Culture, counter-revolution and revolution in Ireland, 1886–1916', in Boyce (ed.), *The Revolution in Ireland, 1879–1923*, London, Macmillan, 1988, p. 127.
15 J. C. Beckett, *The Anglo-Irish Tradition*, London, Faber, 1976, p. 153.

16 W. B. Yeats, 'The Literary Movement in Ireland', in Lady Gregory (ed.), *Ideals in Ireland*, London, At the Unicorn, 1901, pp. 87–102.
17 Yeats's anxiety to get to know the people of Ireland inspired him to contemplate disguising himself as a peasant and wandering through the west of Ireland; Pierce, op. cit., p. 150.
18 Boyce, 'One Last Burial', p. 122.
19 D. G. Boyce, *Nationalism in Ireland*, 3rd edition, London, Routledge, 1995, pp. 269–70.
20 Yeats, 'September 1913', in A. Norman Jeffares, op. cit., pp. 55–6.
21 J. S. Kelly, 'The Fifth Bell', in Komesu and Sekine, op. cit., p. 160.
22 'The Second Coming' in A. Norman Jeffares, op. cit., pp. 99–100.
23 'Meditations in time of civil war', ibid., p. 119.
24 'Parnell's Funeral', ibid., p. 175. See G. Watson, *Irish Identity and Literary Revival: Synge, Yeats, Joyce and O'Casey*, 2nd edition, Washington, Catholic University of America Press, 1994, pp. 108–10.
25 'Politics', in A. Norman Jeffares, op. cit., p. 203.
26 J. S. Kelly, 'The Fifth Bell', op. cit., pp. 166–7.
27 'The Second Coming', in A. Norman Jeffares, op. cit., pp. 99–100. See also E. Longley, *Poetry in the Wars*, Newcastle, Bloodaxe, 1986, pp. 20–1. For the 'myth of the catastrophe' see G. N. Watson, *Politics and Literature in Modern Britain*, London, Macmillan, 1977, Ch. 6.
28 Kelly, 'The Fifth Bell', op. cit., pp. 166–7.
29 'Coole Park and Ballylee, 1931', in A. Norman Jeffares, op. cit., pp. 150–1. For Yeats's flirtation with Fascism see E. Cullingford, *Yeats, Ireland and Fascism*, London, Macmillan, 1965, pp. 207–78.
30 'The statues', ibid., pp. 195–6. See J. S. Kelly, 'The Fifth Bell', op. cit., pp. 173–4.
31 T. Paulin, 'The politics of poetry', *The Times*, 31 May 1986. See L. C. Knights, *Public Voices: Literature and Politics with Special Reference to the Seventeenth Century*, London, Chatto and Windus, 1971.
32 J. A. Morris, *Writers and Politics in Modern Britain, 1880–1950*, London, Hodder and Stoughton, 1977, p. 6.
33 Paulin, 'The politics of poetry', *The Times*, 31 May 1986.
34 S. Spender, *World within World*, London, Hamish Hamilton, 1951, pp. 116–19.
35 Ibid., p. 119.
36 Ibid., p. 207.
37 Ibid., p. 33.
38 Ibid., p. 137.
39 Morris, *Writers and Politics*, pp. 9–11.
40 Ibid., p. 11.
41 Spender, *World within World*, p. 137.
42 Morris, op. cit., p. 29.
43 C. Day Lewis, 'The Magnetic Mountain', in R. Skelton (ed.), *Poetry of the Thirties*, London, Penguin Books, 1988, pp. 61–2.
44 N. Wood, *Communism and British Intellectuals*, London, Gollanz, 1959, p. 104.
45 'The Magnetic Mountain', in Skelton, op. cit., p. 62.
46 Spender, *World within World*, op. cit., p. 137. See also K. B. Hoskins, *Today the Struggle: Literature and Politics in England during the Spanish Civil War*, Austin and London, Texas University Press, 1969, pp. 182–206.
47 Spender, *World within World*, op. cit., pp. 138–9.
48 'A Communist to Others', in Skelton, *Poetry of the Thirties*, op. cit., pp. 54–9.
49 Spender, 'Writers and manifestos', in *Left Review*, 5, 1935, 145–50. See V. Cunningham, 'Neutral? 1930s writers and taking sides', in F. Gloversmith (ed.), *Class, Culture and Social Change*, Brighton, Harvester Press, 1980, Ch. 2.

50 M. O'Neill and G. Reeves, *Auden, MacNiece, Spender*, op. cit., p. 219. See Hynes, *The Auden Generation*, Ch. VIII.

51 Auden, 'Spain', in Mendelson, *The English Auden*, pp. 210–2. For a more hostile interpretation, see G. Watson, *Politics and Literature in Modern Britain*, op. cit., pp. 56–7.

52 Cunningham, in Gloversmith, op. cit., p. 49.

53 Spender, *World within World*, op. cit., p. 225.

54 Ibid., pp. 255–6.

55 Ibid., p. 241.

56 Ibid., p. 242.

57 Ibid., pp. 245–7. See also his *The Thirties and After: Poetry, Politics, People, 1933–75*, London, Macmillan, 1978, pp. 71–9.

58 Spender, *World within World*, op. cit., p. 247.

59 Morris, *Writers and Politics in Modern Britain*, op. cit., p. 60.

60 J. Cornford, 'Full Morn at Tirez: Before the Storming of Huesca', in Skelton, *Poetry of the Thirties*, pp. 137–9.

61 Spender, 'Two Armies', in Skelton, op. cit., pp. 144–5.

62 Spender, *The Thirties and After*, op. cit., p. 25.

63 Mendelson, *The English Auden*, pp. xvii–xix. The Republican Government had moved to Valencia in November 1936.

64 George Orwell was particularly hard on Auden for this phrase; see J. Fuller, *A Reader's Guide to W. H. Auden*, London, Thames and Hudson, 1970, pp. 258–9.

65 For an analysis of the poem's language and structure, see O'Neill and Reeves, op. cit., pp. 216–8; for its politics, F. Buell, *W. H. Auden as a Social Poet*, Ithaca, Cornell University Press, 1973, pp. 148–57.

66 'A Summer Night', in Mendelson, *The English Auden*, op. cit., pp. 136–7.

67 Mendelson, op. cit., p. 406.

68 Pierce, *Yeats' World: Ireland, England and the Poetic Imagination*, op. cit., p. 71.

69 H. Carpenter, *W. H. Auden: A Biography*, op. cit., p. 206.

70 J. Moynahan, *Anglo-Irish: The Literary Imaginations in a Hyphenated Culture*, Princeton, Princeton University Press, 1995, p. 221.

71 Pierce, op. cit., pp. 257–8.

72 D. Cairns and S. Richards, *Writing Ireland: Colonialism, Nationalism and Culture*, Manchester, Manchester University Press, 1988, p. 153; P. Muldoon, '7 Middagh Street', in *Meeting the British*, London, Faber, 1987, pp. 36–60; E. Longley, *The Living Stream*, Newcastle, Bloodaxe, 1994, pp. 265–6.

73 J. S. Kelly, 'The Fifth Bell', p. 160. But see P. Rafroidi, 'Imagination and Revolution: The Cuchalain Myth', in O. MacDonagh et al. (eds), *Irish Culture and Nationalism, 1750–1950*, London, Macmillan, 1983, pp. 137–48.

74 J. S. Kelly, op. cit., pp. 143–4.

75 See Pierce, op. cit., pp. 186–91.

76 'Easter 1916', in A. Norman Jeffares, pp. 93–5.

77 J. W. Foster, *Colonial Consequences: Essays in Irish Literature and Culture*, Dublin, Lilliput Press, 1991, p. 146.

78 'In memory of W. B. Yeats', in Mendelson, *The English Auden*, op. cit., p. 242.

79 Ibid., p. 137.

80 C. Day Lewis, 'Revolutionaries and Poets', in *Left Review*, 9, 1935, pp. 439–42. The Scottish poet, Hugh MacDiarmid, confronted the same problem: 'Are my poems spoken in the factories and the fields/in the streets o'the Toon/Gin there're no', then I'm failing to dae/What I ocht to ha' done.' 'Second poem to Lenin' (1932), in *Complete Poems*, I, London, Matin Brian and O'Keefe, pp. 323–8.

81 Auden, 'September 1, 1939', in Mendelson, op. cit., pp. 245–7.

82 Hynes, *The Auden Generation*, op. cit., pp. 379–80.

83 Spender, *The Thirties and After*, op. cit., p. 17.

84 Ibid., pp. 16–17.

85 MacNiece made this point in a preface to *Modern Poetry*, published at the end of the 1930s. The poet must be 'a maker, not a retail trader. The writer today should be not so much the mouthpiece of a community (for then he will only tell it what it knows already), as its conscience, its critical faculty, its generous instinct.' Quoted in E. Longley, 'Poetry and Politics in Northern Ireland', in *The Crane Bag*, 9 (i), 1985, p. 34.

86 Spender, in *Fact*, 4, July 1937, p. 25. MacNiece came to a similar conclusion; see O'Neill and Reeves, op. cit., p. 2. See also K. B. Hoskins, op. cit., pp. 238–46. *Fact*, a journal launched in 1937 to spread information in an easily understood form, sold 10,000 copies in the first issue.

87 Skelton, op. cit., pp. 722–3. O'Neill and Reeves analyse this poem, op. cit., pp. 73–5.

88 P. Crotty, *Modern Irish Poetry: An Anthology*, Belfast, Blackstaff, 1995.

89 See, for example, the subtle and moving poem by Peter MacDonald, 'Sunday in Great Tew, 8th November 1987', which explores his reaction to the Enniskillen Remembrance Day Massacre; ibid., pp. 416–9.

90 For a critique of Heaney's political verse see Longley, op. cit., pp. 26–40, and her *Poetry in the Wars*, pp. 140–60. See also Cairns and Richards, op. cit., p. 146.

91 J. W. Foster, *Colonial Consequences*, op. cit., p. 73. See his critique of Heaney on pp. 76–7.

92 'A Summer Night', in Mendelson, op. cit., p. 137.

93 Hynes, *The Auden Generation*, op. cit., pp. 251–2.

94 J. Fuller, *A Reader's Guide to W. H. Auden*, op. cit., pp. 258–60.

95 Paulin, 'The politics of poetry', op. cit.

96 Mendelson, *The English Auden*, op. cit., pp. 317–8; for a comparison of the 1930s verse with later revised versions, and for examples of the deletions, see Mendelson with his *W. H. Auden, Collected Poems*, London, Faber, 1976.

97 J. W. Foster, op. cit., pp. 76–7.

98 As Sir Ernest Barker put it in his *National Character*, London, Methuen, 1948: 'We have drawn no kind of division between the "social fact" of nationality and the "political scheme" of the state', p. 255.

99 L. MacNiece, 'Valediction', in *Collected Poems*, London, Faber, 1979, pp. 52–4.

100 M. H. Thuente, *W. B. Yeats and Irish Folklore*, op. cit., p. 253.

101 Crotty, *Modern Irish Poetry: An Anthology*, op. cit., p. 1.

102 Carpenter, *W. H. Auden*, op. cit. pp. 218–19.

Part III
Slavonic jesters

Next, we address the relationship between intellectuals and the communist movement in two distinct ways. In its theoretical aspect, this relationship arises from the Marxian controversy concerning the relative importance of leadership, rather than social spontaneity, in political movements. What is the role of leading political personalities, and how much weight should be given, within Marxian orthodoxy, to the unfolding of predetermined social and economic conditions? In its Leninist version, the intellectual vanguard gains pre-eminence over the outlook of the popular mass, sometimes casually dismissed as 'false-consciousness', particularly when revolution appears to be off the political agenda. In its practical aspect, the connecting image is again from Kolakowski, who defines the jester as 'motivated not by a desire to be perverse but by distrust of a stabilized system'. We consider the destabilizing role of intellectuals as jesters in the demise in Russia of both Tsarism and Communism and in the largest Eastern European country, Poland, in the communist period – from World War II to its collapse in 1989.

Edward Acton puts the fall of the Soviet Union into historical perspective. The intellectual's role is regarded from one particular angle: that of subversion. A distinctive feature of Russian political culture, inherited from the nineteenth century, and some argue even earlier, was the existence of a radical or revolutionary intelligentsia. Wedded to contrasted philosophies of political action – populist, maximalist (Bolshevik), or cautious (Menshevik) – these streams converged in early 1917 to sweep away the old autocracy in the triumphant advance of a popular uprising. Thereafter, they fell out about the nature and future of the revolution which their efforts had done so much to engender. Their pivotal role in 1917 has sometimes been equated with that of Soviet dissidents in the Brezhnev and Gorbachev periods, but Acton considers that this contrast is greatly exaggerated. Compared to the first Russian revolutionaries, the dissidents had little social resonance; on almost all social issues they were isolated: the authorities knew full well how easy it was to turn a distrustful society against a 'privileged' and remote intellectual elite. While true for Russia, Acton notes the rather different position of intellectuals in the non-Russian republics, where intellectuals played a much greater role in keeping alive and reviving a sense of separate culture and distinctive national consciousness.

The second piece traces Polish intellectuals through the stormy shifts of post-war politics. Three phases are identified and distinguished. First Stalinism arrives with the Red Army as a pre-existing socio-economic package. Faced with a patriotic appeal to help rebuild the country devastated by the Nazis, some intellectuals came to support the new cause. But most of them remained incurably revisionist, and lost little opportunity after Stalin's death to subvert official Soviet doctrines and dogmas, such as socialist realism. After Khrushchev's official dethronement of Stalin in 1956, revisionists hoped that communism could be peacefully transformed from within. Hope flowered briefly, but suffered increasing state repression and perished during an attempted anti-intellectual coup of March 1968 which drove many thousand intellectuals – including Kolakowski – into Western exile. An accompanying event, the Warsaw Pact invasion of Czechoslovakia in August, put paid to revisionist ideas. Crucial to the third stage, Solidarity, was the establishment of links between intellectuals and the Polish working class, which led to the birth of a ten-million strong independent trade union in 1980. The links survived martial law (imposed at the end of 1981) and into the first Solidarity government (formed in 1989). Although there remains a scholarly debate about the size and importance of their contribution, it is clear that Polish oppositionists succeeded, where Russian dissidents had not, in forming an alliance between intellectuals and workers which helped to subvert the communist system.

Neil Harding returns to the theoretical legacy. He argues that the founding fathers, Marx and Engels, did identify a working class or proletariat which, from the 1880s formed the natural constituency of socialist political leadership in Europe, until it fractured into fratricidal national conflict in 1914. Thereafter, in particular through the influence of Lukács and Korsch, real linkages between intellectuals and workers dissolved into 'Hegelianizing of Marxism'. From being adjuncts or prompters of the proletariat, left-wing intellectuals imposed impossible expectations upon workers, whose subsequent failure to rebel was attributed to the 'fruits of false consciousness and the entrapments of a hegemonic bourgeois culture'. For Harding, this Gramscian discourse leads into a blind alley. It restricts the field of revolutionary politics to those who had remained faithful: socialist intellectuals themselves. But their Olympian disdain for the working class, as a god that failed, leaves the door open to other political parties of the centre and right which can, with increasing plausibility, present themselves as the real champions of the proletariat.

8 Revolutionaries and dissidents

The role of the Russian intellectual in the downfall of Tsarism and Communism

Edward Acton

Modern Russian history provides rich material for the study of one particular dimension of the intellectual's role: that of subversion. Twice this century, the country has seen oppressive regimes – one Tsarist, the other Communist – generate and confront furious denunciation by disaffected Russian intellectuals. In both cases, the regime eventually came crashing down in ruins. Of course, great caution is needed in drawing conclusions from a comparison between their respective intellectual outlaws. Russian historiography is strewn with beguiling analogies between one period and another, seemingly unbreakable continuities across the centuries, and apparently endlessly recurring historical patterns. The world of Sakharov and Gorbachev was far removed from that of Nicholas II and Lenin. Indeed, the Soviet regime portrayed itself as the very antithesis of its Tsarist predecessor. And clearly its ideology and political organization, as well as the social and economic order and cultural life over which it ruled, differed fundamentally from that of Imperial Russia. Nevertheless, not only did the USSR inherit from late Tsarism the full weight of its political culture, but there were major structural similarities between the two. Both regimes governed a vast land mass extending over one-sixth of the globe. Both regimes were predominantly Russian in complexion, but ruled over a complex multinational society in which in numerical terms Russians enjoyed pre-eminence rather than overwhelming dominance (44.3 per cent in 1897; 52.4 per cent in 1979). While one rested its claim to legitimacy on divine-right monarchy and the other on Marxism–Leninism, both repudiated pluralism, competitive democracy and the claims of national sovereignty. In upholding their authority, both relied in good measure upon coercion, savagely curtailed civil rights, and narrowly restricted political participation in general and free speech in particular. The two regimes faced comparable international problems in being confronted by Great Power rivals which were more advanced in economic terms and which provided refuge and resources for their domestic critics. For all the difference between the societies over which they ruled, both regimes presided over swift and profound social change. Finally, both were abruptly repudiated by popular opinion and overthrown.

When attention is turned specifically to the role played by intellectuals, parallels are again immediately apparent. Other essays in this volume explore some of the problems involved in defining the term 'intellectual'. Not least of these is the fact that while in some periods and societies it is almost value-free and refers primarily to occupation and level of education, in others it is associated with a hostile attitude towards existing authority and used variously as a term of abuse or a badge of pride.[1] In the Russian context, the problem is to some extent simplified by the currency given to the word 'intelligentsia' since the 1860s. It came to be used specifically to denote educated critics of the establishment. Nicholas II, we are told, pronounced the word with the same sneer he used when speaking of syphilis.[2] It stood for all hostile journalists, writers, academics and professionals, for the emergent public opinion he detested. But the concern here is with just one sub-section of the intelligentsia. Excluded are those educated strata who operated within the bounds of the restricted civil liberty permitted by the Tsarist regime; those who sought no more than piecemeal reform; and those whose disaffection was concentrated on religious or sectoral issues. The focus is on members of the intelligentsia, and specifically the *Russian* intelligentsia, who took their critique of the regime to the point of wholesale rejection and direct challenge: the radical or revolutionary intelligentsia. During the Soviet period, the word 'intelligentsia' underwent a considerable transmutation. The regime redefined it to describe a broad social category including all non-manual strata of the working population or, in some contexts, those strata with higher education. In common parlance, it retained some of its old connotations, bringing to mind a literary, artistic, academic and scientific milieu, though no longer necessarily implying hostility to the Establishment. Here, however, the focus is on dissident intellectuals, and specifically those *Russian* dissidents who were not only critical of the regime, but whose hostility went beyond single issues, be it religion or the environment, and who took their protest to the point of direct defiance.[3]

A library could be filled with works devoted to the Russian revolutionary intelligentsia of the Tsarist epoch. Soviet historiography lavished attention on them as the forerunners of the Bolsheviks, the Great October Revolution and the construction of socialism. Western historians, even while debunking Soviet hagiography and differing widely in their own assessments of the revolutionaries, have found themselves powerfully drawn to the subject. The main landmarks of the 'tradition' became almost canonical.[4] The foundations were laid by Alexander Radishchev's (1749–1802) public protest against serfdom at the end of the eighteenth century. The first organized challenge was that mounted by the Decembrist revolt at the time of Alexander I's death in 1825. The 'remarkable decade' of 1838–48 saw philosophical debate spill over into fierce divisions between 'Westerners' and 'Slavophiles' about Russia's future and the adoption of Western socialist ideas by the most radical circles. Following Russia's defeat in the Crimean War (1853–6), there was mounting pressure for the emancipation of the serfs, fed from the far Left by Alexander Herzen's path-breaking emigré journal *Kolokol* smuggled in from London. The terms of the Emancipation Act of 1861 were bitterly denounced and N. G. Chernyshevsky and other radical writers fostered commitment to the revolutionary overthrow of Tsarism and the notion of introducing socialism on the basis of the repartitional peasant commune. From the 1880s, this 'revolutionary populist' call for Russia to avoid capitalism was challenged by Marxists, led by G. V. Plekhanov, who were convinced that the development of capitalism was inevitable, but so too was its overthrow by the proletariat it was spawning. The turn of the century saw the illegal creation of two underground parties, the Socialist-Revolutionary Party, bringing together latter-day populists, and the Russian Social Democratic Workers' Party, which coalesced around the flagship Marxist journal *Iskra*. The latter party promptly split between 'hard-line' Bolsheviks and more patient Mensheviks. Having enjoyed rapid, if brief, growth during the revolution of 1905–7, the three socialist parties re-emerged from the underground to win overwhelming popular support – and engage in fateful mutual conflict – during the revolutionary upheaval of 1917.

Study of Soviet dissidents and the 'human rights' or 'democratic' movement, as participants called it, is naturally much less well-established. Nevertheless, *samizdat* publications, autobiographical narratives by participants, and Western analyses have converged in delineating some of the major landmarks.[5] Khrushchev's 'Secret Speech' of 1956, denouncing Stalin, is commonly regarded as crucial. It deeply disillusioned a generation taught to believe in Stalin's benign genius, and it pointed towards a limited but significant lightening of censorship. The major spur to dissident activity was the move by Khrushchev's successors to halt the cultural 'thaw' of the late 1950s and early 1960s. When two writers, A. D. Sinyavsky and Iu. Daniel, were arrested in 1965 for publishing satirical works in the West, a number of prominent intellectuals protested against what they saw as preparations for the rehabilitation of Stalin and neo-Stalinist repression. Disaffection grew with the trial and harsh punishment of the two in 1966; a second show trial of Iu. Galanskov and A. Ginzburg, in 1968 was followed by the Soviet crushing of the 'Prague Spring' later that year; and 1970 saw the removal of A. Tvardovsky from the editorship of *Novy mir*, the most daring journal of the 'thaw' years. By then *samizdat* ('self-publishing' of uncensored manuscripts by carbon copying) was under way, and in 1968 the flagship of the movement, *The Chronicle of Current Events*, made its appearance.[6] A major dissident achievement was seen in 1971 when Roy Medvedev's devastating account of the Stalin years, *Let History Judge*, was published in the West. In 1972 repression sharply intensified, briefly silencing the *Chronicle*, and in 1974 the most famous dissident, Solzhenitsyn, was forcibly deported. Nevertheless, dissident activity continued, and the Helsinki Accords of 1975 triggered the establishment of Human Rights 'Watch Groups' in several Soviet cities. In 1979, however, the authorities redoubled their efforts against the dissidents; in 1980 the third 'giant' of the movement, Andrei Sakharov, was sent into internal exile in Gorky, and two years later his wife, Elena Bonner, announced that the last Helsinki Watch Group, in Moscow, had been forced to cease activity. Although *samizdat* by no means dried up, and the *Chronicle* continued to appear, if irregularly, the general consensus was that the movement had gone into steep decline by the mid-1980s.[7]

During the Brezhnev period, between the mid-1960s and the early 1980s, Western commentators were highly conscious of the analogy between pre-revolutionary and Soviet intellectual protest. There was a general if tentative assumption that eventually, at some date in the future, the dissidents, like their forerunners, would be vindicated by the downfall of the CPSU.[8] Now that the second regime has indeed collapsed as ignominiously as the first, the temptation to emphasize the apparent symmetry is evidently becoming much stronger. In particular, the view seems to be gaining ground that the dissidents played a role that, in terms of historical significance, matched that of their pre-revolutionary counterparts. This claim is given credence by the heroic stature which the most famous dissident figures achieved in Western eyes. In his influential Reith Lectures on the awakening Soviet Union, Geoffrey Hosking suggested that the Gorbachev reforms were in some sense a response to dissident activity, that it was dissent which 'brought forth' *glasnost* 'which is otherwise impossible to explain',[9] and has concluded that 'the contribution of the human rights movement to the later emergence of independent political associations was vital'.[10] R. V. Daniels argues that the dissidents succeeded in 'de-legitimizing and morally discrediting the regime'.[11] And according to Richard Pipes, they 'played an incalculable role in exposing the falsehoods with which the communist elite suffocated its subjects...[and] accomplished wonders sapping its foundations.'[12]

Before permitting this verdict to assume the status of conventional wisdom, it is worth noting that between 1970 and the mid-1980s, when the foundations were supposedly being 'sapped', Western commentators in fact became increasingly pessimistic about the impact of the dissidents. One measure of this was the manner in which, when using the canonical landmarks of the revolutionary tradition to measure dissident progress, they gradually pushed it further and further back in time. At the beginning of the 1970s, when the dissident movement appeared to be burgeoning and the *Chronicle* had emerged as the flagship *samizdat* publication, the analogy that was made was between it and *Iskra*, the social-democratic journal created shortly before the revolution of 1905.[13] A slightly more cautious estimate at that high tide of dissident activity paired Khrushchev's 'Secret Speech' with the Crimean War, and the impact of the *Chronicle* in the West with that of Stepniak's account of *Underground Russia* in the 1880s.[14] By the mid-1970s, the analogy between the *Chronicle* and *Iskra* seemed fanciful and it was equated instead with publications of a much earlier period, such as Herzen's *Kolokol* in the 1850s.[15] An even more guarded suggestion was that the impact of the dissidents might be regarded as comparable to that of the

Decembrists of 1825.[16] The most detailed treatment of the two 'movements', that of Marshall Shatz published a few years later, found the analogue of the dissidents still further back in time. Noting that active dissent, though now ineradicable, 'remains a very limited fragmented phenomenon, the property of a lonely handful of individuals', he located it as early as the eighteenth century. The comparison he drew was between the impact of Khrushchev's speech on the consciousness of Soviet intellectuals and that of the Enlightenment on the nobility of Catherine the Great's time, and between the dissidents of the late 1970s and Alexander Radishchev, the founder of the revolutionary tradition.[17]

Caution about making grandiose claims for the impact of the Russian dissidents is also counselled by the way in which the role of the revolutionary intelligentsia has been reappraised in recent years. The effect has been to downgrade significantly earlier evaluations of the part disaffected intellectuals played in destroying Tsarism. Whereas treatments coloured by Cold War rhetoric portrayed the revolutionaries as superhuman, whether angelic or demonic, since the 1960s revisionist studies have tended to stress their dependence on the wider social movements which underlay the revolution. Emphasis on viewing the revolution 'from below' has done much to demythologize the revolutionary intelligentsia. It has demonstrated that they by no means generated popular unrest, were in no position to impose their goals upon workers and peasants, and played a decidedly subsidiary role in moulding popular aspirations. It has cut the would-be leaders down to size. Yet, even in their demythologized state, the subversive role of the revolutionary intelligentsia puts that of the Russian dissidents in the shade. This is to take nothing away from the moral grandeur of dissident protest. Indeed, the fact that they were so isolated renders their courage even more impressive.[18] But, in terms of the impact they had upon events, the gulf between them and their illustrious – or notorious – forebears is arresting.

First, a word on direct numerical comparison between revolutionaries and dissidents. Such comparison is fraught with difficulty. A biographical dictionary of pre-revolutionary activists begun in the 1920s was cut short by Stalin and a somewhat comparable dictionary of dissidents published in 1982 made no pretence at being comprehensive.[19] Part of the problem lies in deciding on the criteria, in terms of the nature of the dissenting activity and the level of commitment, for inclusion in a head count. Although arrest for a political offence might seem to provide a clear and verifiable criterion, in fact Soviet dissidents were evidently frequently dealt with under non-political articles of the law. An alternative is to include all who can be identified by name – whether because they joined an illegal party, wrote an illegal political publication, or engaged in explicit oppositional activity. Both approaches require a careful line to be drawn between intelligentsia and others, leave to one side a penumbra of anonymous sympathizers, and are far from satisfactory. Where the number of known political offenders of all nationalities is concerned, current estimates would suggest some 3,000–4,000 each decade from the 1870s, rising steeply in the period of the revolution of 1905. Even less reliable estimates for the Soviet period suggest a figure of 1,000–2,000 for the 1960s, rising until the early 1970s.[20] The editors of the *Biographical Dictionary of Dissidents* collected the names of 10,000 dissidents active between 1956 and 1975, but after discarding those about whose activity there was minimal evidence, they included only some 3,400. In absolute terms, therefore, the numbers in both cases were very small and the disparity between them difficult to measure with any confidence. When consideration is given to the size of the potential pool from which the two groups were drawn, however, a very different picture emerges. Whereas, in the early twentieth century, the number of citizens of the Russian Empire with higher education was around 100,000, by the mid-1980s the equivalent figure in the USSR exceeded 18 million.[21] Had the proportion of the intelligentsia who became openly disaffected under Tsarism been reproduced in the late Soviet period, the number of active dissidents would not have been a few thousand but nearer a million. The disparity is even more marked when, as here, attention is focused specifically upon Russian revolutionaries and dissidents. Given the preponderance of Russians among the educated elite under Tsarism, it is no surprise to find them dominant among the revolutionary intelligentsia.[22] What is surprising is that among Soviet dissidents, although Russians constituted over half the population and were relatively advantaged in terms of access to higher education, they appear to have provided a small minority of known Soviet dissidents.[23] In proportionate quantitative terms, therefore, the Russian revolutionary intelligentsia constituted a phenomenon of incomparably greater significance than Russian dissent in the last decades of the USSR.

In themselves, of course, numbers are hardly the critical issue. But a similar contrast emerges when the two groups of intellectuals are compared in terms of political activity. Pre-revolutionary activists created lasting and viable political organizations which impinged directly upon the regime's political processes. In the 1870s, they launched (as yet unsuccessful) propaganda drives directed at peasants and the emergent industrial working class. In the late 1870s and early 1880s, their terrorist tactics provided the catalyst for a major political crisis. By the 1890s, they were making a significant contribution to agitation for and organization of successive strike waves. They had a hand in articulating the demands and encouraging the popular protests which forced the Tsar to issue the October Manifesto in 1905. By then, they had founded parties which rapidly attracted working-class and to some extent peasant support, and during that year, and again in 1917, they were intimately involved in the creation of soviets, trade unions and an All-Russian Peasant Union. Moreover, popular elections – to the Duma in 1906 and 1907, to soviets between March and October 1917, and to the Constituent Assembly in November 1917 – demonstrated mass repudiation of loyalist parties, fading sympathy for liberal parties which had operated 'within the system', and overwhelming popular support for socialist parties.[24]

The impact of the dissidents scarcely bears comparison with this. Their attempts at underground organization were limited, and those organizations that did emerge were fragile and ephemeral. They created no institutions that bore even a faint resemblance to those of their pre-revolutionary forebears. Indeed, in strictly political terms, they were relatively marginal.[25] Had there been a broad symmetry between the role played by the dissidents and that of the revolutionary intelligentsia before them, one might expect to find that their protest, influence and following had gradually intensified over time and reached a crescendo in the immediate pre-perestroika period. In fact, almost the reverse appears to have happened, with the dissident movement suffering a marked decline in the late 1970s and early 1980s.

The Russian dissidents are equally overshadowed when attention turns from the process of bringing down the old regime to that of replacing it with a new one. The revolutionary intelligentsia – from Lenin and Chernov at the centre to countless provincial figures across the Empire – occupied key roles in the course of 1917. The parties they created were critical players in the political struggles of that year. And their critique of capitalism, the rival view they had developed of how society was to be run, economic life organized and justice delivered, were crucial in the sequel to the revolution. The attempt at central planning and the abolition of commodity exchange after the revolution – and Stalin's 'second revolution' a decade later – cannot be explained as a mere extension of the pre-revolutionary schemes of the intelligentsia. But there is no doubt that important features of those programmes, as well as the language and visionary terms in which they were projected, drew directly on that tradition.

What counterpart may be found in Russian dissident activity? Clearly a number of dissidents joined in pushing forward the scope of glasnost and perestroika once the initiative had been taken from above. Between 1986 and 1989, there were instances of former political prisoners taking a lead in founding new semi-legal journals and informal political grouping.[26] Sakharov's release from internal exile by Gorbachev and his presence on the national stage was of major symbolic importance. But by no stretch of the imagination can their role be equated with that of the revolutionary socialists during 1917. What struck one socialist activist, Boris Kagarlitsky, was how very few dissidents occupied prominent positions in the course of perestroika.[27] Nor was dissident input into post-communist Russian policy commensurate with that of the revolutionary intelligentsia after 1917. It was only when perestroika proved a disastrous economic failure that emergent new elites began to seize upon the market as the solution to all problems – and for that dissident responsibility seems decidedly limited.

The question that arises is why should this have been? Why should disaffected intellectuals have been so much more potent in overthrowing one regime than the other? The most obvious explanation is the sheer intensity of repression. Even when Stalinist terror ceased, it might be argued, there remained a legacy of fear and inhibition for which there is no parallel in pre-revolutionary Russia. And although the instruments of overt terror were reined in after 1953, the regime continued to impose ruthless punishment for political offences – including the horrors of incarceration in psychiatric hospitals. At the same time, the sanctions at its disposal were comprehensive in a sense that even those of regimes such as those of Hitler, Franco and Mussolini were not. Every citizen was, in effect, dependent on the state for housing, education, health care, every form of welfare benefit and, above all, employment itself. Thus, long before a dissident fetched up in prison, he or she put at risk career, current job, status, family, health, security in old age, and peace of mind.[28] Moreover, did the apparatus for surveillance and intervention not become progressively more sophisticated and effective? The state could afford a police and spy network that suffocated the kind of activity engaged in by pre-revolutionary radicals. It succeeded in keeping a much tighter grip on all forms of organization and in preventing any equivalent of the semi-autonomous professional associations that began to emerge under Tsarism. Furthermore, the argument would run, Soviet censorship, ability to vet imported publications, and control of foreign travel was simply much more effective than the often clumsy efforts of Tsarism. The later twentieth century has developed means of silencing intellectual criticism that set it apart from earlier epochs.

Maybe. But there are grounds for scepticism that this alone accounts for the disparity between pre-revolutionary radicals and Russian dissidents. For one thing, the hardships suffered by the Tsar's political victims should not be underrated. Moreover, if these vaunted modern implements of social control were really so overwhelming in Soviet hands, why have countless other repressive regimes of the last quarter-century found them quite inadequate to suffocate organized intellectual and political opposition? Even if the case is accepted that the Soviet regime, though crassly inefficient in so many ways, was in this efficiency itself, it is striking that religious (notably Baptist) and minority nationalist dissenters should have managed to make measurably greater impact and recruited markedly more supporters than did Russian dissidents. Equally, many of the advantages that the KGB enjoyed over the Tsar's Okhrana were offset by the resources potentially available to Soviet dissidents. The pool of articulate, educated personnel from which intellectual dissenters might have been drawn, as we have seen, was much larger in the Soviet period than in the Tsarist. The means of underground communication, of *samizdat*, were significantly more sophisticated. The size of the expatriate, anti-regime Russian communities was much greater than in Tsarist days, and so too, it might be argued, was the moral, technical, financial and political assistance potentially available. The publicity provided by Western radio transmission beamed into the USSR had no pre-First World War equivalent. Nor did the Tsar's domestic enemies enjoy anything like the welcome given dissidents by Western governments and international organizations, or the diplomatic support lent them by the US. And this support was by no means ineffective: anxiety over Western reactions and the risk of jeopardizing détente appears to have played a significant part in inhibiting repression of dissent at least until the 'second Cold War' at the end of the 1970s.[29]

Monstrous though the restrictions and repression of the late Soviet period were, therefore, it is not satisfactory to leave the matter at that. At the very least, a closer look at sources of dissident weakness may highlight the most salient ingredients in the CPSU's recipe for domination. It may also point to other factors at work, other features of the Soviet order, of Russia's place within it, and indeed of the late twentieth century more generally, which contributed to the Russian dissidents' lack of muscle. As an initial step towards exploring the issue, it may be useful to press the comparison with the revolutionary intelligentsia and examine dissident weakness in the light of the explanation historians of Tsarist Russia have developed for the impact made by their predecessors. Three elements of that explanation are particularly suggestive about the source of the dissidents' relative impotence.

The first concerns the genesis of the revolutionary intelligentsia. Crucial here was the clash between the Tsarist state and the educated elite. The state itself had called into being this elite in order to modernize and man the civil and military establishment. But having done so, the regime was anxious lest they absorb and propagate seditious ideas, and it proceeded to curtail free speech and inquiry and inhibit cultural development. Rather than succumbing to pressure from above, however, a minority of the educated elite rebelled. That they had the self-confidence and drive to do so reflected in the early decades the high proportion drawn from the nobility, bred with a relatively strong sense of personal dignity, and in some cases empowered by financial independence.[30] More significant in explaining the rebellion of the socially and financially less advantaged majority was the inherent frustration experienced by intellectuals whose 'species activity' involved a measure of critical inquiry and creative freedom. The effect was to lead them to question and challenge the source of those constraints, and thereby to become involved in political conflict.

On the face of it, the Soviet state might almost have been designed to reproduce the same chain reaction, and indeed a closely analogous mechanism has been cited to explain the emergence of dissent.[31] Compulsory adherence to Marxism–Leninism could not fail to engender intense frustration among at least a minority of intellectuals. Its claims, indeed, were more sweeping and, in many ways, more claustrophobic than those of Tsarist official ideology. As in the nineteenth century, dissent was concentrated among precisely those intellectuals who were best endowed with self-assurance and sense of dignity and who felt the restrictions on cultural life most keenly. In this case, such characteristics were most pronounced among scientists and writers. In part, this was because of the high status they enjoyed and, in part, because it was inherent in the very nature of their calling that they should experience most intensely the need for cultural freedom denied them by the state. Yet, the proportion of this elite who fell foul of the government was, as we have seen, minuscule compared to the proportion under Tsarism. Somehow, the regime had greater success than its predecessor in integrating and incorporating its potential critics into the Establishment. One implication may be that the restrictions and frustrations of intellectual life were less oppressive, and the rewards more attractive[32] than they appear from the outside. This hypothesis gains credence from the evidence of 'permitted dissent' in the later 1950s and 1960s[33] and the intellectual vitality within the academies and research institutes of the late Soviet period. Attention has been drawn to the scope for historiographic debate in the 1960s, the development of sociology and social psychology in the 1970s, the closer links established with Western science and scientists, the presence of independently-minded economists within the academic Establishment, and the loosening grip of 'socialist realism'.[34] It also corresponds to the view of those dissidents who themselves regarded *samizdat* as essentially a by-product of innovative legal publications: 'All the most important phenomena in *samizdat*', remarks Boris Kagarlitsky, 'were engendered by processes that began in *legal* culture.'[35]

A second feature of recent treatments of the revolutionary intelligentsia draws attention to the contrast between the Soviet student body and its Tsarist predecessor. In explaining how the radical subculture and revolutionary underground recruited a 'critical mass' of new adherents year after year, historians have pinpointed the experience of students in higher education.[36] Notwithstanding the growing proportion of plebeian social background, students enjoyed an elevated position at the pinnacle of a steeply hierarchical education system. This developed in them a sense of their own importance and dignity which gave them the confidence to question the conventions of Tsarist society. Young, ebullient and articulate, the student world became highly conducive to the free flow of ideas and encouraged an egalitarian sense of solidarity quite unlike the stratified society outside. It was this which fuelled their increasingly vigorous reaction to the restrictions which a nervous government imposed on student activity and university autonomy. 'The formula, simply put, was dignity plus student solidarity equals resistance.'[37] This resistance was provoked by the authorities' interference over specific student issues – the free speech of professors, the content of the curriculum, the right to form independent student organizations – and most students did not get involved in politics and protests of a more general nature. But in the oppressive conditions of Tsarist Russia, to move from issues of higher education to more general criticism of the socio-political structure was a short step. Radical ideas and illegal literature circulated within student assemblies, cafeterias, libraries, voluntary schools and communes. Thus, there emerged a semi-institutionalized 'school of dissent' which introduced generations of students to a radical subculture and provided a transmission belt for a limited but steady flow of recruits to the revolutionary underground.

On the face of it, many of the ingredients for radical recruitment on the nineteenth-century model were present in higher education in the USSR – relative privilege, youth, illicit protest literature, boring curriculum, irksome interference and constraints by authority. And yet no 'school of dissent' emerged. Indeed, as has frequently been noted, the universities remained remarkably passive throughout the late Soviet period. Soviet students of the pre-Gorbachev decades, remarks Geoffrey Hosking, 'were among the most docile in the world'.[38] Even when social mobility slowed markedly and a shortage developed in opportunities for graduate-status work, there was no upsurge in student radicalism.[39] It may be that the formula which so successfully reconciled most graduates to the status quo was already operative at student level: higher education was first and last a passport into their ranks. Since analogous pressures were at work in Tsarist Russia, more significant may have been the change in the status associated with higher education as it ceased to be the rarefied privilege of a tiny minority and became a mass phenomenon. An increasingly urban and educated society may simply not have conferred on the student body (or the educated elite in general) the same prestige and sense of power that their forerunners had experienced amidst a largely illiterate and peasant society. It is arguable that a student body which had reached five million by the mid-1980s could not reproduce the sense of solidarity, intellectual superiority and social responsibility which had characterized their forebears a century earlier and to which radical leaders had successfully appealed.[40]

This hypothesis relates to a third and central issue: that of language and ideology. Crucial to the influence the revolutionary intelligentsia came to exert, and the prominent political positions they came to occupy, was their success in introducing and disseminating the terminology, the concepts, the discourse through which popular rejection of the Tsarist regime was articulated. The historical, political and economic ideas they developed, the social categories in terms of which they analysed society, were widely adopted, if in simplified form, and played a demonstrable part in delegitimizing the Tsarist regime. Their ideas, their assault upon the hallowed image of the Tsar, upon the arbitrary exercise of authority, and upon the habits and language of social deference, found a response because they spoke so directly to the experience of workers and peasants. The impact made by underground and socialist propaganda is attested by the language of 'class' adopted by workers and to some extent by peasants, by countless factory and village resolutions, by the terms in which many came to think about their own predicament.[41]

On the face of it, the rigid and increasingly barren, almost antiquated, formulae of Marxism–Leninism were acutely vulnerable to the challenge of a rival discourse. And yet, unlike their pre-revolutionary forbears, their critique was for the most part expressed through the language and within the conceptual framework of the regime itself. The central tactic of the human rights movement was to hold the record of the Soviet government up for comparison with its own laws and constitution. Dissident documents denouncing root and branch the Soviet system, Marxism, Marxism–Leninism, or socialism in general, were outnumbered by those urging its purification and the observation of 'socialist legality'. Thus, far from creating a rival discourse, the dissidents relied very largely upon that of the regime. Moreover, their energies were directed specifically towards civil liberties and, in particular, freedom of thought, information and expression – the subject of Article 19 of the UN's Universal Declaration of Human Rights, which from the very first issue was featured in the *Chronicle*. This is not to deny that various individuals and small groups proffered alternative socio-economic programmes and broad indications of the direction in which they wished Russia to move. Attempts at creating a typology of dissident ideologies tended to highlight three broad currents – a 'pure Leninist' one identified with Medvedev, a liberal-democratic one identified with Sakharov, and a nationalist-religious one which came to be identified with Solzhenitsyn.[42] Potentially, it was the last of these which offered a discourse most directly at odds with the principles and language (as opposed to the practice) of the regime.[43] But even among dissidents, its appeal remained strictly limited. In general, the relative dearth of economic and social content in the *Chronicle* reflected the preoccupations of the movement as a whole, and, on the part of some, a deliberate decision not to work towards or develop any specific blueprint for an alternative social order.[44] There were complaints by some activists that the emphasis on freedom of speech was at the expense of developing an agenda for and a vision of the post-Soviet order. 'It is plain that if we don't answer the question as to what kind of society we should have', wrote Andrei Amalrik in the late 1970s, 'it will be answered by those who want to drag us from one totalitarian pitfall into another.'[45]

The Russian dissidents failed to generate an alternative discourse comparable to that of socialism a century earlier. In Weber's terms, these intellectuals did not fulfil the function of formulating a broad vision for overall social change, and took only limited steps towards providing the political, social and moral prescriptions to legitimate demands for such change. There is no doubt that they made an enormous impression on Western public opinion. But comparison with their pre-revolutionary counterparts calls into question the nature of their impact at home. The very enthusiasm with which perestroika was met, and the evident support that Gorbachev enjoyed in his early years, suggests, on the contrary, that despite the best efforts of the dissidents, outright repudiation of the Soviet order was limited. Indeed, even after the revelations of glasnost, even when hope in perestroika had turned to ashes, Gorbachev had become deeply unpopular, and the party had been discredited, opinion surveys revealed the tenacity of some of the principle features of the old system.[46]

Explanations for the ideological vitality and impact of the revolutionary intelligentsia have had a dual focus. Attention has been drawn, first, to the wealth of intellectual capital on which they drew. The radical critics of Tsarism freely imbibed the Enlightenment, democratic and socialist discourse developed in the West. They shared to the full – some would say to excess – nineteenth-century European faith that history was the story of progress, that social processes and social problems could be subjected to scientific analysis, and that a just and free socialist society lay around the corner. From early in the century, when they absorbed the heady brew of German Idealism and Romanticism, through populist philosophers such as Mikhailovsky and Lavrov, to Marxists in the last pre-revolutionary decades, the revolutionary intelligentsia exuded confidence that they were working with the grain of history. Whether expressed in Hegelian formulae, in terms of the inexorable advance of morality or reason, or in terms of historical materialism, the revolutionary tradition was permeated by confidence that the principles and the agenda they propounded arose from superior understanding and conformed to the underlying logic of the historical process. And throughout they were buoyed up by the sense that they were poised to discover its key, to penetrate to the core of social reality, to lay bare the answers to society's problems.

But the currency gained by this socialist discourse was not simply a product of the faith and will-power of convinced intellectuals. Central to recent reappraisals of the ideological role of the revolutionary intelligentsia has been emphasis on their interaction with a restive mass constituency. 'Intelligentsia initiative was successful', concludes Laura Engelstein's study of the 1905 revolution in Moscow, 'only when it reflected... basic popular impulse.'[47] It is first and foremost by underscoring their dependence upon major discontented social groups within Tsarist society – primarily peasants and workers – that such works have demythologized the role they played. What gave them leverage and political significance was their success in aligning their protest with the aspirations of millions. Recent analyses have been at pains to emphasize the two-way process that lay behind this alignment. On the one hand, conscious by the 1890s that the mobilization of popular support was crucial if they were to change the existing order, the radicals were under the most powerful compulsion to adapt their ideas and tailor their programmes to ensure that they had mass appeal. On the other hand, growing numbers of workers and peasants, deprived by the repressive Tsarist order of any forum through which to express and advance their interests, strove to articulate their sense of oppression, insult and injustice. The result was a measure of harmonization and interpenetration between the radical programmes of the intelligentsia and popular aspirations. It was this that enabled the intelligentsia to take a hand in developing and propagating both the language and the organizations – parties, soviets, trade unions – through which workers and, to a lesser extent, peasants came to express their frustrations.

On both scores, the Russian dissidents were sorely wanting. In terms of intellectual capital and confidence, the contrast with the revolutionary intelligentsia was stark. Though they certainly questioned the capacity of the Soviet regime to survive, they did not share their predecessors' faith that their protest would ultimately be vindicated by the laws of reason and history. The regime's apparent stability and sheer longevity (by twentieth-century European standards) seemed, instead, to bear witness to the historical triumph of the irrational and the immoral. If this oppressive, cumbersome, destructive order was the last word in modernity, history in its Russian version at least was indeed a tale told by an idiot. And even for those who were convinced it must eventually disintegrate, it represented too long a historical detour to permit a restoration of the faith in progress enjoyed by pre-revolutionary radicals. Moreover, their experience of a society that proclaimed itself the product of the triumph of reason and scientific planning left them scant faith in either. The regime had succeeded in colonizing the historical record, the conceptual armoury of social analysis, and the very language of protest. For generations the CPSU had worked tirelessly to identify itself with all the most resonant themes in the Russian heritage – from Superpower status to victory in the Great Patriotic War, from the ordeal of the Russian Civil War to the liberation of 1917, from the classics of Russia's literary Golden Age to the heroism and idealism of the revolutionary tradition.[48] It had made its particular reading of history the very basis of its legitimacy, projecting itself as the authentic product of universal laws governing the historical process. It had associated itself, all but inseparably, with the very notion of class analysis and had entrenched a singularly rigid and moribund form of such analysis. It had projected Soviet socialism as the culmination of human progress, the fulfilment of man's aspiration for social justice, altruism, democracy, liberty, equality, international fraternity, solidarity and peace. Each claim, it is true, rang ever more hollow. But the effect was not only to create deep cynicism about the regime but to jaundice an entire discourse, to debase the language of social analysis and historical progress. Nor, after two world wars and the horrors of the Holocaust, did the West provide any equivalent of the overarching explanatory models, optimistic philosophies of history and novel conceptual tools on which the pre-revolutionary intelligentsia had drawn. There, too, the Enlightenment project was in crisis, and neither the resurgence of fundamentalist faith in free-market individualism nor the intellectual pirouette of post-modernism had much resonance in the Soviet context.

Equally, the Russian dissidents engaged in no interaction with a mass constituency comparable to that of the revolutionary intelligentsia. Their isolation was manifest and keenly felt. Speaking in the late 1970s, Medvedev quoted with approval the reproach of an anonymous sympathizer: 'The struggle for human rights will succeed only if the dissidents broaden their horizons and move from an exclusive preoccupation with the persecution of dissidents to a concern with the life and rights of the worker from Tula, the collective farmer from the Vologda region, the librarian from Tetyushi and the vocational-school student in Podolsk.'[49] Comparison with their pre-revolutionary counterparts suggests that the explanation for this lies not only in their impoverished intellectual armoury but also in the nature of Soviet society. The Soviet system rested upon a social structure which rendered the emergence of viable Russian constituencies of protest, capable of developing a broadly-based sense of common identity and interest, much more problematic than under Tsarism. The experience of both Gorbachev and the new Russian political parties of the late perestroika period point to the difficulty of identifying and mobilizing a coherent social constituency within the RSFSR.[50] Collective protest of any kind was inhibited by the almost ubiquitous illicit stratagems, ranging from moonlighting and illegal earnings to petty corruption and slack work-practice, which individuals had developed to cope with the endless restrictions and frustrations of Soviet life. More fundamentally, the abolition of private ownership of the means of production precluded clear-cut class divisions. For all the repression, exploitation, cynicism and friction by which Soviet style 'socialism' was disfigured, it involved an inescapable measure of interdependence. The different strata of Soviet society lacked distinctive objective interests comparable to those which had motivated pre-revolutionary workers and peasants. Each of the major categories in terms of which Soviet society was ritualistically analysed – the working class (sometimes sub-divided between state-farm workers and workers in industry, mining, transport and services), collective farm workers, non-manual employees, and intelligentsia – were internally riven by differences in terms of education, skill, wages, social origins, gender, generation, sector and region and bound to the other categories by the state's ownership and control of the means of production. On the face of it, the most promising mass constituency, potentially the most powerful in terms of numbers and economic leverage, was the working class. Yet it was no less subject to stratification, fragmentation and state dependence than any other 'class'.[51] Equally, no discourse had been more fully appropriated and exhausted by decades of Communist rhetoric and propaganda than that of socialist appeals to proletarian class-consciousness.[52]

The constituencies that were successfully identified and mobilized in the Gorbachev years, of course, were those of the national minorities. Were we to turn from the Russian dissidents to those of the Baltic republics, Ukraine or the Caucasus, a more impressive verdict on their impact might be drawn. There, they did play a very considerable role in laying the groundwork for nationalist protest and faith that independent statehood provided an answer to the problems of the Soviet order. The great majority of Russian dissidents, on the other hand, were ambivalent about nationalism. Apart from anything else, they were aware of the obstacles to using it as a vehicle for opposition to a Russian-dominated order: since Stalin's time, elements within the Soviet

Establishment had successfully exploited chauvinist motifs to rally popular Russian support for the status quo. To the very end, an overwhelming majority of Russians regarded the USSR rather than the RSFSR as their homeland. With that avenue foreclosed, Russian dissidents were unable to break out of their isolation and speak to and for a mass base.

CONCLUSION

There was a sharp contrast between the role played by Russian intellectuals in demolishing two ugly regimes of the twentieth century. In the Tsarist case, they took vital initiatives, provided an alternative language and discourse that was widely adopted, helped to mobilize major constituencies in opposition, and bequeathed a vision of society destined to be highly influential in shaping – or warping – post-revolutionary policy. In the Soviet case, they took few key initiatives, drew largely on the regime's own language, failed to mobilize any viable constituency, and had little impact on immediate post-revolutionary policy. In any explanation for the contrast, the sheer scope of Soviet repression must clearly feature. However, before assuming that this was a sufficient condition for marginalizing disaffected intellectuals in the Khrushchev and Brezhnev years, it is worth considering in more detail the constraints under which anti-Soviet Russian dissidents laboured. Comparison with the revolutionary intelligentsia of the late Tsarist period throws into sharp relief the regime's success in integrating and incorporating the cultural elite; the quiescence of Soviet students and the very different function of higher education in Soviet life; the dissidents' relative lack of intellectual self-confidence; and their inability to discover, still less disseminate, a viable discourse and agenda behind which to mobilize a significant social movement.

The immediate implication concerns the need to maintain a hard-headed sense of proportion when assessing the dissident contribution to the collapse of communist rule. But beyond that, the contrast with their pre-revolutionary predecessors suggests the basis for a more general typology of the conditions which facilitate or preclude subversion by dissident intellectuals. Despite the very different social and political structure prevailing in the West, it is to similar conditions that an explanation for the impotence of radical critics in the post-1968 era must look – the incorporation of the cultural elite, student passivity, the relative diffidence of intellectuals, and their failure to develop a discourse that resonated deeply with any significant constituency.

NOTES

1   In the Anglo-Saxon world, the dichotomy may be traced to Burke's contemptuous attack on the French *philosophes* in *Reflections on the Revolution in France*, London, Penguin, 1982.

2 R. Pipes, *The Russian Revolution*, London, Collins Harvill, 1990, p. 60.

3 The term 'dissent' is of course open to numerous interpretations. For Alexander Shtromas, by defining dissent as refusal to assent to the ideas rather than refusal to comply with the decisions of a governing body, virtually every Soviet citizen was a dissident, see A. Shtromas, 'Dissent and Political Change in the Soviet Union', in E. P. Hoffmann and R. F. Laird (eds), *The Soviet Polity in the Modern Era*, Hawthorne, New York, Aldine, 1984, pp. 717–24. For the distinction between 'subversive' and other forms of opposition, see F. C. Barghoorn, 'Factional, Sectoral and Subversive Opposition in Soviet Politics', in R. A. Dahl (ed.), *Regimes and Oppositions*, New Haven, Yale University Press, 1973, pp. 39–40, 70–82.

4 For one of the last Soviet treatments, written in the Gorbachev years, but still broadly faithful to orthodoxy, see V. Khoros, I. Pantin, Ye. Plimak, *The Russian Revolutionary Tradition*, Moscow, Progress, 1988; for a standard Western introduction, see P. Pomper, *The Russian Revolutionary Intelligentsia*, New York, Thomas Y. Crowell, 1970.

5 A valuable account published shortly before the Gorbachev era and available in English is L. Alekseeva, *Soviet Dissent. Contemporary Movements for National, Religious and Human Rights*, Middletown CT, Wesleyan University Press, 1985.

6 On the *Chronicle*, see M. Hopkins *Russia's Underground Press: the Chronicle of Current Events*, New York, Praeger, 1983; and, for an annotated translation of the first eleven issues, P. Reddaway, *Uncensored Russia. The Human Rights Movement in the Soviet Union*, London, Cape, 1972.

7 C. I. Gerstenmaier, 'Dissidents', in H. J. Veen (ed.) *From Brezhnev to Gorbachev: Domestic Affairs and Soviet Foreign Policy*, Leamington Spa, Berg, 1987, pp. 172–7; see the bleak picture painted by Medvedev in 1980, R. Medvedev, *On Soviet Dissent*, New York, Columbia University Press, 1980, pp. 146–7.

8 For a crisp and lucid study of the parallels between the two 'movements', see M. S. Shatz, *Soviet Dissent in Historical Perspective*, Cambridge, Cambridge University Press, 1980.

9 G. Hosking, *The Awakening of the Soviet Union*, Cambridge MA, Harvard University Press, 1990, p. 13.

10 G. Hosking, J. Aves, P. J. S. Duncan, *The Road to Post-Communism. Independent Political Movements in the Soviet Union, 1985–1991*, London, Pinter, 1992, p. 4.

11 R. V. Daniels, *The End of the Communist Revolution*, London, Routledge, 1993, p. 72.

12 R. Pipes, *Communism: The Vanished Spectre*, Oxford, Clarendon Press, 1994, p. 52.

13 F. C. Barghoorn, 'The General Pattern of Soviet Dissent', in P. J. Potichnyj (ed.) *Papers and Proceedings of the McMaster Conference on Dissent in Soviet Politics*, Hamilton, Ont., McMaster University Press, 1972, p. 13.

14 Reddaway, *Uncensored Russia*, op. cit., pp. 22, 37–8.

15 T. Friedgut, 'The Democratic Movement: Dimensions and Perspectives', in R. L. Tokes (ed.), *Dissent in the USSR. Politics, Ideology, and People*, Baltimore MD, Johns Hopkins University Press, 1975, p. 133.

16 H. L. Biddulph, 'Protest Strategies of the Soviet Intellectual Opposition', in Tokes (ed.), *Dissent in the USSR*, p. 115.

17 Shatz, *Soviet Dissent*, op. cit., pp. 136–37, 140, 152.

18 See J. Rubenstein, *Soviet Dissidents. Their Struggle for Human Rights*, Boston, Beacon Press, 1985, for a powerful celebration of their struggle.

19 S. P. Boer, E. J. Driessen and H. L. Verhaar (eds), *Biographical Dictionary of Dissidents in the Soviet Union, 1956–1975*, The Hague, Mijhoff, 1982.

20 For the late Tsarist period, see V. R. Leikina-Svirskaia, *Intelligentsiia v Rossii vo vtoroi polovine XIX veka*, Moscow, Mysl', 1971, pp. 308–19 and *Russkaia*

intelligentsiia v 1900–1917, Moscow, Mysl', 1981, pp. 249–54; for the late Soviet period, see the summary in F. C. Barghoorn, 'The Post-Khrushchev Campaign to Suppress Dissent: Perspectives, Strategies, and Techniques of Repression', in Tokes (ed.), *Dissent in the USSR*, pp. 85–6.

21   Leikina-Svirskaia, *Intelligentsiia v Rossii*, pp. 69–70, estimates that on top of the 20,000 with higher education by the beginning of the 1860s, another 85,000 had graduated by the end of the century; for the Soviet figure, see D. Lane, *Soviet Society under Perestroika*, London, Unwin Hyman, 1990, pp. 138–9.

22   Overwhelmingly so among Bolsheviks and Social Revolutionaries. See D. Lane, *The Roots of Russian Communism*, London, Robertson, 1975, pp. 39–46; M. Perrie, 'The social composition of the Socialist-Revolutionary Party before 1917', *Soviet Studies*, 24, 1973, pp. 223–50. From the late nineteenth century, there was a steep rise in the Jewish proportion, see R. Brym, *The Jewish Intelligentsia and Russian Marxism*, London, Macmillan, 1978, pp. 2–3.

23   Their under-representation is suggested by the *Biographical Dictionary of Dissidents*: of the entries where nationality was established (just over one-third), Russians constituted little more than 20 per cent. Given the numerous factors that may have distorted the representative character of the entries (drawn largely from the 10,000 names appearing in the *Chronicle* and the 30-volume collection of *samizdat* documents collected by Radio Liberty), this evidence is little more than impressionistic .

24   On recent work on the Russian revolution, see E. Acton, *Rethinking the Russian Revolution*, London, Edward Arnold, 1990.

25   See A. Brown, 'Gorbachev and the Reform of the Soviet System', J. Bloomfield (ed.), *The Soviet Revolution*, London, Lawrence Wishart, 1989, pp. 63–84 for perceptive comments on the limited impact of the dissidents.

26   Hosking, Aves, Duncan, *The Road to Post-Communism*, op. cit., pp. 1–28; for a similarly positive evaluation though with rather less evidence, see N. N. Petro, 'Perestroika from below' in A. J. Rieber and A. Rubinstein (eds), *Perestroika at the Crossroads*, Armonk NY, M. E. Sharpe, 1991, pp. 103–5.

27   B. Kagarlitsky, *The Disintegration of the Monolith*, London, Verso, 1992, p. 26. S. Mitrokhin and M. U. Urban, 'Social Groups, party Elites and Russia's New Democrats', in D. Lane (ed.), *Russia in Flux. The Political and Social Consequences of Reform*, Aldershot, Hants, Elgar, 1992, shows that as of April 1991 only 6 per cent of the elite of two emergent parties, the Democratic Party of Russia and the Social Democratic Party of Russia, claimed to have been politically active before 1986, pp. 75–7. D. Bakry and B. D. Silver, 'Soviet Citizen Participation on the Eve of Democratization', *American Political Science Review*, 84, 1990, pp. 821–47 suggests a strong measure of continuity between those who became politically active in the early Gorbachev years and those who had been active (if, doubtless, often frustrated) participants in the official institutions and politics of the late Brezhnev period.

28   F. C. Barghoorn, 'The Post-Khrushchev Campaign to Suppress Dissent: Perspectives, Strategies, and Techniques of Repression', in Tokes (ed.), *Dissent in the USSR*, op. cit., pp. 35–95.

29   P. Reddaway, 'Dissent in the USSR', *Problems of Communism*, 32, 1983, no. 6, pp. 1–15.

30   See the seminal essay by M. Raeff, *The Origins of the Russian Intelligentsia*, New York, Harcourt, Brace and World, 1966, and the study of Herzen's youthful rebellion in M. Malia, *Alexander Herzen and the Birth of Russian Socialism 1812–1855*, Harvard, Harvard University Press, 1961.

31   Shatz, *Soviet Dissent*, op. cit., pp. 138–48.

32   See the thoughtful discussion by G. Feifer, 'No Protest: the Case of the Passive Minority', in Tokes (ed.), *Dissent in the USSR*, op. cit., pp. 418–37.

33   See D. R. Spechler, *Permitted Dissent in the USSR. 'Novy mir' and the Soviet Regime*, New York, Praeger, 1982.

34   See, for example, M. Lewin, *Political Undercurrents in Soviet Economic Debates: From Bukharin to the Modern Reformers*, London, Pluto, 1975; M. Lewin, *The Gorbachev Phenomenon. A Historical Interpretation*, London, Radius, 1988; R. D. Marwick, 'Catalyst of Historiography, Marxism and Dissidence', *Europe–Asia Studies*, 46, 1994, pp. 579–96; J. Gooding, 'Perestroika as Revolution from Within', *Russian Review*, 51, 1992, pp. 36–57.

35   B. Kagarlitsky, *The Thinking Reed. Intellectuals and the Soviet State from 1917 to the Present*, London, Verso, 1988, p. 272.

36   D. R. Brower, *Training the Nihilists: Education and Radicalism in Tsarist Russia*, Ithaca NY, Cornell University Press, 1975; S. D. Kassow, *Students, Professors and the State in Tsarist Russia*, Berkeley CA, University of California Press, 1989.

37   Brower, *Training the Nihilists*, op. cit., p. 139.

38   G. Hosking, *A History of the Soviet Union*, London, Fontana, 1990, p. 403.

39   E. Gloecker, 'Underemployment and potential unemployment of the technical intelligentsia: distortions between education and occupation' in D. Lane (ed.), *Labour and Employment in the USSR*, Brighton, Wheatsheaf, 1986.

40   A similar argument has long been adduced to account for the post-1968 decline in political commitment among Western students.

41   See, for example, S. A. Smith, *Red Petrograd. Revolution in the Factories 1917–1918*, Cambridge, Cambridge University Press, 1983, and D. Koenker, *Moscow Workers and the 1917 Revolution*, Princeton NJ, Princeton University Press, 1981, on workers, and S. J. Seregny, *Russian Teachers and Peasant Revolution: Politics and Education in 1905*, Bloomington IN, Indiana University Press, 1989 and O. Figes, *Peasant Russia. Civil War. The Volga Countryside in Revolution (1917–1921)*, Oxford, Clarendon Press, 1989, on peasants.

42   For attempts to categorize the often highly volatile ideological positions adopted by different dissidents, see R. L. Tokes, 'Varieties of Soviet dissent: an overview', in Tokes (ed.), *Dissent in the USSR*, op. cit., pp. 11–16; V. Krasnov, 'Images of the Soviet Future. The Emigration and *Samizdat* Debate', in A. Shtromas and M. A. Kaplan (eds), *The Soviet Union and the Challenge of the Future* Vol. 2, New York, Paragon House, 1989, pp. 390–1.

43   See J. B. Dunlop, *The New Russian Revolutionaries*, Belmont MA, Nordland, 1976, for a detailed study of one such group.

44   Reddaway, *Uncensored Russia*, op. cit., pp. 24–8.

45   A. Amalrik, *Notes of a Revolutionary*, London, Alfred A. Knopf, 1982, p. 49. For a negative assessment from the dissident Left, see Kagarlitsky, *The Thinking Reed*, pp. 211–16.

46   See the illuminating set of papers in J. R. Millar and S. L. Wolchik (eds), *The Social Legacy of Communism*, Cambridge, Cambridge University Press, 1994, and for attitudes in the immediate pre-Gorbachev years, B. D. Silver, 'Political beliefs of the Soviet citizen: Sources of support for regime norms', in J. R. Millar (ed.), *Politics, Work and Daily Life in the USSR*, Cambridge, Cambridge University Press, 1987, pp. 116–32; see also S. White, G. Gill, D. Slider, *The Politics of Transition. Shaping a Post-Soviet Future*, Cambridge, Cambridge University Press, 1993, pp. 14–19.

47   L. Engelstein, *Moscow 1905. Working-Class Organization and Political Conflict*, Stanford CA, Stanford University Press, 1982, p. 14. On peasants, see T. Shanin, *Russia, 1905–7. Revolution as a Moment of Truth. The Roots of Otherness: Russia's Turn of Century*, Vol. 2, London, Macmillan, 1986, pp. 120–37. For a broader theoretical analysis drawing on the Russian example, see R. Brym, *Intellectuals and Politics*, London, Allen and Unwin, 1980.

48　See J. Bergman, 'Soviet Dissidents on the Russian Intelligentsia, 1956–1985: The Search for a Usable Past', *Russian Review*, 51, 1992, pp. 16–35 for dissident references to the revolutionary intelligentsia: it is arguable that what is striking is how little, rather than how much, Russian dissidents made of the revolutionary tradition, reflecting, no doubt, the regime's success in colonizing the legacy of that tradition.

49　Medvedev, *On Soviet Dissent*, op. cit., p. 135.

50　See M. E. Urban, 'Party formation and deformation on Russia's Democratic Left', in R. T. Huber and D. R. Kelly (eds), *Perestroika-era Politics: The New Legislature and Gorbachev's Political Reforms*, Armonk NY, M. E. Sharpe, 1991, pp. 129–50; O. Cappelli, 'The short parliament 1989–91: political elites, societal cleavages and the weakness of party politics', in S. White, R. de Leo, O. Cappelli, *The Soviet Transition: From Gorbachev to Yeltsin*, London, Frank Cass, 1993, pp. 109–30.

51　See the discussion in A. Pravda, 'Is there a Soviet Working Class?', *Problems of Communism*, 31, 1982, no. 6, pp. 1–24.

52　See E. Teague, *Solidarity and the Soviet Worker. The Impact of the Polish Events of 1980 on Soviet Internal Politics*, London, Croom Helm, 1988, pp. 159–92 on the gulf between workers and Soviet dissidents.

9 Politics and the Polish intellectuals, 1945–89

Tony Kemp-Welch

Few countries have been more preoccupied than Poland with the role of intellectuals. It has been a recurrent theme in public life for at least a century and a half.[1] The Polish notion of intelligentsia – a word probably imported from German around 1841[2] – was political from the outset, though this was camouflaged as simple patriotism to circumvent the censorship. The first use in print states 'Polish society expects from those who might be called the intelligentsia, an understanding of the national cause: to love, work and sacrifice for it'.[3] Thus understood, the intelligentsia took upon itself a leading role in the national struggle to regain independence during the country's tripartite partition. On the eve of the 1863 uprising against Russian occupation, the poet Norwid contrasted the deficiency of Poland 'as a society' with the supreme patriotism of Poland 'as a nation' at vital moments of history. Furtherance of the fatherland was 'the collective duty of the intelligentsia'.[4] The insurrection was crushed, yet romantic patriotism triumphed. As with the uprising of 1830–1, the failure entered national mythology, expressed in legends, songs and literature, both within the country and in – often acrimonious – Western exile. The romantic myth of a crucified nation entered the national consciousness: God was testing the nation, scourging it with the 'whips of the Mongols'[5] but one day Poland would achieve resurrection. This patriotic imperative survived well into the twentieth century. Partially suspended during Polish inter-war independence, it was cruelly revived by the Warsaw Uprising of 1944, and perhaps finally laid to rest only with the restoration of state sovereignty in 1989.

Romantic insurrectionism always had an alternative: organic work, whose origin lay in the perceived interconnection between the lack of independent statehood and shortcomings in Polish culture. It blamed the unruliness of national character for the partitions, and tried instead to cultivate sober and pragmatic calculation. Proponents set about supplying reason, progressive thought, and above all science, to a backward society. They became physicians in the face of ill-health and teachers in confronting popular obscurantism – which their Russian counterparts called 'going to the people'. An important role in this movement was played by women. Thus Narcyza Zmichowska noted 'the most precious blood of the nation drained away through two veins: emigration and underground activity'.[6] However heroic it might have been, such conspiratorial activity left 'not a trace behind'. She argued that society needed an intelligentsia that would 'train itself up' through the professions into positions of responsibility from which it could influence state policy and public opinion. Where a loosening of the legal system permitted, non-clandestine activity could revive society's sense of autonomy, thus rescuing it from the torpor and helplessness into which it had sunk. Informal intelligentsia 'circles' (*srodowiska*)[7] thus became a source of practical initiatives, most notably in Galicia where Austrian occupation put fewest constraints upon such associations. This second tradition is revived in the 1970s as part of the opposition to communist rule.

A third approach, openly anti-intellectual, is usually associated with the Polish anarchist Machajski (Russified as Makhaev and later demonized under Stalinism as *makhaevshchina*). Its key idea was that intellectuals 'exploit' socialist ideas for their own purposes.[8] The thesis was set out in an exile pamphlet in Russian, read by Trotsky (who told Lenin of it) in 1902. The intelligentsia is seen as an economic class with a vested interest in continued exploitation of the proletariat. Socialism, and especially Marxism, which had arisen to defend and promote workers' interests, had been turned into an intelligentsia ideology whereby the 'socialization of the means of production' would bring itself to power, while leaving the position of exploited workers largely unchanged. Machajski regarded the intelligentsia as not *declassé*, but as a distinct group of non-manual workers: white collars or (as he preferred to put it) white hands, which enjoyed 'a robber's income no smaller than that of the middle- and large-scale capitalists'. As managers or engineers they control production: this is more important than actual ownership. They run industry in order to create surplus value which they appropriate to educate their offspring, thereby establishing a 'hereditary monopoly of knowledge'. Orthodox Marxism had thus to be modified: the new capital was knowledge, accumulated and as jealously guarded by the intelligentsia as by the capitalist. Their 'family quarrel' with the bourgeoisie became redundant: Why destroy capitalism now? Who else could manage the complex industrial economy of a post-revolutionary state? His solution – the antidote to counter the 'conspiracy of intellectuals' – was a 'workers' conspiracy' to foment a universal general strike to promote equality of income and educational opportunity. Machajski thought Marx's famous phrase about the 'first phase of communism' (before full communism arrived) was a euphemism for the enshrinement of state capitalism under the management of a socialist intelligentsia.[9] He thus predicted that a new form of tyranny *over* the workers would be established in their name: an eloquent prophecy of Stalinism.

STALINISM IN POLAND (1945–54)

Stalin had always recognized that Polish communists faced a cultural challenge. In a handwritten note to Roman Zambrowski (1 September 1945), he suggested inter-Party coordination of plans for political literature and cinema.[10] The correspondence recognized that the Polish Party (PPR – later PZPR) faced social isolation. It confronted a population that had recently emerged from the longest occupation in World War II, and had, arguably, engaged in the least collaboration with the invaders. Jan Gross has shown the alternative forms of collective life that emerged in response to the social control exercised by the occupier.[11] The Nazi programme left no prospect for the Polish population other than subjugation or extermination. Most of those intellectuals who had survived the initial round-ups and deportations of 1939–40 entered the underground. A parallel society was created through a vast network of informal social institutions, including the largest clandestine press in occupied Europe. As Kazimierz Wyka put it, Poles behaved so far as possible 'as if' there were no Germans present in daily life.[12] A split reality emerged in which the occupiers were circumvented and ignored, so that they existed rather as inanimate objects, or a natural calamity, than as part of the social system. Such exclusion, however, was harder to sustain under Stalinism.

For Polish society, mindful of the Katyn massacre and the Gulag, Stalinism was – as Krystyna Kersten points out – 'primarily a symbol of satrapy and oppression'.[13] It was an alien imposition. By contrast, Soviet Stalinism had been indigenous and without a predecessor. Old Bolsheviks were warning at the end of the 1920s against a premonition: once the possibility had become reality it was too late. However, Stalinism in the USSR was the outcome of a distinctive political process to which the Old Bolsheviks had themselves contributed. The fate of their most prominent theorist, Bukharin, illustrates the tragic impotence of an intellectual in politics.[14] Post-war Polish intellectuals, however, could have no such delusions. Stalinism arrived as a pre-existing package, delivered by the Red Army, with the Allied seal of approval. The political monopoly, previously sanctioned at Yalta, was duly established.

Stalinism in Poland might be considered 'mild' by neighbouring standards. It lacked some elements of the Soviet 'model', such as 'show trials' of top Party leaders and full-scale (*sploshnaya*) collectivization, though they might well have been imposed had Stalin lived longer. None the less, society experienced terror as a central aspect of everyday life. The psychology of terror is complex and the outsider should not presume to judge. We know from research on Soviet intellectuals in the 1930s, that a 'moral anaesthetic' may be necessary for the psychological self-defence, or even physical survival, of those trying to cope. It can take various forms: underestimating the extent of official violence, rejecting criticism of the state as a 'provocation', shutting one's eyes to individual acts of repression or trying to explain them away as 'untypical'. Many Soviet citizens believed there had to be a reason for terror. 'They must know what they are doing', even though their great reasons of state could not be revealed to 'little people' down below.[15] To believe that terror was mindless madness, orchestrated from the centre, meant there was no hope,[16] a prospect human self-preservation perhaps instinctively rejects.

Polish research into this aspect of Stalinism is in its infancy. Pioneering indications are set out by Hanna Swida-Ziemba.[17] She argues that terror was internalized. Since almost everyone was threatened with arrest, even death, this was bound, over the years, to create conformity. Nazi terror, though even more violent, had not been internalized to the same degree. She agrees with Wyka that it was an external imposition, not part of the social system. By contrast, creators of Stalinism often delegated the 'responsibility' of de-masking enemies to the public at large. Denunciation became a social duty. Neutrality 'in conditions of capitalist encirclement' was tantamount to capitulation. Society was subjugated by rupturing the natural pattern of human relationships. The policy was to atomize individuals by closing down contexts for free association and conviviality. Workers would be arbitrarily transferred from one department to another, so that sustained social contact was precluded. The outcome was ideologized as the formation of a 'collective': in fact an empty shell manipulated by management. The state proclaimed the 'revolutionary march' of an abstraction: a mass society without personal contacts or human bonds. 'Working class' itself became an empty formula. Of course, any rapid industrialization is bound to cause disjunction, as large numbers move from the countryside to towns, bringing with them a whole baggage of rural norms and expectations. 'Peasant-workers' had a dual consciousness: estranged and isolated, and also 'urbanized'. Inter-generational conflict was also fostered. The young, of a 'new era', were encouraged to consider their elders as 'reactionary remnants' (*przezytki*), 'enemies of the revolution', who might include elderly relatives, or even parents.

But Poland's Stalinists did have some positive cards to play. Their propaganda differentiated themselves from the pre-war regime. An old order, gone for ever, was being replaced by the new, whose promising features included democratization of schools, development of press and publishing, and social advancement of young workers and peasants through further studies. The sociologist Chalasinski accepted such systemic change as progress overcoming 'reaction'.[18] The Party's dichotomies, old versus new, for 'us' against 'them', accorded well with Cold War simplicities. Moreover, accommodation with the new regime was not necessarily dishonourable. There *was* a devastated country to restore. In undertaking to lead this task, liberators from the Nazis could call upon patriotism and egalitarian beliefs. They were able to confront intellectuals with quite sharp choices: would they stand aloof, or, alternatively, use their skills and services in national reconstruction?

Some Polish intellectuals resisted the temptations and went into actual or inner emigration. We should here note the outstanding importance of the emigré magazine *Kultura*, smuggled back in from France. This single journal broke the state publishing monopoly and provided uncensored commentary and debate on events taking place 'in the country'. It preserved links with Western culture which were being officially severed, apart from a handful of 'progressive' Western leftists who continued to be carefully cultivated. Even these could be unreliable. Western delegates to the World Congress of Intellectuals For Peace (Wroclaw, August 1948) became insubordinate and a few even voted *against* the Congress's 'anti-imperialist' resolutions.[19]

Others played the game of camouflage so brilliantly analysed by Czeslaw Milosz. He calls it 'Ketmanism' after a traditional philosophy of Persia. The performance consists in acting out a series of public roles while masking one's private opinions: 'a constant and universal masquerade'. Thus 'National Ketman' means sounding loud approval of Russian achievements in all realms of human endeavour, while personally feeling 'unbounded contempt for Russia as a barbaric country'.[20] 'Aesthetic Ketman' professes total devotion to the lofty doctrine of socialist realism and tosses off Odes to Stalin on appropriate occasions. But in the privacy of the author's own four walls, rented at low cost from the state, 'one finds (if he is a well-situated intellectual) reproductions of works of art officially condemned as bourgeois, recordings of modern music, and a rich collection of ancient authors in various languages. This luxury of splendid isolation is pardoned him so long as his creative work is effective propaganda'.[21] How can such a person justify their hypocritical performances in public? Thus: 'One's life on earth is not judged by transitory panegyrics written out of necessity'.

According to the Stalin model, a social structure can be remoulded 'from above' by promotion out of previously excluded classes. As Stalin had put it in 1928: 'We need hundreds and thousands of new Bolshevik cadres capable of mastering the most diverse branches of knowledge.'[22] An intelligentsia of a new type was consciously created. The Stalinist programme of forced industrialization created numerous positions in a new social hierarchy, occupied by those 'pushed up' through the Party and higher technical schooling. A recent Polish handbook calculates the impact of a similar operation. Starting from a figure of a few thousand in the nineteenth century, and 150,000 at the turn of the century, the Polish intelligentsia increased to 862,000 by 1939. Despite the ravages of the Second World War, the intelligentsia had grown to 3.5 million by 1986. Included in this overall figure were intellectual elites, leaders of economic, political and cultural life, technical and other specialists (teachers, doctors, journalists), professionals and state officials, and numerous employees in services, trade and bureaucracy.[23]

Many memoirs from the Stalin period relate the stories of young people in their twenties who were appointed to top jobs in state-run enterprises, engineering, the Party apparatus and journalism. The sociologist Maria Hirszowicz has identified their common ethos:

(a) unreserved loyalty to, and faith in, the party leadership
(b) rejection of any personal or group loyalties that might conflict with the interests of the party
(c) readiness to adjust personal plans to the whim of the party bosses
(d) abdication of their critical faculties and humble submission to official ideology.[24]

As she notes, these requirements ran counter to the traditional independence of the intelligentsia, but provided compensation in terms of job security and personal rewards:

> There was the feeling of belonging to the elite, the taste of power, the joy of participation in a chosen group that was arbitrarily reshaping society, the privilege of prying into other people's lives, the exhilarating experience of acting beyond the law and beyond the social rules that limited the freedom of ordinary citizens.[25]

One source of eager young Stalinists were writers and critics grouped around the periodical *Kuznica*. Their defiant manifesto (1 June 1945) demanded:

> Will the creators of national culture – from rural teachers, engineers, doctors, architects, university professors, to actors, writers and composers – remain in an atmosphere of eclectic marasmus, mysticism and pessimism, elitist escapism, turning their cowardly backs on reality, refusing to disclose their true attitudes?

It rejected 'all notions of a separation or opposition between the Polish intelligentsia and the radical movement of workers and peasants'. As they put it, 'We welcome the inevitable process of promoting up a new intelligentsia from peasants and workers... Our task is to assist this process of forming new intellectual strata from the progressive and radical elements of our culture'.[26] Class militancy would be assured by jettisoning 'snobbish dependence on everything already extinct abroad' and by solidarity with contemporary Russian culture and radical thought in the West.

Such cultural debates resemble early Soviet ones. The Russian *rappovtsi*[27] and Polish *kuznicowi* both re-examine the relevance of tradition (heritage) to current culture. There was similar discussion of the *Proletkul'tist* view[28] that the working class could create a culture of its own. Both groups try to redefine the relationship between elite and mass culture, and hence determine the scope, if any, for an artistic avant-garde. The Polish programme, given the ambitious title 'cultural revolution',[29] aimed to democratize cultural life 'to accord with the ideals of progress and popular democracy' and to make 'past attainments and contemporary achievements of culture' accessible to workers and peasants.[30]

To coordinate the initiative, a Central Committee Department of

Education and Culture was established, on the basis of the Propaganda Department.[31] Its fifth meeting (28 March 1947) heard a report on the journal *Mysl Wspolczesna* (*Contemporary Thought*) intended to 'group together respected scholars on the left with democrats of the Kotarbinski and Chalasinski type'. The spokesman complained that although the editorship 'rests in our hands', there had been a dearth of original Marxist articles. Some comrades were neglecting the subject and others were even criticizing it.[32]

Such intellectual 'debates' were run on military lines as 'struggles for hegemony' on the particular 'front'. It was decreed that party-mindedness (*partyjnosc*) should prevail in social science which should be practised exclusively by the Higher Party School. Natural science had to submit its services to the planned economy. Its standards were relevance and practicality, in accordance with the demands of the Stalinist state. Even pronouncements in philosophy – however apparently remote – gained paramount place in Stalinist ideology. They established the context within which all other discussions could (or could not) be conducted.

This trend was bravely challenged by Stanislaw Ossowski. Anticipating much later work, Ossowski noted in 1948:

> Marxism now takes on certain notions peculiar to *religious systems*: sectarianism, orthodoxy, and heresy, for which are coined such terms as revisionism and deviation; from which arises the fear that violations of doctrine, particularly in the theoretical sphere, will devalue the organised workers' movement.[33]

Such developments, he predicted, would lead to expulsions for apostasy reminiscent of Catholic doctrinalism. Asking how one elevates a theory from a chamber group to the level of millions of people, Ossowski answers: only by retarding its development in order to preserve its 'social function as a unifying doctrine/ideology of the whole proletariat'. State imposition of a common ideology, and the idea it is infallible, were designed to create social bonds. But Marxism's dual functions, as science *and* ideology (or religion as seen above), are bound to clash, for they require different psychological approaches. Marx and Engels were well aware of the danger and insisted that historical materialism was a method *not* a dogma. The Party's insistence on unanimity of doctrine might have been favourable in certain circumstances, but it becomes harmful in the long run. For Marx's method must be applied to the history of Marxism itself. The dialectic is fruitful if not reduced to rote or attached to a petrified ideology. Theoretical tasks in respect of current Marxism were, therefore, to reduce its intuitive–metaphorical statements to scientific form; to clarify its concepts, especially those whose role in the Marxist system had changed through time; and to systematize the doctrine by separating out its *a priori* assertions, laws and empirical generalization and its historical hypothesis.[34]

The article provoked a number of rejoinders[35] which indicated that

Marxism had become unfavourable territory for intellectual debate. Senior ideologists had earlier complained that current discussion of Marxism was boring: when it became interesting they closed it down.

Changes in the structure of higher learning were enacted to ensure, as one critic put it from abroad, 'the teaching of all subjects conformed to the official doctrine of dialectical materialism, and included specific fallacious theories which enjoyed the support of the Communist Party'.[36] The right to teach was withdrawn from the sociologist Ossowski, his wife Maria Ossowska, the aesthetician Roman Ingarden and philosopher Wladyslaw Tatarkiewicz. Former chairs of sociology and philosophy became chairs of logic and the history of social thought. Independent philosophical publications were closed down and replaced by *Mysl Filozoficzna*, whose inaugural editorial[37] declared an ideological struggle on all fronts from 'harmful philosophical schools including: Thomist, Christian philosophy; phenomenology (idealist and reactionary) – Husserl, Ingarden on the theory of literature and art' to Florian Znaniecki's school of empirical sociology.[38]

The politicization of historiography proceeded apace. A Central Committee Department of Party History was established (26 January 1949) under the 'direct control of Party leader Bierut'.[39] The Politburo envisaged the construction in Warsaw of a Central Museum of the 'progressive–revolutionary tradition of the working-class and Polish nation', which would illustrate its close links with 'the Russian revolutionary movement, the Party of Lenin–Stalin and the History of the CPSU'.[40] The First Congress of Polish Science (1951) was told that:

> Marxist historical thought is guided by the genius of Lenin and Stalin, forging a methodological conception for all Polish Marxist historians, establishing the basis for a Marxist–Leninist contemporary history of Poland, blazing the trail towards a truly Marxist–Leninist historical science in Poland.[41]

One common agitprop technique was the celebration of 'safe' anniversaries of heroes from the socialist movement. But some were safer than others. Instructions for the eightieth anniversary of Rosa Luxemburg's birth (March 1951) ordered minimal publicity – a short biographical sketch for the press and a discussion internal to the Central Committee School and Academy and added that 'the entire action must be accompanied by sharply critical exposure of Luxemburgism and all theories derived from it'.[42]

As Stalinism developed, a whole army of 'glorifiers' began to 'work over' established intellectuals in every field. Accusers demanded recantations; those who obliged were required to confirm their sincerity by accusing others. One had to join the hunt to protect oneself from being unmasked as a witch. What could be more convincing proof of purity than to denounce one's former friends? Demonology developed. The Party dispatched lecturers to big enterprises and 'intellectual circles' to explain Stalin's colossal contribution to intellectual understanding.[43] Enormous coverage was given to Stalin's *Essay on Linguistics* (1950) which includes the brilliant observation that language is 'a means of communication'. The public was advised to study the *Short History of the Bolshevik Party* (*Historia WKP(b) Krotki Kurs*) (Warsaw, 1948), available in 140,000 copies, and the *Collected Works* of Lenin and Stalin (editions of 250,000 plus).

Officials slogans for higher educational meetings in honour of Stalin's seventieth birthday (December 1949) declared:

1   Long live comrade Stalin, Leader (*vozhd'*) and Teacher of the Toiling Masses of the Whole World!
2   Long live the Great Friend of Poland – Joseph Stalin!
3   Long live the Organizer of the Victory over Fascism – Leader of the World Camp of Peace – Generalissimo Joseph Stalin!
4   Long live the Continuer of the Immortal Works of Marx, Engels, Lenin – The Great Stalin!
5   Glory to the Builder of the world's first socialist state – to Great Stalin!
6   Long live the Leader of the World Camp of Peace, Democracy and Socialism – the Great Stalin!
7   Stalin – Freedom and Peace amongst nations!
8   The Name of Stalin is Indissolubly linked with the two-fold Liberation of the Polish Nation!
9   The Science of Stalin shows the whole of humanity the infallible path of struggle and work for a better tomorrow!
10   Supported by the science of Lenin and Stalin – the Polish working class is leading the nation to victorious socialism!
11   The Disseminated science of Lenin and Stalin – is educating the nation in the sprit of progress, genuine patriotism and internationalism![44]

It is difficult to tell how seriously such propaganda was taken. Wider social attitudes towards Stalinism remain obscure. Research into patterns of consent and approval, of self-policing, denunciation and other aspects of popular opinion are only now beginning.

REVISIONISM (1955–68)

Since deities do not die, the 'Stalin cult' might have ended in March 1953. But its embodiment in political practices and social structures of the Polish state meant that Stalinism could not be eliminated so easily. None the less, rather later than in neighbouring communist countries, there started to appear social pressure for change. This movement, loosely known as revisionism, still looked upon communist parties as potentially reformable. The aim was to replace their apparatus with more open-minded people, willing to challenge some of the Stalinist shibboleths such as the absolute primacy for heavy industry for production over the need of consumers, and the absolute primacy over intellectual life of *mat–dia* (the Stalinist reformulation of Marxism–Leninism). It importantly included a striving for cultural space, closed by Stalinist dogmatism. In Poland, a literary harbinger of revisionism in other spheres was the anti-Stalinist 'Poem for Grown-Ups' by Adam Wazyk,[45] which spoke eloquently of the disillusionment of an erstwhile supporter. Also in 1955, radical young intellectuals transformed the boring Communist Youth Union (ZMP) journal *Po prostu*, into an important social forum.[46] But the real impetus for de-Stalinization followed Khrushchev's 'secret speech' denouncing Stalin at the Twentieth Congress of the CPSU (14–25 February 1956)[47] whose most devastating initial impact was upon former believers.

Reporting back to the Central Committee, Morawski cited Khrushchev's statement to foreign delegates that the struggle with the 'cult of the individual' was by no means over but would continue until all remnants had been eradicated from social life, including science, education, art and literature. 'Distortions to which it gave rise went deep into the life of the Party and of the country.' Manifestations of the cult included 'stubborn, petrified bureaucracy', suppression of criticism, disregard for 'the needs and views of the population', servility, conformism and – crucially for the intelligentsia – the prohibition of independent thought and initiative. Morawski noted: 'Each of us speaks about this with bitterness. We developed this cult in ourselves.'[48]

The high priest of Polish Stalinism, Adam Schaff, complained that party rank-and-file members had not understood the 'secret speech'. Fortunately, intellectuals in the Higher Party School (later Institute of Social Science) were better informed and ready to explain matters that had hitherto been 'top secret', or at least 'confidential', to 'students, the creative intelligentsia and the wide mass of intellectuals'. But, most regrettably, intellectuals were now raising further questions: How is the Party directing science and culture? What is 'dogmatism' and is it connected with the 'cult of the individual'?[49] Subsequent speakers called for free debate. The philosopher Baczko saw the Congress sparking off an ideological revival, political and moral, personal and collective, against the prevalent cynicism of public life. Another said such cynicism emanated from the Party *apparat* and corrupted the whole social environment.[50] After a fortnight's turmoil, the decision was taken – uniquely amongst the East European communist states – to publish and make widely available the Khrushchev speech.

The popular response was enormous. A leading journal of the day noted:

> Like all other newspapers, the radio service and every institution for propaganda on the so-called 'ideological front' – which is becoming simply a tribunal for open discussion between people – we now receive hundreds of letters. They pour in like an avalanche.[51]

Similarly, the volume of letters received by the Party itself increased many fold: some 18,000 arrived in April alone. This ferment was positive and welcome to revisionists seeking to change the Party. Morawski told a conference on culture and education:

We now have a lively, heated discussion in the Party on issues raised by the Twentieth Congress, a very sharp and critical discussion. Its focus is a struggle for democracy in every sphere of life.[52]

As always in a political crisis, there was a dramatic revival of professional associations. The Party noted 'particularly wide discussion in literary circles, with a whole wave of meetings. Writers speak with great vehemence on the problems of freedom of expression'.[53] The report noted 'a challenge to communist writers (Kott, Woroszylski, Braun and others) and their young followers, from liberal critics (Sandauer, to some extent Przybos and others) who deny their right to continuing authority in literary affairs and call for 'people with clean hands'.[54]

Several hundred attended an 'open meeting' of the Writers' Union (27 April 1956). It was a stormy session with frequent interruptions. An attempt to defend Party privileges, including special shops exclusively for its use, came in for ridicule. 'It is not right that ministers and other activists working 14–16 hours a day in offices, should have to queue to get a kilo of meat (*laughter in the hall*).'[55] Another speaker condemned multi-roomed villas for Party families of two or three, holiday homes, and priority access to scarce goods for 'those working in the military, security services, bureaucrats, ministers and Central Committee members'. How could one talk of 'justice for all' in such circumstances? There had been much talk about dignitaries, but what about their dependants and hangers-on? Should ministers' children be driven to school or kindergarten in official limousines? Foreign travel paid by the state was 'junketing abroad, all official – go as cultural attaché!'. Social inequalities were rife: 'When hospital waiting-lists are long and the sick lie for ages in corridors, is it any wonder that public irritation is aroused by the spectacle of luxuriously equipped and spacious polyclinics reserved for the elect?' (*prolonged applause*). Years of negative selection (promotion of those with loyalty rather than ability) had resulted in the 'cult' of the incompetent.[56]

Sandauer deplored the triumph of incompetence in culture: careerism, cunning and cynicism, 'teaching us for a decade that the highest virtue is the absence of firmly-held beliefs'. Culture had been eliminated at record speed: imposing uniformity on the periodical press, gagging publishers, and threatening writers with a ban on publication or starvation. But, he argued, anti-Stalinist speeches were not enough. Freedom was not attainable when it depended upon individual whim, but only through legal guarantees. The 'thaw' in culture would remain a façade until there developed a new type of institution reorganizing literary life on the basis of collegiality. He warned that Stalinists, who had conducted terror campaigns against the intellectuals, could hardly be transformed into democrats overnight. 'Our Writers' Union was closed for eight years to those who did not agree with its harmful and mistaken policies.'[57]

Po prostu published a signed editorial which rallied the young intelligentsia to social protest. It noted 'students always played a gigantic role in Polish revolutionary movements' and called for a contemporary action programme:

> to struggle together with the whole of our Party, for restoration and development of communist norms of life in building socialism. Over the last decade, our official organizations developed many sores and wounds. They will be hard to cure. The cult of Stalin deformed the system, introducing many elements alien to the ideology of Marxism-Leninism, such as the dictatorship of individuals, in varied spheres and varying degrees, the paralysis of democracy, jamming of Western broadcasts, contempt for the masses.[58]

Groups from all over Poland empowered the Warsaw Club of the Crooked Circle (KKK) to act as Secretary 'to organize and support existing groups and help new ones arise, and to represent their interests to the authorities and institutions (particularly where local authorities were being obstructive)'.[59] Discussion clubs mushroomed: for music (including jazz), sculpture and film appreciation. Student theatre and satirical reviews appeared in Gdansk, Lodz, Krakow and elsewhere. Young people deserted the official Youth Union in droves.[60]

Long accustomed to regard themselves the vanguard of a nation faced with political and cultural oppression, the intellectuals now found themselves simply one part – and not always the most advanced – of a universal protest. In the late summer and autumn of 1956, the entire Polish nation took up against Soviet power. The communist authorities were only able to survive by restoring to the Party its former leader Gomulka, dismissed in 1948 and later imprisoned as a 'right-wing deviationist', and despite threatened Soviet military intervention, installing him as First Secretary. Because of his past persecution, and apparent willingness to stand up to Russian intimidation, Gomulka became a national hero. But the dual act of satisfying Polish and Soviet demands could not be sustained. The years 1956–7 proved to be the high point of Polish revisionism.

The revisionist position was expounded in a series of articles by Kolakowski. In one sense repentant Stalinism, in another they represented a reconsideration from within. 'Current and Outmoded Notions of Marxism' tries to separate out the two. On one hand, Marxism was:

> not a universal system but a vital philosophical inspiration affecting our whole outlook on the world, a constant stimulus to the social intelligence and social memory of mankind. It owes its *permanent validity* to the new and invaluable points of view opened before our eyes, enabling us to look at human affairs through the prism of universal history.[61]

Such insights illuminated the economic and social in history, showing how man in society is formed by the struggle against nature; the simultaneous process by which man's work humanizes nature; the de-masking of 'myths of consciousness' as the outcome of earlier alienation 'traced back to their real sources'. These are compatible with the view that human history is and will continue to be a record of progress. On the other hand, as with other doctrines inherited from the nineteenth century, much of Marxism had been absorbed into conventional wisdom. Some of its tenets were commonly accepted by non-Marxists. Others had not stood the test of time and had been discarded. This was not a 'defeat' for Marxism, but the triumph of eminent scholarship which had lost its exclusivity by merging with the 'very tissue of scientific life and becoming an elementary part of it'.[62]

A further article, for the Party monthly, entitled 'Intellectuals and the Communist Movement' suggested that the degree of participation of a 'pedagogic intelligentsia' in a system of rule was inversely proportional to the extent of police repression. 'The less one is capable of ruling by intellectual means, the more one must resort to the instruments of force.' In consequence, however, the intellectuals attract a disproportionate and instinctive animosity of the forces of 'law and order'. Marxist intellectuals, however, faced an important challenge – echoing Ossowski:

> The reconstruction of a Marxism adequate to the needs of this era – the era of the atom bomb, of imperialism in its current phase, of contemporary bourgeois culture, and of the existence of the socialist camp made up of various states – is a task which may have a decisive influence on the future of communism.[63]

Such analyses could only be conducted in absolute freedom of discussion. They required the rebirth of sociology as an independent science, instead of a collection of banalities. 'Without it, the Party cannot know or foresee the real consequences of its own decisions.' But intellectuals had further tasks including the creation of 'a socialist culture in its most diverse forms, but above all in intellectual and artistic aspects'. This included identifying the tendencies of historical evolution leading to the destruction of capitalism that are brought about 'as a result of the struggle of the exploited classes'.[64]

As this formulation showed, the revisionists were engaged in a rearguard theoretical action to remain within the canons of Marxism while simultaneously resisting those who would silence its deliberations. At the heart of their critique was the Stalinist dogma of 'untouchable truths that are excluded from discussion' which allowed 'non-scientific points of view to have a monopoly over science'. Yet the political *inspiration* of the communist movement, the entire tradition of European rationalism, could not be at odds with an objective knowledge of the world or with alleged 'truths' settled in advance, or served up as a matter of faith alone. Kolakowski's attempt was later repudiated as an 'anachronism' based on the hope that 'intellectual honesty might be restored [*sic*] within this orthodoxy or might bring it back to health'. In his English translation (1971) the author announced his abandonment of such hope and declared, 'I am certain I was mistaken in cherishing it'.[65]

Not long after the 'Polish October' revisionism was officially proscribed. *Po prostu* and *Nowa Kultura* were both shut in 1957. Intelligentsia discussion was banished to cafés, the Club of the Crooked Circle (banned in 1962),[66] and thereafter to private apartments.

The revisionist dilemma concerned the compatibility, or otherwise, of the Party with democracy. From its outset, the Polish Communist Party (which dared not even adopt this name) faced social isolation. There was the likelihood that the new holders of political power would find themselves vanquished by the conquered. As Gorky had anticipated for the early Soviet period: 'Bolshevism will be swallowed up in the ocean of old Russia like a grain of salt in a muddy pool.'[67] The events of 1956 had shown that this anxiety was very real. Thereafter, Party orthodoxy argued for a rigid structure to hold the ring against recalcitrant social forces, while, as revisionism reminded it, an accommodation with some sections of society could hardly be avoided.

The ensuing impasse was exposed in an 'Open Letter to the Party' (1965). Jacek Kuron and Karol Modzelewski's outspoken and extraordinarily courageous manifesto declared 'nothing has replaced the official Stalinist doctrine which was shattered in 1956–57'. Society of the mid-1960s was still ruled by a bureaucracy seeking to cloak its own class interest in the guise of 'national interest'. Having no coherent ideology to offer, but insisting on the monopoly of ideological expression, the bureaucracy was forced 'to eliminate all signs of ideological independence in a time of general crisis'. This had catastrophic consequences for 'the creative intelligentsia whose social function is the scientific formulation of social thought and the artistic expression of ideas'. All attempts at intelligentsia independence were snuffed out by administrative repression:

> Engaged scholars, writers and artists are discriminated against by publishing houses and cultural policy-makers. They are denied access to mass media, that is the chance to practise their profession: socio-literary periodicals which exhibit even a minimum degree of independence are replaced by publications which are then boycotted by the most eminent creative people; the intensification of censorship narrows down still further the already small margin of professional freedom among the creative intelligentsia. In this way, the ideological crisis becomes a crisis in cultural creativity.[68]

The remedy was revolution. The working class was compelled by its hopeless position to overthrow the bureaucracy. Although Machajski was not mentioned, there is a clear reflection of his premonition that a socialist elite would become a new ruling class.

As Krzysztof Pomian – a philosopher in emigration on a recent return journey – puts it, 'Revisionism did not play a political role, nor did it engage in practical activity'. However, it did assert the autonomy of 'culture against ideology' and of 'ethics against politics'. This broke the stranglehold of

Stalinist totalitarianism. Revisionism had very positive results in the universities and in keeping open intellectual contacts (though not travel) between Poland and the West, for instance through translation and publications. It thereby 'eroded the "leading role" of the party and undermined the concept of *partyjnosc* in culture and science'.[69] Yet the poverty of revisionism was cruelly revealed in 1968. First, the Polish Party, far from reforming, fell into the hands of its most cynical and primitive elements and launched a campaign against Jewish communists and citizens, forcing many from office and into exile. The impact upon academic life was particularly severe. These 'March events'[70] were followed by the crushing of the Czechoslovakian reform movement in August. For many young intellectuals, the combination was decisive: the Party could no longer be regarded as a credible vehicle for political change. Its inspiration would have to be sought elsewhere.

SOLIDARITY (1968–89)

An alternative had already been explored by some members of the lay-Catholic intelligentsia. In the aftermath of October 1956, the 'Znak' group offered its support to Gomulka in exchange for specific concessions: the right to run discussion clubs for Catholic intellectuals; return of the weekly newspaper *Tygodnik Powszechny* (given to the pro-government 'PAX' in March 1953) and the monthly *Znak* (shut in 1949) and admission of five 'Znak' deputies to the *Sejm* (parliament) following elections in January 1957.[71] These activities had a significance out of all proportion to their scale. In effect, they were the only example of political pluralism during the Gomulka period. They could not, however, be described as oppositional: they styled themselves neo-positivists.

Building upon the ideas of Emmanuel Mounier, whose journal *Esprit* was the model for the monthly *Wiez*, edited by Mazowiecki, from 1958 a forum for lay Catholic discussion in Poland, they advocated a form of Catholic personalism. This outlook holds that, faced with the tragedy and inhumanity of the twentieth century, in defending oneself against totalitarianism, there is no need to return to individualism. Besides the dangers of the omnipotent state, lie also the perils of rapacious individualism. A distinction is drawn, from Jacques Maritain, between an 'individual', a material being possessed of intelligence and will to serve such a being, and a 'person', with a spiritual existence affirmed through knowledge and love. Personal development is achieved through relationships with others. To realize human dignity, it is necessary to advance the dignity of others: personalist humanism is thus social humanism. Such an outlook has both social and political implications. The social aspect concerns human dignity in all spheres, including that of labour, as spelled out by the Vatican during the Solidarity Congress, above all in the encyclical *Laborem exercens* (1981). Society does not exist *sui generis* but should be created and sanctioned through persons exercising their civil and political rights. The state should serve society by promoting the freest possible development of social groups with their own rights and liberties. Consequently, Polish workers should strive, in cooperation with all classes, for the restoration of their rights. This can only be achieved when communities are 'as autonomous as possible from the state'.[72] While rejecting any Marxism, they sought every opportunity for understanding, rather than conflict, with the state. They sought to mediate between the Party and the population. As we shall see, this opportunity materialized dramatically in the summer of 1980.

An important prelude arose in 1976. A great source of political stability for Poland and its neighbouring states was the inability of the workers and intellectuals to act together, and the mutual antagonisms that could be stirred up to keep them apart. Thus workers stood aside in 1968, when intellectuals had protested against the cultural policies of the state. So far as they were involved at all, it was as a Party-organized 'angry workers' demonstration' against the intellectuals. Likewise, the workers' uprising of December 1970, in which large numbers were killed, received scant response from the intelligentsia beyond an appeal from the 'Znak' group for an impartial investigation into the disturbances. Following further protests in June 1976, however, intellectuals denounced maltreatment of the protesters and proposed the reform of workers' representation in a letter to the *Sejm*. Then, in September, fourteen intellectuals formed a Committee for Defence of Workers ('KOR')[73] to offer medical, financial and legal help to those persecuted and their families. Against all expectations, their initiative was stunningly effective. All workers sentenced for their part in the protests had been released within a year and reinstated, though often to lesser positions at work. This was the first great success of inter-class collaboration. Rather than falling redundant, however, as the authorities perhaps hoped, the Committee then broadened its scope to the protection of the whole society (KSS), retaining the label 'KOR' for nostalgic reasons.

Despite Western critics, who were inclined to dub the Polish opposition 'Marxist', KSS 'KOR' subscribed to no all-embracing ideology. On the one hand, Marxism propounded by the state was regarded as an ineffectual catechism unrelated to social reality; on the other, much Western Sovietology was considered irrelevant to Eastern European experience. But interesting collaboration took place between members of 'KOR' and their journal *Krytyka* and Hungarian writers.[74] In their mutual critique of state socialism, in its Polish and Kadarist variants, there was the shared assumption that social pressure, rather than socio-philosophical cogitation, would be more likely to influence the authorities.

'KOR' members ranged in age from students brought into politics by the university protests of 1968 to the veteran economist Professor Edward Lipinski, who styled himself 'a socialist since 1906'. The great majority had outstanding records of resistance to one or other forms of authoritarian repression. Thus five were veterans of the Russo-Polish War (1920); thirteen took part in the underground resistance to Nazi occupation; many others were victims of the show trials in the Stalin and post-Stalin eras.[75] Despite the efforts of official sources to present 'KOR' as an isolated band of renegades and traitors, this small group of intellectuals – which resolutely resisted creating any formal structure or organization – set new standards of social behaviour. It became apparent, first to themselves and then to wider constituencies, that Polish communist claims to subservience and obedience could be resisted. It *was* possible to say 'no' to demands of the state. Of course, workers in their June 1976 protests – forcing the government overnight to abandon price increases – had shown the way. But now the intellectuals' refusal of state demands moved into society as a whole, creating ever deeper space for activity no longer controlled by the political authorities.

As the release of workers and their intellectual supporters in July 1977 showed, public opinion, so often considered a virtual impossibility within a communist state, could be effective. Its mobilization requires a specific target, if possible endorsed from abroad. Thus, after the June 1976 events, Jacek Kuron addressed an open letter on repression to the Italian Communist leader Enrico Berlinguer, successfully using one communist Party to influence another.[76] 'KOR' and other human rights groups used the Helsinki agreements of 1975, and their subsequent international monitoring, to gain Western publicity and encourage their own government to play more than lip service to international covenants into which it had entered voluntarily. It transpired that preconditions for pressure group activity, often thought of as an exclusively liberal-democratic preserve,[77] proved to exist in Poland. To mobilize it, 'KOR' and other groups fostered a vigorous clandestine literature circulating outside the censorship. At first, this concentrated simply on informing the general public of information withheld by censored publications. The extraordinary extent of the state's powers over publishing was revealed by the dramatic defection of a censorship official to neutral Sweden with the censor's rule book and massive documentation of the censor's intervention.[78] Similarly, the state's monopoly over higher education was contested by the re-opening of the 'Flying University', a traditional institution under occupation, offering lectures and seminars on subjects that official institutions treated as taboo. Seven courses were offered in the first session: politics since 1945, economic thought, sociology, contemporary political ideologies, social psychology, literature and culture. Kuron summed up this aspect of the activity of 'KOR' as 'the struggle for pluralism in every area of social life, in schools, scientific institutions, in film and literature, in the Church, in peasant households and amongst friends'.[79]

At the heart of 'KOR's philosophy was an ethos of non-violence. The programme was simple: to reconstruct civil society from below, to revive all the spheres of social life that had perished under the communist regime.

Appeals for insurrection or revenge were absolutely rejected: it was not considered permissible to advocate any action that could lead to death or suffering. As Adam Michnik acknowledges, 'KOR' emulated the great prototype institution of resistance to the would-be totalitarian state: the Catholic Church.[80] This was not to say that all 'KOR' members were Catholics, far from it, but rather to recognize a forerunner – and uneasy partner – with enormous experience in the fostering of a community's ability to self-organize around a joint goal, such as construction of a church without official permission – reminiscent of the village bridge-building in *News from Nowhere*.

Thus, a Students' Solidarity Committee was formed (May 1977) 'to operate outside the officially sanctioned forms of socio-political activity, which are dependent on the communist party'. It sought to encourage further 'independent self-organization of Polish students beyond officially recognized institutions'.[81] As the intellectual discussion group 'Experience and the Future' explained, the fundamental problem of public institutions founded since the war was their lack of popular legitimacy. 'Over this whole period, the regulations and norms of social life were not accepted.' The ordinary citizen had no focus of loyalty beyond the family and immediate social circle: all the intermediary institutions had been swallowed up by the state. This had the catastrophic consequence that every protest took on the form of a general uprising – there were no shock-absorbers, no mediating institutions. Indeed, law itself, 'in a great many cases plays a quasi-class role. It serves to defend privilege and inequality, it is an instrument for the dictatorship of groups and individuals whose aim is unfettered legal authority put to the service of egotistical self-advantage, even though the essence of a legal order is to limit arbitrariness.'[82]

The role of intellectuals in fostering the Solidarity movement remains contested. Important antecedents were certainly the news-sheet *Robotnik* (*Worker*), assembled by 'KOR' intellectuals from materials sent in by regional correspondents. It reached workers in all major industries and was at one stage distributed openly at factory gates. The hawking of *Robotnik* was one of Lech Walesa's first contacts with the political opposition. However, the editors did not imagine that a single imprint could transform Polish politics. They thought, rather, that the attempt to build channels of communication between workers themselves would enable them to share and generalize experiences. To this end, a Charter of Workers' Rights was drawn up, including as appendices the rights of workers to form associations (guaranteed by Poland's accession to ILO conventions) and the right to strike. It obtained signatories from twenty-two cities.[83] When protests resumed, in August 1980, those workplaces that had contacts with the intellectual opposition were often first in the field and best prepared for negotiations with management. However, the treatment of Solidarity as somehow 'intellectual-inspired' would not be accepted by its alleged progenitors.

'KOR' took the view that it was an enabling association, showing the way by its very existence for the self-organization of others. The idea of doing more, acting as some form of Leninist vanguard for a workers' movement, was profoundly repugnant. Intellectual ambitions were frequently overtaken by worker militancy and institutional imagination. As Kuron readily admits, the demand of the Gdansk shipyard workers in August 1980 for trade union independence seemed entirely unrealistic.[84] Likewise, the first intellectual advisers invited to the shipyards (by Walesa) to assist workers in their negotiations arrived with far more restricted expectations. As the economist Tadeusz Kowalik recalls, 'We almost all arrived in Gdansk with grave doubts about the feasibility of Point One of the strikers demands' (the call for independent, self-governing trade unions, separate from the state).

> When I raised the question, Mazowiecki emphasized that our status did not permit us to change the content of the strikers' demands; Geremek advised us newcomers to form our opinion after talking to the workers on strike... I must add that during the course of a whole week's negotiations, I did not meet a single striker or delegate from other enterprises who was willing to consider any compromise on this vital issue.[85]

During the Gdansk negotiations, the intellectuals found themselves treated as 'experts' by the striking workers. Kowalik suggests that the choice of term 'experts', made by the strikers themselves, was perhaps influenced by 'some myth of intellectual expertise'. He mentions the manner in which the formation of a 'Commission of Experts' was announced to the shipyard workers. Members were introduced according to their academic qualifications: in economics, sociology and – above all – law, 'believed to be essential for the conduct of negotiations'.[86] However, the specializations of those in history (Geremek) and philosophy (Cywinski) were not mentioned. Following the successful negotiations, the role of 'experts' in Solidarity developed considerably. Indeed, its National Committee had a team of experts officially attached. This body was regularly addressed by intellectuals, and regional committees established research groups to report on a wide variety of social and economic issues. The charge came to be made, especially when the authorities began to renege on the Gdansk and other agreements, that the 'experts' were somehow to blame. As Jacek Kurczewski notes, this was very prevalent (as an alibi) in most regional branches of Solidarity, though Walesa himself never made 'experts' into scapegoats.[87]

Jerzy Jedlicki wrote in May 1981 that protests against intellectuals were short-sighted, above all when they had argued for caution. 'Perhaps we have in us subtler antennae for detecting dangerous areas. And perhaps we are better able to formulate the longer-term aims which this movement needs to discover as it develops.'[88] Contrasting this with the view (advocated by the sociologist Jadwiga Staniszkis) that experts should be so far as possible a neutral bank of knowledge, to be called on when needed, Jedlicki was still thinking 'in terms of the intelligentsia as a social category with a special vocation deriving from their intellectual potential'.

In Kurczewski's view, 'the "expert" is a figure of interest in so far as he or she mediates between two forces and two worlds'. The Solidarity experts spoke as though they had power:

> and in fact they did. It consisted in the will to represent those same millions whom the union activists wished to represent. This common will was behind both the power of the experts and those whom they advised. I think this is the deepest lesson to be learned, even if it is not new.[89]

The lesson was that men of learning and men of power could, by reference to a common stock of values, take an opportunity for exchange 'in which the experts serve as mediators in an ultimate fulfilment of their vocation'. The two functions were interdependent: one could not operate without the other.

The apparent failure of Solidarity, crushed by 'martial law' after only sixteen months of legal existence, lead to retrospective debate about its origins and nature. American commentators remain divided. David Ost sees the Solidarity movement as the culmination of earlier opposition to the Leninist state. In particular:

> KOR played the central role, providing a direct link from the radicals of the sixties to Solidarity in the eighties. Moreover, although the idea of forming independent trade unions was first raised by the striking workers of Gdansk and Szczecin in 1970, it was KOR that did the most to perpetuate the idea in that decade. Not only did it endlessly propagate the idea of independent civic initiatives in general, but it was KOR, as well as independent leftists collaborating with it, that organized the influential Committee for Free Trade Unions in Gdansk in 1978, the leaders of which became leaders of Gdansk Solidarity two years later.[90]

But while these intellectuals nurtured a 'civil society', the breakthrough of 1980 was hindered for Ost by its 'politics of anti-politics'. Solidarity was unable to realize its ideals because it lacked an 'institutional model for political intervention'. In its fervent wish to differentiate itself from the communist authorities, the opposition was inclined to eschew politics altogether. However, once Solidarity had been born, the question of the state had to be confronted. 'But at that point, Solidarity was unprepared, because its ideological origins had considered by-passing the state.' This led to the calamity of December 1981, when the legal Solidarity union was so easily crushed.

By contrast, Lawrence Goodwyn and Roman Laba accuse the intelligentsia of hugely exaggerating its own role. For them, Solidarity is not the outgrowth of opposition but an autonomous social movement with its own origins and history in the activity of ordinary working people. Goodwyn focuses on 'social movements'[91] in which people break through the barrier of fear into democratic self-assertion. Laba identifies and condemns an 'elite thesis' in the Western literature and argues that in 1980 workers showed themselves capable of independent self-organization. He provides empirical evidence from earlier uprisings (above all 1970) and argues that there is an independent social history of Polish workers. It was coherent and self-identified without outside help. The bridge between 1970 and 1980 is collective memory, kept alive partly through symbolic activities, though he notes interestingly that negative symbols – hate figures – were absent from the Solidarity iconography. The political culture of working-class resistance to the Leninist state integrated the national insurrectionist tradition (fraternity) and the social revolutionary tradition (equality). This was a creative synthesis 'not just nationalism repackaged as workerism'. He concludes that intellectuals did play some part: 'There would not have been a Solidarity without the intellectuals, but the Solidarity they joined was built on the framework developed by workers themselves.'[92]

The role of the intelligentsia in post-war Polish politics culminated in the spectacular abdication of communist power in 1989. Intellectuals were instrumental in convening the 'round table' which negotiated the peaceful transfer. The refusal to use force had geopolitical roots – the decision by Moscow (probably taken in 1986 and announced – to general disbelief – in spring 1987)[93] which empowered the East European communist governments to make what compromises with society they deemed necessary to remain in power without the ultimate sanction of Soviet tanks. Most of the ruling parties seem to have misunderstood, or ignored, this opportunity. However, the Polish communists acceded to the compromise and invited interested parties, including a re-legalized Solidarity, to a 'Round Table' discussion of future political arrangements. Michnik considers this was 'probably intended as a kind of trap for Solidarity, to gain legitimacy for its own authority, or perhaps an attempt to co-opt some segments of the democratic opposition into the camp of the authorities in order to gain credibility in the community'.[94] In fact, the device made it possible for Poland 'to use elements of the Spanish route to democracy, a scenario in which the reform wing of the ruling camp could find a common language with the democratic opposition, which does not desire a confrontation and understands that political compromises are a necessary condition for democratic order'.

The convening of a 'Round Table' was greatly assisted by mediators. Over a hundred intellectuals had met in a Warsaw church, at Walesa's invitation, on 18 December 1988. They adopted the title a 'Citizens' Committee at the side of Solidarity's Chairman' and proposed to draw up an action programme, in consultation with independent public opinion. Fifteen commissions were established, headed by those on Trade Union Pluralism (Mazowiecki) and Political Reform (Geremek), to prepare and present their programmes within three months. The Round Table eventually opened on 6 February 1989. As in the 1980 negotiations, there was an underlying assumption that an agreement could be reached. Mazowiecki again put forward the notion of reciprocity – according to which a compromise is seen as a step forward rather than a concession, and each side makes positive commitments. The principle 'respect your partner' excluded 'hard-heads' on either side. Once again, both sides agreed to scale down some of their demands and to respect the rights of others through joint guarantees. As in 1980, they made mutually binding undertakings.

In addition to lay Catholic advisers, an important role was played by the Church itself. Bishop Dabrowski described the Church's role as that of a witness and observer, not taking sides. 'This is because it does not want to be a political force; it must not replace society in deciding the fate and future of the nation. At a time when society was deprived of its identity, and even voice, it [the Church] had to take its place out of necessity... When the dialogue finally came about, the Church's role as a substitute was over.'

As a result of the 'Round Table', the former opposition and many leading Solidarity 'expert' advisers formed the first post-communist government. Prime Minister Mazowiecki's acceptance speech gave a lapidary summary of Solidarity's thinking over the previous few years. It promised a 'government of all Poles' based on the rule of law ('subordinated to political objectives for forty-five years'). Poland could afford no more ideological experiments. Devastation of the national economy could be overcome only through partnership – telling society the truth and enabling public opinion to be heard. The state could not be omni-competent. Its scope had to diminish: 'It cannot deal with everything, guarantee everything. It should formulate and regulate.' The transfer from 'monopoly to pluralism' was indispensable. 'We are crossing out the past with a thick line.'[95]

But within a matter of months the new elite was regarded as 'them' by many members of the working class. Why had this happened? In part, by drawing so sharp a line under the communist past, and avoiding recriminations, the Mazowiecki government seemed open to the charge of exonerating those guilty under the old regime. So, too, was the 'shock therapy' of market-type reform pushed through parliament, with little public discussion, under the 'Solidarity umbrella' and during the euphoria of political liberation. But a more subtle, and unanticipated, set of changes was transforming the social structure, which Andrzej Tymowski calls the 'unwanted social revolution'.[96] In a few months, the intellectuals' traditional posture was undermined. Their previous moral stance as social and political critics was vitiated by entering government. They became 'the authorities'[97] calling upon society to face hardship and make the sacrifices which had previously been their contribution to its future well-being. Roles had been reversed. The jesters had become the priests in post-communist politics.

NOTES

1 Important overviews are provided by A. Gella, 'The life and death of the old Polish intelligentsia', *Slavic Review* (30) March 1971, pp. 1–27 and (edited) *The Intelligentsia and the Intellectuals*, Beverley Hills, Sage, 1976.

2 Cited in A. Kijowski 'Pryczynek do dyskusji o inteligencji', *Zapis* (London and Warsaw) (5) January 1978, p. 91.

3 See A. Walicki *Philosophy and Romantic Nationalism: the case of Poland*, Oxford, Clarendon Press, 1982, p. 177.

4 A. Walicki, 'Three traditions in Polish patriotism', in S. Gomulka and A. Polonsky (eds) *Polish Paradoxes*, London, Routledge, 1990, pp. 32–3.

5 Mickiewicz, quoted by J. Jedlicki, 'Holy ideals and prosaic life, or the devil's alternatives', in *Polish Paradoxes*, p. 46.

6 J. Jedlicki, 'Holy ideals and prosaic life', pp. 51–3. See also the aesopian monographs on the nineteenth-century Polish intelligentsia: J. Jedlicki, *Klejnot i bariery spoleczne* Warsaw, 1968 and B. Cywinski, *Rodowody niepokornych* Warsaw, 1971.

7 On this social pattern, see J. R. Wedel (ed.) *The Unplanned Society*, New York, Columbia University Press, 1992.

8 Waclaw Machajski (Volskii) is the author of *Umstvenniye Rabochi*, 2 Vols, Geneva, 1905.

9 M. Nomad, *Rebels and Renegades*, New York, Macmillan, 1932.

10 Archiwum Akt Nowych (hereafter, AAN) – National Archives in Warsaw, Odzial VI (former Central Archive of the PZPR) p. (paczka) 112, t. (tom) 25, p. 19. Sections of the archive are being renumbered. References given here are to the classifications found at the time of use.

11 J. T. Gross, *Polish Society Under German Occupation. The Generalgouvernement 1939–1944*, Princeton NJ, Princeton University Press, 1979, p. xi.

12 K. Wyka, *Zycie na Niby: Pamietnik po Klesce*, Warsaw, 1959 and excerpt 'The excluded economy' (1945), in Wedel, *The Unplanned Society*, op. cit., pp. 23–61.

13 The pioneering work on Polish Stalinism is by K.Kersten, *Narodziny systemu wladzy, Polska 1943–1948*, independently published by *Krytyka*, Warsaw, 1984; trans. *The Establishment of Communist Rule in Poland, 1943–1948*, Berkeley CA, University of California Press, 1991.

14 Some of these dilemmas are described in A. Kemp-Welch (ed.) 'Introduction', *The Ideas of Nikolai Bukharin*, Oxford, Clarendon Press, 1992, pp. 21–2.

15 G. T. Rittersporn, 'The omnipresent conspiracy: on Soviet imagery of politics and social relations in the 1930s', in J. A. Getty and R. T. Manning (eds), *Stalinist Terror: New Perspectives*, Cambridge, Cambridge University Press, 1993, pp. 99–115.

16 See N. Mandelstam, *Hope Abandoned*, London, Collins, 1974.

17 H. Swida-Ziemba, 'Stalinizm i spoleczenstwo polskie', in J. Kurczewski (ed.), *Stalinizm*, based on a session (18 November 1988) at the Instytut Profilaktyki Spolecznej i Resocjalizacji, (University of Warsaw, 1989) pp. 15–95.

18 J. Chalasinski, *Spoleczna genealogia inteligencji polskiej*, Studium probemow chlopskich i robotniczych, Warsaw, 1946; 'Zagadnien kultury wspolczesnej', *Przeglad Socjologiczny*, (11) 1957, pp. 11–52.

19 Special issues of *Kuznica*, (34/35), 1948 and *Novy Mir*, (Moscow), (49), 1948.

20 C. Milosz, *The Captive Mind*, London, Secker and Warburg, 1953, reprinted with new 'author's note', London, Penguin Press, 1985, p. 61.

21 Milosz, *The Captive Mind*, pp. 64–5.

22 J. V. Stalin, Speech to the Eighth Congress of Komsomol (16 May 1928), *Sochineniya*, XI, Moscow, 1950, pp. 70–4.

23 'Inteligencja' in W. Sienkiewicz, *Maly slownik historii Polski*, Warsaw, Wiedza Powszechna, 1991, pp. 54–5.

24 M. Hirszowicz, *The Bureaucratic Leviathan. A Study in the Sociology of Communism*, Oxford, Martin Robertson, 1980, p. 182.

25 Hirszowicz, *The Bureaucratic Leviathan.*

26 *Kuznica* (1) 1945; also S. Pollak, 'Problemy inteligencji w ZSRR i u nas' *Kuznica*, (40) 1945; Z. Zabicki, *'Kuznica' i jej program literackie*, Krakow, 1966.

27 On the Russian Association of Proletarian Writers (1928–32) – the 'Rappovtsi' – see S. Sheshukov, *Neistovye revniteli: Iz istorii literaturnoi bor'by 20-kh godov*, Moscow, Moskovskyi rabochii, 1970.

28 Z. Sochor, *Revolution and Culture: the Bogdanov–Lenin Controversy*, New York, Cornell University Press, 1988.

29 For the equivalent stage in Soviet history, S. Fitzpatrick (ed.) *Cultural Revolution in Russia, 1928–1931*, Bloomington, Indiana University Press, 1978, and *Education and Social Mobility in the USSR, 1921–1934*, Cambridge, Cambridge University Press, 1979. A recent Polish overview is H. Palska, *Nowa Inteligencja w Polsce Ludowej. Swiat przedstawien i elementy rzeczywistosci*, Warsaw, 1994.

30 J. Kott, 'Gorzkie obrachunki', *Kuznica* (31/32) 7 August 1947; W. Sokorski, 'Zagadnienie walki o nowa kulture' *Odrodzenie* (32) 10 August 1947.

31 AAN 295 (Central Committee PPR)/XVIII/43 (27 February 1947).

32 AAN/XVIII/43 (Spychalski).

33 S. Ossowski, 'Teoretyczne zadania marksizmu. Szkic programu' (marked 'artykul dyskusyjny' by the editors), *Mysl Wspolczesna*, (1) 1948, pp. 3–18.

34 S. Ossowski, 'Doktryna marksistowska na tle dzisiejszej epoki', *Mysl Wspolczesna*, (12) 1947, pp. 501–13.

35 For instance: J. Hochfeld, 'O znaczeniu marksizmu', *Mysl Wspolczesna* (4) 1948 and A. Schaff, 'Marksizm i rozwoj nauki', *Mysl Wspolczesna*, (6/7) 1948. Ossowski responded in 'Na szlakach marksizmu', *Mysl Wspolczesna*, (8/9) 1948, pp. 19–34.

36 Z. A. Jordan, *Philosophy and Ideology. The Development of Philosophy and Marxism–Leninism in Poland since the Second World War*, Dordrecht, Sovietica, 1963, p. 158.

37 'Od Redakcji', *Mysl Filozoficzna* (1) 1950, pp. 7–15.

38 See F. Znaniecki, *The Social Role of the Man of Knowledge*, New York, Octagon, 1965. For parallels with the Soviet experience, see T. Kemp-Welch, 'Stalinism and Intellectual Order' in T. H. Rigby et al. (eds), *Authority, Power and Policy in the USSR: Essays presented to Leonard Schapiro*, London, Macmillan, 1983.

39 AAN 237/XXI (Department of Party History)/1.

40 AAN 237/XXI/6. Also, C. Bobinska, 'O przelom w nauce historycznej', *Nowa Kultura*, (2) 1950; 'Stalin a pewne zagadnienia metodologii historii' *Przeglad Historyczny*, (40) 1950.

41 Zanna Kormanowa, 'with the assistance' of Nina Assorodobraj, Aleksander Gieysztor and Tadeusz Manteuffel, 'Referat Podsekcji Historii, Sekcji Nauk Spolecznych i Humanistycznych, Kongresa Nauki Polskiej', *Kwartalnik Historyczny*, (3/4) 1951, pp. 253–326. See P. Hubner, *1 Kongres Nauki Polskiego jako forma realizacji zalozen polityki naukowej Panstwa ludowego*, Polish Academy of Sciences, Warsaw, 1983 and *Polityka naukowa w Polsce w latach 1944–1953. Geneza systemu*, Wroclaw, Polish Academy of Sciences, 1992, 2 vols.

42 AAN 237/ XX1.

43 AAN 237/ XXI.

44 AAN/237/XIX (Press and Publications Department)/55. A recent monograph is R. Kupiecki, *'Natchnienie milionow': kult Jozefa Stalina w Polsce, 1945–1956*, Ministry of National Education, Warsaw, 1993.

45 A. Wazyk, 'Poemat dla doroslych' *Nowa Kultura* 19 August 1955. For the protests it evoked, see 'Verses in a political storm' (trans. A. and W. Kemp-Welch), *Encounter*, June 1976, and *Polityka* (Warsaw) (1) 1981.

46 See W. Wladyka, *Na czolowce. Prasa w Pazdzierniku 1956 roku*, Warsaw-Lodz, 1989; A. Friszke, *Opozycja polityczna w PRL, 1945–1980*, Aneks, London, 1994, pp. 67–77 and its theoretical prelude, A. Friszke and A. Paczkowski (eds), *Opozycja i opor spoleczny w Polsce (1945–1980)*, Institute of Political Studies, Warsaw, 1991. For a memoir account of *Po prostu*: B.N. Lopienska and E. Szymanska, *Stare numery*, Warsaw, 1990, pp. 63–77.

47 A report of Khrushchev's speech appears in *The Anti-Stalin Campaign and International Communism. A Collection of Documents* edited by the Russian Institute, Columbia University, New York, 1956, pp. 2–89. It is likely many criticisms of Stalin's foreign policy (particularly towards China) were omitted from the Russian text. His 'violations of socialist legality' excluded those concerning the '"Peoples" Democracies'.

48 AAN VI p. (paczka) 112, t. (tom) 26, pp. 15–18.

49 AAN 237/V/231 (Adam Schaff).

50 AAN 237/V/233 (Bronislaw Baczko).

51 A. Braun, editorial *Nowa Kultura*, (17), 1956.

52 AAN 237/VIII/438, 'Narada aktyw' (17 April 1956).

53 AAN 237/XVIII (CC Department of Culture)/150. On the censorship, see D. Nalecz, *Glowny Urzad Kontroli Prasy 1945–1949*, Warsaw, Institute of Political Studies, 1994. For publishing, S. A. Kondek, *Wladza i wydawcy. Polityczne uwarunkowania produkcji ksiazek w Polsce w latach 1944–1949*, Warsaw, Biblioteka Narodowa, 1993.

54 AAN 237/XVIII/119 'Sektor Literatury'. The general background is given by B. Fijalkowska, *Polityka i tworcy (1948–1959)*, Warsaw, 1985. For the responses of writers, J. Trznadel, *Han'ba Domowa: rozmowy z pisarzami*, Lublin, 1990.

55 AAN 237/V/303, stenographic account pp. 60–2.

56 Ibid., p. 63.

57 Ibid., pp. 128–30.

58 'Co robic?', editorial *Po prostu*, 8 April 1956.

59 AAN/XVIII/161, p. 24.

60 For party anxieties, see Z. Zemankowa, AAN 237/V/204 pp. 90–3 (29 March 1956).

61 Kolakowski, *Marxism and Beyond*, op. cit., p. 205.

62 Kolakowski, *Nowe Drogi*, Warsaw, September 1956.

63 Kolakowski, *Marxism and Beyond*, op. cit., p. 178.

64 Ibid., p. 179.

65 Ibid., p. 6.

66 The standard account by a member is W. Jedlicki, *Klub Krzywego Kola*, Kultura, Paris, 1965; Warsaw, 1989.

67 A. M. Gor'kii, *O russkom krest'yanstve*, Berlin, 1922.

68 J. Kuron and K. Modzelewski, *An open letter to the party*, Pluto Press, London, no date (1965).

69 K. Pomian, 'Nieudana proba intelektualnej modernizacji Polski', *Mowia wieki*, (10) 1991, pp. 1–6. The best overview is A. Friszke, *Opozycja polityczna w PRL, 1945–1980*, Warsaw, Aneks, 1994, pp. 133–68.

70 The standard account is J. Eisler, *Marzec 1968: geneza, przebieg, konsekwencje*, Warsaw, Krytyka, 1991.

71 See A. Micewski, *Wspolrzadzic czy nie klamac? Pax i Znak w Polsce, 1945–1976*, Libella, Paris, 1978.

72 A valuable study is S. S. Miller, 'Catholic Personalism and Pluralist Democracy in Poland', *Canadian Slavonic Papers*, (25–3), pp. 425–39. See also J. Baluka,

'Dzialalnosc kola poslow katolickikh "Znak" w sejmie PRL 11 kadencji (1957–1961)' *Przeglad Sejmowy*, 1996, 1 (13).

73 The standard account by a founder member is J. J. Lipski, *KOR*, London, Aneks, 1983, trans. as *KOR. A History of the Workers' Defense Committee in Poland, 1976–1981*, Berkeley, University of California Press, 1985.

74 'From opposition to Marxism', *Krytyka*, (Warsaw) (5) Winter 1980. See also G. Konrad and I. Szelenyi, *The Intellectuals on the Road to Class Power*, Brighton, Harvester, 1979.

75 See J. Kay (A. Kemp-Welch), 'The Polish Opposition', *Survey*, Vol. 24, No. 4 (109), Autumn 1979, pp. 7–20.

76 *L'Unitá*, 20 July, 1976.

77 L. B. Schapiro, 'Introduction', *Political Opposition in One-Party States*, London, Macmillan, 1972.

78 *Czarna ksiega cenzury PRL*, London, Aneks, 1977–8, 2 vols.

79 *Bratniak* (Gdansk) (16) Spring 1979.

80 See A. Michnik, *Kosciol, Lewica, Dialog*, Warsaw, 1983.

81 Students' Solidarity Committee, 'Statement', June 1979.

82 Translated as M. Vale (ed), *Poland. The State of the Republic*, London, Pluto Press, 1981.

83 *Robotnik* (Warsaw) (35), Special Issue 18 July, 1979.

84 J. Kuron, *Gwiazdny czas*, London, Aneks, 1991.

85 T. Kowalik, 'Experts and the working group' in A. Kemp-Welch, *The Birth of Solidarity. The Gdansk Negotiations, 1980* Macmillan/St Antony's Series, London, 1983; 2nd enlarged edition 1991.

86 T. Kowalik, 'Experts and the Working Group', op. cit.

87 J. Kurczewski, 'Power and wisdom: the expert as mediating figure in contemporary Polish history', in Ian Maclean et al. (eds) *The Political Responsibility of Intellectuals*, Cambridge, Cambridge University Press, 1990, pp. 77–100.

88 Quoted by Kurczewski, idem., pp. 90–2. See also J. Jedlicki, 'Heritage and collective responsibility' in Maclean, *The Political Responsibility*, pp. 53–76.

89 Kurczewski, 'Power and Wisdom', op. cit.

90 D. Ost, *Solidarity and the Politics of Anti-Politics. Opposition and Reform in Poland since 1968*, Philadelphia, Temple University Press, 1990, pp. 10–11, p. 57.

91 L. Goodwyn, *Breaking the Barrier. The Rise of Solidarity in Poland*, Oxford, Oxford University Press, 1991.

92 R. Laba, *The Roots of Solidarity. A Political Sociology of Working-class Democratization*, Princeton NJ, Princeton University Press, 1991. Reviewers had many reservations: M. Bernhard, 'Reinterpreting Solidarity', *Studies in Comparative Communism* (24) 1991, pp. 313–30; J. Kubik, 'Who done it. Workers, intellectuals, or someone else?', *Theory and Society* (23) 1994, pp. 441–66.

93 A. Kemp-Welch, 'The Polish Paradigm' in D. Spring (ed.), *The Impact of Gorbachev*, London, Frances Pinter, 1990.

94 A. Michnik, 'The Moral and Spiritual Origins of Solidarity', in W. M. Brinton and A. Rinzler (eds) *Without Force or Lies. Voices from the Revolution of Central Europe in 1989–90*, San Francisco, Mercury House, 1990, pp. 239–50.

95 Mazowiecki, in *Uncensored Poland* (London) (6) 1989, p. 6.

96 A. W. Tymowski, *The Unwanted Social Revolution: From Moral Economy to Liberal Society in Poland* (unpublished manuscript, 1995).

97 I. Grudzinska-Gross, 'Post-Communist Resentment: or the Rewriting of Polish History' *East European Politics and Society*, (6–2) Spring 1992, pp. 141–51.

10 Intellectuals and socialism
Making and breaking the proletariat

Neil Harding

> I have satisfied myself of one thing, that it is a society of genuine working men but that these workmen are directed by social and political theorists of another class.
>
> Interview with Karl Marx, the head of L'Internationale,
The World, New York, 18 July 1871.[1]

One of the signal contributions of socialist theory in the latter half of the twentieth century has been its painstaking, and often illuminating, exploration of the varied sites of power within contemporary (bourgeois) society and their complex interaction. The state has been brought back in by writers such as Miliband, Poulantzas and Therborn.[2] Althusser, Marcuse and Raymond Williams have broadened the field to examine the way in which cultural hegemony is exerted through a dominant ideology with the purpose of manufacturing consent, or creating a condition of repressive tolerance.[3] In doing so, they have, in a sense, continued where Gramsci signed off. The seemingly neutral social institutions dealing with the sick, the insane and the criminal have been shown, by Michel Foucault, to be themselves agencies of control and surveillance whose inner logic are forms of knowledge that themselves embody and perpetuate social oppression.[4] The critique goes deeper yet, for radical feminists insist that the basic power relation within society is gender-based and is produced and reproduced within the (patriarchal) family. Here, in the celebrated phrase, 'the personal is the political'. System-sustaining power, it is argued, seeps down into our very language and into personal relations; it reaches 'into the very grain of individuals'.[5]

It had, of course, long been recognized by Marxists that ideology itself was perhaps the single most important source of power in bourgeois society, permeating and justifying all the particular institutional bodies through which power was exercised within the economy, in society and in the state. The whole point of Marx's critique of bourgeois society was to reveal what was presented (and broadly accepted) as the fixed and permanent 'nature of man' as no more than the set of characteristics necessary for the vindication of a historically transient, exploitative and inhumane society. The same applied to the so-called 'economic laws', the social hierarchy and the political structure. Ideology, in the Marxist account, is always and everywhere an expression of class or particular interest. It seeks to justify a particular ordering of power relations as the general or universal interest.

'HEY, YOU THERE!' ALTHUSSER ON CALLING PEOPLE'S NAMES

It is regrettable that, with some distinguished exceptions, these careful Marxist-inspired analyses of the sites of power in bourgeois society have not been applied to Soviet-type societies or to the functioning of Marxist parties.[6] These would, at least at first sight, appear to be extraordinarily fertile areas in which to apply Marxist critique. It is equally regrettable that Marxist insights into the nature of ideology in general should not themselves have been applied specifically to the development of Marxism. For some, no doubt, such an exercise could have no meaning. They would invoke Althusser's contention that Marxism (at least as correctly read) was a body of scientific knowledge 'which tries to break with ideology, in order to dare to be the beginning of a scientific (i.e. subject-less) discourse on ideology'.[7] It was, in this account, to the great credit of Marxism that it had set itself the task of discovering the reality of the world that was disguised and veiled by men's 'imaginary representation of that world'.[8] As an inclusive project, Marxism spoke to a genuine human universality. It could, therefore, have no place for the imaginary constructs, myths and mystifications whose real purpose was to guarantee and reproduce the power of a particular group or class. Its object being the *elimination* of power relations, it had no need of arguments to *justify* them. Social, economic and political power relations are other people's problems. Ideology as a partial and particular set of claims is transcended by the universalism of socialism and it, too, then becomes someone else's problem. It is part of an enduring political convention that acolytes of a given system of thought arrogate to themselves the title of faithful portrayers of reality whilst castigating competing systems as ideological. In order to go beyond mere assertion, we need to establish more precisely what it is that is constitutive of ideological thought, and here Althusser himself has provided a penetrating and influential analysis.

Ideologies, according to Althusser, establish as their indispensable core an abstracted Subject – 'a Unique and central Other Subject'.[9] Liberalism has the autonomous individual, conservatism the community expressed through its traditions, nationalism the nation defined by blood, language or culture. The most perfected of ideologies (the one chosen, therefore, as Althusser's model) is religion, with God as the uniquely powerful Subject. The power of ideology, in Althusser's account, resides in its ability to get ordinary individuals (the concrete subjects) to recognize as their own the life situation, interests and future prospects set out in the programmatic parts of the ideology. The Subject 'calls these individuals by their names...it interpellates them in such a way that the subject responds: "*Yes, it really is me!*" ... it obtains from them the *recognition* that they really do occupy the place it designates for them as theirs in the world ... it obtains from them the recognition of a destination'.[10] Interpellation (or the hailing of the individual by the Subject) prompts recognition of role, place and destination by the one so called. Even when individuals refuse to recognize themselves when called, refuse to be inserted into ideological practices or ritual, or flagrantly defy them, they still are not lost; the Subject still claims them and calls them to atone for their transgressions. 'God needs men, the great Subject needs subjects, even in the terrible inversion of his image in them (when the subjects wallow in debauchery, i.e. sin).'[11] If there were no sin then God would not be needed, its ever-threatening presence is precisely the premise of His existence. The subject, far from being denied by recalcitrance, is confirmed by it, and spurred to contrition and atonement.

It is entirely obvious (but, none the less, worth remarking) that there is and must be both a notional and physical separation between the one doing the hailing and the one who is hailed. Further, it is abundantly clear that the one who is hailed can play no part in the constitution of the hailer but is, on the contrary, constituted by him.

What the Subject does, in order to ensure the continued compliance of the individuals successfully hailed, and in order to guarantee the reproduction of his own power, is to involve them in a complex and organized pattern of activities and rituals. In this way, the individual subject quickly discovers that '*his ideas are his material actions inserted into material practices governed by material rituals which are themselves defined by the material ideological apparatus from which derive the ideas of that subject*'.[12]

Ideological apparatuses are then the organizing and coordinating foci in which the ideas and values sustaining the ideological Subject are constantly confirmed in the daily lives and activities of the individual subjects. These apparatuses are many and varied and they comprehensively embrace the people's lives. They include religious, educational, family, legal, political, trade union, cultural and communications apparatuses.[13] Ideology must therefore express itself in organizational form; 'an ideology always exists in an apparatus, and its practice or practices. This existence is material'.[14] There is always structure, discipline and hierarchy in ideology whose purposes are to guarantee the dominance of authoritative personnel.

The cycle of dependence and subjection of the concrete subjects is completed when they accept and voluntarily enact the roles specified for them by the ideological Subject. The net effect of this is that the promise of freedom, or realization of individual capacities that ideological patterns of thought routinely make, turns into its inverse. The individual is comprehensively subordinated to and dominated by the very ideological Subject that promised him fulfilment:

> the individual *is interpellated as a (free) subject in order that he shall submit freely to the commandments of the Subject, i.e. in order that he shall*

(freely) accept his subjection, i.e. in order that he shall make the gestures and actions of his subjection 'all by himself'. *There are no subjects except by and for their subjection.*[15]

It was Althusser's contentious claim that Marxism was a science and not an ideology and, as such, it had no place for a potent Subject bestriding history. In order, however, to establish whether or not Marxism itself created a domineering Subject, we need to begin by applying Althusser's own account of the oppressive logic of ideological discourse to Marxism itself. At the risk of pre-empting the conclusions of this chapter, I will go on to argue that Marx did indeed locate the proletariat as the Subject of his distinctive ideological position; further that he inserted the intelligentsia as its proxy. The development of twentieth-century Marxism under the pervasive philosophical influence of Lukács and Gramsci (and, via them, of Hegel) conspired to elevate the universality of the proletarian Subject and the potency of the intellectuals and, therewith, to emasculate the actual working class.

MARX, CONJURING THE SUBJECT, INSERTS THE INTELLECTUALS

So long as Marx confined himself to characterizing the proletariat as an abstracted universal ('the abstraction of all humanity, even of the semblance of humanity')[16] that served the purpose of a philosophical and categorical Other to the bourgeois–capitalist order he so despised, the question of agency – what the Subject was to do and how it was to do it – barely arose. It was already given that its goal (indeed its *raison d'être*) was the total overthrow of the very premises upon which modern society was constituted.[17] To state a goal was not, however, to state a mode of activity. Only when Marx, for the one and only time in his career, descended to the programmatic level of outlining a transitional strategy with enumerated concrete proposals, did he quite self-consciously step out of philosophical and social critique into the discourse of ideology. He therefore had to construct a political Subject, i.e. one that was capable of conscious, directed and therefore organized activity. The proletarian Subject now had to be attributed consciousness (i.e. awareness of the real causes of its present plight, and of its revolutionary transformative goals), articulation (i.e. the ability to formulate and propagate its proximate and long term aspirations), and organization on at least a national basis (i.e. the capacity to mobilize, enthuse and marshall its constituents in such force as to achieve its strategic goals). It is significant that these attributes of the proletarian Subject were not systematically elaborated until the writing of *The Manifesto of the Communist Party*. This was the definitive moment of transition from the philosophical to the political Subject; it was the point at which Marxism, for the first time, expressly interpellates the workers of the world to recognize themselves in the account given of their situation in the *Manifesto* and to unite and organize themselves around the programme there set out for them. It is, similarly, far from coincidental that this is the point at which the party is not only inserted; it now appears as a necessary quality of the Subject – becomes constitutive of it.

The party has, over the mass of actual proletarians, 'the advantage of clearly understanding the line of march, the conditions, and the ultimate general results of the proletarian movement'. Its members are 'the most advanced and resolute section' who 'bring to the front the common interests of the entire proletariat'.[18] The party, therefore, far from merely aggregating the felt interests of the workers, expresses its immanent strivings in the realms of a public and national discourse about state power and who should dispose of it. It is, in short, not merely the political expression of the class but its central constitutive element as historical actor, i.e. as Subject. The class cannot be a class 'for itself' without consciousness, organization and articulation – the characteristics given to it by its constitution as a party: 'This organization of the proletarians into a class and, consequently, into a political party'.[19] The class as historical actor is only constituted in its existence as political party for the good reason that it is only in its political struggles that it overcomes its petty localisms and craft divisions. In confronting the generalized expression of bourgeois power revealed in the law and the state, the proletarian Subject is itself obliged to generalize its claims and, therefore, its organizational structure. It must have a national extension and it must confront its bourgeois opponent on the generalized plane of national politics. All local struggles have therefore to be centralized 'into one national struggle between classes. But every class struggle is a political struggle'. It follows that the proletariat only constitutes itself as the Subject by becoming a Party. It is equally clear that, from the outset, there must be separation and distance between class and party.

It comes as no surprise that Marx acknowledges that the party will be largely recruited from the ranks of the declassed bourgeoisie, 'in particular, a portion of the bourgeois ideologists, who have raised themselves to the level of comprehending theoretically the historical movement as a whole'.[20] It is they who 'supply the proletariat with fresh elements of education' or, in the English edition, 'elements of enlightenment and progress'.[21]

The audacious conjuring trick has now been accomplished: the proletariat exists as a class properly 'for itself' only to the extent that it conforms to the characteristics attributed to it by Marx and realized in the party. The dominance of the intellectuals within Marxism is, therefore, given by the initial construction of the proletarian Subject and was consistently reproduced within Marxist parties. The line of succession from Marx to Plekhanov and Kautsky, and thence to Lenin, Lukács and Gramsci, is an unbroken one. With each retelling of the tale the Subject is refined, acquires new attributes, making of it an ever more perfect and God-like being. As the epitome of valour and revolutionary dedication, the Subject calls to account the human lapses of its votaries and their lack of resolve. As the fount of perspicacity and prescient awareness of the future, it impugns their short-termism. It always represents the general class interest as they, too often, express particular and conflicting claims and even bourgeois views. There is a permanent tension, therefore, between the Subject and the interpellated. The latter must recognize themselves, not as they presently are, but as they yet might be. Really existing empirically given working men and women cannot be the measure and model for the construction of the Proletariat. They are dehumanized and brutalized by the work process, deprived of leisure and the opportunity to reflect upon their conditions, and subject to the all-pervasive dominance of the ideas of the ruling class. Their consciousness, their aspirations and goals, must be imputed or attributed from outside, they cannot be in any way clarified by a mere aggregation of what working men currently feel or think:

> It is not a question of what this or that proletarian, or even the whole of the proletariat, at the moment *regards* as its aim. It is a question of *what the proletariat is*, and what, in accordance with this *being*, it will historically be compelled to do. Its aim and historical action is visibly and irrevocably foreshadowed in its own life situation as well as in the whole organization of bourgeois society today.[22]

It is in the gap between actual and potential that the power and authority of the party resides (just as Althusser noticed that the power of religion is confirmed rather than negated by the evidence of sin and dereliction among its followers). Actual subjects purge their derelictions through acts of atonement – they display their contrition as a condition for entering, once again, into a state of grace.

In the career of Marxian socialism in the twentieth century, no actual working class was ever able to realize the exacting specifications established for it by the successive generations of intellectuals who established and refined the proletarian Subject. A premonition of this was given by Marx himself who despaired of England as the nurturing ground, not only of a bourgeois bourgeoisie but a bourgeois aristocracy and a bourgeois proletariat. Plekhanov, the founder of dialectical materialism and self-styled guardian of Marxist orthodoxy, proclaimed that 'the mere possibility of a purposeful movement of the Russian working class' depended upon the organizational and ideological work of the socialist intelligentsia.[23] Kautsky was blunter still, providing the authoritative texts upon which Lenin was to pin his theory of the party and his crucial distinction between a proletarian and a theoretical mode of knowing. 'The vehicle of science', Kautsky insisted, 'is not the proletariat, but the bourgeois intelligentsia', and nowhere was this truer than in the case of the distillation of the science of socialism.[24] The production of the ideology of socialism (the ideology of the emancipation of the working class) could not, Lenin concluded, be the outcome of the thought and reflection of the working class itself. It would have to be imported into the working class in order to arrest its natural tendency to follow the line of least resistance and rest content with partial amelioration. The acquisition of the appropriate level of culture and intellectual sophistication in order to make contributions to the development of socialist ideology was, Lenin maintained, quite beyond the capacity of ordinary workers.[25] Althusser similarly reminds his readers that a prolonged apprenticeship is obligatory for all those who would enter the arduous trade of 'theoretical practice'.[26] He is unequivocal that:

> Without the efforts of intellectual workers there could be no *theoretical* tradition (in history or philosophy) in the workers' movement of the nineteenth and twentieth centuries. The founders of historical and dialectical materialism were intellectuals (Marx and Engels), their theory was developed by intellectuals (Kautsky, Plekhanov, Labriola, Rosa Luxemburg, Lenin, Gramsci). Neither at the beginning nor long afterwards could it have been otherwise – it cannot be otherwise, neither now nor in the future.[27]

No matter how seemingly 'liberal' or innovatory in thought, the acid test for Marxists (particularly for intellectual Marxists) in the twentieth century remained their attachment to the autonomy of the party vis-à-vis other parties and, as emphatically, its organizational separation and intellectual distance from the class. For many 'external' commentators, this commitment to the party appeared to be a curious act of abnegation by traditionally independent and eccentric intellectuals to the constraints of discipline and the general line. Another way of seeing it, however, is in terms of their necessary solidarity to sustain their group power over the labour movement.[28] Theirs was the conceit born of the assertion that without them the working-class movement could never ascend to adequate consciousness or create an organization capable of transforming society. Theirs, too, was the sobering awareness that without the support of the workers the radical anti-bourgeois intelligentsia would appear as faintly ridiculous and certainly superfluous. Plekhanov, as ever, was quite candid about the instrumental purposes which the proletariat was called upon to fulfil: 'The workers' party alone is capable of solving all the contradictions which now condemn our intelligentsia to theoretical and practical impotence.'[29]

The party was, therefore, of crucial importance to the intellectuals. It had, by the conjuring trick already noticed, inserted itself as an indispensable categorical feature of the Subject itself. Without the party, the proletariat could not be the proletariat, and it only was such to the degree that its actions and attitudes conformed to the Party's specification.

LUKÁCS: POWERLESSNESS OF MASS, POTENCY OF TOTALIZING SUBJECT

The dubious honour of filling out Marx's accounts of class, consciousness, and the role of organization, fell to the trained philosopher and revolutionary adventurer Georg Lukács. However much he might later have disavowed or qualified his stance in *History and Class Consciousness*, his essays remained the fullest, most complex and most influential treatment of these matters in the canon of Marxism. Lukác's arguments were presented in a highly Hegelian form, but their content differs little from what Lenin had earlier maintained, or from what Gramsci was later to write on these matters; more to the point, there was little he said that had no warrant in Marx's original. His sin (if that it was) was to be explicit where Marx had been elliptical about the role of the intellectuals in creating the proletarian Subject.

Lukács has a decidedly bifurcated view of the proletariat. Its consciousness was, he asserted, 'divided within itself'.[30] There is, on the one hand, the empirically given evidence of its divisions, short-sightedness and concern with narrowly economic objectives. On the other hand, the constraints of theory demand that a unified, conscious and therefore organized proletarian force, must assume the role of overthrowing a contemptible bourgeois reality and creating a new society. There was, in short, an 'antagonism between momentary interest and ultimate goal'.[31]

The portrait that Lukács painted of the empirically given proletariat was, frequently, unflattering to a point; dismissive and contemptuous might be more accurate epithets. In almost Hobbesian terms, he laments their 'brutal egoism greedy for fame or possessions'. These men, 'who have been brought up in and ruined by capitalist society', have been reduced to 'automata' and 'slaves of routine'[32] and 'deprived of the practice and tradition of acting independently and responsibly'[33] as well as overdeveloped in their individual consciousness. Trapped in the toils of bourgeois ideology, 'broad sections of the proletarian masses still feel that the state, the laws and the economy of the bourgeoisie are the only possible environment for them to exist in'.[34] In such a social and intellectual milieu, it is hardly surprising that many workers fall prey to the insidious message of opportunists, or vulgar Marxists, that rejects the dialectic and revolutionary struggle, that separates economic from political objectives and is concerned in any case with the proximate demands of the class rather than its ultimate goal. In the more abstruse terminology in which he dressed his discussion, Lukács deploys the dialectical pairing of the empirical with the immanent consciousness of the proletariat – the first is reified, dwelling in separateness, quantification and rational calculation ('mere facticity' Lukács calls it). It concentrates on individuals, things and quantities and is unable to go beyond their immediate appearances. It is static and cannot conceive of the present other than as given, necessary and inevitable. Above all, it cannot grasp process, change and interconnection. Its form of consciousness mimics and reinforces the consciousness of a divided working class that has not yet seen beyond the veils of bourgeois ideology. Its powerlessness and inertia are functions of its internal divisions and its entrapment in its immediate environment.

To remedy this situation Lukács has to invoke epistemological categories that transcend the merely given and the immediate, and the most central of these is his notion of totality. 'The whole system of Marxism', he asserts, 'stands and falls with the principle that revolution is the product of a point of view in which the category of totality is dominant.'[35] No single object, no single 'fact', can be rendered intelligible unless 'we grasp their function in the totality to which they belong'. Marx's method, according to Lukács, was falsely represented by 'vulgar Marxists' as the primacy of economic motives over all others; in fact, it resided in the 'all pervasive supremacy of the whole over the parts'.[36] Nothing, therefore, has significance outside the whole, whilst the whole is enclosed in the story of the smallest part. Without the capacity to comprehend this universal inter-connectedness of things and ideas, 'the "facts" of history must remain – notwithstanding their "value-attributes" – in a state of crude uncomprehending facticity'.[37]

The struggle to embrace totality involved, as Lukács freely conceded, an enormous intellectual labour, for a universal history must embrace all the moments and all the aspects of the past, present and future of mankind's development. The events of the present must, in this account, be seen as universal history and that must be the starting point of the self-knowledge of the proletariat.

> Marx says: 'In order to understand a particular historical age we must go beyond its outer limits'.
>
> When this dictum is applied to an understanding of the *present* this entails a quite extraordinary effort. It means that the whole economic, social and cultural environment must be subjected to critical scrutiny.[38]

The only process of thought capable of comprehending, ordering and integrating these huge theoretical and historical labours is the dialectic. There is, oddly, little that Lukács has to say about the operative principles of this crucial mode of thought and this despite the fact that his book is subtitled 'Studies in Marxist Dialectics'. He contents himself more with assertions than with demonstrations. We are simply invited to assent to the paired propositions that, since totality expresses the essence of Marx's system, the method of its attainment – the dialectic – must be just as integral to revolutionary Marxism: 'the knowledge of reality provided by the dialectical method is likewise inseparable from the class standpoint of the proletariat'.[39] Here, Lukács makes common cause with Lenin who, in 1914, had come to the same conclusion with regard to the centrality of Hegel's dialectic in correctly understanding Marx's method. They were agreed that the fatal methodological error of the revisionists and vulgar Marxists (who had lately betrayed the revolutionary cause and thrown in their lot with their imperialist governments) was precisely that they had adopted mechanical or evolutionary conceptions of development.[40] Bernstein and his acolytes were, in Lukács's view, unable to 'go beyond the immediate simple determinants of social life'.[41] Revisionism, he opined, in a classic Hegelian aphorism, 'elevates mere existence to reality'.[42] The vulgar Marxists and opportunists always and everywhere impugned the validity of the dialectic – that was diagnostic of the slide from militant Marxism to revisionism which itself became a species of bourgeois liberalism. 'Orthodoxy', Lukács insisted, 'refers exclusively to *method*. It is the scientific conviction that dialectical materialism is the road to truth'.[43]

We are told a good deal about what the dialectic can do as 'the science of the general laws of motion', but it is never explained quite how the dialectic does it. It is, emphatically, concerned to step back from the immediate or empirical reality in order to be able to understand the structure and process immanent within it. The dialectic acts to *mediate* the existing or immediate; it mediates between the isolation and divisiveness of the empirical world and the unified totality: above all, it mediates between the incomplete, undeveloped consciousness of the proletariat and its unified all-embracing consciousness that 'is synonymous with the possibility of taking over the leadership of society'.[44] It was, in short, only the totality disclosed by the dialectic that could redeem the empirical powerlessness of the proletariat.

The proletariat's ascent to adequate consciousness was not to be attained purely (or even predominantly) by contemplation. On the contrary, it was central to the case of the whole revolutionary Marxist tradition that it was through its own experience of action that the proletariat came to know its world. This was an activist theory of cognition that was distinct from the path to knowledge of the intellectuals. Not all action could, however, count in this regard. The wrecking activity of Luddites could never generate proper consciousness. Such 'spontaneous, unconscious actions born of immediate despair' generated no constancy of activity, no reflection upon it, and no organization to contain it. Proletarian action to be effective, i.e. to develop and refine consciousness, had therefore to be directed at exposing the contradictions of contemporary society, teasing out its immanent tendencies, and revealing its processes of development. But this is to say that consciousness for the mass can arise only as the *outcome* of action that itself must be informed by adequate consciousness, i.e. a grasp of the totality of existing society and its place in universal history. The proletariat comes to consciousness only *after* the event, only through reflecting on its *praxis* (or mode of activity). Its consciousness, Lukács frequently lamented, was always *post festum*. But just as no single object can be comprehended without a comprehension of totality, so no single meaningful action (i.e. an action tending to refine and develop class consciousness) can be undertaken without precisely the same knowledge.

The way out of this conundrum is, predictably enough, the same as the one discovered by Marx – it is the Party that appears as the indispensable facilitator of all the mediations between the class as it is and the class as it should and must be. 'The form taken by the class consciousness of the proletariat is the *Party*...the Party is assigned the sublime role of bearer of the class consciousness of the proletariat and the conscience of its historical vocation.'[45]

It is abundantly clear from Lukács's whole methodology that the Party, as the repository of adequate consciousness, cannot distil this consciousness from the achieved level of consciousness of the proletarian mass. Adequate consciousness is not 'the inherent or natural possession of the proletariat as a class'.[46] It will advance the matter not one whit to undertake opinion surveys or average out the expectations and aspirations of the empirically given working class. With all of Marx's authority behind him,[47] Lukács declares that 'an organization that bases itself on an existing average is doomed to hinder development and even to reduce the general level.[48] ... This consciousness is, therefore, neither the sum nor the average of what is thought or felt by the single individuals who make up the class.'[49] Not even the most revolutionary worker is capable of overcoming the limitations of his own consciousness or of bridging the distance that separates it from 'the authentic class consciousness of the proletariat'.

A number of important conclusions follow from this analysis of consciousness. In the first place, it has no empirical referents. It is indeed likely to be contaminated if its base line is set by empirical surveys. It follows, as Lukács concedes, that its premise is not an existing consciousness but the evidence of an all-pervading unconsciousness: 'class consciousness implies a class-conditioned *unconsciousness* of one's socio-historical economic condition'.[50] Consciousness within the proletariat has, therefore, to be imputed rather than measured. This, in its turn, is the premise for the existence and activity of the party for if, as Plekhanov had correctly observed, consciousness was a natural or inevitable attribute of the proletariat then the party would have no function. It was precisely the function of the party to bring consciousness to the class. In this respect, as Lukács acknowledges, he agrees with the Marxist orthodoxy of Lenin, who had earlier insisted that consciousness 'would be implanted in the workers "from outside" '.[51] It is for these reasons that the party has to be independent of the class. Lukács has to go further, since for him the development of consciousness is an autonomous process that does not and cannot depend upon empirical evidences either for its formulation or its verification:

> Historical materialism grows out of the 'immediate, natural' life-principle of the proletariat; it means the acquisition of total knowledge of reality from this point of view. But it does not follow from this that the knowledge of this methodological attitude is the inherent or natural possession of the proletariat as a class (let alone of proletarian individuals). On the contrary.[52]

Only vulgar Marxists and reformist social democrats could base their strategy and tactics on the baseline of the ephemeral and unreflected views of actual working men. They trivialize and emasculate Marxism by ignoring the fact that the first and last word of Marxism consists in the recognition of the proletariat as an ideal philosophical category. Only the party, and only the party controlled and led by intellectuals capable of abstracting what must be from what is, is capable of realizing the future. And this will be the realization of philosophy.

In its own existence, therefore, the party must reveal not what the proletariat is, but what it yet might be. 'The Communist Party must exist as an independent organization so that the proletariat may be able to see its own class consciousness given historical shape.'[53] It has to preserve its organizational separation from the class in order to guard against infection by immediacy, facticity and the merely empirical. Lukács's careful formulation of the party's role is clearly designed to avoid these pitfalls: 'The Communist Party is an *autonomous form* of proletarian class consciousness serving the interests of the revolution.'[54]

To apostrophize the proletariat as a purposeful historical actor is to credit it with the ability to represent and articulate its own interests. Throughout the whole of the Marxist tradition a very basic assumption has to be made to the effect that the proletariat disposes of, or distils for itself, a single undivided will. Whether it is conscious of it or not, the proletariat expresses 'The category of totality'.[55] It is the party that is the body that articulates and represents the will of the proletariat – that that will is axiomatically indivisible and single is central to the party's claims to be the *sole* party of the class. To admit of any legitimate pluralism of views in the sense of debates between rival formulations of what is to be constitutive of the socialist project – all this was, to the very last, flatly rejected by orthodox Marxism. The proletarian Subject, to be a potent historical Subject, has to be credited with singleness of purpose. The Communist Party, therefore, 'presupposes unity of consciousness, the unity of the underlying social reality'. The role of the Party 'can be understood meaningfully only if the proletariat's objective economic existence is acknowledged to be a unity'.[56] It is, however, once again clear that there is abundant evidence of gradations and economic rivalries within the class, varying and conflicting accounts of the nature of the situation of the working class and how to alleviate or transform it. For Lukács, it is precisely the existence of such division and dissent that makes it all the more important to insist upon an 'objective' unity. In the linguistic displacement that is so characteristic of Marxism, 'objective' in this usage tends to be used instead of 'immanent' which, to the cynic or critic, might be read as pious projections or system-sustaining prophecy. It is, perhaps, in this light that we can penetrate the murk of such statements as *The objective theory of class consciousness is the theory of its objective possibility.*[57]

The proletarian Subject has, in the words of Lukács, been brought, in and through the Party, almost to its perfected expression, but there is one step to take. Just as the Subject effaces dissent and division in order to express, not an aggregation of wills, but the single unified proletarian will, so the Subject requires of those individuals who recognize their names when called total commitment and perfect subordination. They must be clear that the realm of freedom, which is the goal of the whole movement, imperatively demands the renunciation of all claims to individual freedom. As the consciousness of the class cannot be the aggregation of individual consciousnesses, so the freedom of the class cannot be identified with the sum of individual freedoms. The mass must learn the virtues of subordinating themselves to Party discipline for:

> Only through discipline can the party be capable of putting the collective will into practice... even for the individual it is only discipline that creates the opportunity of taking that first step to the freedom... This is the freedom that works at overcoming the present.[58]

Again, it would seem, the principle of totality and integral unity must be manifest within the thought and actions of the individual whose 'whole personality' must be involved and committed. The extensiveness of the transformative struggle demands 'the *active engagement of the total personality*'.[59] And so it follows that within 'the discipline of the Communist Party, the unconditional absorption of the total personality in the praxis of the movement was the only possible way of bringing about an authentic freedom'[60].

According to Althusser, it was in the nature of ideological constructs to promise freedom but actually to produce the comprehensive subordination of the subjects to the concrete organizational apparatuses that successful ideologies necessarily develop. In the case of Lukács, we see how perfectly his power-laden discourse conforms to the model: to be free entails renunciation of individual freedom and wholehearted identification with the superior will and consciousness that has its material embodiment in the Party:

> The *conscious* desire for the realm of freedom can only mean consciously taking the steps that will really lead to it. And in the awareness that is contemporary bourgeois society individual freedom can only be corrupt and corrupting because it is a case of unilateral privilege based on the unfreedom of others, this desire must entail the renunciation of individual freedom. It implies the conscious subordination of the self to the collective will that is destined to bring real freedom into being... This conscious collective will is the Communist Party.[61]

What Lukács attempted to achieve was to marry Marx's political and ideologized Subject (the class warrior proletariat solidifying itself and learning from its struggles how to eliminate exploitation) to his philosophical Subject (the unalienated, dereified proletariat blessed with a totalizing knowledge of history and society). In the process there was no doubt as to which emerged superior – the former was wholly subordinated to the latter. So much was this the case that the manner in which the class warrior proletariat was supposed to learn (i.e. acquire consciousness) from its actual experience of struggle is conspicuously ignored in *History and Class Consciousness*. The history that is recounted is the history of philosophy. Of Kant and Hegel there is a great deal, but of the conditions and possibilities of actual working-class struggle there is virtually nothing. The immediacy, 'facticity', and divisiveness of the life situation of the proletariat was, indeed, for Lukács, the source of its permanent powerlessness – unless, of course, it was leavened by an intellectual elite that could successfully enlist it to the cause of totality and freedom. But the price that the empirical proletariat had to pay in order to achieve its historical and philosophical empowerment was disciplined subordination to the party, i.e. to the organized philosopher intellectuals. It was much the same message that Antonio Gramsci was to canvass in his *Prison Notebooks*.

ANTONIO GRAMSCI CONSECRATES THE HEGEMONY OF THE INTELLECTUALS

Gramsci, like Lukács, is a man driven by the dream of totality, unity and coherence. He is, if anything, even more rigorous than Lukács in insisting upon the close articulation of the patterns of control through which alone these objectives can be achieved. Hierarchy and stratification, levels of coherence and consequent gradations of power penetrate Gramsci's work through and through. At the apex of the whole system lay the state and at the base the proletariat or the mass, and the mediation between the two was, predictably, the Party.

Every state is, in Gramsci's account, 'ethical in as much as one of its most important functions is to raise the great mass of the population to a particular cultural and moral level, a level (or type) which corresponds to the needs of the productive forces for development'.[62] This instrumentalist relativism with regard to the state and ethics was, as we shall see, to have grave implications for the labouring masses. They were, if necessary, to be ruthlessly remade in their attitudes, physical attributes, and even in their sexual inclinations, in order to fit themselves for the most modern work processes. The ethical state was, further, 'one which tends to put an end to the internal divisions of the ruled, etc., and to create a technically and morally unitary social organism'.[63] The ruthless, authoritarian voice of the Modern Prince resounds throughout Gramsci's writings; Machiavelli sits uneasily beside Marx. On the crucial issue of the nature and function of the state, it was Machiavelli that he found the more congenial. Like Machiavelli, he had a 'realist' and sombre view of the intellectual, moral and political capabilities of the mass. They were, for the foreseeable future, incapable of attaining and exercising that civic virtue which would fit them for the exercise of state power. They were internally divided, had no autonomous will and had not enjoyed 'a long period of independent cultural and moral development on their own'; for such people 'a period of statolatry is necessary and indeed opportune'.[64] The ending of internal divisions and the forging of an intellectually and morally unified society is then the essential role of the state but so, too, in the contemporary context, is the direction of persons and things within the productive process upon which this unity will establish itself. The state here appears not so much as the agency of a specifically national regeneration but rather as the vehicle of industrial modernity. It must, and this is its 'Marxist' integument, be the champion of the most modern productive techniques (Taylorism, Fordism, automation, rationalization, etc.) and must construct those educative and coercive apparatuses necessary to the goal:

> of creating new and higher types of civilization; of adapting the 'civilization' and morality of the broadest popular masses to the necessities of the continuous development of the economic apparatus of production; hence of evolving even physically new types of humanity. But how will each single individual succeed in incorporating himself into the collective man, and how will educative pressure be applied to single individuals so as to obtain their consent and collaboration turning necessity and coercion into 'freedom'?[65]

These were, for Gramsci, the crucial problems of the structure. They express a distinctly illiberal agenda and Gramsci does not flinch from the most illiberal means for their implementation.

The very possibility of establishing the 'technically and morally unitary organism', which is Gramsci's objective, depends upon there being some individuals who cannot only conceive of the project, but who also have the force of will to realize it. The demands made on them are exceptional. They must apprehend the past and present moments of society, not as a mere aggregation of discrete instances, but as a unitary whole. There are few that are by ability, training or inclination equal to this task, but we know their name; they can only be the intellectuals in the traditional sense of the term. In this sense of the term, they are also pre-eminently philosophers, for it is precisely the domain of philosophy to grasp the interconnectedness and unity of things and to make coherent the disparate views about them. It is the philosopher–intellectual alone who can grasp reality at this level of abstraction and generality. He alone has critical consciousness, but:

> To criticise one's own conception of the world means therefore to make it a coherent unity and to raise it to the level reached by the most advanced thought in the world. It also means criticism of all previous philosophy, in so far as this has left stratified deposits in popular philosophy.[66]

At this, the most rarefied level, only the most advanced and developed intellectuals, with a thorough grasp of the historicity and successive phases of cultural, philosophical and social evolution, will be able to grasp the unity and coherence of the present. Only they can actually initiate and innovate, because only they have a purchase on the future. The 'creation of an elite of intellectuals' is, therefore, an absolute prerequisite for the creation of consciousness in the mass and the management of state power. This elite of traditional intellectuals is, indeed, the demiurge of history, for without it:

> A human mass does not 'distinguish' itself, does not become independent in its own right without, in the widest sense, organising itself; and there is no organisation without intellectuals, that is without organisers and leaders, in other words, without... a group of people 'specialised' in conceptual and philosophical elaboration of ideas.[67]

The argument and the arrogance is the same as in Lukács – in both, the discourse of intellectuals is uniquely privileged because only they can grasp totality and this, in turn, confers the right to lead and direct. There is an evident circularity in their argument that if the nature of the project is philosophical (pursuit of totality, universality, end to reification, identity of subject and object...) then only philosophers can lead it, for they alone can conceive and formulate it. The noxious consequences of this stance are common to all such schemes that would prostitute politics to philosophy. The mass (the largely forgotten proletariat) is conceived of in a purely instrumental way. It becomes the passive plastic material that must imperatively be re-formed in order that it may fulfil the role prescribed for it by the state – that is, its share in 'freedom'.

Within Gramsci's conspectus of knowledge there is a second gradation of intellectuals whose competence is of a particular, technical and specialized sort. They do not ascend to the heights of a properly unified conception of the whole, but can participate in its realization so long as they accept their role as executants of a 'philosophical culture'.[68] This group (called variously the 'urban intellectuals' or the 'organic intellectuals') are the 'subaltern officers' to the philosophers' General Staff.[69] The organic intellectuals (unlike the 'traditionals') have the virtue of being embedded in the world of work and production, they are technicians and overseers – professional men who have the capacity for leadership, but only within the framework of an articulated plan and vision. They must, however, recognize their own limitations and be subject to the 'iron discipline' of their intellectual superiors. We already have the construction of a distinctively ideological hierarchy of institutions and disciplinary procedures at the apex of which stand the philosopher–intellectuals.

The third level is the level of the mass. It is crucial to the power of ideology that they, too, should be credited (however notionally) with the capacity to participate in the task of realizing philosophy. The people in the mass can also be admitted to the ranks of the intellectuals if only because they do have *some* ideas. They do, after all, have language, and language itself is a web of ideas and values. At this minimal level all can be admitted *in potentia* to the ranks of intellectuals.[70] They are admitted, however, so that they will be obliged to respond to their names when called, and so that they will be obliged to admit to the poverty of their patchy and eclectic views. The Party, as we shall see, admits them as members of the class only to the extent that they renounce everyday 'common sense', renounce their loyalties to non-Party organizations (themselves the sources of eclecticism), and reform themselves to fit the demands of the modern industrial process.

The formlessness of mass 'common sense' derives in part from the very variety of its sources; tradition, religion, magic and custom. It is a function of the plethora of associations to which individuals belong, each generating separatism and demarcation. 'When one's conception of the world is not critical and coherent but disjointed and episodic, one belongs simultaneously to a multiplicity of human groups.'[71] It is precisely the pluralism of civil society that must be overcome for the good reason that it generates a plurality of identifiers and views and perpetuates superannuated ideas ('Stone Age elements', Gramsci calls them).[72] The dense and diverse structures of civil society, far from being admirable bulwarks against the pretensions of the state, represent for Gramsci so many earthworks and defences which must be stormed and sacked in order that a coherent (therefore unitary) consciousness and organization can be achieved. The diverse, inchoate and incoherent ideas of the mass and their supportive plethora of social organizations, embody so many obstacles to be overcome in the progress towards universality and coherence. They are affronts to organic wholeness and totality. The mass features here as the dramatic foil to the intellectuals; it is the necessary Other to the attributes of philosophy – in every particular it is *not* what the other *is*, and society stands to the Party in exactly the same relationship. Society is fractured and fractious, it is divided within itself and cannot, therefore, distil a 'collective will tending to become universal and total'.[73] Only the Party as proto-state, only this Modern Prince, can provide such a unitary ethical and organizational framework for society. The Party–State itself now features as the supreme standard of the good:

> any given act is seen as useful or harmful, as virtuous or wicked, only in so far as it has its point of reference the Modern Prince itself, and helps to strengthen or oppose it. In men's consciences, the Prince takes the place of the divinity or the categorical imperative.[74]

To be organizationally total the Party–State must also create a form of life that satisfies all its subjects' aspirations. As there can be no alternative morality to appeal to, so there must be no tolerance of autonomous or partial associations, each fostering its alternative focus of loyalty. There is but one focus of loyalty and no intermediate (partial or sectarian) groups can be allowed to insert themselves between the individual and the state.

It always happens that individuals belong to more than one private

association, and often to associations which are objectively in contradiction to one another. A totalitarian policy is aimed precisely at: (1)
ensuring that the members of a particular party find in that party all the
satisfactions that they formerly found in a multiplicity of organizations,
i.e. at breaking all the threads that bind these members to extraneous
cultural organisms; (2) destroying all other organizations or at
incorporating them into a system of which the party is the sole
regulator.[75]

Individualism 'is merely brutish apoliticism, sectarianism is apoliticism'[76] in
that neither has risen to the plane of generality and inclusiveness that is the
state idea. They are both principal targets of the Party which must secure the
integral homogeneity of the class it represents, and homogeneity between
leadership and rank and file, as preconditions for establishing hegemony
over society as a whole. The Party–State aspires to be a homogeneous,
monolithic and totalitarian structure which must be overseen by 'new
integral and totalitarian intelligentsias'. To be effective, to retain its cohesion
and unity of will, the Party must guard itself against the permanent threat of
intellectual and organizational dissent.

For the power of the intellectuals and the party to be total (even
'totalitarian', for Gramsci does not blush at the term),[77] it follows as a
necessary premise that the impotence of the mass must similarly be total. On
this point, as on many others, Gramsci is disarmingly frank. The complex
and lengthy process of creating a 'philosophy which is also politics, and a
politics which is also philosophy'[78] is also the process of the creation of the
intellectuals, and this whole process has its logically necessary counterpoint:

> It is the conception of a subaltern social group, deprived of historical
> initiative, in continuous but disorganic expansion, unable to go beyond a
> certain qualitative level, which still remains below the level of the
> possession of the State and of the real exercise of hegemony over the
> whole of society which alone permits a certain organic equilibrium in the
> development of the intellectual group.[79]

The ordinary mass of people can think nothing, do nothing and be nothing
without the intercession of the intellectual elite. It feels, but does not
understand; it has a spontaneous character, but no consciousness; activity,
but no awareness; it comprehends through faith not reason, so that
didactically the only means of reaching it is through the endless repetition
of the same message wrapped in different coverings. Its province is the
folklore of philosophy, no more than common sense laced with religion.
The mass, it would seem, has the same limited comprehension as
Aristotle's slave, and is, indeed, credited with the same qualities of loyalty
and discipline and the same incapacity to function as an autonomous
being. What human identity they have, Gramsci insists, is given to them
only as members of an inclusive corporate body – the collective worker, or

integral society, or, at the apex, the State. Devoid of creative spirit or organizational ability and incapable of innovation, the mass is unable even to conceive that its own history might be of possible importance. By themselves, they are plastic but inert – a subaltern mass, a turbulent chaos, or an 'impotent diaspora'[80] which, without the theoretical, organizational and disciplining force of the intellectuals would 'vanish into nothing'.[81] The objective of the intellectual elite is, therefore, 'to give a personality to the amorphous, mass element',[82] and to do so the elite has to insert the mass into politics. The 'simple'[83] must be hailed and obliged by a judicious mixture of coercion and consent to answer their names and promise to make themselves anew. They must imperatively recognize that what is needed is 'a new type of worker and of man'.[84]

The transformation required of the 'simple' 'man-in-the-mass' is quite awesome for it entails a comprehensive change of attitude towards work, society, sex and leisure, so that the 'collective worker' can be imprinted by the Party (or the State) with the responses and dispositions required by the latest technology and consequent organization of the work process. Gramsci recognizes that there will be a considerable number of recalcitrants in the grip of the old Adam, seduced by outmoded notions about the dignity of labour and misplaced attitudes concerning the application of individual 'intelligence, fantasy and initiative' within the work process. They fall prey, in short, to superannuated notions that 'humanism' has got something to do with the world of work. It was against such ideas that the 'new industrialism', with Gramsci as its fulsome apologist, was fighting.[85]

In the era of comprehensive mechanization, it is 'the timed movements of productive motions connected with the most perfected automatism that must be developed'.[86] These new methods of work 'are inseparable from a specific mode of living and of thinking and feeling life'.[87] They demand a much more intrusive and all-embracing surveillance and control of the 'private' habits of the individual worker. 'These new methods demand a rigorous discipline of the sexual instincts (at the level of the nervous system) and with it a strengthening of the "family" in the wide sense... and of the regulation and stability of sexual relations.'[88] The worker, it seems, must subject himself to the tutelary regime exacted of a professional athlete by his coach: 'The principle of coercion, direct or indirect, in the ordering of production and work is correct.'[89] The worker, therefore, cannot be allowed to 'squander his nervous energies in the disorderly and stimulating pursuit of occasional sexual gratification'.[90] He or she must be disciplined or coerced to forgo the exhausting dissolution characteristic 'of the petit bourgeois and the Bohemian layabout'. 'Womanizing', Gramsci gravely warns, 'demands too much leisure'[91] and the new age and new demands made on the worker counsel a return to the unaffected sexual mores of the stable monogamous peasant household. 'The truth is that the new type of man demanded by the rationalization of production and work cannot be developed until the sexual instinct has been suitably regulated and until it too has been rationalized.'[92] Gramsci has similar strictures against alcohol, 'the most dangerous agent of destruction of labouring power',[93] or indeed any other libidinous, bibulous, or otherwise exhausting, leisure time pursuit: 'Someone who works for a wage, with fixed hours, does not have time to dedicate himself to the pursuit of drink or to sport or evading the law.'[94]

It was, in Gramsci's puritan universe, part of the historic progressiveness of industrialization not only to submerge the individual in the corporate endeavour, but also, unwittingly perhaps, to subserve the advance of philosophy. Philosophy, in this particular notation, was the ascetic ideal lauded by Plato of the cultivation of reason and the concomitant taming of the instinctive, appetitive, sensuous and acquisitive instincts characteristic of man's animality. The term 'philosophy', Gramsci reminds us, has 'a quite precise meaning: that of overcoming bestial and elemental passions through a conception of necessity which gives a conscious direction to one's activity'.[95] The moral regeneration that the new industrialism made necessary was, therefore, replicating on a social scale, the painful progress of self-mortification that the individual philosopher had to endure in order to become a philosopher. The proletarians too, it seems, were to be called upon to 'make dying their profession':[96]

> The history of industrialism has always been a continuing struggle (which today takes an even more marked and vigorous form) against the element of 'animality' in man. It has been an uninterrupted, often painful and bloody process of subjugating natural (i.e. animal and primitive) instincts to new, more complex and rigid norms and habits of order, exactitude and precision which can make possible the increasingly complex forms of collective life which are a necessary consequence of industrial development.[97]

It was, according to Gramsci, one of the merits of fascism that it had successfully begun to discipline the mass to conform to the dictates of the new industrialism. Disciplining ourselves to the demands of industrialization happily coincides with realizing philosophy in the world, and that, for Gramsci, was the role we played in universal history.

It was to a joyless land, *sans femmes, sans bières* and *sans sports*, that the worker was summoned by the intellectual elite now dressed in state power, dangling the incentive of high wages. As incentives go, this must have appeared unconvincing even to Gramsci himself for, if the quintessential pleasures of working-class life (or any life for that matter) were now on the socialist Index, upon what was the worker to spend his or her increased wage? Gramsci had thought that one out – the workers would become savers with the state so that further capitalization, automation and integral rationalization on a vaster scale could then take place.

Gramsci is too much of a realist to expect that the dangling of these withered carrots would tempt the donkeys from their comfortable (if malodorous) stalls – as a country lad he knew how much more efficacious was the stick. Now Gramsci's tone becomes ominous and his policies draconian. Far from recoiling from the punitive work regime, of which he must have had first-hand experience in the Soviet Union, he is happy to endorse its harsh precepts. Even Trotsky's extreme proposals of 1920 for the militarization of labour in order 'to give supremacy in national life to industry and industrial methods, to accelerate, through coercion imposed from the outside, the growth of discipline and order in production, and to adapt customs to the necessities of work',[98] were wholly valid and correct in so far as they sanctioned state violence against recalcitrants.

Gramsci was clear that this phase of the restructuring of the workers would be intense and more brutal than earlier phases, but the objective, 'the creation of a psycho–physical nexus of a new type, both different from its predecessors and *superior*',[99] warranted the anguish. There was no doubt that, 'A forced selection will ineluctably take place; a part of the old working class will be pitilessly eliminated from the world of labour and perhaps from the world *tout court*'.[100] There is no agency that Gramsci's state will not endorse, no instruments that it will not employ, and no limits that it will recognize, in the business of suborning the workers to the demands of philosophy.

Through the familiar process of Marxist abstraction and sophistry, Gramsci proceeds to demonstrate that the coercive disciplining of the working class, in so far as it 'is exercised by the *élite* of the class over the rest of that same class', can be construed as 'self coercion and therefore self-discipline'.[101] In any case, if the new form of production relations objectively necessitates this moral, psychical and physical regeneration, then the workers themselves must recognize that imperious necessity. But this recognition of necessity is, according to Gramsci, no more than the recognition of the ensemble of productive and social relations in constant change in which we have our being and define our individuality. Human nature lies 'not within the individual but in the unity of man and material forces. Therefore the conquest of material forces is one way, and indeed the most important, of the conquest of personality'.[102] My self-adaptation to the changing demands of the 'material forces' in which I am embedded is, therefore, at once a necessity for my progress and for theirs. It is the recognition of these objective conditions and possibilities that makes me free and confirms my individuality. I can rejoice at being forced to be free.

Gramsci's moral relativism is matched by his institutional relativism. What matters is the integrity of the Party–State, its monolithic character and unchallengeable authority. What matters is its untrammelled power to impose its will (for the Prince is 'the man who wills something strongly [and] can identify the elements which are necessary to the realisation of his will')[103]. Politics expresses itself as 'the intervention of the State (centralised will) to educate the educator, the social environment in general'.[104] The principal task in hand is, therefore, to re-educate and re-form the degenerate mass, to lead the 'simple' into a higher form of life, and to oblige them through coercion and inducements, to play the part allotted to them in the processes of modern industrialism superintended by the state. Politics now reduces itself to an organizational and institutional matter of ensuring the compliance of inferior agencies to superior ones and the optimal articulation of relations between the directive, executive, and surveillance functions of the state:

> The maximum of legislative capacity can be inferred when a perfect formulation of directives is matched by a perfect arrangement of the organisms of execution and verification, and by a perfect preparation of the 'spontaneous' consent of the masses who must 'live' those directives, modifying their own habits, their own will, their own convictions to conform with those directives and with the objectives they propose to achieve.[105]

It is in the thought of Antonio Gramsci that the arrogance of the intellectuals in the Marxist tradition reveals itself as their untrammelled power which signals the nemesis of the proletariat as historical subject. Within Gramsci's social dialectic of interaction between intellectuals and the mass there is the same zero sum game going on as in the general Marxist analysis of the relationship between state and society – the power of the one is a function of the impotence of the other. This, in turn, is no more than a re-specification of Althusser's formulation of the relationship between the Subject and his subjects – as ideology becomes more perfected (compare Feuerbach and Marx on the God–man relation) so the Subject grows in power and the subject is made conscious of his subjection. In Gramsci, this process is pursued to its barbarous theoretical limits. The proletarian subject is stripped of the last remnants of his original Promethean potential and, to signal the metamorphosis, is now contemptuously referred to as the man-in-the-mass or 'the simple'. This refractory mass, far from being the authors of its own destiny (the ruling class), becomes instead the object to be transformed by the imperious will of the intellectuals concretized in the hegemonic state.

CONCLUSION

I have accepted throughout this chapter that the power of ideology is to be found in the gap between what its subject *is* and what it could be or must become. I have further maintained that Marx, at the one point when he self-consciously presented his ideas as an ideological statement, astutely avoided presenting his subject as a philosophical category. Indeed, in the *Manifesto* Marx pours scorn on all those utopian schemata (his own past endeavours included) that based themselves upon one or other variant of the eternal characteristics of human nature. The subject he presented and the constituency he addressed was now precisely located historically and grounded in contemporary economic and sociological reality: it was, of course, the proletariat. This ideologized subject, far from being universal and inclusive, was distinctive – its badge was the exploitation that it suffered. This subject knew its enemies for it confronted them on a daily basis. It would learn how to overcome its enemies in the course of the broadening struggles it would be compelled to mount to protect and guarantee its own existence. The Party was inserted as a crucial step in this progression in that it entered into the very specification of class existence. Ideology, as Althusser reminds us, always has a material, organizational embodiment. It is, none the less, plausible to believe that the industrial worker, as described by Marx, could recognize himself when hailed. Exploitation and deprivation were very palpable things, they could be chronicled (as Engels's *Condition of the Working Classes in England* and Marx's *Capital* demonstrated). It was in history, economics and sociology that Marx located his ideologized subject and it was, therefore, to those disciplines that Marx overwhelmingly devoted himself. It was clearly crucial that the proletariat be empirically constituted. Its lived life, its deprivations and aspirations, its housing, education and sanitary provision, its rates of pay, hours of work and prospects for security were all essential elements of its being, and they were all explored by Marx (and Engels) often in the most detailed way.

It was from the directly recognizable setting of their lived life that the proletarian subjects of the Second International were called to recognize their name and, in their millions, they did so. The 1890s and early 1900s were the salad days of European socialism when all was bright and brotherly and the irresistible growth of the movement made the socialist future a racing certainty. This was the period of the broadest dispersion of socialist ideas, of the exponential growth of party members and the organizational consolidation of socialist parties. All of this was won largely because the workers enthusiastically recognized themselves in the portrait painted by social democratic propaganda and agitation. They recognized their vital interests in the demands for the eight-hour working day and for minimum rates of pay.

It was the First World War that saw the fracturing of socialism and the demise of the Second International; the workers flocked to the colours, nation set on nation, fratricide consumed fraternity, the class struggle was declared suspended for the duration. For Marxists, particularly intellectual Marxists, some explanation had to be found for this wholly unanticipated collapse and 'betrayal'. It was, almost exclusively, Marxists from a high bourgeois intelligentsia background and who had, moreover, little contact with the practical politics of mass democratic movements, who initiated this analysis (Lenin, Korsch, Lukács). For them, the apostasy of the socialist leaders of the Second International proceeded precisely from their preoccupations with the partial, economic and short- or medium-term interests of their constituents. These preoccupations had, quite naturally, generated an overt (or, more generally, an unspoken) presumption that capitalism would increasingly evolve into socialism through the utilization of democratic means for the attainment of state power. Their errors, the critics concluded, were fundamental. They were errors of method and of objective. Methodologically they had substituted a vulgar (and inherently bourgeois) evolutionary determinism for the vitality and interactiveness of Marx's dialectic. They had fallen prey to the giveness of their social and economic environment, they had become entrapped in 'mere facticity'. Sociology was, for Lukács and later for Gramsci, emblematic of this decline and they treated its methods and conclusions with withering scorn. In severing or ignoring the tie of the Marxist dialectic to its Hegelian roots, the economistic Marxists of the Second International had conspired to emasculate its revolutionary force. They had either frankly jettisoned the idea of a qualitative and abrupt transformation (the 'leap' which, according to Lenin, constituted the essence of Marx's method) or else they rhetorically invoked it as a distant abstraction. They had, above all, quite failed to guard the integrity of Marxian socialism as the categorical Other of bourgeois society – the negation of all its values, structures, and justifying principles. The demands of militant Marxism, the critics concluded, had to be pitched in such a way that they *could not* be satisfied by bourgeois society. They would, moreover, have to be pursued in a way that would rupture the existing structures of bourgeois society. What was required was a transcendent tactic and a sublime goal.

All of this necessarily assumed a theoretical prescience that was itself able to step outside of and to reflect upon the giveness of a cultural and economic environment – a consciousness unconstrained by the determined limitations of its own social being. As was the case with Marx's original setting (or convenient sidestepping) of this problem, it was only the intellectuals who could possibly fulfil the vital regenerative role. Critical Marxism of this sort was foundationally dismissive of the economic and social environment of its subject; from such settings treachery and emasculation had proceeded. The subject that was now insisted upon (by Lukács and Korsch) was, explicitly, the philosophical subject – the free, unalienated, defetishized individual who would, in his own person, transcend the pervasive antimonies of bourgeois philosophy. It was the proletarian subject who would finally put paid to the diremptions of freedom and necessity, subject and object, individual and collectivity, and so on. This was, they could plausibly maintain, no more than a restitution of the philosophical humanism of genuine Marxism that had been so trivialized and violated in the career of the Second International.

It is a matter of principle for Lukács that the subject that now appears has no empirical referents. It neither derives from nor is it justified by sociological or economic analysis. A Marxist can indeed accept that 'every one of Marx's individual theses', *all* of Marx's propositions and prophesies in these fields, were mistaken and void without feeling himself in any way challenged in his method.[106] Gramsci is less emphatic in principle, but in practice he almost wholly ignores the lived-life experience and felt needs of the working class. For him such things can play no part in the construction of a genuinely proletarian subject, which is the product of a wholly discrete theoretical practice. Gramsci, too, inveighs against the stultifying entailments of sociological method, rounding on the 'vulgar evolutionism' of Bukharin's attempts to situate the proletarian subject.[107]

The Hegelianizing of Marxism, the restitution of dialectical method and the recovery of Marx's philosophical humanism in the reconstruction of the proletarian subject was, and continues to be, greeted as a profoundly liberatory departure for socialism – particularly, of course, by the intellectuals. In retrospect this was hardly surprising for, from first to last, it was a current of thought that uniquely privileged their discourse. The transmutation of ideology into philosophy necessarily entailed their permanent tutelage. The very idea that the least cultured, least educated class in contemporary society defined itself solely in terms of its capacity to realize the transcendent philosophio–historical goals of Hegelianized Marxism was, at one level, specious nonsense. At another level, it was an ideal vehicle for the reproduction of the power of the intellectuals. They laid upon the slender shoulders of the workers such an intolerable weight that they were bound to buckle and fall. And each time that they did so they could be, and were, arraigned for their frailty – theirs always was the fault and the guilt. And the felt interests of working people – for a degree of security, for a glimpse of luxury for themselves and a better future for their children – all this was studiously ignored or rejected as the fruits of false consciousness and the entrapments of a hegemonic bourgeois culture. As Rudolf Bahro tartly remarks: 'All Marxist discussions since 1914 lead to the conclusion that the interests on which workers actually act are not their real interests.'[108] From the Olympian heights of a high bourgeois background it was easy to be contemptuous of such modest demands and to urge total commitment to the total transformation. But all that this yielded was an open door to the parties of the right and centre who could, more plausibly, present themselves as the workers' champions.

Far from revitalizing Marxism, this arrogant and illiberal movement of critical Marxism became, in the Frankfurt School, ever more abstruse, ever more distanced from the working class, and ever more contemptuous of them as a vehicle of emancipation. Finally, they were condemned by the intellectuals to the dustbin of history as being unworthy of the role allotted to them as the vehicle for the realization of philosophy (and the concomitant rule of philosophers). The idle venture of construing a philosophical politics, the fundamental subversion of ideology by philosophy was, predictably, revealed as illiberal, elitist and profoundly anti-democratic. More to the point, it was shown to be politically irrelevant and wisely rejected by those it had treated with such arrogant contempt.

NOTES

1 Facsimile of front page of the *Massachusetts Review*, vol. xii, no. 3, Summer 1971, facing p. 444.

2 See, for example, R. Miliband *The State in Capitalist Society*, London, Weidenfelt and Nicolson, 1969, *Marxism and Politics*, Oxford, Oxford University Press, 1977 and *Class Power and State Power*, London, Verso, 1983; N. Poulantzas, *Political Power and Social Classes*, London, New Left Books, 1973 and *State, Power, Socialism*, London, New Left Books, 1978; G. Therborn, *The Ideology of Power and the Power of Ideology*, London, Verso, 1980.

3 Gramsci's *The Modern Prince* and his *Prison Notebooks* were deeply influential in the development of modern Marxism and are published in A. Gramsci, *Selections from Prison Notebooks*, ed. Q. Hoare and G. N. Smith, London, Lawrence and Wishart, 1978. On Althusser, texts referred to include *Lenin and Philosophy and other Essays*, London, New Left Books, 1971 and (with Etienne Balibar) *Reading Capital*, London, Verso, 1979. For Marcuse on the state, see particularly *Soviet Marxism*, London, Routledge and Kegan Paul, 1958 and *One Dimensional Man*, London, Routledge and Kegan Paul, 1964. Raymond Williams's *Culture and Society*, London, Chatto and Windus, 1958 and *The Long Revolution*, London, Chatto and Windus, 1961 were also key texts.

4 M. Foucault, *Madness and Civilization*, London, Tavistock, 1971; *The Birth of the Clinic*, London, Tavistock, 1973.

5 M. Foucault, *Power, Knowledge: Selected Interviews 1972–1977*, ed. C. Gordon, Brighton, Harvester, 1980, p. 39.

6 One of the most distinguished exceptions is *Dictatorship Over Needs*, Oxford, Blackwell, 1983 by F. Feher, A. Heller and G. Markus.

7 L. Althusser, *Lenin and Philosophy*, op. cit., p. 162. I make no attempt to reconcile Althusser's views on ideology as expressed here with his very different views on the subject earlier expressed in *For Marx*, (London, New Left Books, 1965), see particularly pp. 231–5.

8 L. Althusser, *Lenin and Philosophy*, op. cit., p. 153, cf. p. 155.

9 Ibid., p. 156.

10 Ibid., p. 166.

11 Ibid., p. 167.

12 Ibid., p. 158.

13 Ibid., pp. 136–7.

14 Ibid., p. 156, cf. p. 158.

15 Ibid., p. 169.

16 Karl Marx, Frederick Engels, *Collected Works*, London, Lawrence and Wishart, 1975, Vol. 4, p. 36. The quotation is from *The Holy Family*.

17 Marx/Engels, *Collected Works*, Vol. 3, p. 186.

18 Marx/Engels, *Collected Works*, Vol. 6, p. 497.

19 Ibid., p. 493.

20 Ibid., p. 494.

21 Ibid., p. 494, see footnote (a)

22 Marx/Engels, *Collected Works*, Vol. 4, p. 37.

23 G. Plekhanov, *Selected Philosophical Works*, London, Lawrence and Wishart, 1961, Vol. 1, p. 404.

24 K. Kautsky, 'Programme for the Social Democratic Party of Austria', quoted by Lenin in *What Is To Be Done?*, *Collected Works*, London, Lawrence and Wishart, 1960–70, Vol. 5, p. 383.

25 I have discussed at length the orthodoxy of Lenin's views on proletarian consciousness in my *Lenin's Political Thought*, Vol. 1, London, Macmillan, 1977.

26 'It is essential to realise that this is a real difficulty that can only be surmounted by an apprenticeship in scientific abstraction and rigour', Althusser, *Lenin and Philosophy*, op. cit., pp. 76–7.

27 L. Althusser, *For Marx*, op. cit., p. 24.

28 It was of course this analysis that pervaded the anarchist critique of Marxism from Bakunin's critique in *Statism and Anarchy* (*Gosudarstvennost i Anarchiya*, Archives Bakounine, Vol. III, Leiden, E. J. Brill, 1967) to Machajski's *Umstvenniye Rabochi*, 2 vols, Geneva, 1905. A more modern variant of some of these themes is Konrad and Szelenyi *The Intellectuals on the Road to Class Power*, Brighton, Harvester, 1979.

29 Plekhanov, *Selected Philosophical Works*, Vol. 1, p. 389.

30 G. Lukács, *History and Class Consciousness*, London, Merlin, 1968, p.70.

31 Ibid., p. 73.

32 Ibid., p. 335.

33 Ibid., p. 267.

34 Ibid., p. 262.

35 Ibid., p. 29. Compare Althusser's exposition of *The Process of Theoretical Practice* which is itself an elaboration of Marx's proposition that 'The concrete totality as a totality of thought, as a thought concretum is in fact a product of thought and conception', Althusser, *For Marx*, op. cit., p. 182.

36 Lukács, *History and Class Consciousness*, op. cit., p. 24.

37 Ibid., p. 171.

38 Ibid., p. 261.

39 Ibid., p. 21.

40 The principal source is Lenin's *Philosophical Notebooks* in *Collected Works*, Vol. 38. I discuss at some length the nature of this methodological shift in Lenin's thought and the impact it had upon his politics in my *Leninism*, London, Macmillan, 1996; see particularly Chapter 9.

41 Lukács, *History and Class Consciousness*, op. cit., p. 9.

42 Ibid., p. 22.

43 Ibid., p. 1.

44 Ibid., p. 228.

45 Ibid., p. 41.

46 Ibid., p. 20.

47 At the beginning of his crucial chapter on class consciousness, (p. 46) Lukács quotes, as his prefatory text, Marx's immanentist appraisal of the proletariat from *The Holy Family* (cited earlier in Note 16), p. 51.

48 Lukács, *History and Class Consciousness*, op. cit., p. 327.

49 Ibid., p. 51.

50 Ibid., p. 52.

51 Ibid., p. xviii.

52 Ibid., p. 21.

53 Ibid., p. 326.

54 Ibid., p. 330.

55 Ibid., p. 174.

56 Ibid., p. 324.

57 Ibid., p. 79.

58 Ibid., p. 316.

59 Ibid., p. 319.

60 Ibid., p. 320.

61 Ibid., p. 315.

62 Gramsci, *Selections from Prison Notebooks* op. cit., p. 258.
63 Ibid., p. 258.
64 Ibid., p. 268.
65 Ibid., p. 242.
66 Ibid., p. 324.
67 Ibid., p. 334.
68 Ibid., p. 345.
69 Ibid., p. 14.
70 Ibid., p. 3.
71 Ibid., p. 324.
72 Ibid., p. 324.
73 Ibid., p. 129.
74 Ibid., p. 133.
75 Ibid., p. 265.
76 Ibid., p. 148.
77 Ibid., p. 148.
78 Ibid., p. 395.
79 Ibid., p. 396.
80 Ibid., p. 152.
81 Ibid., p. 152.
82 Ibid., p. 340.
83 Ibid., p. 33.
84 Ibid., p. 302.
85 Ibid., p. 303.
86 Ibid., p. 305.
87 Ibid., p. 300.
88 Ibid., p. 300.
89 Ibid., p. 301.
90 Ibid., p. 305.
91 Ibid., p. 304.
92 Ibid., p. 297.
93 Ibid., p. 303.
94 Ibid., p. 304.
95 Ibid., p. 328.
96 'Then it is a fact Simmius that true philosophers make dying their profession';
   Plato, *The Last Days of Socrates* Harmondsworth, Penguin, 1969, p. 113.
97 Gramsci, p. 298.
98 Ibid., p. 301.
99 Ibid., pp. 302–3.
100 Ibid., p. 303, cf. p. 298.
101 Ibid., p. 300.
102 Ibid., p. 361.
103 Ibid., p. 171.
104 Ibid., p. 403.
105 Ibid., p. 266.
106 Lukács, *History and Class Consciousness*, op. cit., p. 1.
107 Gramsci, *Prison Notebooks*, op. cit., p. 426.
108 R. Bahro, *The Alternative in Eastern Europe* Brighton, Harvester, 1978, p. 244.

Part IV

American agnostics

Ever since Alexis de Tocqueville's *Democracy in America* and his analysis of the tyranny of the majority there has been an awareness that the egalitarian and democratic society of America brings with it a mass culture that finds little room for the intellectual. Burgeoning economic power, imperial ambitions and the dominance of the television and film industries have served to increase the intellectual's marginalization, fostering the anti-intellectual intellectualism of someone like Irving Kristol. Further, the growth of higher education has drawn independent intellectuals into the universities, producing, critics argue, the demise of the 'public' intellectual.

As elsewhere, intellectuals in America have faced the dilemma posed by the conflicting demands of autonomy and commitment, most obviously in the inter-war exchange with Marxism. But much more than elsewhere, they have confronted the pervasive influence and energy of popular culture, feeling themselves alternatively obliged to uphold the standards of high culture and seduced by the desire for public acclaim. In Richard Hofstadter's terms, the 'tragic predicament' of the American intellectual is found in the conflict between ideals and personal interests.

In this sense, the situation of the intellectual in America is more complex and varied than in other countries and continents. There is no immediate and automatic model to be followed. What it means to be an intellectual has been subject to constant reformulation. The sites occupied by intellectuals have changed. Agendas have been reinvented. Personnel and ethnic groups have evolved. In America, in short, intellectuals have never constituted a unitary class with a fixed sense of mission and goal.

More recently, there has been the charge that America has seen its last intellectuals. The ivory tower of academe, it is claimed, has drawn their fangs, leaving such Vietnam war protest figures as Noam Chomsky in a small minority who continue to voice radical criticism. According to Russell Jacoby, one of the most acute commentators on American intellectual life, America's professoriate is now politicized, yet apolitical. The culture wars in the classroom have replaced the classical political issues of welfare, the economy, the environment and foreign policy as sources of engagement. Rhetoric has replaced substance. One sign of renewal has been the recent emergence of black writers as public intellectuals speaking to a new public about issues that have come to the fore in our post-Cold War world. But even here it is asked if these intellectuals operate too comfortably in the cultural mainstream and too easily at the centre of the elite academic establishment to remain oppositional figures and to avoid becoming media pundits.

What is certain is that American agnosticism about the role of the intellectual is destined to continue. Presently, Michael Walzer's 'connected critic' sits by the side of Richard Rorty's 'ironist' and the 'self-imposed marginality' of Cornell West's 'critical organic catalyst'. No doubt other models will emerge. What forms they will take and in what circumstances they will appear is a matter for future speculation.

11 Freedom, commitment and Marxism
The predicament of independent intellectuals in the United States, 1910–41

Steven Biel

On the eve of the First World War, Randolph Bourne sounded a perennial theme in American intellectual life: the problem of crafting a public role without sacrificing autonomy. 'Our "intellectuals" will have to sharpen up their knowledge, and stiffen their fibre a good deal', he wrote from Paris in 1914, '... before they can take the commanding place of leadership which they fill in France'.[1] Bourne undoubtedly knew that this problem (and its corollary – that European intellectuals had figured it out) extended well back into the nineteenth century, when Emerson grappled with the relationship of the thinker to antebellum reform. Yet Bourne phrased it generationally, as an exhortation to young intellectuals for whom the dilemma of freedom and commitment took shape in the specific historical context of the early twentieth century.

In seeking to resolve the dilemma, Bourne and his generation looked away from the newly established centres of American intellectual life – the universities – which they found too arid and aloof. Ivory tower irrelevance and ineffectuality, they believed, merged with timidity and institutional pressures to produce a climate in which neither engagement nor autonomy was possible. Rejecting the universities, these young intellectuals chose to become free-lancers. They shunned specialization and the cult of expertise in favour of the roles of generalist and prophet. As early as 1910, Bourne and his generation set upon the task of bringing the life of the mind into a more dynamic relationship with the life of society.

Intellectual Marxism is best understood as part of their diverse and continuous effort to find the connection between ideas and action and to make literature and criticism serve the purposes of social change. While we tend to associate this effort with a later generation – the New York intellectuals who gravitated around the *Partisan Review* in the 1930s – it was Bourne's contemporaries (though not Bourne himself) who first saw in Marxism an end to intellectual isolation and marginalization. Marxism offered visions of an expanded community of opposition in which intellectuals and workers would join together as historical agents. Community, criticism and effectiveness all seemed possible within Marx's framework – a framework that suggested the progression from the critique of bourgeois society to an active participation in its overthrow. Though the precise nature of the intellectuals' role in bringing about social transformation was the subject of extensive debate, Marxism seemed to furnish a perspective from which intellectuals could finally make themselves matter. Their struggles serve as a case study in the promises and pitfalls of engagement.

Until the Russian Revolution, Marxism had to compete as one among many possible paths toward regeneration and intellectual commitment. The writers for the *Masses* – the pre-World War I voice of Greenwich Village socialism – possessed at least a superficial familiarity with Marx, but as Leslie Fishbein has argued, his ideas merely blended into an eclecticism that offered 'no coherent theory of social change'. From the beginning, however, Marxism had one advantage over competing perspectives: an aura of realism. When Max Eastman was introduced to Marx and Engels in 1911, his inclination 'toward a kind of pastoral utopia' immediately yielded to a body of ideas that seemed to consider 'the hard facts of human nature' and the real forces at play in the material world.[2] The claim of realism was essential to those like Eastman who wanted to distance themselves from the ivory tower.

With the October Revolution, Marxism's appeal grew dramatically. There could be no greater confirmation of its realism than the fact that it had worked. As Eastman's colleague John Reed gushed, the Revolution had not come 'as the *intelligentsia* desired it; but it had come – rough, strong, impatient of formulas, contemptuous of sentimentalism; *real*'.[3] Reed's reaction represented an ever-present strain in intellectual Marxism. The identification of the working class (or its organized party) as the only genuine force for revolution produced a denigration of the 'intelligentsia' as possessing any superior knowledge or any unique social role. One side of Reed – and of many of his contemporaries – was so eager to join the course of history that he veered into a sometimes strident anti-intellectualism.

In the immediate aftermath of the Revolution, Eastman displayed this anti-intellectual side as he engaged in several exchanges over the proper position for intellectuals to take. By way of an open letter to the French novelist and critic Romain Rolland, published in the *Liberator* in December 1919, Eastman insisted that Marx's division of society into 'the capitalists and the proletariat' precluded all other social groupings. '[M]orally it is distasteful to me to treat of myself, and to see you and those associated with you treat of yourselves, as "intellectuals", and conceive of yourselves as thus forming a separate class', he told Rolland. There was, according to Eastman, 'no independent intellectual class, any more than there is an independent class of drygoods merchants'. The only matter of choice for the so-called intellectuals was to merge into one class or the other, and historically 'the most eminent wholesalers and retailers of intellectual goods' had tended to be 'capitalist–nationalistic in their position'. Eastman's prescription was to drop all claims to an independent standing in society. After the decision to enlist with 'the wage-laborers of the earth', intellectuals should acquiesce in their leadership. 'I would put more trust in the ignorant', advised Eastman, for they were not biased by 'culture and wealth of knowledge' towards conservatism.[4] The class struggle seemed to demand that intellectuals abandon their identity as such and re-emerge as workers who happened to labour with their minds and pens.

He returned to this theme several months later, when it was suggested that the *Liberator* join the international movement *Clarté*, led by the French writer Henri Barbusse. Responding to this call, Eastman announced his 'humble respect' for *Clarté's* roster of intellectuals but confessed to feeling 'alien and opposed' to the whole idea of the organization. In what was the most serious indictment a student of John Dewey could make, he said that the movement smacked of 'bad science – or complete lack of science' because it failed to recognize Marx's substitution of material forces for ideas as 'the real motor forces in social evolution'. Those who clung to the Hegelian fantasy that ideas could have any impact per se were merely trying to assert an impossible claim for themselves as 'natural leaders and light-bringers in a revolutionary age'. Against *Clarté's* conception of a role for thinkers as illuminators of reality, Eastman urged a sober surrender of 'the pretense of revolutionary and intellectual leadership'.[5]

When he heard in June 1921 that *Clarté* had 'purged its ranks of reformers and amateur socialists' and 'accepted the principle of the class-struggle in its full meaning', Eastman was able to treat the movement more kindly. He may also have begun to recognize that he was writing himself into a corner – that his attacks on intellectuals were a form of self-immolation; he was now willing to concede writers a unique place in the revolutionary ranks. Propaganda and education (which were synonymous in Eastman's view) were best left to the party and its publications. So then what could writers contribute to the cause? 'There is no single word for it,' he explained, 'but in my own vocabulary I call it poetry.' As he had argued in *Enjoyment of Poetry* in 1913, 'literary and artistic people' were 'distinguished' by their 'ability to realize – to feel and express the qualities of things'. These 'experts in experience', by conveying reality, could contribute 'something indispensable to the practical movement – something that we might call *inspiration*'.

Whatever concessions Eastman had made to intellectual independence, however, were not sufficient to satisfy those who insisted on a freer and more decisive role for writers. Van Wyck Brooks, whose professed socialism was never anything more than vague, chafed at Eastman's ambiguous statements about the leadership of the Communist Party and rejected the secondary status that writers continued to hold in Eastman's scheme. An inspirational role was not enough, Brooks argued, if autonomy and leadership had to be surrendered to others. Eastman was wrong to suggest that 'literary and artistic people have no grounds for setting themselves up as leaders'. After all, it was the artists and intellectuals – the Pushkins, Tolstoys, Dostoyevskys, Shaws, Wells, Webbs, Morrises, and Ruskins – who made 'the statesmen, the economists and the scientists' possible by creating the 'desire' that 'precedes function'. Neither the working class nor its politicians could ever be awakened except for the words and thoughts conveyed in literature and criticism; without intellectual leadership the masses would remain 'so unconscious as to behave almost as if it were automatic'. And for this leadership to assert itself required nothing 'less than absolute freedom'. From here, the Eastman–Brooks debate devolved into an argument over semantics. Eastman's response, titled 'Inspiration or Leadership', granted that literature might 'sometimes in great hands inspire the workers in a practical movement towards a richer and more universal life for all'. If Brooks wanted to call this leadership rather than inspiration, that was fine. But the workers were still the true agents of change, and presence of artists and intellectuals was probably incidental to the success of any revolution.[6] For all his concessions and the much gentler tone of 'Inspiration or Leadership', Eastman refused to admit what the whole exchange had made abundantly clear: that Marxism had not yet done anything to clarify the intellectuals' social role.

Against the tendency toward anti-intellectualism, a competing strand of intellectual Marxism affirmed rather than denied the motive power of the creative intelligence. The Russian Revolution, according to this affirmative vision, did not point to the submergence of the intellect in the class struggle; instead, announced Floyd Dell in 1926, it offered writers 'the possibility, in the nature at present of a religious hope, of shaping the whole world nearer to the heart's desire'. In Dell's view, the Revolution signalled the end to a century of intellectual and artistic resignation that had followed in the wake of the French Revolution and persisted in the climate of determinism produced by Darwin and the theory of evolution. Even Marx's philosophy, when rigidly interpreted by resigned intellectuals, had served until 1917 as another excuse for 'fatalism'. But the Bolsheviks, Dell explained, had exploded the narrow determinism of the nineteenth century and restored the belief 'that the Great Change was to be effected by a sweeping conversion of men's minds'.[7] In other words, the Russian Revolution had demonstrated the place of human volition – and the centrality of intellectual leadership – in the historical process.

Lenin was the figure who seemed to confirm these beliefs and came to function as a particular kind of hero and model for Marxist intellectuals in America. Even as he was scoffing at the idea of intellectual leadership in his responses to Rolland and *Clarté*, Eastman apotheosized Lenin for his ability to guide and shape the Revolution. In a 1918 poem entitled 'To Nicolai Lenin', Eastman celebrated his hero for bringing 'light' (precisely what he mocked in his attacks on *Clarté*) and 'mountain steadiness of power' to the cause. He returned repeatedly to Lenin in the 1920s as an example of what he termed 'a statesman of the new order', whose supreme trait was that he knew how to think. 'He has the habit of defining a problem before he enters it', Eastman observed, 'and he enters it with the trained equilibrium of one who knows the true relation between facts and ideas in scientific thinking'. Lenin was, in short, the quintessential pragmatist – a thinker constantly aware of the 'concrete situation' and able 'to refocus his powerful will, and to readjust his wealth of ideas, to new states of fact' in order to produce results. As Lenin applied it, Eastman argued, Marxism was flexible rather than dogmatic and permitted the kind of intellectual freedom necessary to ensure its efficacy. In fact, Lenin was so complete a pragmatist – so independent in his thinking because so committed to translating ideas into action – that he did not even consider 'the Marxian theory as anything other than a scientific hypothesis in process of verification'. What his critics called his 'dogmatism' was really the pragmatist's clear identification of an end to be pursued, and what they called his 'opportunism' was simply the flexibility needed to reach this end. When Lenin died in 1924, Eastman eulogized him as 'the first great historic engineer – the first leader of mankind who, instead of unconsciously expressing the dominant social forces of his time, analysed those forces and understood them' and guided 'the one he believed in to its goal'. He was the supreme example of the free but focused intellect as a force for social change.[8]

In less elaborate form, Eastman's intellectual associates joined him in the cult of Lenin. John Reed, who in some places minimized the importance of any leadership, celebrated Lenin as 'the locomotive of history' and a 'strange popular leader – a leader purely by virtue of intellect'. Like Eastman, he took particular notice of the Bolshevik leader's willingness to experiment. Floyd Dell, in a review of Reed's *Ten Days That Shook the World*, focused almost exclusively on the 'towering' figure of Lenin. 'Not by eloquence but by knowledge he becomes the prime mover of revolutionary events', Dell wrote; because of a thorough understanding of reality gleaned from calm and open-minded investigation, everything 'is done as he says – for he is right'. As late as 1936, when Eastman was irretrievably out of favour with Stalinists such as Joseph Freeman, Freeman still paraphrased Eastman on Lenin: 'He was a man who had aroused a class, an entire country to the meaning of scientific knowledge'.[9] For American intellectuals, part of the mystique of the Russian Revolution lay in the decisive role that Russian intellectuals, with Lenin in charge, had played. Here was proof that the critical, creative and socially-conscious intelligence could assert its presence in the thick of vital events.

While no American intellectuals were so hubristic as to see themselves as potential Lenins, many derived from the example of Russia's revolutionary leadership the conviction that they could participate meaningfully in the work of social transformation. Dell joyously proclaimed a new 'era' that would stand out 'among all others in the history of the world for its gigantic conscious effort at political reconstruction'. Within this broad effort, intellectuals and artists, combining 'high philosophic calm' with a 'warm and rich humanity', could take on the responsibility for stating 'the nature of the task which mankind may accomplish'. In its content, as Michael Gold also insisted in his early advocacy of proletarian literature, revolutionary writing could teach the masses 'courage and confidence', lead them 'to scorn the ideals of bourgeois and capitalist society', strengthen the 'sense of community' among workers, and contribute to 'an indomitable will to victory and freedom'.[10]

More importantly, the *act* of literary expression could provide glimpses into the life of fulfilling work and human freedom that would emerge from the revolution. Dell poked fun at Gold's 'romantic delusion that he belongs to the working class' and his apparent shame at 'not being a workingman' as signs of a self-defeating and socially unproductive kind of anti-intellectualism. In April 1922, Gold had publicly refused to review Harold Stearns's *Civilization in the United States* on the grounds that even in skimming the book he had smelled 'the faint, acrid aroma of intellectual irony' and aloofness. The proletariat, he argued, had 'no time to think or lead full-orbed lives', and so the intellectuals, in urging a life of 'Art and Culture', were guilty of bourgeois sympathies. Dell retorted that, like it or not, 'Comrade Mike' was 'a literary man, an intellectual', and that there was 'nothing to be ashamed of in that'. The writers' revolutionary task of explaining, encouraging and teaching could only be accomplished if they were 'free from the necessity of toiling eight to fourteen hours a day'. It was only with 'leisure', Dell instructed Gold, that artists and intellectuals could make their contributions; and it was in demonstrating the creative possibilities of both work and leisure that they made their most substantial contribution to the revolution. The free life of the artist–intellectual was the only existing model for the life of all in the classless society. 'He has come back from the stoke-hold talking about how beautiful Strength and Steam and Steel and Noise and Dirt are', Dell remarked of Gold. 'If so, I say, why abolish capitalism?'[11]

Such varying conceptions of the writer's relation to the revolution continued to form a sub-theme of intellectual discourse through the 1930s. A manifesto prepared by Edmund Wilson, Lewis Mumford, Waldo Frank and John Dos Passos in 1932 expressed the belief that 'in imaginative works, in philosophic thought, in concrete activities and groups, the nucleus and the framework of the new society must be created *now*'. The purpose of 'the social–economic revolution', they contended, was to 'release the energies of man to spiritual and intellectual endeavor'. Through the practice of their craft, writers could see to the other side of the revolution, where self-interest has surrendered to self-expression and community, and could pass this vision on to the masses.[12]

The belief, not only that criticism, free inquiry and creativity were possible within a Marxist framework, but that they were essential to revolutionary progress, informed the efforts of American intellectuals to publicize and interpret the class struggle in the middle and late twenties. By the fall of 1922, with Max and Crystal Eastman living abroad, the *Liberator* had exhausted its funds, and Michael Gold expressed his concern that it would have to be turned over 'to some individual or some party that can put it on its feet'. Despite their wish 'to maintain the independent character of the Liberator', Gold, Dell and Freeman failed to find an alternative source of income and finally agreed to surrender control to the Communist Party. Almost immediately after the disappearance of the *Liberator*, its former staff and contributors began to perceive the need for a new magazine of independent radicalism.[13]

To rally support behind the venture, the organizers made explicit reference to the *Masses* – a name certain to resonate among American intellectuals as a symbol of free expression. The aim was to put together as diverse and impressive a roster of contributing editors as possible and to make clear from the start the new magazine's commitment to open discussion. Among those who worked actively to launch the publication were Frank, Freeman, Gold and Dos Passos; the list of less active supporters included Eastman, Brooks, Mumford and Wilson.[14]

The official announcement of *New Masses* placed the magazine firmly within a tradition of intellectual independence by claiming, under the heading 'Our Inheritance', a direct descent from the old *Masses*. 'Its sympathies', the editors declared, 'will be frankly radical, but it will have no affiliations with any political party and be committed to no special propaganda'. The first issue, which appeared in June 1926, seemed to confirm the announced policy by featuring an enormous list of contributing editors and a debate between Dos Passos and Gold on the meaning of intellectual independence. Dos Passos stated his concerns about 'phrases, badges, opinions, banners imported from Russia or anywhere else'. The *New Masses* had to be 'a highly flexible receiving station', 'full of introspection and doubt' rather than 'an instruction book'. Gold did not disagree. He merely accused Dos Passos of wanting to 'revolt blindly' rather than with 'full, bold, hard consciousness'. He was not, he insisted, urging slavishness; it was absurd to think that American intellectuals would 'take their "spiritual" commands from Moscow'. But neither would he 'deny that Soviet Russia and its revolutionary culture' formed 'the spiritual core' around which all genuinely committed artists and writers were 'building their creative lives'. For Gold, the Marxist framework was broad enough to allow for flexibility and indigenous expression while providing the 'scientific' perspective without which all artistic and intellectual efforts were doomed to insignificance.[15]

Events in the Soviet Union soon forced Gold to define more clearly how much independence Marxism permitted before the cause of revolution was jeopardized. It was his old friend Max Eastman, back from Europe and openly siding with Trotsky against Stalin, who tested the sincerity of the commitment of the *New Masses* to open discussion. Eastman's name had appeared on the masthead from the beginning, not because he was making any direct contribution to the magazine, but because he, as its editor from

1912 to 1917, could lend the prestige of the old *Masses* to the effort. When he returned to the United States in 1927, he looked to the *New Masses* as a forum for his views, only to find that his critical opinions of the Stalin dictatorship were unwelcome. In his letter of resignation, Eastman argued that he had joined the *New Masses* in the understanding that it would be 'independent of all dictation – a "free revolutionary magazine" '. He had discovered, however, that 'through fear of the loss of patronage or circulation, or through mere fear of stating the facts of life', the editors were either directly or indirectly obeying 'the dictation of party heads'. In Eastman's view, 'this confused and pussy-footing policy' showed a 'lack of intellectual force and courage' and was 'harmful to the advancement of a genuinely revolutionary culture in America'. By excluding criticism and dissent, the magazine was abandoning its function of interpreting American conditions and fashioning a revolutionary course in keeping with these conditions.[16]

Worried that Eastman's complaints would jeopardize the magazine's funding, the editors tried to clarify its politics. The *New Masses*, they explained, was not an official party publication, but they drew the line at any views that might threaten its place within the revolutionary movement. The inclusion of anti-Soviet opinions would put the *New Masses* outside the realm of influence. While it remained 'dedicated to the job of drawing together the progressive radical elements, not widening their differences', there were limits to what was genuinely progressive or radical; independence must not interfere with effectiveness. Michael Gold's dismissal of the Trotskyites in 1930 summed up this line of reasoning. 'They are', he wrote, 'separated from the main stream of history', and nothing was more distasteful to Gold than the thought of being relegated to the periphery.[17] While Eastman now believed that a critical Marxism was the only path towards meaningful change, Gold and his *New Masses* colleagues were reaching the conclusion that the commitment to free discussion stopped short of permitting ideas that endangered the revolution or went against the apparent course of history. By the end of 1929, Floyd Dell had also resigned and earned Gold's eternal enmity. In October 1933, the Communist Party took control of the *New Masses* and thus brought a conclusive end to the experiment in independent Marxism.[18]

Eastman carried on his pursuit of a scientific Marxism despite the opposition of the *New Masses*. In V. F. Calverton's *Modern Quarterly* and in his books, Eastman produced a critique of Marxist orthodoxy that would, he believed, serve as the first step toward the creation of a more legitimate alternative.[19] He was guided in this task by a hostility to Stalin which extended as far back as Lenin's death. Eastman had, in effect, declared his independence in 1925, when he published Lenin's testament – a document that suggested Lenin's hatred of Stalin and his wish to be succeeded by Trotsky. The crisis in the Soviet Union compelled Eastman to search out its causes, which he discovered to be intellectual in nature; there had to be something wrong with Marx's *ideas* to produce such unfortunate results. In a curious interpretation of political developments, Eastman insisted that flaws in philosophy were responsible for Stalinism, and this, in turn, implied that a revision of Marx was necessary to produce a true socialism. By an intellectual tour de force, Eastman made his own work the key to revolution.

Marx and Lenin: The Science of Revolution (1927) was the fullest and most intelligent discussion of Marxist philosophy produced to date by any American intellectual of Eastman's generation. The book did not offer a new assessment of Lenin, whom Eastman still presented as the leader of a corps of 'scientific revolutionary engineers', but Eastman was no longer prepared to view Marxism as an inherently scientific framework. Rather, he argued, Lenin was heroic precisely because he had gone against the essentially religious thrust of Marx's thought. Marx had never been able to cure himself completely of the 'mental disease' of Hegelianism, described by Eastman as 'an unintelligible mixture of emotional mysticism and psychological half-truth'. In retaining the dialectic, even after substituting materialism for idealism, Marx and Engels perpetuated the belief that history was unfolding 'in a congenial direction'. Marxism thus possessed 'the essential features of a religious psychology' – the faith 'that the universe itself is producing a better society' and that people need 'only to fall in properly with the general movement of this universe'. In short, wishful thinking – what Eastman called the 'animistic habit' – lay at the heart of Marxist orthodoxy. Dialectical materialism identified the goal of a communist society with the inevitable course of history.[20]

Eastman was most disturbed by the apparently fatalistic quality of Marxist metaphysics. Marx and Engels had failed to recognize that human purpose, not 'History', was what really produced social revolution; they lacked any conception of 'true science', of 'defining a purpose and compelling the external world into its service'. Eastman could not tolerate any system that seemed to deny the creative potential of thought, and the rigid economic determinism that he attributed to Marx and Engels implied such a denial. Their failure to differentiate between conditions and causes had produced a false view of history as a process beyond human control, shaped solely by unmanageable economic forces. In reality, Eastman contended, economic forces merely suggested the boundaries of human intervention and, if properly understood, contributed to the kind of scientific outlook that allowed people 'to control history to the fullest possible extent'. This was Lenin's genius. Lenin, according to Eastman, had no real interest in the dialectic; if he believed in it at all, he managed to escape from its deleterious effects by disguising his experiments in 'practical engineering' as parts of some inevitable historical process – in other words, without letting it be known, he was 'heretical', and the Bolshevik Revolution, a product of scientific thinking, 'was a violation of Hegelian Marxism'. Lenin temporarily transformed Marxism from a religion into a science, which, as Eastman described it, met all the criteria of Dewey's instrumentalism.[21]

After Lenin's death, however, Soviet Marxism turned back towards religion. Eastman concluded *Marx and Lenin* by connecting the bureaucratic statism of Stalin's Russia with a return to dialectical materialism. Either through his own ignorance, or in a conscious effort to consolidate his power, Stalin was using Marx's belief in the inevitable progress of history toward communism (the withering away of the state) to justify his counter-revolutionary actions. As Eastman viewed it, 'animistic mysteries have always been employed by an aristocracy to befuddle the masses', and in this case, they were being used to postpone or avoid the building of true communism.[22] In its orthodox form, Eastman was suggesting, Marxism could justify any evil. The salvation and extension of the revolution demanded that Marxism be revised from a religion into a science. *Marx and Lenin*, presumably, was the first step.

By the late twenties, Eastman had completely abandoned his earlier assumption that intellectuals would do best to blend inconspicuously into the proletariat. He now insisted that intellectual independence was crucial, not so much for its own sake as to provide intelligent guidance to the processes of social change. Though isolated from many of his old colleagues, Eastman could take solace in the apparent fact – by his own reasoning, at least – that he still had an important role to play in the revolutionary movement. It was the critical Marxist, the scientific Marxist, who was the sole hope for the revolution.

The Depression pushed more of Eastman's contemporaries toward Marxism, but the shift toward an explicitly Marxist critique of capitalism did not signal the repudiation of the long-standing goal of intellectual autonomy. Appealing as they were in providing context and structure, Marx's ideas were equally attractive for their apparent incompleteness and flexibility. In explaining his move to the left after 1929, Waldo Frank confessed that the desire 'to play a role of action' was paramount. But Frank and others responded to the promise of involvement in the belief that this need not preclude independence. The Communist movement required the 'vision' that only writers could provide; the function of the intellectual as fellow traveller was 'gradually to win' the Communists 'to a deepening of their doctrine'. Frank approved of Edmund Wilson's demand that American writers 'take Communism away from the Communists' – that they take the lead in producing an independent Marxism better suited to American conditions. In the first half of the 1930s, there was reason for intellectuals to hope that they were on the verge of creating an autonomous yet decisive social role for themselves.[23]

Amid such hopes, independence was a persistent matter of concern. Though he felt drawn to the left as early as 1930, Wilson resisted what he saw as the alien, religious character of Communism. He had tried 'to become converted to American Communism in the same way that Eliot makes an effort to become converted to Anglo-Catholicism'. But there was something artificial about Communism as it was currently constituted in the United

States; it was somehow 'unrelated to real life' – foreign rather than indigenous and ritualistic rather than adaptable.[24] He was not convinced, however, that these problems were insurmountable. In the *New Republic* symposium of 1931 in which he called upon intellectuals to rescue Communism from the Communists, Wilson pressed for a resurgent opposition that would 'not be afraid to dynamite the old shibboleths and conceptions and to substitute new ones as shocking as possible'. Presumably, this would differ from previous iconoclasm by substituting the sharper knowledge of society gleaned from Marx for a vague discontent and by recognizing that it was the 'social system' itself that was responsible for America's lack of a 'common purpose' and 'common culture'. With a clearer focus and a potential audience shocked into the realization that life in capitalist America was 'meaningless', criticism stood a better chance than ever of becoming an authentic social force. The key to effectiveness, however, was intellectual integrity; there was no room for hackneyed phrases and borrowed ideas. 'Who knows', Wilson asked, 'that if we spoke out now with confidence and boldness, we might not find our public at last?'[25]

The articles that followed Wilson's in 'The Position of the Progressive' series continued to insist on the necessity of intellectual independence. Matthew Josephson argued that intellectuals were uniquely capable of feeling and exposing the ills of capitalism. 'I have always believed that the intellectual classes combat the profit-making order', he wrote, 'not only because of their increasingly small part in it, but also because of the moral nightmares it gives them. The moment you are disinterested, as scientist, artist or teacher, you are hemmed in, jostled and harassed on every side by the stupefying principle that determines the whole environment: buy cheap and sell dear.' By Josephson's reasoning, the fact that capitalism conspired against disinterestedness automatically placed intellectuals in opposition to bourgeois society and meant that disinterested thinking was, by its very nature, of service to the revolution. The intellectual's function was twofold: to agitate and convert. Through 'the method of moral indignation', intellectuals aroused the public; daring ideas, conceived by minds that functioned outside the profit-making order, possessed 'psychological appeal' and 'practical force'. As a class apart, neither interested in the preservation of capitalism nor beaten down by it, 'dissenting thinkers' were equipped to attack the status quo and to 'imagine and picture the new state in all its forms'.[26]

Benjamin Ginzburg went even further in defending the autonomy of intellectuals while insisting on the practical value of 'cultural activity'. Ginzburg warned against the tendency among 'professional intellectuals' towards 'a depreciation of their intellectual crafts in favor of a mysticism of social action' and criticized 'the anti-intellectualism of the American intellectual, who is overawed by the practical sweep of American life'. In one of the most perceptive self-analyses produced by an American critic in these years, he observed that 'in no country is the intellectual so preoccupied with affecting the course of politics to the exclusion of his intellectual interests. The less power he has of determining conditions, the more passionate, it would seem, is his will-o'-the-wisp quest of political influence'. The alternative to this 'messianic inversion of values' was to recognize that the 'real connection' between intellectual endeavour and social change could occur only when the autonomy of 'intellectual and cultural activities' was absolute. These were the activities that 'form the cradle of values, from which emerge the forces of spiritual generosity, freedom and disinterestedness that become crystallized, however slowly, in politics'. From Ginzburg's perspective, preserving 'intellectual values' was a vital precondition for 'intelligent action'.[27] On this point, at least, the participants in Wilson's forum were in agreement. No matter how great the allure of commitment, few among Wilson's contemporaries were willing to sacrifice their identities as critics to the cause of revolution; nor, as their hopeful statements suggested, did such a sacrifice seem necessary. The revolution would not only tolerate, but in fact seemed to demand, independent voices.

The idea that Marxism was pliable, that it lent itself to adaptation and revision for purposes of efficacy, surfaced often in the writings of intellectuals for whom Marx was a relatively recent discovery. Waldo Frank, for example, trumpeted his independence at the beginning of *Dawn in Russia*, an account of his Soviet travels published in 1932. Frank insisted on the role of 'intelligence and will' in shaping revolution and thus felt an obligation to improve upon Marx; the book was a combination of reportage and Frank's own version of Marxism – the somewhat formless theory he later termed 'integral Communism'. Enamoured of Russia, he was concerned, nevertheless, that its 'militant ideology' would harden into dogma. 'What', he asked, 'may become of the relative truths of great men like Marx and Lenin – men who were the first to disclaim dogma and to stamp their doctrines as a method of action bound to shift as the scene of action shifted?' Like Eastman, Frank identified dialectical materialism as the troublesome component of Marxism. Frank's concern, however, was not with the dialectic, but with materialism. Because Marx had been forced to wage war upon traditional religion, Frank argued, he had adopted a terminology which emphasized the hard facts of existence and the mechanics of life. The danger was that once the 'first battles' to alter material conditions had been won, there was little in Marx to guide the revolution away from material values, 'from the economic stage of proletarian dictatorship into the cultural stage of Communism'. Somebody had to supply 'a vision of life as deep and broad and flexible as growing life itself' to carry the revolution beyond the 'mechanical and lifeless'. In contrast to Eastman, whose revisions were intended to make Marxism less rather than more religious, Frank took it upon himself and his fellow writers and artists to add this spiritual dimension to Marxism: 'to make it the religious movement for which the world is passionately crying'. The greatest possible betrayal of the revolution would be for intellectuals to stop interpreting and to accept Marxism as a closed system. 'To be a good Marxian', Frank bluntly put it in the September 1932 *New Masses*, 'is to be creative enough to go beyond Marx'.[28]

If intellectuals brought well-established concerns about autonomy into their considerations of Marxism, direct observation of Communist Party activities and troubling information about Soviet attempts to control the literary sphere deepened these concerns. After Wilson witnessed party organizers at work during the miners' strike in Harlan County, Kentucky, he 'came back convinced that if the literati want to engage in radical activities, they ought to organize or do something independently – so that they can back other people beside the comrades and so that the comrades can't play them for suckers'. By June 1932, he was willing to agree with Dos Passos and to advise Frank, who had also been to Harlan County, that their proposed intellectual manifesto had to avoid following 'the Communist formulas too closely'. Wilson veered between the belief that 'serious revolutionary work' was 'impossible' without 'obedience to central authority' and the sense that nothing valuable could be accomplished by 'mere parrots of the Russian party and yes-men for Stalin'. The furthest he would go in submitting to party 'discipline' was to vote the Communist ticket in the November 1932 presidential election.[29]

A more detailed statement of the threats to independence came from the embattled Max Eastman, a party member for a short period in the early twenties, who now emphatically rejected any such compromises of autonomy. In *Artists in Uniform* (1934), Eastman returned to his favourite theme of the evils of dialectical materialism – the 'veritable theological bludgeon with which men of independent thought and volition are subdued to silence and conformity'. Because the success of the class struggle depended upon an 'inflexible integrity of vision and speech', the spectacle of writers and artists slavishly submitting to the commands of the Comintern was profoundly unsettling. Eastman's specific target was the staff of the *New Masses*, whose 'enthusiastic approval' of its own 'dressing-down' by the International Union of Revolutionary Writers was the most disturbing example yet of 'the dwindling dignity of the literary mind' and of 'political (and financial) abjection parading as leadership in the creation of a new culture'. Writers like Michael Gold were 'sickly and unsound', Eastman wrote; 'they do not believe either in science or art or in themselves'. Their subservience represented a betrayal of their calling and, ultimately, of the revolution itself. If the purpose of the revolution was to set people free, the surrender of artistic and intellectual freedom was pointless at best and counter-revolutionary at worst. By 1934, the critic who had blasted Rolland and Barbusse for their bourgeois delusion that writers were a class unto themselves was instructing his colleagues to refuse to join any 'practical organization' and to 'assert with self-dependent force' their 'own sovereignty'.[30]

Those who attended the first American Writers' Congress in April 1935 did not heed Eastman's advice about organizations, but they did conceive of the Congress as an effort to establish writers as a sovereign force in the revolutionary struggle. While the Communist Party viewed the Congress and its offshoot, the League of American Writers, as components of the new Popular Front strategy, many of the participants used the occasion to advance the cause of intellectual independence under the Marxist rubric. Joseph Freeman may have acted cynically when he spoke in only the most general terms about writers being 'an integral part of the working-class movement' and argued that their best work would emerge 'out of active identification with it', but he had Eastman's *Artists in Uniform* specifically in mind and knew that he had to contend with questions about autonomy. What is most striking about the proceedings of the Congress is the amount of attention paid to issues of free expression. There was, of course, considerable discussion of the subject of Malcolm Cowley's address: 'What the Revolutionary Movement Can Do for a Writer'. Cowley and others celebrated the movement's value in carrying writers 'outside themselves, into the violent contrasts and struggles of the real world'. There was also, however, frequent discussion of the participants' other major concern. Cowley himself touched on the problem of independence when, in the vein of Eastman (*persona non grata* at the Congress for being too outspoken on Stalin and the party), he referred to Marx and Lenin as 'scientists of action' and thus implied the value of flexibility and critical inquiry.[31]

The most direct comments on this matter came from Dos Passos, Frank and Kenneth Burke. Dos Passos warned against 'letting the same thuggery in by the back door that we are fighting off in front of the house' and urged openness in place of 'minute prescriptions of doctrine'. Frank, who was elected chairman of the League, insisted again that the embrace of Marxism must not preclude intellectual independence: 'We have to believe in our own work and in the necessity of the autonomy of our own work as craftsmen and writers.' Burke's paper, with its controversial claim for the importance of symbols as well as material forces, and its call to replace 'workers' with 'people' in revolutionary discourse, was itself an example of intellectual autonomy. 'Revolutionary Symbolism in America' spoke simultaneously to the issues of independence and efficacy by contending that a formulaic 'proletarian' approach would unnecessarily constrain writers while alienating 'the unconvinced', who could be enlisted only by using '*their* vocabulary, *their* values, *their* symbols'. Burke even tried to rescue the term 'propaganda' from its negative connotations of rigidity and uniformity. The function of revolutionary intellectuals was to 'propagandize by inclusion, not confining themselves to a few schematic situations, but engaging the entire range of our interests'. Generalists, rather than dogmatists, as Burke saw it, were the most effective propagandists.[32]

Despite the later belief among many of those who attended the Writers' Congresses and joined the League that they had been 'duped', the decision to participate was usually made in the same spirit as the decision to stay out.

Participation did not necessarily indicate a lapse in judgement or a capitulation for the sake of a sense of involvement. Burke, Frank, Dos Passos and Cowley believed that their presence would help give the organization an independent stature and that this, in turn, would bind the intellectual community together as a sovereign social and political force. It was such a conviction that allowed Brooks to belong to the League while lashing out at doctrinaire Marxist criticism for denying 'the independence of the literary mind'.[33] Edmund Wilson, on the other hand, chose 'to keep as far from the whole business as possible' in the belief that writers were best off avoiding all chances of getting dragged into petty party squabbles and doctrinal disputes. Wilson's advice to Dos Passos, whose address to the Congress he admired, was to leave 'political controversy' to the Communists and merely do the important work of the independent writer. To denounce obstructions to free expression within the context of such an organization was 'to enter into politics oneself and to have to take political responsibilities'. Why not function outside the League and write on one's own terms? Wilson declared his own independence by resigning 'from everything that I was aware of being associated with' and by writing to the officials of the Writers' Congress 'that they either ought to include the members of heretical groups or change the wording of the sentence in their program about inviting "all revolutionary writers" '.[34] For both Wilson and Dos Passos, however, the desideratum was the same: critical discussion in the service of social reconstruction.

Even the party members among Wilson's contemporaries felt compelled to wrestle with the issue of intellectual and artistic freedom. Perhaps Michael Gold's statement at the first Writer's Congress that there was 'room in the revolution' was merely lip service to attract a wider range of writers under the emerging Popular Front programme. But Gold, for all his willingness to advance the party line, was also a product of the old *Masses* and an intellectual culture that placed a high value on independence. Lewis Mumford, who had attended City College with Gold, spoke even after being vilified by his old friend of 'something vehement, defiant, deeply human ... that made his conversion to communism and his acceptance of its regimentation of mind deeply foreign to his character'.[35] In his own effort to reconcile thought and action, Gold no doubt came down on the side of action – often to the point where he verbally liquidated writers who struck him as bourgeois or counter-revolutionary. Yet, he too was trying to discover a role for the 'revolutionary intellectual' and the 'activist thinker' that would allow for the preservation of intellectual identity while also forwarding the class struggle. Thus, he admired John Reed, who had succeeded, in Gold's view, in combining the careers of 'active revolutionist' and 'pioneer revolutionary writer'. For Gold, 'proletarian literature' was a broad enough rubric to permit a maximum of artistic freedom and still fulfil a revolutionary purpose. The sole constraint upon the revolutionary writer, Joseph Freeman argued in a direct attack on Eastman, was not to be 'remote from the revolution' and not to write about 'the self-indulgences of the philistine'.[36] Gold, Freeman and others who were willing to link their fortunes with the Communist Party did so in the belief that what Freeman referred to as the fusion of art and life demanded it. In their minds, this choice did not represent a repudiation of intellectual independence so much as a channelling of independence into socially productive channels. It was only the freedom to be irrelevant that they despised.

After 1935, in what was more a gradual dawning than an epiphany, American intellectuals abandoned the conviction that Marxism lent itself to revision and criticism. Revelations about the Moscow trials, Communist activities in the Spanish Civil War, the vilification and assassination of Trotsky and the Nazi–Soviet pact functioned to undermine the assumption that Marxism permitted dissent and invited intellectual autonomy. By 1941, Gold and the few remaining Stalinist intellectuals in the United States were forced to give up the pretence of flexibility and to declare emphatically that writers were best off when they submitted to the direction of the party. In an attempt to rewrite recent American literary history in light of the Hitler–Stalin agreement, Gold credited the 'strong, able and culturally developed' Communist movement with saving 'the majority of American intellectuals' from the fate of becoming 'fools, dupes, and fascists' and giving 'these groping intellectuals a form and philosophy for their inchoate disillusionments and rebellions'. If it was 'a Communist "dictatorship" ' that had 'forced the writers out of the bourgeois caves of class blindness and despair', then he was all for it; the alternative, it seemed, was 'lackeyism to capitalism'.[37]

Most of Gold's contemporaries agreed with him only to the extent that they, too, came to see Marxism as incompatible with intellectual independence, and few accepted his conclusions about the benefits of submission. The literary production that best embodied this shift in understanding was Wilson's magnum opus of the 1930s, *To the Finland Station*. Though he did not complete the book until 1940, Wilson published the first chapters in the *New Republic* as early as 1934 and conducted part of his research on a Guggenheim Fellowship in the Soviet Union in 1935. Before departing, he confided the purpose of his work to Dos Passos. 'What is needed', he wrote, 'is to see Marx and Lenin as a part of the humanistic tradition which they came out of' – the tradition of the Enlightenment and the French Revolution that had divided in the nineteenth century into the bourgeois pessimism of writers such as Taine and the revolutionary hopefulness of Marx and Engels.[38] Wilson conceived of the project as a necessary recontextualization of Marxism to save it from the dogmatists and party officials and to demonstrate, as he put it in *Travels in Two Democracies* (1936), that 'the socialist ideal is more natural to us than to the Russians'.[39]

An important step in the recasting process was to demonstrate that Marx and Engels themselves were not doctrinaire when it came to explaining the place of writers in society. Marx, Wilson wrote in his essay 'Marxism and

Literature' (1938), never 'worked out a systematic explanation of the relation of art to social arrangements', and he did not treat literature as 'wholly explicable in terms of economics'. Rather, he and Engels tended to see these as activities that worked 'to get away' from their 'roots in the social classes' and to develop their own 'discipline' and 'standards of value, which cut across class lines'. Set free from narrow economic and social determinants, literature and art might then 'reach a point of vitality and vision' where they could 'influence the life of the period down to its very economic foundations'. It was Wilson's contention that Marx and Engels recognized the possibility of ideas acting as independent historical forces and that, true to the spirit of the founders, Lenin and Trotsky had 'worked sincerely to keep literature free'. Stalin, on the other hand, had corrupted 'every department of intellectual life, till the serious, the humane, and the clear-seeing' were forced to 'remain silent'.[40]

To the Finland Station further wrestled with the problem of the superstructure – the independence and motive force of ideas – that Wilson had begun to explore in 'Marxism and Literature'. In the spring of 1938, Wilson read Eastman's *Marx and Lenin*, which he praised as 'the best critical thing' he had encountered on the 'philosophical aspect of Marxism', and began to reconsider his assumptions about the humanistic character of Marx's thought.[41] While he still admired Marx and Engels for their attempts 'to make the historical imagination intervene in human affairs as a direct constructive force' and for their 'sense of a rich and various world', he recognized in the dialectic a competing element of 'mysticism' and German intolerance. Following Eastman's argument, Wilson discovered a dangerous religious tendency in Marx's effort 'to harness the primitive German Will to a movement which should lead all humanity to prosperity, happiness and freedom'. The 'disguise of the Dialectic' – 'a semi-divine principle of History' – had made it possible to evade 'the responsibility for thinking, deciding, acting'. Wilson continued to distinguish between Marx and Engels and 'the crude pedants and fanatics' who claimed to be their followers, but he also found in the dialectic a component of Marxism that 'lends itself to the repressions of the tyrant'.[42]

Because it was written over a six-year period, *To the Finland Station* turned out to be an ambiguous book. The admiration for Marx, Engels and Lenin was tempered by Wilson's arrival at the conclusion that the dialectic was a built-in excuse for totalitarianism. His method of resolving this dilemma was consistent with the implications of 'Marxism and Literature'. Wilson argued, in effect, that Marx, Engels and Lenin were heroic figures precisely because they ignored one of the principal features of Marxism; in other words, they were sufficiently flexible to transcend Marxism itself. Stalin and Trotsky were not. Trotsky abandoned 'the exploratory spirit' that characterized Marx, Engels and Lenin, and his work revealed a 'dogmatic Marxism' that contrasted starkly with the ideas of these other men. Wilson managed to salvage something of his original purpose by claiming that, for a moment, in the person of Lenin, 'history acted and history written' had converged to a positive end. But what Wilson had begun as a celebration of ideas, becoming social and historical forces, finally emerged in a much more ambivalent form. An individual who believed that he 'was carrying out one of the essential tasks of history' could do more harm than good if he lacked the exceptional qualities of a Marx or Lenin; and Marxism, as a body of ideas capable of influencing the historical process, was to be feared as much as admired – especially now, in its period of 'decadence'.[43]

If Wilson hedged on whether Marxism tended inevitably toward dogmatism and totalitarianism, Eastman did not. By the mid-1930s, his disillusionment had grown to include Trotsky, whom he had looked upon since 1924 as the leader of a more democratic and scientific communist movement. When he published a revised version of *Marx and Lenin* under the title *Marxism: Is It Science?* in 1940, Eastman included Trotsky and Lenin in his condemnation of the 'dialectic religion'. Much of the book was identical to the 1927 edition, and Eastman continued to link the 'scientific attitude' to 'the general aim of a more free and equal society'. But his answer to the question posed in the new title was a resounding 'no'. By 1940, Eastman no longer saw Marxism as a flexible system of thought which could be saved from Marx and purged of its religious orientation. A note added to the old section on Lenin as a scientist of revolution captured Eastman's change of mind: 'Lenin's faith in the dialectic philosophy was more vital to his thinking, and more disastrous, than I realized.' Eastman now believed that Lenin's embrace of the dialectic had allowed him to equate the dictatorship of the Party with progress toward Communism, when in reality it had led to Stalin. In a companion volume, *Stalin's Russia and The Crisis in Socialism*, also published in 1940, Eastman charged that the dialectic's ability to justify everything as a step toward the withering away of the state and the triumph of socialism had permitted Stalin to construct a totalitarian regime and purge his enemies in the name of socialism; the dialectic had allowed Stalin to portray 'etymological' finesse as real social change.[44]

Eastman intended the last section of *Stalin's Russia* to lay the foundation for a revised socialism. Without Lenin as a model, however, his alternative was even less substantial than before, and the most he could suggest was the substitution of the word 'radical' for 'revolutionary' to indicate that 'the attitude of experimental science' had replaced 'an imported revolutionary metaphysics'. Eastman explained his vagueness by claiming that 'of the two main ingredients of wisdom, practical action and detachment', he had 'for some years cultivated only the latter'. But he could say with certainty that what was needed now was 'a movement of hard minds, loyal to the oppressed', and 'disillusioned' with 'evangelism' and 'self-consoling ideologies'. Most of all, they had to know the 'errors as well as the truths in Marxism' and 'the lessons of the Russian revolution and the fate of the Third International'. What truths remained in Marxism, Eastman did not say. *Marxism: Is It Science?* and *Stalin's Russia* seemed to suggest instead that Marxism and 'honest intelligence' were fundamentally incompatible and that, at most, Marxism could point to underlying historical conditions – not to a legitimate praxis.[45]

By 1941, Wilson was able to perceive the end of a phase of American intellectual history. In a tribute to Eastman, he argued that the intellectual attraction to Marxism had been little more than desire masquerading as realism:

> The fact that Marx and Engels combined an un-examined idealism with real and great intellectual genius has made it possible for American intellectuals to whoop it up for the Marxist religion, under the impression that they were applying to the contemporary world a relentless intellectual analysis; and strong in the reassurance of standing right with the irresistible forces of History, the Marxist substitute for old-fashioned Providence, they have felt confident that History would see them through without further intellectual effort on their part.

If this was primarily an attack on the Stalinists, it was also a piece of self-criticism – a recognition that the conception of Marxism as expansive and non-dogmatic was based more on a wish than on critical thought. Like Eastman, Wilson found Marxism salvageable only as an interpretative tool, not as a prescription for change. Marx and Engels had provided a 'technique' for studying historical and contemporary problems with reference to their social and economic context, but because of their German background, they had 'tended to imagine socialism in authoritarian terms'.[46] Intellectuals, he implied, would have to be more sceptical, more vigilant about preserving their independence, in the future. They had to know the risks involved in the quest to assert their social presence and foster change, even if this meant modifying their expectations in the interests of autonomy.

The deep-seated concerns about independence that shaped this generation's sense of the intellectual vocation led to comparatively early breaks with Stalinism – some in the 1920s, most in 1936 or 1939. Only a few diehards like Michael Gold held out until the final disillusionment of 1956. Yet the investment in the Soviet Union, and the tendency after 1940 to conflate Marxism and Stalinism, also produced political enervation. Eastman's virulent anti-communism signalled the end to any positive idea of change. Wilson, though nominally a democratic socialist, moved toward an increasingly dark perspective on history in which the world seemed to be locked into 'a competition for power for its own sake'.[47] After the Second World War, he no longer spoke of the redeemed America he had dreamt of in the thirties. Despite its ostensible pragmatism and openness, there was an all-or-nothing quality about intellectual Marxism that exhausted its adherents' attempts at engagement. Freedom and commitment seemed more dichotomous then ever, and they opted for freedom.

Only those like Mumford who had never staked much on Marxism could continue to articulate a vital alterative vision. From Mumford's perspective, his generation had taken a wrong turn; instead of talking about 'Americanizing' Marx – and never really doing it – American intellectuals should have been bold enough to bypass him entirely. Mumford's consistent regionalism, his call for decentralization and redistribution rather than bureaucratization and destructive growth, his demand for the humanization of technology, made him less prone to the exhaustion that characterized other critics after 1940. Defending the dream of personal and social regeneration in 1950, he held to the conviction that 'it is better to sink one's last hopes in such a dream than to be destroyed by a nightmare'.[48] For Mumford, genuine intellectual independence – the ability to speak truth to power in all its destructive forms and to imagine untried possibilities against the pressures of 'realism' – did not stand in opposition to engagement. By thinking in terms of diverse audiences rather than mass constituencies, by grounding utopian aspirations in the concreteness of community and participatory democracy rather than the abstractions of the proletariat and revolution, by projecting these aspirations over time rather than pretending that they had already been realized overseas, Mumford showed how intellectuals might find that freedom and commitment are synonymous after all.

NOTES

1   Randolph Bourne to Prudence Winterrowd, 11 March 1914, Randolph Bourne Papers, Rare book and Manuscript Library, Columbia University.
     For a broader exploration of this problem among members of Bourne's generation, see Steven Biel, *Independent Intellectuals in the United States, 1910–1945*, New York, New York University Press, 1992.
2   Leslie Fishbein, *Rebels in Bohemia: The Radicals of The Masses, 1911–1917*, Chapel Hill, University of North Carolina Press, 1982, p. 39; Max Eastman, *Enjoyment of Living*, New York, Harper, 1948, pp. 354–5.
3   John Reed, *Ten Days That Shook the World*, New York, Modern Library, 1935 [1919], p. 133. The emphasis is Reed's.
4   Max Eastman, 'A Letter to Romain Rolland', *Liberator*, December 1919, pp. 24–5.
5   Max Eastman, 'The Clarté Movement', *Liberator*, April 1920, pp. 40–2.
6   Max Eastman, 'Clarifying the light', *Liberator*, June 1921, pp. 5–7; Van Wyck Brooks, 'A reviewer's notebook', *Freeman*, 29 June 1921, pp. 382–3; Max Eastman, 'Inspiration or leadership', *Liberator*, August 1921, pp. 7–9. The emphasis is Eastman's. For other discussions of the Rolland and Clarté debates, see Daniel Aaron, *Writers on the Left: Episodes in American Literary Communism*, New York, Octagon, 1979 [1961], pp. 50–5, and James Burkhart Gilbert, *Writers and Partisans: A History of Literary Radicalism in America*, New York, John Wiley and Sons, 1968, pp. 45–7.
7   Floyd Dell, *Intellectual Vagabondage: An Apology for the Intelligentsia*, New York, George H. Doran, 1926, pp. 150, 257.
8   Max Eastman, 'To Nicolai Lenin', *Liberator*, November 1918, p. 17; Max Eastman, 'Lenin – a statesman of the New Order', *Liberator*, September 1918, p. 10; Max Eastman, 'Lenin – a statesman of the New Order II', *Liberator*, October 1918, p. 28; Max Eastman, 'About dogmatism', *Liberator*, November

1920, p. 8; Max Eastman, 'Hillquit repeats his error', *Liberator*, January 1921, p. 21; Max Eastman, 'The wisdom of Lenin', *Liberator*, June 1924, p. 8.

9   John Reed, 'Soviet Russia now', July 1920, in *An Anthology*, Moscow, Progress Publishers, 1966, pp. 230–1; Reed, handwritten note on Lenin [July 1920], published in *Anthology*, opp. page 56; Reed, *Ten Days*, p. 125; Floyd Dell, 'Lenine [*sic*] and His Time', *Liberator*, May 1919, p. 45; Joseph Freeman, *An American Testament: A Narrative of Rebels and Romantics*, New York, Farrar and Rinehart, 1936, p. 501.

10 Floyd Dell, 'My political ideals', in *Looking at Life*, New York, Knopf, 1924, p. 149; Floyd Dell, 'Art under the Bolsheviks', *Liberator*, June 1919, p. 18. See also, for example, Michael Gold, 'Two critics in a bar-room', *Liberator*, September 1921, pp. 28–31.

11 Floyd Dell, 'Explanations and apologies', *Liberator*, June 1922, pp. 25–6; Michael Gold, 'Thoughts of a great thinker', *Liberator*, April 1922, [n.p.].

12 The manifesto, which the authors decided not to publish at the time, appears with a letter from Wilson to Theodore Dreiser, 2 May 1932, in Edmund Wilson, *Letters on Literature and Politics, 1912–1972*, Elena Wilson (ed.), New York, Farrar, Straus and Giroux, 1977, pp. 222–3.

13 Gold to 'the Trustees of the Garland Fund', [n.d.], Roger Baldwin to Freeman, 21 September 1922, Lewis S. Gannett to Baldwin, 29 September 1922, *Report of The American Fund for Public Service, Inc. for the First Six Months of Operation: July 1922–January 31, 1923*, American Fund for Public Service [AFPS] Records, Rare Books and Manuscripts Division, New York Public Library, Astor, Lenox and Tilden Foundations.

14 Mumford to Maurice Becker, 17 February 1925, Dos Passos to Becker, [n.d.], List of committee members of 'Dynamo', 23 March 1925, AFPS Records.

15 *New Masses* official prospectus, December 1925, AFPS Records; John Dos Passos, 'The New Masses I'd like', *New Masses*, June 1926, p. 20; Michael Gold, 'Let it be really new!', *New Masses*, June 1926, pp. 20–1.

16 Eastman to 'The New Masses', 27 January 1928, AFPS Records.

17 Egmont Arens to Baldwin, 31 January 1928, AFPS Records; Michael Gold, 'Trotsky's pride' (June 1930), in *Mike Gold: A Literary Anthology*, Michael Folsom (ed.), New York, International Publishers, 1972, p. 195.

18 On Dell's resignation, see Douglas Clayton, *Floyd Dell: The Life and Times of an American Rebel*, Chicago, Ivan R. Dee, 1994, pp. 252–4.

19 On Calverton's significant role as an editor in supporting independent Marxism in the United States, see Leonard Wilcox, *V. F. Calverton: Radical in the American Grain*, Philadelphia, Temple University Press, 1992, especially chapters 9 and 10.

20 Max Eastman, *Marx and Lenin: The Science of Revolution*, New York, Albert and Charles Boni, 1927, pp. 22, 25, 37–9, 41.
    John P. Diggins praises Eastman's critique in *Up from Communism: Conservative Odysseys in American Intellectual History*, New York, Harper and Row, 1975, especially p. 40. Eastman's debate with a younger Dewey student, Sidney Hook, is recounted in Richard Pells, *Radical Visions and American Dreams: Culture and Social Thought in the Depression Years*, New York, Harper and Row, 1973, pp. 127–35.

21 Eastman, *Marx and Lenin*, op. cit., pp. 39, 63–4, 128, 148–9, 162.

22 Eastman, *Marx and Lenin*, pp. 203, 211.

23 Waldo Frank, *Memoirs of Waldo Frank*, Alan Trachtenberg (ed.), Amherst, University of Massachusetts Press, 1973, pp. 185, 194, 197; Edmund Wilson, 'An appeal to progressives', *New Republic*, 14 January 1931, p. 238.

24 Wilson to Allen Tate, 28 May 1930, in Wilson, *Letters on Literature and Politics*, op. cit., p. 196.

25 Wilson, 'Appeal to progressives', op. cit., pp. 236–38.

Lewis Mumford apparently did not believe that Wilson was doing enough to take communism away from the Communists. In refusing to sign a petition circulated by Wilson and Malcolm Cowley in support of the Party's presidential candidate in 1932, Mumford wrote to Waldo Frank: 'There is something unhealthy in the way in which the younger generation are *accepting* communism: they must *create* communism: it is not a patent breakfast food that was pre-digested by Marx and warmed over by Lenin'. Mumford to Frank, 18 September 1932, Waldo Frank Collection, Special Collections, Van Pelt-Dietrich Library Center, University of Pennsylvania.

Several months earlier, when Mumford, Frank and Wilson were working together on a more general manifesto of the intellectuals, the participants agreed that they should avoid 'the usual communist clichés'. But they never managed to come up with language that all three writers (and John Dos Passos, whom Wilson consulted) found satisfactory; Mumford to Wilson, 25 March 1932, Edmund Wilson Papers, Yale Collection of American Literature, Beinecke Rare Book and Manuscript Library, Yale University.

26 Matthew Josephson, 'The road of indignation', *New Republic*, 18 February 1931, pp. 13–15.

27 Benjamin Ginzburg, 'Against messianism', *New Republic*, 18 February 1931, pp. 16–17.

28 Waldo Frank, *Dawn in Russia: The Record of a Journey*, New York, Scribner's, 1932, pp. 4, 24, 158, 246, 252, 260, 264, 270, 272; Frank, *Memoirs*, p. 192; Waldo Frank, 'How I came to Communism', *New Masses*, September 1932, p. 7.

29 Wilson to Dos Passos, 29 February 1932, Wilson to Frank, 17 June 1932, in *Letters on Literature and Politics*, pp. 222–3; Edmund Wilson, *The Thirties: From Notebooks and Diaries of the Period*, Leon Edel (ed.), New York, Farrar, Strauss and Giroux, 1980, pp. 208, 212–13.

30 Max Eastman, *Artists in Uniform: A Study of Literature and Bureaucratism*, New York, Octagon, 1972 [1934]), pp. 6, vii–viii, 24–25, 27, 29; Max Eastman, 'Art and the life of action', in *Art and the Life of Action with Other Essays*, New York, Alfred A. Knopf, 1934, pp. 81–2, 84.

31 Joseph Freeman, 'The tradition of American revolutionary literature'; Malcolm Cowley, 'What the Revolutionary Movement can do for a writer', in Henry Hart (ed.), *American Writers' Congress*, New York, International, 1935, pp. 58, 59, 62.

32 John Dos Passos, 'The writer as technician'; Waldo Frank, 'Values of the revolutionary writer', 'Discussion and proceeding'; Kenneth Burke, 'Revolutionary symbolism in America', in *American Writers' Congress*, pp. 72, 75, 80–81, 90–1, 92, 93–4, 190. The emphases are Frank's and Burke's. On Burke and the First Writers' Congress generally, see Aaron, *Writers on the Left*, Chapter 10.

33 Brooks to Alfred Harcourt, 2 January 1938, Van Wyck Brooks Collection, Special Collections, Van Pelt-Dietrich Library Center, University of Pennsylvania; Malcolm Cowley, 'Notes on a Writers' Congress', 21 June 1939, in *Think Back On Us... A Contemporary Chronicle of the 1930s*, Henry Dan Piper (ed.), Carbondale, Southern Illinois University Press, 1967, p. 170.

34 Wilson to Dos Passos, 9 May 1935, in *Letters on Literature and Politics*, pp. 263–8.

35 Mumford to Daniel Aaron, 17 January 1959, Lewis Mumford Collection, Special Collections, Van Pelt-Dietrich Library Center, University of Pennsylvania.

36 Michael Gold, 'Discussion and proceeding', *American Writers' Congress*, pp. 166–7; Michael Gold, 'John Reed and the real thing' (1927), in *Mike Gold: A Literary Anthology*, p. 154; Joseph Freeman, 'Introduction,' in Granville

Hicks, Michael Gold, Isidor Schneider, Joseph North, Paul Peters and Alan Calmer (eds), *Proletarian Literature in the United States: An Anthology*, New York, International Publishers, 1935, pp. 9, 12, 16.

37 Michael Gold, *The Hollow Men*, New York, International Publishers, 1941, pp. 31, 46–7, 98.

38 Wilson to Dos Passos, 31 January 1935, in *Letters on Literature and Politics*, op. cit., p. 259.

39 Edmund Wilson, *Travels in Two Democracies*, New York, Harcourt, Brace, 1936, p. 252.

40 Edmund Wilson, 'Marxism and literature', in *The Triple Thinkers: Ten Essays on Literature*, New York, Harcourt, Brace, 1938, pp. 266–7, 269, 274, 276–7, 289.

41 Wilson to Eastman, 5 October 1938, Max Eastman Papers, Lilly Library, Indiana University.

42 Edmund Wilson, *To the Finland Station: A Study in the Writing and Acting of History*, New York, Harcourt, Brace, 1940, pp. 162, 187, 189, 196–97, 213, 216.

43 Wilson, *To the Finland Station*, pp. 197, 428, 437.

44 Max Eastman, *Marxism: Is It Science?*, New York, W. W. Norton, 1940, pp. 215–16, 282; Max Eastman, *Stalin's Russia and The Crisis in Socialism*, New York, W. W. Norton, 1940, pp. 9, 45.

  Floyd Dell, whose career as critic and novelist had faltered in the thirties and who was now working for the WPA., praised Eastman for 'doing simple logical justice to the subject' of Marxism and for translating into written form Dell's own 'bitterness, anger, suspicion and resentment at having been swindled'; Dell to Eastman, February 1940, Eastman Papers.

45 Eastman, *Stalin's Russia*, pp. 136, 139, 245, 250, 255.

46 Edmund Wilson, 'Max Eastman in 1941', 10 February 1941, in *Classics and Commercials: A Literary Chronicle of the Forties*, New York, Farrar, Straus, 1950, p. 65; Edmund Wilson, 'Marxism at the End of the Thirties', 22 February–1 March–8 March 1941, in *The Shores of Light: A Literary Chronicle of the Twenties and Thirties*, New York, Farrar, Straus and Young, 1952, pp. 742–3.

47 Edmund Wilson, *Patriotic Gore: Studies in the Literature of the American Civil War*, New York, Oxford University Press, 1962, p. xxxi.

48 Lewis Mumford, 'In the name of sanity' (1950), quoted in Paul Boyer, *By the Bomb's Early Light: American Thought and Culture at the Dawn of the Atomic Age*, New York, Pantheon, 1985, p. 351.

12 The tragic predicament

Post-war American intellectuals, acceptance and mass culture

George Cotkin

In his explosively controversial memoir *Making It* (1964), Norman Podhoretz claimed to have blown the lid off the hidden secret of intellectuals. Recalling his early years as a member of the 'family' of New York intellectuals in the 1950s, Podhoretz wryly introduced himself as 'a man who at the precocious age of thirty-five experienced an astonishing revelation: it is better to be a success than a failure... it was better to be recognized than to be anonymous'.[1] Podhoretz understood what Thomas Kuhn had been saying in a way about the structure of scientific communities and what Pierre Bourdieu and his followers would later argue about intellectual distinction.[2] Of course, many at the time found distasteful, or at least misleading, Podhoretz's Horatio Alger imagery of his rise to intellectual acceptance and sometimes even fame – it undermined the symbol of the intellectual as someone unencumbered by pecuniary or status concerns. Yet Podhoretz was surely near the target in realizing that it is the nature of the intellectual to make distinctions (between high, middle and lowbrow cultural pursuits, between who is and is not an intellectual) and to attempt to be distinguished in the making of such distinctions.

If Podhoretz's reflections lacked depth and subtlety, then the evaluation of historian Richard Hofstadter must be seen as more satisfactory and cognizant of another truth about intellectuals. Hofstadter, who employed the concept of status anxiety in his historical analyses, found intellectuals to be both desirous of popular acclaim yet also antagonistic to such acceptance: 'when bourgeois society rejects them [intellectuals], that is only one more proof of its philistinism; when it gives them an "honored place", it is buying them off. The intellectual is either shut out or sold out.'[3] For Hofstadter, this situation constituted 'the tragic predicament that faces any man who is in one way or another caught between his most demanding ideals and his more immediate ambitions and interests'.[4] This tension between ideals and interests could not be resolved, according to Hofstadter. Nor should it be. From this 'tragic predicament' – at times almost comic, since it seemed so overwrought with the type of manic anxiety felt by characters in a Saul Bellow novel – might arise a middle-ground position, one not based on foundational alienation nor clawing acceptance of power.

Instead, the intellectual would have 'primary responsibility to truth or to his creative vision, and he must be prepared to follow them even when they put him at odds with his society'.[5]

In many ways, Hofstadter's ideal of the intellectual anticipates the recent formulation of the 'connected critic', as developed by Michael Walzer.[6] Walzer maintains that the intellectual or critic should proudly complain, not out of ontological alienation, but rather with responsibility to both a particular community and to abstract values. Walzer, as much as Hofstadter, views the critic as in a tense position. Numbing, tragic alienation can be avoided or lessened so long as the intellectual remains bonded to a larger community and to the pursuit of truth and justice. Hofstadter and Walzer's formulations may sound quaint in this Foucauldian era of suspicion of the universal intellectual and of recourse to ideals of 'responsibility to truth', as if truth were unproblematic or unrelated to the exercise of power. But to post-war intellectuals, upholding intellectual and cultural standards, however vague they might appear, seemed to be both a noble and an absolutely critical endeavour.

There is absolutely no reason why the intellectual – as either Podhoretz's man 'on-the-make', Hofstadter's tragically conflicted thinker or Walzer's 'connected critic' – cannot be engaged in important intellectual work. After all, on one level such creative production would obviously win for him or her intellectual distinction, respect and status from one's peers. Irving Howe admitted that one could find among New York intellectuals 'petty greed or huckstering, now and again a drop into opportunism'. But, rightly concluded Howe, he and other intellectuals were driven by 'a gnawing ambition to write something, even three pages that might live'.[7]

While, in the post-war years, American intellectuals often succeeded in penning a few 'pages that might live', they also spent an inordinate amount of time trying to define boundaries, to make distinctions, to establish their authority in opposition to the foes of mass culture and anti-intellectualism. These intellectuals sought to define themselves, in part, by their choice of enemies, both real and imagined. The definition of membership, function and status in the intellectual community was not carried out only in highbrow journals such as *Partisan Review*, *Commentary* and *New Republic*. The process of establishing status and place for the intellectual in American society was also a creation of the instruments of the mass culture that intellectuals found so distasteful. Mass culture played a critical role in the representation of the intellectual, in defining what constituted a highbrow thinker. Not surprisingly, many intellectuals were unusually sensitive and wary of such presentations.

The harried, often intemperate, attacks launched by post-war intellectuals against mass and popular culture – film and comic strips, no less than popularizations of highbrow cultural forms such as symphonic concerts – were critical, then, more for their role in the acts of exclusion and self-definition than for their insight and depth. For post-war intellectuals, status and subject were bound together. To be a serious intellectual in America required that one be opposed to the insidious, levelling forces of mass culture; showing too much respect for mass culture (except as a threat) could even bring forth doubts about one's own intellectual credentials. Such anxiety generally blinded post-war intellectuals to the richness of mass and popular culture; it forced intellectuals to overstate the lines dividing elite and popular culture. In the post-war years, the distinguishing marks of the intellectual, the distinctions that he or she was moved to generate were vague matters of taste that paraded as unassailable standards. And even the expression of such distinctions, in the process marking oneself off as an intellectual, also proved particularly incapable of bringing satisfaction or surcease from doubts about status to the intellectuals making them.[8]

Dangers to the life of the mind, to the strenuous ideal of highbrow cultural enterprise lurked everywhere. Delmore Schwartz's famous quip that 'sometimes even paranoids have real enemies' may be taken as paradigmatic of the world-view of post-war thinkers as they confronted the impossible problem of self-definition in the face of the presumed threats of mass culture, McCarthy era anti-intellectualism, and even adulation. All too often, post-war intellectuals drew up the following equation: mass culture = kitsch; high culture = intellectuals. In attempting to maintain their identity as intellectuals, in general opposition to mass culture, post-war thinkers ultimately cordoned themselves off from much that was rich, challenging and experimental in American popular culture. As Susan Sontag warned in 1964, in 'Notes on "Camp" ', a crucial document that marked a shift away from the post-war antagonism to popular culture: 'there are other creative sensibilities besides the seriousness (both tragic and comic) of high culture and high style of evaluating people. And one cheats oneself, as a human being, if one has *respect* only for the style of high culture'.[9] But post-war intellectuals were incapable of dropping their faith in the redeeming power of high culture. In the process, they ironically undermined their own status and power as intellectuals. By sharpening too fine a point to the pencil of their own tastes, they became less self-critical, overly resistant to innovation and experimentation in the life of the mind. If today the complaint about political correctness is that there is too much cant about race, class and gender, then for the post-war intellectuals fighting on the culture front, their ideals of 'irony, paradox, ambiguity, and complexity' took on their own talismanic and limiting connotations.[10]

This closing of the mind of post-war intellectuals – condemned by Harold Rosenberg as 'The herd of independent minds'[11] – is best perceived in their strident protests against mass culture. To be sure, there were valid reasons behind the attack. In part, the critical concern with mass culture may well have been indicative of the shift of intellectuals away from Marxian and radical political criticism toward non-political cultural criticism. But for many intellectuals, whatever their political positions, mass culture appeared to be dangerously antagonistic to the purity of highbrow ideals; it threatened to reduce serious thinking into a commodity for mass consumption, corrupting both idea and thinker. If the social life of the post-war world, as captured in the suburban phenomenon of inexpensive but bland housing, represented the future as conformity and complacency, then so too might mass culture promise a Levittown[11a] of the mind. Cultural degeneration in society at large appeared to be mimicked in the huge numbers of students flocking into the universities and colleges, many supported by the GI Bill.[11b] To meet the demands of the new students, many of whom might be perceived as not the most intellectually gifted, it was feared by many intellectuals that the educational system would be forced to spoon-feed information, to transform highbrow cultural monuments into middle-brow products made for easy and pleasant consumption.

But, it must be remembered, this almost hysterical concern with mass culture on the part of post-war intellectuals was caught up in the question of the status, prerogatives and very definition of the intellectual.[12] And, given the horrors of recent history, the crimes of Stalin, the excesses of the Popular Front ideology of the 1930s and 1940s (itself an exercise in the creation of an artificial cultural construct) and totalitarianism, American intellectuals were wary not only of their own positions in America, but also of the danger of mass culture feeding into a frenzy of anti-intellectualism.[13]

To be sure, there is justice in emphasizing as the defining themes of the post-war intellectuals their movement from radicalism to conservatism, from an adversarial to a celebratory stance vis à vis America, or from ideological commitments to the ideal of an 'end of ideology'.[14] Such concerns are readily apparent, for instance, in the famous symposium 'Our Country and Our Culture', organized in 1952 by the editors of the *Partisan Review*. The American economy's apparently successful evolution from scarcity to abundance, and the demands of international anti-Communist politics, helped to explain the sudden willingness of intellectuals to affirm American life and institutions. Distinguished theologian Reinhold Niebuhr noted that the dangerous ideals of the 1930s, utopianism and progress, might now be recalled by mature intellectuals in the 1950s as little more than 'an adolescent embarrassment'.[15] The symposium editorial statement found that 'the tide has begun to turn, and many writers and intellectuals now feel closer to their country and its culture'.[16]

The discussions in the symposium were also redolent with concerns about the challenge of mass culture and the status of the intellectual. In addition, opinion differed as to whether it was actually a good thing for intellectuals to begin to feel comfortable, to attain success in America. The issue of success did not simply mean the danger of the intellectual being corrupted by wealth or being led into complacency by academic appointments. It also raised the spectre of how might an intellectual remain an intellectual when his or her thoughts were no longer part of what the critic Lionel Trilling had once proudly referred to as an adversarial culture.[17] The interplay between success, alienation and mass culture defined the extended conversation carried on by post-war intellectuals about their own function and fate.

To understand the post-war intellectuals' assault on mass culture, it is first necessary to consider two critical texts that helped to define the issue and to frame questions for them: Clement Greenberg's 'Avant-garde and kitsch' (1939) and Hannah Arendt's *The Origins of Totalitarianism* (1951). Both works pivot around mass culture and its affinity with totalitarianism. Of equal importance, both works assay the ruins of modernism and the nature of alienation: themes that predominated in the work of post-war thinkers.[18]

Greenberg's first major essay reveals many of the formulations that later became his signature in theorizing abstract expressionism: form over content, and emphasis on the evolution of the medium. Yet the essay is drenched in the politics of anti-Stalinism and anti-totalitarianism. Still a Trotskyist when he wrote the essay, Greenberg was in a foul mood about the possibilities of social change to save high art. Indeed, he closed his essay with the faint hope that 'Today we look to socialism *simply* for the preservation of whatever living culture we have right now'. The forces of doom – capitalism, fascism and Stalinism – were all guilty of trafficking in kitsch, which Greenberg viewed as serving powerful interests. Greenberg upheld the ideal of the avant-garde, but he recognized that avant-garde abstractionism was based on a shift 'away from subject matter of common experience' toward 'the medium of his [the artist's] own craft'.[19] Modern art became difficult and inaccessible; alienated, uneducated masses were logically estranged from high art. In such a situation, the worker would be drawn to the familiar representationality of kitsch. Kitsch was 'ersatz culture...the epitome of all that is spurious in the life of its times'. Prepackaged, predictable, sentimental, kitsch required none of the reflection demanded to appreciate high art. Kitsch was imperialistic and seductive. It 'converts and waters down a great deal of avant-garde material for its own uses and its enormous profits are a source of temptation to the avant-garde itself, and its members have not always resisted this temptation'.

Kitsch then worked as a corrupting agent, spreading itself throughout the culture, undermining the avant-garde artist, highbrow culture and the authority of intellectuals. Vigilance against the 'virulence of kitsch' was demanded of the intellectual. Yet at this historical conjuncture, the problem confronting the intellectual was more than kitsch as an abstract entity, to be quarantined off into a sanitary closet so that high culture might thrive. Greenberg emphasized that kitsch faithfully and powerfully served the totalitarian state as a vehicle for propaganda and legitimation: 'Kitsch keeps a dictator in closer contact with the "soul" of the people.' While dictators such as Mussolini might flirt briefly with high modernism, they were inexorably moved to repudiate artistic experimentation in favour of kitsch which supported the illusion of the masses being in control. Thus, Italian modernists 'are sent into the outer darkness, and the new railroad station in Rome will not be modernistic'.[20]

In his connecting totalitarianism (and capitalism) with kitsch art production, Greenberg had outlined the dangerous logic of mass culture and the shaky future of the avant-garde. Such concerns had not been centrally discussed during the war years. But with the conclusion of the Second World War, and the publication of Arendt's massive tome, *The Origins of Totalitarianism*, the emphases of Greenberg on art and politics, kitsch and avant-garde, mass culture and totalitarianism, again came to the fore.

Arendt's volume achieved canonical status among post-war intellectuals because of the authority of her prose, from the authenticity of her experiences as a survivor of the Nazi assault on culture, the sparkle of her big ideas, and out of her exalted position among New York intellectuals. As Alfred Kazin remembered, Arendt 'became vital to my life...it was for the *direction* of her thinking that I loved her, for the personal insistencies she gained from her comprehension of the European catastrophe. She gave her friends...intellectual courage before the moral terror the war had willed to us'.[21] Such cultural capital was joined by a personal power that 'bristled with intellectual charm, as if to reduce everyone in sight to an alert discipleship', recalled Irving Howe: 'Rarely have I met a writer with so acute an awareness of the power to overwhelm'.[22]

Arendt documented, in a metaphysical as much as a historical sense, the destructive wake of the decline of the national state, the rise of imperialism and, finally, how totalitarianism offered to resolve the state of chronic loneliness of modern men and women. In the end, the specific interpretations and the sweeping structure of the argument were less important to post-war American intellectuals than the nightmarish, numbing vision that Arendt painted on her canvas. The category of class, once so central to the social theories of intellectuals, had been demolished by the alienation of individuals from their own class and by the power of the totalitarian state to transcend class boundaries. Appeals to class were now viewed as divisive and counter-productive, helping to create the orgies of destruction that made the totalitarian turn all the more confounding and frightful.[23]

Historian Wilfred McClay is certainly on target when he notes that 'For American thinkers, the disturbing postwar vision of totalitarianism [as developed by Arendt, as well as by Erich Fromm] disclosed some of the anxieties and projections of the free-floating intellectual trying to find his way in a democratic social order'.[24] Alienation, loneliness, the atomized individual, superfluity, are the figures of expression that stalk the barren landscape, seared by the horrors of totalitarianism. Not surprisingly, while Arendt used these images to explain the plight of modern man in the mass society, intellectuals would employ these same terms to define their own status. Thus, when intellectuals interrogated the implications of mass culture, they were also looking inside themselves and pondering their own fates.[25] Thus, Arendt bequeathed to post-war intellectuals a heightened fear of the seductive and pervasive power of mass culture. She strikingly detailed how the elite and mob coalesced in totalitarian movements to 'destroy respectability'.[26] As Greenberg had noted with kitsch, so too did Arendt consider the massification of society to topple the solidity of tradition and the high ideals of European culture. Her analysis of the power of propaganda in the hands of the totalitarian state drove home, as did Orwell's *1984*, the ability of dictatorial regimes to manufacture truth and to disseminate it to the masses, who were all too eager to accept falsehood and absurdity so long as it was cloaked in the cape of authority and fantasy. Even more frightening, perhaps, Arendt demonstrated that avant-garde culture's attack on 'all traditional values and propositions' had served the forces of reaction. Thus, ironically, 'the only political result of Brecht's "revolution" was to encourage everyone to discard the uncomfortable mask of hypocrisy and to accept openly the standards of the mob'.[27]

The outlines of the post-war intellectuals' critique of mass culture are sufficiently familiar and consistently blurry. Raised most persistently by Dwight Macdonald in a series of essays published over a ten-year period, mass culture was conceived of as an 'infection [that] cannot be localized'.[28] Macdonald compared popular culture (he would later come to prefer the term 'mass culture') with fascism. In the competition for the hearts, minds and tastes of the mass, kitsch art and fascism proved too formidable for the producers of high culture. But equally disconcerting, popular culture refused to allow high culture to maintain its own sphere of influence and dominance. 'Good art competes with kitsch, serious ideas compete with commercialized formulae'. The serious producer of art finds his or her services suddenly in demand by the organs of mass culture. This led to what Macdonald called 'phoney-Avant-Gardism' which 'is not a raising of the level of Popular Culture, as it might superficially appear to be, but rather a corruption of High Culture. There is nothing more vulgar, in fact, than sophisticated kitsch', said Macdonald, simply repeating Greenberg's earlier formulation.[29]

Macdonald and his allies lamented that 'If there were a clearly defined cultural *elite*, then the masses could have their *kitsch* and the *elite* could have its High Culture, with everybody happy'. Macdonald failed to recognize how impossible was the task of having a clearly defined intellectual elite since the lines between high and low culture are by nature shifting, constructed rather than pre-existent. Especially troublesome to Macdonald was the imperialistic nature of mass culture and kitsch, as opposed, presumably, to the benign attributes of high culture. The political, as much as the aesthetic, dangers of this were apparent to many post-war intellectuals. Bernard Rosenberg, one of two editors of an influential volume on mass culture published in 1957, proclaimed that 'At its worst, mass culture threatens not merely to cretinize our taste, but to brutalize our senses while paving the way to totalitarianism'. Mass culture produced likely specimens for totalitarianism by cheapening life, by denying to human beings 'any really satisfying experience'. Kitsch arose, Rosenberg stressed, in the tradition of Greenberg, out of industrialization and increased literacy, along with the decline of the aristocracy and the rise of democracy. Little hope for avoiding the infection of mass culture and kitsch appeared on the horizon, only greater dehumanization of the individual, deadening of sympathies, and objectification of men into kitsch.[30]

Intellectuals, whether radical or conservative in their personal politics, came together on few issues as much as on mass culture. Radical Irving Howe, borrowing imagery from the Frankfurt School, went so far as to announce that Donald Duck was 'a frustrated little monster who has something of the SS man in him and whom we, also having something of the SS man in us, naturally find quite charming'.[31] Conservative Ernest Van Den Haag emphasized the 'invasion' of popular on high culture. Middlebrow culture, which attempted to make available to the masses predigested versions of great works of art and literature, was assured popular acclaim but was doomed to ultimate aesthetic failure. 'Bach candied by Stokowski, Bizet coarsened by Rodgers and Hammerstein...Shakespeare spliced and made into a treacly musical comedy.' Nor should apostles of mass education take succour in the ideal that through this type of initiation into 'high' culture might the masses flock to encounter the 'real thing'. Quite the contrary. 'Even if a predigested version were to lead to the original work, the public would be confronted with ideas and tropes which in their adulterated form have become counterfeit.' In the end, all high culture, under the weight of mass production, is reduced to 'familiar cliches'.[32] But 'familiar cliches', more than a willingness to discriminate and evaluate the mass culture of the 1950s, became the note that post-war intellectuals sounded all too often. In playing this song over and over again, intellectuals were demarcating their territory and attempting to establish their own credentials as the guardians of what might be valuable in culture. 'No intellectual life', wrote Niebuhr, 'can be at ease with the massive spiritual, moral, and cultural crudities, which seek to make themselves normative in a civilization'. The intellectual, warned Niebuhr, must not allow such 'crudities' and 'the synthetic and sentimentalized art of Hollywood or even the lower depths' of television to become normative.[33]

To be sure, not all intellectuals in America faced mass culture with abject fear and trembling. While mass culture had, as Arendt clearly indicated, aided totalitarianism, American social scientists emphasized that such a state would not happen here because of the pluralistic, group-centred nature of American life. Daniel Bell even questioned the heuristic value of the notion of mass society as 'very slippery. Ideal types, like the shadows in Plato's cave, generally never give us more than a silhouette'. Bell found that Arendt's description of the modern age of the masses failed to account for 'the complex, rightly striated social relations of the real world'.[34] For Bell, as much as for sociologists David Riesman and Edward Shils, the structures of American society – family, church, neighbourhood, trade unions – served as buffers against massification. Riesman proclaimed that 'I see no evidence of the alleged increasing power of the mass media producers...American culture constantly outdistances its interpreters'.[35] Moreover, Riesman stressed, mass cultural productions while powerful, were not passively encountered by their intended audiences. All works of popular culture, no less than high art, were reinterpreted by the individual. In his 'Listening to popular music' (1947), Riesman demonstrated that the presumed 'mass' of teenagers listening to popular music were divided in allegiances and tastes. This 'training' in choosing what type of music they liked, argued Riesman, allowed teenagers to express 'consumer preferences' and, in unsophisticated form, to both 'talk about music' and 'to talk about other things'. Thus the concluding theme of *The Lonely Crowd*, autonomy through the ability to make conscious choices, was not undermined so much by mass culture as made possible by it.[36]

However, Bell and Riesman did worry about the negative effects of middlebrow and mass culture on high culture. Although calling for more study of mass culture's limiting stereotypes, Riesman admitted 'that there is a lot to be said for the position held by the critic Clement Greenberg and many others that the social mobility of the middlebrow...has damaged and deranged high culture'.[37] And historian Howard Brick notes that Daniel Bell, especially in the 1940s, 'worried over the totalitarian propensities of frustrated masses' and mass culture. Ours is 'a time', Bell wrote, 'when our emotions are drained from us by the repetitiveness of horror and their place is pumped in the euphoric sentimentalism of the standardized entertainments'.[38] Although art critic Harold Rosenberg found Dwight Macdonald's assault on mass culture to be a bit too earnest and hysterical, a case of 'the intellectualization of kitsch', he refused to become a cheerleader for kitsch. 'There is only one way to quarantine kitsch', wrote Rosenberg, and that is 'by being too busy with art'.[39] While conservative sociologist Edward Shils pooh-poohed his fellow intellectuals' denigration of kitsch, he admitted that 'it would, of course, be frivolous to deny the aesthetic, moral, and intellectual unsatisfactoriness of much of popular culture or to claim that it shows the human race in its best light'.[40]

Perhaps the most important subtext for discussions of mass culture in the 1940s and 1950s revolved around the implications of mass culture for the status and function of the intellectual. In this dialogue, post-war American intellectuals were engaging in one of the proper enterprises of the intellectual, the examination of his or her own *raison d'être*. Discussion began well before the end of the Second World War and continued into the 1950s, as American thinkers fretted about what, C. Wright Mills asked, should be 'The social role of the intellectual'? Intellectuals, in Mills's analysis, were threatened by bureaucratic co-optation and tragic inwardness. Bureaucratic society increasingly 'dwarfed' the individual and drew the thinker into its powerful grip, thus limiting expression and independence. Yet the response of some intellectuals to this encroachment on the ideal of the intellectual as critic or outsider, had also been mistaken, resulting in an impotent idealization of a politics of distance. Emphasis on the tragic view of life sanctioned personal escape and estrangement over social commitment. The cult of alienation, Mills prophesied, would only grow stronger; while valuable 'in the pursuit of truths', alienation must not become 'a political fetish'.[41] But if Mills was strong on the problems confronting the intellectual in the dawn of the post-war world, his essay was less forthcoming about what the specific role of the intellectual should be, or at least how the intellectual might achieve the ideal of critical independence without sacrificing a radical politics of commitment. Despite all the print that was spilled on this issue in the late 1940s and 1950s, no one really resolved the issue.

After the war, Mills and a host of other American intellectuals constantly returned to examine the social role and future of the intellectual. Irving Howe's highly influential essay, 'This age of conformity' (1954), considered the 'whole position and status of intellectuals', finding them, in the face of a mass society, sadly 'responsible and moderate. And tame'. An intellectual edge traditionally had been provided by Bohemia and the avant-garde, which 'at least in America, is becoming extinct'.[42] Two years later, in 1956, historian H. Stuart Hughes wondered 'Is the intellectual obsolete?' For Hughes, the pull of academic conservatism and the continuation of anti-intellectualism in America conspired to undermine the ideal function of the intellectual as a 'freely speculating mind'. While Hughes concluded that intellectuals were not obsolete just yet, they faced at best 'a dubious future', marked by a critical public and 'subtle pressures' to conform 'to the role of a mental technician'.[43] At the heart of the intense fascination and fear of mass culture on the part of intellectuals, literary critic Leslie Fiedler noted, was that 'fear of the vulgar is the obverse of the fear of excellence, and both are aspects of the fear of difference'.[44] This fear reflected intellectuals' own uncertainty about their place in an American society that appeared to be increasingly given to mass education and popular entertainments. In many ways, Irving Howe captured these concerns in his criticism of kitsch and conformity while also indicating how the critical perspective of post-war intellectuals became ossified and problematic, thereby undermining their ability to be attuned to shifts in American culture and made their cultural capital deflationary by the mid-1960s.

Howe is an intriguing figure in these debates about the status of intellectuals and the question of mass culture, in part, because he was, at least in retrospect, his own best critic. Writing in 1970 about the prevalent post-war critique of mass culture, Howe noted that it 'was tightly drawn, almost an intellectual and analytical cul-de-sac'. Moreover, Howe recognized, that for many intellectuals the critique of mass culture had replaced an earlier critique of capitalism, only this time the masses were blamed for the failure of socialism in America: 'If you couldn't stir the Proletariat to action, you could denounce Madison Avenue in comfort'.[45]

Post-war intellectuals, through the critique of mass culture, as Howe understood, were attempting to define themselves in the face of greater security and acceptance in America. As noted earlier, Howe believed that by the mid-1950s intellectuals had become too tame in their criticism, too connected to institutions of power or conservatism. Academe forced intellectuals 'not only to lose their traditional rebelliousness but to one extent or another *they cease to function as intellectuals*'.[46] The critique of mass culture helped to define the programme of intellectuals, allowed them to remain 'outsiders' without politically stigmatizing them as leftists.

Howe, a professed anti-Stalinist radical, believed that intellectuals needed to be alienated from mass culture. This did not negate their ability to accept, in general, American society, certainly in comparison with other available systems; but it did not excuse the intellectual from criticizing the society. For Howe, the intellectual was, by definition, alienated from any society, not from oneself. This constituted the honourable tradition of the intellectual. Alienation, it seemed, promised to offset the dangerously seductive and corrupting power of middlebrow and mass culture on the intellectual and to blunt the barbs of McCarthyite anti-intellectualism. Such an attitude of alienation, when tied to the ideals of complexity and nuance and to the social and political reading of literature, promised Howe the tools with which to resist conformity.[47]

When Howe surveyed the academic mind in the 1950s, he found too much highbrow conformity. Conformity in concerns and methods had, in the hands of the New Critics, resulted in an orthodoxy riven with 'ideological motifs' that served to hermetically separate literature from society.[48] The few scholars who had escaped the orthodoxy of the New Critics and the antiquarianism of academic criticism, tumbled into another mode of conformity, an emphasis on Original Sin that promised, for literary men, the chance to 'relish disenchantment' and to revel in a 'sense of profundity and depth'. Divorced from society, enchanted with his or her own disenchantment, the scholar had moved too comfortably into a stance of estrangement and political impotence.[49] Alienation had come to the intellectuals, but not with the bite that Howe had imagined or desired.

Howe desperately dreamed of a new avant-garde, working 'in behalf of critical intransigence'. While Howe might attempt to realize this ideal, without having to have any truck with middlebrow or popular culture, his own ideal of an avant-garde was problematic. In essence, his committed brand of criticism, anchored in his social reading of literature and the admittedly decaying ideals of modernism, was a mode of exercising intellectual authority, of creating canons of interpretation, 'perspectives of observation'.[50]

In a famous essay discussing African-American writers – Richard Wright, James Baldwin and Ralph Ellison – Howe attempted to force his political and aesthetic values on Ellison. The naturalistic power of Wright, Howe opined, was in his ability to make 'his readers confront the disease of our culture' – racism.[51] This was not central to Ellison's work. Certainly Howe appreciated Ellison's imaginative skills in *Invisible Man* (1952). Ellison 'is richly, wildly inventive; his scenes rise and dip with tension, his people bleed, his language sings. No other writer has captured so much of the hidden gloom and surface gaiety of Negro life.' But, Ellison fails on political grounds; he is guilty of a 'sudden, unprepared and implausible assertion of unconditioned freedom'.[52] Given the social reality of blacks in racist America, Howe found this a dangerous illusion, a complacent concept. Freedom must be fought for, it cannot be proclaimed in a novel. Thus, Howe condemned Ellison for creatively positing existential freedom for a black man in a society which, according to Howe, prevented that very possibility from being realized. His social reading of the creative spaces of the novel was unrelentingly narrow and harshly blind to the greatness of the work *as* a work of art. In this sense, Howe was reducing Ellison to a formula, itself an act of kitsch criticism.

Ellison did not appreciate Howe's political scolding. In contrast to Howe, Ellison was compulsively and proudly a creative writer, without a hint of highbrow antagonism to mass culture. Comfortable in his role as an intellectual and artist, Ellison did not need to make a fetish of his alienation, race or politics – although all spoke in his artwork. He gyrated marvellously between a blues idiom and knowing political and philosophical commentary. The need to distinguish himself as a thinker, to assert himself in terms of practical politics or sociological analysis, was not present in Ellison as it was in Howe and other post-war, anti-Stalinist intellectuals. Ellison refused to be a representative for the Negro condition. As an African-American trying to be a creative artist and thinker, Ellison consciously cultivated his own voice and freedom. Surely the black writer functions in conditions not of his own choosing, wrote Ellison, but 'He is no mere product of his socio-political predicament'. The black writer, proclaimed Ellison, 'in a limited way, is his own creation'.[53]

If Howe's comprehension of the function of the intellectual as politically engaged dissenter and his ideal of the social construction of literature were somewhat limiting, so too were his aesthetic ideals unable to cope with new forms of art and mass culture. While Howe enjoyed baseball because of its leisurely manner and the ability of fans present at the game to interact with one another, he damned the darkened chambers of the movie theatre as isolating and dangerous – productive of a fascist mentality![54] By the late 1960s and early 1970s, Howe had wrapped himself in the ideals of complexity, 'nuance and ambiguity', distanced reason and the necessity of tragedy to attack the culture of the New Left, which Howe found rent with 'relaxed pleasures and surface hedonism'. Howe thus railed against the threat of mass culture and the 'high priests' of 'neo-primitivism' – Norman Brown, Herbert Marcuse, Marshall McLuhan, Allen Ginsberg and Norman Mailer. The new culture, in Howe's estimate, 'devalues the word...favors monochromatic cartoons, companionate grunts and glimpses of the ineffable in popular ditties. It has humor, but not much wit. Of the tragic it knows next to nothing...it arms itself with the paraphernalia of post-industrial technique and crash-dives into a Typee of neo-primitivism'.[55]

Howe's impassioned complaints captured the danger inherent in the intellectual enterprise – the problem of needing to delimit the 'proper' scope of the life of the mind to categories of acceptable and non-acceptable. The process may be necessary but it promotes – as in Howe's reaction to Ellison and Ginsberg – a type of stagnation and close-mindedness.[56] Howe was hardly alone in these qualities; the challenge of the 1960s counter-culture also brought forth the ire of Diana Trilling as well as Norman Podhoretz's famous attack on the Beat writers. Writing in the *Partisan Review*, Podhoretz found the Bohemianism of the 1950s to be 'hostile to civilization; it worships primitivism, instinct, energy, "blood"'. In the end, the Beats were condemned not only as anti-intellectual, but also as suffering 'from a pathetic poverty of feeling as well'. Podhoretz found an adolescent, 'suppressed cry' in Kerouac's books that shouted: 'Kill the intellectuals who can talk coherently.' On the one side, then, stood the primitivism and anti-intellectualism of the Beats; on the other side were arrayed the faithful guardians of civilization, the intellectuals. In sum, the dispute, according to Podhoretz, was about 'being for or against intelligence itself'.[57]

The battle lines were drawn around both political views and intellectual styles. Especially central was the desire of the post-war intellectuals to maintain their distinction as intellectuals by excluding those who did not seem to warrant inclusion, according to preconceived criteria of high versus low culture. In the end, the walls of the post-war intellectual world toppled in the 1960s. Norman Mailer, Susan Sontag, and even Dwight Macdonald defected, and with the rise of a new set of thinkers associated with the founding of *The New York Review of Books* in 1963 and with the counter-cultural style of the New Left, the fear of mass culture and the prerogatives of the older group of intellectuals faded into the sunset.

If, by the 1960s, the post-war intellectuals were in a well-deserved state of anxiety about the counter-cultural assault, this was hardly a new position for them to occupy; indeed, it might be said that they had long been accustomed to manning the barricades of high culture against the unruly mass. What made the assault of the New Left so painful to the post-war intellectuals was that many intellectuals seemed to be acting in the name of anti-intellectualism. This stance not only challenged the cherished ideals of Howe and his compatriots, but it wreaked havoc with their sense of the function of the intellectual. Certainly post-war intellectuals had grown self-satisfied, secure in their positions as the arbiters of highbrow taste and culture. Although they had denounced the seductiveness of academic positions, even Howe, within a year of his famous critique of academe in 1954, was teaching at Brandeis University. But, in fairness to the post-war intellectuals, they had from the outset placed themselves in a no-win position. Try as they might to define the function of the intellectual, they failed to find any resting place. They were stymied not simply by the inability of abstract ideas to resist changing social conditions, but also by their own conflicting views about what it meant to achieve success in American society. They craved adulation and respect, but shivered when it came from middlebrow culture.

The silent disease of acceptance, as much as antagonism from mass culture or hippies, frightened post-war intellectuals. Although Hofstadter documented many instances of anti-intellectualism in the McCarthy Red Scare era and throughout American history, he realized that anti-intellectualism was a given in an egalitarian, democratic society. But popular antipathy to the life of the mind in America was generally accompanied by the intellectuals' own gnawing fear of being accepted with open arms into the American mainstream. As Hofstadter remarked, intellectuals were caught in an essential paradox: 'while they do resent evidences of anti-intellectualism, and take it as a token of a serious weakness in our society, they are troubled and divided in a more profound way by their acceptance'.[58]

The two sides of this equal fear of acceptance and of alienation are displayed in intellectuals' reaction to middlebrow representations of intellectuals in the 1950s. To be sure, during the McCarthy years, anti-intellectualism was rife and debilitating. Intellectuals, although often in the forefront of anti-Stalinism and pro-Americanism, nevertheless were viewed by the public as fostering a questioning attitude that aided subversive activities or weakened the resolve to fight Communism. And intellectual questioning undermined the moral fibre of America, according to evangelist Billy Graham, by promoting 'reason, rationalism, mind culture, science worship, the working power of government, Freudianism, naturalism, humanism, behaviorism, positivism, materialism and idealism', ending in the view 'that morality is relative – that there is no norm or absolute standard'.[59]

Yet, it must be noted, the early years of the 1950s were also salad days for American intellectuals, the time when they began to achieve greater status and influence. Whether such a change was good or bad was discussed regularly, but all agreed that improved status was undeniable. Lionel Trilling, who thought it a good thing for intellectuals to be connected with the wealthy classes, and especially vice versa, noted that in America 'Intellect has associated itself with power as never before in history, and is now conceded to be itself a kind of power'.[60] This formulation, of intellectuals as an interest group within American society, became part of the general theory of group interest and pluralism that dominated sociological thought throughout the 1950s.[61]

Fears of success are more intriguing than anxiety about rejection. Even before the Soviet launching of Sputnik put a premium on the power of intellectuals and scientists in the Cold War, the image of the intellectual in the popular culture of early-1950s America was hardly a nightmare vision of narrow-minded populist bigots ranting and raving about the sins of intellectuals. Even the designation that at first seemed to most denigrate the intellectual – the egghead – underwent a series of subtle transformations that reveal the increasing status and acceptance of the intellectual in this period.

Intellectuals, despite their obvious ability to wield ideas, create images and prepare narratives, do not control their own image. The cultivation of an image is a bottom or middle-up, quite as much as a top-down, enterprise. In 1952, at the same moment when the 'Our Country and Our Culture' symposium was trumpeting the intellectuals' appreciation of America, signs were also present that America was not quite so enthused by the intellectuals. Louis Bromfield, in the rabidly anti-communist journal of opinion *The Freeman*, defined an 'Egghead' as:

> A person of spurious intellectual pretensions, often a professor or the protégé of a professor. Fundamentally superficial. Over-emotional and feminine in reactions to any problem. Supercilious and surfeited with conceit and contempt for the experience of more sound and able men . . . A self-conscious prig, so given to examining all sides of a question that he becomes thoroughly addled while remaining always in the same spot. An anemic bleeding heart.

Such 'eggheads', Bromfield further proclaimed, had supported traitors like Alger Hiss, allowed Stalinism to thrive in America, and appeased Communism abroad.[62]

While Bromfield attempted to use the term 'egghead' to condemn intellectuals, the notion was not always scrambled in that manner. Egghead entered the American political lexicon during the presidential contest of 1952, which pitted Democrat Adlai Stevenson, Governor of Illinois, against Republican Dwight D. Eisenhower. As numerous reporters noted, Stevenson's well-crafted and intelligently nuanced speeches had gained him a reputation for intellectuality. A good number of college-educated Americans, and certainly many intellectuals, came to identify with Stevenson, perceiving his candidacy, in the words of Arthur M. Schlesinger Jr, as a vehicle 'not to attain public objectives or even to affect public policy, but to affirm an interior sense of admiration and of belief'.[63] As both Republican and Democratic intellectuals flocked to support Stevenson, pro-Eisenhower forces recognized the defection of intellectuals, but without especial worry. Following a particularly strong Stevenson speech on the complicated issue of atomic energy, an Eisenhower stalwart admitted that intellectuals were drawn to Stevenson: 'But how many egg-heads do you think there are?'[64] Eisenhower's smashing victory in the 1952 election drove home the obvious fact that intellectuals were not a significant portion of the electorate.

Defeat for the intellectuals and their sainted candidate turned into bitterness, as they felt themselves buffeted about by populists, McCarthyites and anti-intellectuals of all stripes. In a particularly heated observation, Schlesinger moaned that 'the word "egghead" seemed to detonate the pent-up ferocity of twenty years of impotence' on the part of the business interests. The Babbitts of America had arisen and smote down the intellectuals, repudiating the hope and image that intellectuals might continue to contribute their expertise to the national government, as they had done under the New Deal and wartime administration of Franklin D. Roosevelt. While Schlesinger admitted that Eisenhower was not an anti-intellectual himself – he had after all served as president of Columbia University – many leading Republicans 'were less admiring of the life of the mind' and were attempting 'to convert the Democratic defeat into an egghead rout by tracking the intellectual down to his final stronghold, the university'.[65]

What makes this statement appear so much of a tempest in a teapot is that it perfectly captures the anomalous position of the intellectual. Under attack, the intellectuals cried out that they were in danger – but in danger of what? Of losing jobs to the forces of reaction? To be sure that happened; all too often. But what Schlesinger failed to acknowledge, as Irving Howe and C. Wright Mills perfectly comprehended, was that acceptance by the public was not unproblematic. Success also brought difficulties and anxieties, albeit of a different kind, to the intellectual. The allure of power, the seduction of status threatened intellectuals in a manner that Schlesinger in 1952 failed to countenance. Thus, the danger of antagonism on the part of the populace to the intellectual represented an ironic flip side to the dangerous celebration of the intellectual on the part of the populace.

In 1954, *Time* magazine, a proudly middlebrow publication, decided to address the status of the intellectual in American society. Only a couple of years after the Stevenson débâcle, and while the stench of McCarthyism still filled the air, *Time* magazine pictured on its cover a bona fide intellectual, David Riesman. The article was largely an accessible consideration of the American character, a synopsis of the inner and other directed concept of the individual that Riesman had written about in his *The Lonely Crowd* and that he returned to in 1954 with the publication of *Individualism Reconsidered*.[66] In typical *Time* fashion, the essential ideas of personality types developed by Riesman were glibly laid out. Faced with the dilemma that Riesman had grappled with in his concluding chapter of *The Lonely Crowd* about how to achieve autonomy in a culture that was organized to stress getting along and manipulation rather than to rely on the gyroscope of the self-sufficient, autonomous individual, *Time* turned to Riesman for advice. More play and expertise as a consumer of the arts would aid the individual to focus on what might be potentially important to him. This need not necessarily lead the intellectual or average citizen away from politics; it would grant both a larger, more energetic perspective. Moreover, Riesman advised his fellow intellectuals to stop being so prissy in their antagonism to mass culture, and 'to stop worrying about whether their judgments are approved in the market place or the ballot box, to pursue truth as independent men, affecting society as models of autonomy, not as victors on this public issue or that'.[67]

As important as the ideas that Riesman presumed to communicate for *Time*, was the image that he was given by middlebrow culture. In an information box entitled 'An Autonomous Man', the magazine offered biographical information that highlighted Riesman's breadth of knowledge, the non-specialized 'lingo' of his prose, and his refusal to rise in the hot air balloon of pure theory. Riesman became the intellectual as Everyman, comfortable with his large and active family, living in Chicago with two servants and summering on a Brattleboro, Vermont dairy farm. He was also a 'vigorous, competent' tennis player, a man attuned to clothing, food, good wine and a fan of movies ('but not "message" movies, because movies' proper message is the "enrichment of fantasy" ').[68] Indeed, the *Time* profile had transformed the alienated intellectual into a parallel version of the then emerging 'Playboy' male, but softened by a pinch of the ideal father, for better consumption and appreciation by middle-class readers.[69]

By 1956, again before Sputnik had been launched, the reformation of the image of the intellectual was well under way. Articles appeared in two exemplary middlebrow publications that announced the intellectual a major, positive force in American cultural and political life. A *Newsweek* cover depicted an egg wearing a pair of dark-framed glasses. The accompanying story found that intellectuals – affectionately viewed as eggheads – were now 'in the limelight, and somewhat favorably so'. In fact, even President Eisenhower, when a reporter noticed that he had a Latin motto on his desk, was able to joke, 'That proves I'm an egghead'. Not only could Eisenhower now claim egghead status, but as *Newsweek* clearly indicated, eggheads were powerful forces within both parties, picturing Republican intellectuals 'on the firing line' and important Democratic thinkers, including Arthur M. Schlesinger Jr and John Kenneth Galbraith.[70]

In the same year, *Time* magazine chipped in with a cover story entitled 'America and the Intellectual: The Reconciliation', with Columbia University cultural historian Jacques Barzun and the flame of knowledge burning brightly on the cover. The upshot of this story, mimicking the emphasis of the symposium 'Our Country and Our Culture', was that America's important intellectuals – Barzun, Niebuhr, Walter Lippmann, Trilling, Sidney Hook and Paul Tillich – had moved from 'protest' to 'affirmation'. Equally important, intellectuals, in embracing America, were discovering that America was more than willing to hug them in return. The intellectual is, concluded *Time*, closer than ever before to assuming the role he originally played in America: 'the critical but sympathetic – and wholly indispensable – bearer of America's message'. Barzun characterized the essential property of this message, borrowing a phrase from F. Scott Fitzgerald, as 'a willingness of the heart'.[71]

One would presume that American intellectuals, as presented by *Time* and *Newsweek*, would at last rest comfortably with their ideal function of connected critics, 'critical but sympathetic'. After all, wasn't that precisely what Schlesinger had bemoaned with the defeat of Stevenson and the turn against the intellectuals in 1952? Yet the intellectual response to this newfound celebration of the intellectual, by Schlesinger and others, was agitated rather than excited. Schlesinger found the recent articles on intellectuals to be too strong on reconciliation and insufficiently appreciative of the responsibility of intellectuals to criticize at the drop of the hat. Thus, Schlesinger announced the need (one that the popular journals had underplayed) of recognizing the variety of functions and views of intellectuals. Different functions were required at different historical moments. Presently most in need, according to Schlesinger, was 'the Intellectual as Gadfly'. Echoing the ideas of Howe, with whom Schlesinger shared strongly anti-Stalinist feelings but relatively little else, Schlesinger proclaimed that in an age of conformity and complacency 'the grouch and the grumbler, the sour puss and the curmudgeon, the non-constructive critic, the voice of dissent and the voice of protest' were most necessary. Strange musings coming from a Stevenson confidant and intellectual, who had a few years earlier published a book that attempted to revitalize liberalism as *The Vital Center* (1949). Apparently Schlesinger wanted to be wanted, as much as he desired the electorate to have had the sense to elect Stevenson. But when the middlebrow public started to 'affirm' the value of intellectuals not unlike Schlesinger, albeit as affirmers more than dissenters, Schlesinger quickly distanced himself. Similarly, in the 1960s, the self-proclaimed apostle of the avant-garde, Irving Howe, had sheltered himself from the avant-gardism of the counter-cultural generation.[72]

Today we have travelled a considerable distance from the anxieties about status, distinctions between cultural forms, and fear of mass culture that defined the post-war intellectuals. Now, it is a given that the lines between high and low culture are artificial constructs, matters of fluid relations rather than fixed categories. If the post-war intellectuals used the figure of mass culture as a bogeyman, as something vague but dangerous, in order to define themselves as intellectuals engaged in worthy pursuits, the intellectual of today occupies no such position of antagonism or anxiety. Now we find intellectuals as respectful of the blood drenched 'oeuvre' of Quentin Tarantino as of the novels of James Joyce, of the lyrics of Killdozer as of the music of Mahler. And, not surprisingly, we encounter Princeton University professor of literature Elaine Showalter talking about 'Benign dysfunction and unrequited love in the all-male household' of the latest Batman movie in a *TLS* review.[73]

What, then, distinguishes the intellectual of today? In what vault does his or her intellectual capital reside? The ability to navigate between levels of culture, without worrying to distinguish between them, appears to be the mark that defines the function of the 'postmodern' intellectual, both within and outside academe. The primary imperative of the intellectual is to engage in brilliant flights of interpretation of whatever strikes his or her fancy. The condemnation that Harold Rosenberg once uttered against Dwight Macdonald, that he was a 'kitsch' critic because he spent so much time grubbing around kitsch artefacts has lost its sting.[74] Today the intellectual brings the equipment of interpretation wherever he or she travels.

Yet it should not be presumed that the anxiety of success that plagued post-war intellectuals has vanished, although it may now express itself in a form different from the 'tragic predicament' that Hofstadter posited. Often secure in their academic bailiwicks, relatively well off financially, the current generation of successful academic intellectuals wander with their tools of interpretation throughout the cultural landscape, the mountains as well as the valleys, but they remain concerned that such treks be politically relevant, fully concentrated critiques of power. If academic intellectuals increasingly seem incapable of taking pleasure in the text of great works of art, they seem also to be increasingly concerned about the danger of enjoying popular culture too uncritically. This leads to a new version of Rosenberg's 'slumming' about in popular culture with the purpose of demonstrating brilliantly and at tiresome length its negative aspects, or at least, its dialectical propensities.

As for the anxiety of the successful intellectual in search of relevance, that enterprise is expressed in the current fascination with being a 'public intellectual', with speaking to a wider audience, with making a difference both within and outside the academy. This is a new version of the intellectuals' search for authority. Thus have academic intellectuals in the last decade in America transformed themselves into warriors for political correctness and diversity. Of course it is better to be correct than incorrect, diverse rather than monolithic. But in their zeal to prove their worth, to question the very institutional forum that has allowed them a modicum of success and comfort, many academic intellectuals risk falling into line as a 'herd of independent minds', without a deliciously developed sense of the irony, angst and distance that helped to define post-war intellectuals. Perhaps, in time, the post-war intellectuals' non-absolutist but authoritative discourse, deifying the ideals of the modernist avant-garde, upholding the transformative power of great literature against barriers of class, race and gender, and speaking in terms of traditions of criticism and alienation might make a comeback. If so, then the tensions and concerns that the post-war intellectuals exemplified may prove to be productive, if their stale descent into a deeply dug interpretive ditch can be avoided.

NOTES

1 N. Podhoretz, *Making It*, New York, Random House, 1964, p.xi.
2 Although the post-war situation in Paris was quite different from New York, or the United States in general, Bourdieu's concept of distinction and intellectual field are powerfully conveyed in Anna Boschetti, *The Intellectual Enterprise: Sartre and Les Temps Modernes* trans. Richard C. McCleary, Evanston, Northwestern University Press, 1987.
3 R. Hofstadter, *Anti-Intellectualism in American Life*, New York, Alfred A. Knopf, 1963, p. 417. In even stronger fashion, Christopher Lasch found

'fantasies of omnipotence' along with 'fears of hostility and persecution' as the dualities in the frame of mind of intellectuals in America, leading to ·'the isolation of American intellectuals, as a class, from the main currents of American life'. C. Lasch, *The New Radicalism in America, 1889–1963: The Intellectual as a Social Type*, New York, Alfred A. Knopf, 1966, p. 349.

4 Hofstadter, *Anti-Intellectualism*, p. 417.

5 Ibid., p. 419.

6 M. Walzer, *Interpretation and Social Criticism*, Cambridge, Harvard University Press, 1987, pp. 36–40. A less impressive consideration of this issue is in Edward Said, *Representations of the Intellectual*, New York, Pantheon Books, 1994.

7 I. Howe, 'The New York intellectuals', in I. Howe, *Decline of the New*, New York, Harcourt, Brace and World, 1970, p. 240.

8 In contrast, thinkers who practise currently in the field of cultural studies, are blessed (or damned) with highly specialized vocabularies and theoretical constructs which permit them to maintain their status as intellectuals. No matter how much time a cultural studies scholar spends analysing, and valorizing, popular culture, there is never any danger of he or she being considered as anything but an intellectual.

9 S. Sontag, 'Notes on "Camp" ', (1964) in *Against Interpretation*, New York, Delta, 1966, pp. 286–7.

10 Daniel Bell, *The End of Ideology: On the Exhaustion of Political Ideals in the Fifties*, revised edition, New York, Free Press, 1962, p. 300.

11 The term is used to title a section of his book, *The Tradition of the New*, Chicago, University of Chicago Press, 1960.

11a This term has come to designate a form of inexpensive, uniform mass housing (eds).

11b The so-called GI Bill approved government funding for war veterans designed to provide university education (eds).

12 These connections between concern with status and the rise of mass culture are reductionistically offered in Herbert J. Gans, *Popular Culture and High Culture: An Analysis and Evaluation of Taste*, New York, Basic Books, 1974.

13 On the relation between anti-Stalinism, Popular Front ideology and the critique of mass culture, see Andrew Ross, *No Respect: Intellectuals and Popular Culture*, New York and London, Routledge, 1989, pp. 15–64.

14 On the symposium and the mixed legacy of the post-war intellectuals, see Richard Pells, *The Liberal Mind in a Conservative Age: American Intellectuals in the 1940s and 1950s*, New York, Harper and Row, 1985. For hints on how post-war New York intellectuals attempted to redefine the nature of the term intellectual, based largely on anti-Stalinist precepts, see Neil Jumonville, *Critical Crossings: The New York Intellectuals in Post-war America*, Berkeley, University of California Press, 1991. Also helpful are Alexander Bloom, *Prodigal Sons: The New York Intellectuals and Their World*, New York, Oxford University Press, 1986; Alan M. Wald, *The New York Intellectuals: The Rise and Decline of the Anti-Stalinist Left From the 1930s to the 1980s*, Chapel Hill, University of North Carolina Press, 1987; Terry A. Cooney, *The Rise of the New York Intellectuals: Partisan Review and Its Circle, 1934–1945*, Madison, University of Wisconsin Press, 1986. Trilling called liberalism 'the sole intellectual tradition' in America; Lionel Trilling, *The Liberal Imagination: Essays on Literature and Society*, New York, Viking Press, 1950, p. ix. On the centrality of this text, see Thomas Bender, 'Lionel Trilling and American culture', *American Quarterly* 42 (June 1990), pp. 324–47.

15 R. Niebuhr in 'Our country and our culture', *Partisan Review* 19, n. 3, (May–June 1952), p. 301.

16 'Editorial statement', in 'Our country', p. 282.

17 Especially helpful on Trilling's later ambivalent relationship to modernism's adversarial culture is Mark Krupnick, *Lionel Trilling and the Fate of Cultural Criticism*, Evanston, Northwestern University Press, 1986, pp. 135–54.

18 C. Greenberg, *The Collected Essays and Criticism: Perceptions and Judgments, 1939–1944*, John O'Brien (ed.), Chicago, University of Chicago Press, 1986; H. Arendt, *The Origins of Totalitarianism*, Cleveland, Meridian Books, 1962. A third critical text for post-war intellectuals should be noted: *Escape From Authority* by Erich Fromm (New York, Rinehart, 1941). This work, with its emphasis on the alienated mind and anxious individual in search of meaning and community (alas, too often found in totalitarian movements) deeply influenced both Daniel Bell and David Riesman. But Fromm played, on the whole, less of a central role in the formulations of post-war intellectuals, especially those in New York. For a first-rate analysis of Fromm's influence, see Wilfred M. McClay,*The Masterless: Self and Society in Modern America*, Chapel Hill, University of North Carolina Press, 1994, pp. 253–8.

19 C. Greenberg, *The Collected Essays and Criticism*, op. cit., pp. 8–9.

20 Ibid., pp. 12–21.

21 A. Kazin, *New York Jew*, New York, Alfred A. Knopf, 1978, p. 195.

22 I. Howe, *A Margin of Hope: An Intellectual Autobiography*, San Diego, Harcourt Brace Jovanovich, 1982, p. 270.

23 On Arendt, see Elisabeth Young-Bruehl, *Hannah Arendt: For Love of the World*, New Haven, Yale University Press, 1984, pp. 220–1. Young-Bruehl is excellent on noting some of David Riesman's hesitations about Arendt's thesis, pp. 252–6. On the metaphysical aspects of Arendt's analysis, see Jeffrey C. Isaac, *Arendt, Camus, and Modern Rebellion*, New Haven, Yale University Press, 1992, p. 60.

24 McClay, *The Masterless*, p. 263.

25 This is not to limit the scope of Arendt's influence. Her work on the ideology and form of totalitarianism influenced the 'end of ideology' debate; Daniel Bell and other social scientists – drawing upon their own leftist anti-Stalinist backgrounds and from European theory – detailed the dangers of the mind prone toward absolutes.

26 H. Arendt, *The Origins of Totalitarianism*, op. cit., p. 333.

27 Ibid., p. 335.

28 The language employed by Macdonald and other post-war critics of mass culture bears a striking similarity, it must be admitted, to the anti-Communist rhetoric that was central to Cold War America, especially in its use of the terms infection, invasion, virus – all of which must be contained. On the culture of the Cold War and its language, see Ross, *No Respect*, op. cit., pp. 42–64; Elaine Tyler May, *Homeward Bound: American Families in the Cold War*, New York, Basic Books, 1988.

29 D. Macdonald, 'A theory of "popular culture" ', *Politics* 1 (February 1944), pp. 20–2. Also see Macdonald, 'A theory of mass culture', (1953) reprinted in *Mass Culture: The Popular Arts in America*, Glencoe, Illinois, Free Press, 1957, pp. 59–73; 'Masscult and Midcult', *Partisan Review* 27 (Spring 1960), pp. 203–33 and (Fall 1960), pp. 589–631. On Macdonald and Mass Culture, see Barry D. Riccio, 'Popular culture and high culture: Dwight Macdonald, his critics, and the ideal of cultural hierarchy in modern America', *Journal of American Culture* 16 (Winter 1993), pp. 7–18; Michael Wreszin, *A Rebel in Defense of Tradition: A Life and Politics of Dwight Macdonald*, New York, Basic Books, 1994, Ch. 12.

30 Bernard Rosenberg, 'Mass culture in America', in *Mass Culture*, op. cit., pp. 3–12.

31 I. Howe, 'Notes on mass culture', (1948) in *Mass Culture*, p. 499.

32 E. Van Den Haag, 'Of happiness and despair we have no measure', in *Mass Culture*, pp. 524–5.

33 Niebuhr, 'Our country and our culture', op. cit., pp. 302–3.

34 Bell, *The End of Ideology*, op. cit., pp. 22, 25.

35 Riesman, 'Our country and our culture', op. cit., pp. 312–13.

36 D. Riesman, 'Listening to popular music', in *Individualism Reconsidered*, Glencoe, Illinois, Free Press, 1954, pp. 183–93.

37 D. Riesman, 'Culture: popular and unpopular', in *Individualism Reconsidered*, pp. 180–1. For a finely modulated analysis of the benefits and debits of middlebrow culture, see Joan Shelley Rubin, *The Making of Middlebrow Culture*, Chapel Hill, University of North Carolina Press, 1992.

38 Howard Brick, *Daniel Bell and the Decline of Intellectual Radicalism: Social Theory and Political Reconciliation in the 1940s*, Madison, University of Wisconsin Press, 1986, p. 139.

39 H. Rosenberg, 'Pop culture: kitsch criticism', in Rosenberg, *The Tradition of the New*, op. cit., p. 263.

40 E. Shils, 'Daydreams and nightmares: reflections on the criticism of mass culture', (1957) in *The Intellectuals and the Powers and Other Essays*, Chicago, University of Chicago Press, 1972, p. 261.

41 C. Wright Mills, 'The social role of the intellectual', in *Power, Politics and People: The Collected Essays of C. Wright Mills*, Irving Louis Horowitz (ed.), New York, Oxford University Press, 1963, pp. 295, 301.

42 I. Howe, 'This age of conformity', *Partisan Review* 21 (January–February 1954), pp. 8, 9. Howe followed publication of his essay by founding a new journal, aptly called *Dissent*, dedicated to the spirit of protest and organized against the complacency and conformism of 1950s culture.

43 H. S. Hughes, 'Is the intellectual obsolete? The freely speculating mind in America', *Commentary* 22 (1956), pp. 318, 319.

44 L. Fiedler, 'The middle against both ends', (1955) in *Mass Culture*, op. cit., p. 547.

45 I. Howe, 'The New York Intellectuals', op. cit., pp. 226–7.

46 Howe, 'This age of conformity', op. cit., p. 13.

47 Howard Brick brilliantly demonstrates how alienation and estrangement served as essentials in 'the process of deradicalization' and political impotency. See Brick, *Daniel Bell*, op. cit., p. 13.

48 Howe, 'This age of conformity', p. 21. For a later, similar evaluation of the ideological character of Cold War criticism, see Tobin Siebers, *Cold War Criticism and the Politics of Skepticism*, New York, Oxford University Press, 1993, pp. 29–70.

49 Howe, 'This age of conformity', pp. 23–5.

50 I. Howe, *Politics and the Novel*, New York, Meridian, 1957, p. 16.

51 I. Howe, 'Black boys and native sons', *Dissent* (Autumn 1963), p. 355.

52 Ibid., pp. 363–4.

53 Ellison, 'The world and the jug', in *Shadow and Act*, New York, Vintage, 1995, pp. 112–13.

54 Howe, 'Notes on mass culture', op. cit., pp. 497–8.

55 Howe, 'The New York intellectuals', op. cit., p. 256.

56 For a brilliant, if sometimes too harsh, evaluation of the post-war intellectuals, see Morris Dickstein, *Gates of Eden: American Culture in the Sixties*, New York, Basic Books, 1977, pp. 8–10.

57 N. Podhoretz, 'The know-nothing Bohemians', (1958), reprinted in T. Parkinson (ed.), *A Casebook on the Beat*, New York, Thomas Y. Crowell, 1961, pp. 204, 211, 212.

58 Hofstadter, *Anti-Intellectualism*, p. 393.

59 Quoted in Hofstadter, *Anti-Intellectualism*, p. 15. Hofstadter titled one of his chapters: 'On the unpopularity of the intellect', pp. 24–51.

60 Trilling, 'Our country and our culture', op. cit., p. 320.

61 Typical of this view, see Seymour Martin Lipset, *Political Man: The Social Bases of Politics*, New York, Doubleday, 1960, Ch. 10. Also, Lewis A. Coser, *Men of Ideas: A Sociologist's View*, New York, Free Press, 1965, Part 3.

62 Louis Bromfield, 'The triumph of the egghead', *The Freeman* 3 (1 December 1952), p. 158.

63 Arthur M. Schlesinger, Jr, 'The highbrow in American politics', *Partisan Review* 20 (March–April 1953), p. 158.

64 On the introduction of the term into the 1952 election, see Joseph and Stewart Alsop, *The Reporter's Trade*, New York, Reynal, 1958, p. 188.

65 Schlesinger, 'The highbrow in politics', op.cit., p. 161.

66 D. Riesman, with Reuel Denney and Nathan Glazer, *The Lonely Crowd: A Study of the Changing American Character*, New Haven, Yale University Press, 1950. McClay, *The Masterless*, op.cit., pp. 236–57.

67 'What is the American character?' *Time* 64 (22 September 1954), p. 25.

68 Ibid., p. 24.

69 On the Playboy ideal in the 1950s, see Barbara Ehrenreich, *The Hearts of Men: American Dreams and the Flight From Commitment*, New York, Doubleday, 1983, pp. 42–51.

70 'The egghead: who he is and who he thinks he is', *Newsweek* 48 (8 October 1956), 53.

71 'America and the intellectuals: the reconciliation', *Time* 67 (11 June 1956), p. 70.

72 Schlesinger, '*Time* and the intellectuals', *The New Republic* 135 (16 July 1956), p. 17. Similarly, Dan Wakefield, 'Branding the eggheads: but the brand won't stick', *Nation* 183 (24 November 1956), pp. 456–8.

73 E. Showalter, 'Dracula lite forever', *The Times Literary Supplement* n. 4816 (21 July 1995), p. 16. On Killdozer, see Clint Burnham, *The Jamesonian Unconscious*, Durham, Duke University Press, 1995.

74 Rosenberg, 'Pop culture: kitsch criticism', in *The Tradition of the New*, op. cit., p. 263.

13 Are intellectuals a dying species?

War and the Ivory Tower in the postmodern age[1]

David L. Schalk

I doubt if I am alone among my colleagues, who have the pretentiousness or the folly to call themselves 'intellectual historians', in admitting how easy it is to get stuck at square one with the question of definition, and hence face real difficulties in beginning any serious analysis. Few of us are absolutely certain that we know precisely what an intellectual is, even if we have sensitive antennae which tell us when we meet someone whether we think he or she is a member of the species.

Of all the attempts to arrive at a satisfactory working definition of this vaguely delimited social grouping we know as 'the intellectuals', there are two I find especially interesting and useful. The first is universal in scope and comes from Sandy Vogelgesang's excellent study of the American Intellectual Left during the Vietnam era – intellectuals are: 'men and women of ideas who explore and challenge the underlying values of society. Theirs is a normative function: to prescribe what ought to be'.[2] This definition could be applied without undue strain to such diverse individuals as George Orwell and Simone de Beauvoir, Friedrich Nietzsche and Hannah Arendt. The second definition does not really contradict the first, but is a specific and time-bound addendum to it: '*Intellectual*, noun, masculine gender, a social and cultural category born in Paris at the moment of the Dreyfus Affair, dead in Paris at the end of the twentieth century; apparently was not able to survive the decline of belief in Universals.'[3]

This is an imagined entry from a hypothetical dictionary to be published in the year 2000, as formulated by the 'New Philosopher' and media personality Bernard-Henri Lévy, in his intriguing little book which appeared in 1987, *Éloge des Intellectuels*. Lévy's definition struck a lot of sensitive nerves, and has been cited on both sides of the Atlantic, usually as an epigraph without additional commentary.[4] The context around which Lévy devised this definition is of interest.

As observers of the contemporary French scene know, Lévy has moved beyond (or beneath) *l'Idéologie française*, which appeared in 1981, a quite powerful and important polemic which found echoes in much of the debate about Vichy France in recent years. A decade later he brought out the rambling and incoherent *Les Aventures de la liberté: Une histoire subjective des intellectuels.* In 1993, the painfully dull and tortuously pedantic investigation of the relation between the sexes, *Les hommes et les femmes,* which Lévy co-authored with Françoise Giroud, was for a while the number one best seller in France, whatever that says about the literary tastes of the French *grand public.*[5]

Back in 1987, however, Lévy was more provocative and informative. On the occasion of the publication of *Éloge des Intellectuels,* he told the *New York Times* in an interview that 'France is a country where the glory of literature has always been linked by a concrete, massive engagement in the affairs of the century'.[6] Now, he added, engagement has ended, intellectuals are no longer hated and assaulted as they were in earlier times. Looking back to the age of engagement, Lévy referred very specifically to the period of the Algerian War, 1954–62. The crisis intellectuals were going through in the 1980s was, he thought, a quiet collapse, a 'débâcle', intimately linked with their withdrawal from the public stage and their return to the ivory tower.[7]

While on the subject of definitions, and the point will become important in the argument of this chapter, let us remember that the ivory tower is not just the university, as it is sometimes understood to be, in the United States at least, but in its original nineteenth century derivation referred more generally to the intellectual's home. As Flaubert wrote to Louise Colet in 1852, in the modern world of a developing mass culture which he so detested, 'we must, independently from that humanity which rejects us, live for our vocation, climb into our ivory tower, and remain there alone with our dreams'. Already, in 1837, Sainte-Beuve spoke of the poet Alfred de Vigny as 'the most secretive of poets, who before noon retires to his ivory tower'.[8]

According to Bernard-Henri Lévy the generalized and irrevocable retreat into that very place, which he observed in the 1980s, and few commentators would question the accuracy of this perception, was going to produce an effect which Flaubert could neither have imagined nor would have desired: namely the intellectuals' disappearance as a distinct social grouping. Already, Lévy argued, surviving intellectuals suffer from a sense of unreality; in the country of Voltaire and Zola, businessmen, singers, and actors are now consecrated as *'maîtres à penser'.*[9]

There appears to be a close though complex link between the intellectual (as opposed to the 'mandarin', or 'specialist') and engagement, and that *the one may be impossible without the other.* That the very appearance of intellectuals, and thus manifestation of engagement, of critical dissent, might prove to be a 'passing phenomenon, born on the streets of Paris (at the height of the Dreyfus Affair) in 1898, and dying there exactly seventy years later' was suggested in my 1979 volume, *The Spectrum of Political Engagement.*[10] I was thinking, of course, of the notorious events of May 1968, when the students, apprentice intellectuals if you will, took their elders and nominal mentors by surprise. For a brief, euphoric, and most would argue never to be repeated, moment those students seemed to 'rule' Paris in a spirit of joyous anarchy.[11]

After 1979, when disengagement (*dégagement*) was already widespread though not universal, the question of the continued existence of the class to which I belonged would not let go of me, nor I of it, but I could not figure out a way to come to grips with it in an intelligible manner. Gradually, I came to the conclusion that a single case study offered the most fruitful possibilities. Given my professional training as a Europeanist, the topic with the greatest potential seemed to be the wave of intellectual engagement that began in November 1954 in response to France's undeclared war in Algeria. I wanted to find out what kind of a wave it was – an exceptionally large one in a series, or solitary and unrepeatable – and how it related to the status and possibly the survival of the intellectual class.

It was at this precise moment that I had what a religious person might call a 'moment of epiphany', or an 'oceanic experience'. I conceived the extravagant, perhaps foolhardy, notion of drawing the parallels between Algeria and America's war in Vietnam, from the perspective of the responses of the respective intelligentsias to both tragic and divisive wars. So I embarked on the project, assuming that as a trained historian I could at least subdue if not eliminate my own extremely powerful feelings about America in Vietnam, not to mention my less intense, vicarious as *un étranger*, but none the less very real emotional response to the Algerian war.[12] The direct result of that moment is *War and the Ivory Tower: Algeria and Vietnam*. The primary purpose of this essay is to revisit and update the arguments of that book before the Gulf War very briefly (for the last time?) stirred up the American intelligentsia.

In *War and the Ivory Tower*, I was clearly, perhaps nostalgically, looking back to modernity and away from the surrounding postmodernity. Hence, the imagined dictionary definition from the year 2000 I offered towards the end of the book, turning Bernard-Henri Lévy on his head: 'Intellectual, noun [from the French, *intellectuel*], a social and cultural category first described in Paris at the moment of the Dreyfus affair and quickly adopted into English. Refers to men and women given to the exercise of the intellect, but also prone to periodic intervention in public life. See Engagement.'

Perhaps some brief observations on when our fabled postmodern age began are in order here. Surely in France by 1978, with the publication of François Furet's *Interpreting the French Revolution*, and perhaps in 1974 when the influential review *Tel Quel* broke with Maoism. What we can say with a fair degree of certainty is that the postmodern age began in earnest with the death of Jean-Paul Sartre in 1980, and his celebrated mass funeral was the last – at least up to this writing in January 1996 – echo of an earlier age of significant intellectual engagement. Every commentator on French and American intellectual affairs, on both sides of the Atlantic now agrees that we are immersed (or sunk, depending on one's evaluation) into postmodernity, however one wishes to define that elusive term.

Turning now to the arguments of *War and the Ivory Tower*, any discussion of the striking – one might want to use the word haunting – similarities between what I have called the two cycles of engagement, means beginning with the wars themselves, to which the intellectuals were responding.

Let us remember that these were long (eight and nine years respectively) and undeclared wars, separated exactly by a decade. Similarities between the two conflicts were discovered very early, at least by December 1964, only four months after the Tonkin Gulf Resolution which signalled the escalation of the conflict in Vietnam.

In the *New York Review of Books* (henceforth *NYRB*), later to become known as the 'Bible of Vietnamese Dissent', the British novelist and critic D. A. N. Jones reviewed a work by Lieutenant Pierre Leuillette entitled *Saint Michael and the Dragon: Memoirs of a Paratrooper*. The book had been published four years earlier in French and is an account of Leuillette's service in the Algerian war. The paratroop units with their snappy berets and leopard camouflage uniforms were the toughest and most brutal in the French army, and under General Jacques Massu they took charge of the 'pacification' of the city of Algiers in 1956.

Leuillette's memoir had been quite controversial, for it openly admitted that the French forces employed methods of interrogation and retaliation 'for which German war criminals were universally execrated and finally hanged'. The second step, drawing the parallel between their Algerian and our Vietnam wars, was already taken. Jones observed that the Algerian war was almost as savage as the campaign that had been waged on behalf of the South Vietnamese dictator Diem. Leuillette, as would General Massu himself a few years later, calmly stated what French anti-war intellectuals had been ardently claiming since 1955, that torture had been widely employed by their army in Algeria, especially by the paratroops. To read his account, Mr Jones asserts, is 'to feel dirty'. The French, he stated, lost their war, and deservedly.

In 1964, news photographs were already being shown in England of 'Free World' tortures at work in Vietnam. Jones felt that it would be difficult to win European support for the American war in Vietnam, 'except among those who enjoy cruelty'. Leuillette's account, Jones thought, 'preaches the lesson which it took him too long to learn, that there are certain ways of hurting which are not tolerable, which will strip you of your manhood and your will to win'.[13] Obviously, field commanders in Vietnam did not subscribe to the *NYRB* and, if they read Leuillette, they did not understand the implications of his message. But the issue of torture is raised, two months *before* the February 1965 decision was made to send ground troops to Vietnam on a massive scale.

Briefly, other parallels which have been drawn range widely – from a global perspective that views both bitter struggles as episodes in a larger historical process of decolonization, to a specific focus on political, diplomatic and military matters.

The political approach emphasizes the changes of regimes after four years of war in both countries, in 1958 and 1968, with more conservative governments than those under which the wars began ultimately making peace. In this context, I cannot resist citing an example, little known but which I can fully document, of what we might term the 'sedative' or 'soporific' use of history. In his anguish and uncertainty over how to terminate the war which Lyndon Johnson had bequeathed to his administration, President Richard Nixon was calmed by 'stories of the torturous and deceptive extrication' accomplished a decade earlier by President Charles de Gaulle. The storyteller was none other than Henry Kissinger.[14] This anecdote was corroborated from a different angle by Redha Malek, former Algerian ambassador to France and to the United States, prime minister from the summer of 1993 to the spring of 1994, and erstwhile candidate for the Presidency of Algeria in 1995. Louis Joxe, the principal French negotiator of the Evian accords of March 1962 ending the Algerian war, informed M. Malek, who had been on the opposing negotiating team, of a visit by Henry Kissinger to Paris in 1969. Kissinger came to enquire about techniques which M. Joxe had employed in negotiating with the FLN, which he, Kissinger, could transfer to his upcoming negotiations with the Vietnamese NLF (National Liberation Front).[15]

Military comparisons include the size of the expeditionary forces, a half million in both cases at their peaks, the use of draftees, the blind and persistent optimism of the commanding officers (in the French case, the stock phrase was 'the last fifteen minutes' (*le dernier quart d'heure*); in the American, 'the light at the end of the tunnel'). There were similar, essentially identical, techniques of 'pacification', including relocation of vast civilian populations, the use of free fire zones (*zones interdites*) and, probably most tragically, even horrifically, the same techniques of torture, not to mention similar debates over war crimes and the drawing of the Nuremberg parallels.

Indeed the surface similarities are so dramatic that somewhat less attention has been paid to certain obvious differences. Perhaps the most significant was the presence of a settler population of nearly a million in Algeria. A not unimportant fact is that since television only became a fixture in French households in the 1960s, Algeria was not the 'living room war' that Vietnam later became.

Were there similarities in *actions against* the two wars, efforts to halt the spread of the syndromes, especially on the part of engaged intellectuals; and did the Americans draw any lessons of value from the French experience? These questions lay at the heart of my research. An analysis of the nature and extent of these similarities forms the core of *War and the Ivory Tower*.

My research led me to conceive of these two cases of intellectual engagement in terms, first, of varieties, then as patterns, and finally as cycles – cycles that are remarkably similar, if not identical. The view of history as cyclical goes back a long way, at least to the great Italian Giovanni Batista

Vico (1668–1744). My own training and thinking has always been linear and progressivist and I had difficulty accepting what I was discovering, but the evidence, at least for the period from 1954–73, is very strong, even if it should prove true that the sequence of cycles has now ended and that we are in a period of complete and steady disengagement for the foreseeable future.

During Algeria and Vietnam, the cycles of engagement operated in the following manner: once the condition of disengagement was abandoned, there were three stages, or levels, each of which can be quite precisely delineated. The first was composed of calm, rational, frequently scholarly, presentations, in an effort to persuade the leaders of the governments in question of the errors of their ways. I call this stage 'pedagogic'. Under the pressure of events, this was transformed gradually into a second stage, which I term simply the 'moral': a condition of outrage, distress, shame, and a sentiment of confusion and impasse – and uncertainty as to the form that engagement must now adopt.

By the third year of full-scale American military involvement in Vietnam – 1966 – a large percentage of the American intelligentsia had moved to the second level, as had their French compatriots in response to the Algerian situation exactly a decade earlier.

A powerful example of this stage in the United States may be found in Elizabeth Hardwick's almost unbearably poignant 'We are all murderers', from the issue of 3 March 1966 of the *NYRB*. Ostensibly a review of Jean-Paul Sartre's play, *The Condemned of Altona*, Hardwick's article actually addressed the moral questions raised by our presence in Vietnam. Sartre's great political drama, first performed in Paris in 1959, was a perfect vehicle for this message, since the play, which superficially is about German guilt during World War II, was in actuality an allegorical representation of French guilt for atrocities committed during the Algerian War.

Hardwick attended the American première at the repertory theatre of Lincoln Center, and noted that the audience did not seem to grasp Sartre's message. In the intermission she heard people speaking of the 'Condemned of Altoona [Pennsylvania]', and she wondered if we could 'ask ourselves to make the leap from Germany to Algeria to ourselves'.

Parenthetically, I think that for many Americans of the Vietnam generation at least, Altoona symbolizes the middle-American spirit which arguably, if it did not lead my country into the Vietnam disaster, kept us there until 1973, or 1975, depending on whether one prefers the cut-off date of the end of direct American military involvement, or that of the military defeat and collapse of the South Vietnamese government. One thinks also of Michael Cimino's magnificent and gripping 1978 film, *The Deer Hunter*, much of which takes place in an industrial city of Pennsylvania, 'Clairton', which could easily be substituted for Altoona, and I believe answers Norman Mailer's question of 1967, 'Why are we in Vietnam?', better than any single work of art with which I am acquainted.[16]

Ms Hardwick observed that American theatregoers are not accustomed to dramas like Sartre's, and that plays which 'seek a greater historical and social engagement' have had little success on our stage. We prefer dramas of individual neurotic tensions (I assume she had Eugene O'Neill and Tennessee Williams in mind). Maybe, she adds, our external situation has changed, our historical experience may be pushing us to a 'true meeting with guilt, leading us to suffering, to acquaintance with the sorrows and mysteries and miseries to which *hubris* and power have led other nations'. But we are not quite ready yet. None of us understands in 1966 what is happening here in 'Altoona', nor what happened some decades ago in 'Altona'.[17]

When the French and American intelligentsias reached the third stage, which they had largely by 1957 and 1967 respectively, they did understand what happened in Altona and Algiers, and later in Altoona and Saigon.

The third level of engagement, which I term 'counter legal' in my book, led in both cases to an invocation of the precedents believed to be established by the Nuremberg trials, and the personal acceptance and public advocacy of a variety of 'illegal' means in an effort to end wars which many had come to view as leading fatally to genocide.

In both countries, there was a wide range within the spectrum of 'illegal' activities. There were bitter and sometimes even vicious debates between those who insisted upon a non-violent approach, such as pouring blood on draft files or burning them with home-made napalm, and those who accepted violence and even aid to forces which were *de facto* enemies of France and the United States, if not *de jure*, since we recall that both wars were never formally declared.

Most French and American intellectuals remained *engagé* rather than becoming what I like to term *embrigadé*, that is fully abandoning their critical spirit in the unquestioning support of a political cause.

In the United States, we did not enter completely into the third stage until after the publication in the *NYRB* in February 1967, and wide circulation thereafter, of the programmatic essay by Noam Chomsky, 'The responsibility of intellectuals', which had a major impact, and led to a flurry of responses which appeared in the *NYRB* and elsewhere. Of special note was an exchange of letters between Chomsky and the eminent critic, essayist and Cambridge professor George Steiner. Steiner praised Chomsky for his powerful exposure of the 'mendacities that surround us.... But what then? You rightly say that we are all responsible, you rightly hint that our future status may be no better than that of acquiescent intellectuals under Nazism, but what action do you urge or suggest?' Steiner wonders whether Chomsky will 'help his students escape to Mexico (as Jeanson helped his students leave France during the Algerian Crisis)'[18] Steiner, not being fully attuned to the American scene, would have been more accurate had he written 'Canada', the country of exile chosen by most American draft resisters. Steiner was referring to Francis Jeanson, former protégé of Sartre, and philosopher turned anti-war activist. During the Algerian war, Jeanson was most famous, or infamous if one prefers, as the elusive leader of the 'suitcase brigade' (*les porteurs de valises*), whom the French police were never able to apprehend. It was in October 1957 that Jeanson went underground. *Les porteurs de valises* were amazingly effective in funnelling money contributed by Algerian workers across the border into Swiss banks, from which it was spent on weapons for the Algerian independence forces.

Chomsky gave an ambivalent answer to Steiner's query, indicating his own painful doubts. Up to that time, he had committed only non-violent acts of witness, refusing to pay his income tax. Like many French intellectuals during the Algerian war, he refused to advocate draft refusal publicly, 'since it is a rather cheap proposal from someone my age'.[19] Whether Chomsky later became *embrigadé* is debatable; his subsequent actions were certainly counter legal. He was arrested a few months later during the march on the Pentagon of October 1967, as marvellously described in Norman Mailer's *The Armies of the Night*.

Finally, the cycles draw to a close, and at the end of both wars we observe a rapid return to what appears to be the ordinary life of academics, if not all intellectuals – the calm and comfort of the ivory tower.

Is this disengagement as permanent as Bernard-Henri Lévy intuits and other scholars have argued after considerable research? As early as 1977, Paul Sorum, in his book *Intellectuals and Decolonization*, concluded that the activities of French intellectuals during the war in Algeria 'may prove to be the final great battle in the long tradition of France's "engaged" intellectuals'.[20] From our vantage point nearly two decades later, it would be extremely difficult to claim that the French intelligentsia has moved since the early 1970s even to stage one. For many observers, myself included, it is difficult to find factors in French society which would suggest that a new cycle of engagement will begin any time soon. Some scholars – such as Pascal Ory and Jean-François Sirinelli in their extremely useful and informative general history of French intellectuals in the twentieth century, first published in 1986 – were less certain. They saw flux and reflux, but a generally ascending curve of engagement as this century wore on.[21]

Already, in 1986, they admitted to having some difficulty explaining the extended period of disengagement which began in 1971, when a kind of 'lassitude' set in following the period of intense activism, largely student initiated, which peaked in 1968. They suggested very astutely that intellectuals in France were in a stage of *échaudement*, which I might translate loosely as 'burnout', when, 'judging themselves to have been deceived by one or several previous engagements, the intellectuals refuse any new mobilization'.[22] While Ory and Sirinelli are historians, not futurologists, and they hesitated to make predictions, it was clear that in 1986 they expected the period of 'burnout' to be overlong already, and that some form of engagement was due to reappear fairly soon.

By 1990, Sirinelli, in his very important and provocative study of the petition as a key ingredient in intellectual engagement, *Intellectuels et passions françaises*, had shifted his views considerably, and could write that

French anti-*Vietnam* war engagement of the late 1960s and early 1970s was a 'swansong'.[23] We should note that *this* engagement was somewhat conflicted and never as clearly focused as our own, for obvious reasons. President de Gaulle was himself firmly opposed to American involvement in Vietnam, and said so publicly on a number of occasions, including in a highly controversial 1966 speech delivered nearby in Phnom Penh, Cambodia.

Sirinelli then develops a very convincing sequential argument. The 'ideological crisis' of the mid-1970s, triggered by the Solzhenitsyn affair, and the final removal of ideological blinders and the full recognition of the true nature of Soviet society as symbolized by the Gulag, was followed for the intellectuals by an 'identity crisis'. At this point Sirinelli suggests, though will not yet definitively posit, that we may be 'at the end of the trail', (*la fin de la piste*) after nine decades of 'dense engagement'.[24] And Sirinelli is willing in 1990 to go as far as to ask the question, though as a professional historian rather than a polemicist he will not hazard an answer, of whether the time has come to sound the death-knell of the intellectuals, *Faut-il sonner le glas des intellectuels?*[25]

It is fascinating to move ahead a scant two years and look at the concluding chapters of the *second* edition of Ory and Sirinelli's history of the intellectuals. By 1992, of course, the Berlin Wall had come down, and the Soviet Union had broken apart. The authors were now willing to admit that the French intelligentsia had entered a real and perhaps more permanent state of crisis, both of ideology and of identity.

Many of Ory and Sirinelli's insights are extraordinarily enlightening, and persuasive; I cannot discuss them here in any detail, but simply would recommend their second edition to francophone readers, and hope that it finds an English translation. I shall mention just two or three of their most intriguing arguments. First, they observe that it is possible that we may be misreading the situation, and that French intellectuals may not be totally disengaged, but rather simply 'less heeded' (*moins écoutés*).[26] They add that French society has now become sceptical about intellectuals – and, I would note parenthetically, as American society has always been, when it has not been downright hostile. Ory and Sirinelli are certainly on the mark in observing that whatever conclusions one wants to draw, the silence of the intellectuals in their homeland still 'makes some noise in French society' (*fait du bruit dans la société*).[27] I would suggest two reasons for this 'noisy silence'. Doubtless, the absence of engagement still seems surprising to many observers, themselves intellectuals, and thus is the subject of much commentary. Also, one must not forget the long-lasting and doubtless still residual tradition of the high prestige enjoyed by French intellectuals; I recall being taught in the 1950s that France was 'the intellectual's paradise'.

Finally, to bring matters as up to date as possible, in October 1995, Sirinelli brought out a major work, *Deux Intellectuels dans le siècle: Sartre et Aron*. The heart of this book is a comparison of two of France's greatest twentieth-century intellectuals, briefly friends and for many years quite bitter ideological enemies. Sirinelli struggles valiantly, and in this reader's view generally successfully, to make his clear preference for Raymond Aron irrelevant to his analysis and interpretation. For our purposes, what is most interesting are Sirinelli's conclusions, where he returns to the general question of the French intellectual class, and its very existence as a coherent group. He now believes that enough time has elapsed for us to see that the period of intense activism represented by the Algerian war was 'a sort of Indian Summer for French intellectuals'.[28] By 1995, it has become apparent that, beginning in 1975, there has been 'an incontestable crisis in the French intellectual class' (*une crise incontestable de la cléricature française*).[29] For the 1945–75 period, it has become possible, Sirinelli believes (much as economic historians do for the sectors they study), to speak of a *Trente Glorieuses* in the history of French intellectuals. Definitively, by 1975, what first appeared to be a phase of retreat (*repli*), began the so-called *années orphelines*. Though Sirinelli does not build upon this metaphor, one could hypothesize that a principal problem of our postmodern age for orphaned intellectuals is that no satisfactory substitute parents have been located.

So, Sirinelli argues, in 1995 we are witnessing the termination of a 'secular *trend* which began with the Dreyfus Affair and during which the intellectual had ruled with majesty' (*trôné en majesté* – a phrase which in everyday American discourse might be better rendered as 'arrogantly ruled the roost').[30] Sirinelli is willing to admit that the time seems to have passed for passionate debates among intellectuals (*des grandes joutes entre clercs*). He resists nostalgia, but he thinks that clearly 'a period has come to an end' (*une période s'est refermée*).[31] For Sirinelli, the burial of Sartre in April 1980 may be viewed as symbolizing the end of an epoch.

In my country, since the end of the Vietnam war, the intellectuals have remained almost constantly at the level of complete disengagement. As early as 1974, Sandy Vogelgesang suggested in her remarkable book *The Long Dark Night of the Soul*, published while the Vietnam War was still raging (though without direct American military involvement, which had ended in January 1973), that 'the leftist intellectuals' opposition to the Vietnam War may have been a rear-guard exercise in futility against the Age of Technology'.[32]

In the 1980s, President Ronald Reagan enjoyed a brilliant success in suppressing intellectual engagement against his administration and his person. He kept a lot of very smart people, who perhaps unwisely scorned him, at bay. Polls that I have seen suggest that around 80 per cent of the professoriate remained opposed to him, and voted against him in 1980 and 1984. It is almost as if Reagan, unlike Johnson and Nixon, possessed an intuitive sense that told him when to stop. One thinks of the invasion of Grenada – a very rapid action, just one day; or Reagan's policy toward Nicaragua – just enough aid to maintain the Contras, but never enough to mobilize the American intelligentsia.

President Bush's actions in Panama, and even the somewhat more extensive though still remarkably brief war with Iraq in February 1991, followed his predecessor's model. We should remember that it was the domestic economy, and not Bush's international adventuring, that cost him the presidency in 1992. Whether these lightning military 'victories' cured the 'Vietnam syndrome' is a separate question, which, as noted above, is not directly relevant to this analysis.

My own view concerning the American intellectual class, though tempered and far less certain, remains essentially unchanged from 1990. I would argue that, in the post-Cold War era, the American intelligentsia is not really moribund, but rather, similar to France, in what Ory and Sirinelli called in 1986 a period of 'mutation'.[33] Exactly what forms those mutations might take are of course open to a variety of speculation.

I submit that we could see in the United States a resurgence of engagement, and hence a confident re-emergence of the intellectual class, if two factors are simultaneously present.

First, a government has to do something stupid and evil enough to elicit a profound moral reaction. Given any acquaintance with the long span of recorded human history, one would surely conclude that this is not an impossibility.

The second factor, which would lead from a moral response to a counter-legal one and to a full cycle of engagement, is, I readily admit, more problematic. The way this factor operates can be well illustrated by returning to America during the Vietnam war era. Let us not forget that for several years, especially between 1966 and 1970, significant numbers of intellectuals, ranging from graduate students to professors nearing retirement, from ministers, nuns, and priests like Father Daniel Berrigan, from physicians to artists, novelists and poets, were willing to take the third step into full engagement. Why did they volunteer to help young men escape to Canada? Why did they travel to Hanoi like Susan Sontag, Mary McCarthy, and Noam Chomsky and a number of others (not just Jane Fonda!), risking popular hatred, to say nothing of legal action?

Mary McCarthy herself admitted in a letter to the *NYRB*, shortly after her return from Hanoi, that the 'power of intellectuals, sadly limited, is to persuade, not to provide against all contingencies. They are not God.' And they are rarely politically gifted: 'What we can do, perhaps better than the next man, is smell a rat.'[34] Maybe we can agree that intellectuals do possess an acute olfactory sense, but this would boil down to the first factor already mentioned, a moral sensibility.

I submit that there is a distinct second ingredient which is necessary, namely that intellectuals will *not* move into full engagement (in significant numbers and organized in some fashion, however loosely) if the external situation which calls them out of their ivory towers, rationally examined, appears totally hopeless. This may be an absolutely central point; in this country there have been eloquent and forceful appeals, as of this writing completely unheeded, for academic intellectuals at least to re-emerge from their somnolence and become engaged, largely in protest against the expected devastating cuts in funding for educational and cultural activities which are expected to be voted by the Republican-controlled Congress. There is a widespread sense of the danger to American intellectual life and free discourse represented by the Republican right wing, and especially by the activities and policies of the Speaker of the House, Newt Gingrich, who as a failed academic appears to have an unusually virulent detestation of the class to which he once, albeit marginally, belonged.

To illustrate the argument for the second ingredient, I shall return to the Vietnam era, to a brilliant statement by Michael Ferber, 'On being indicted', published in the *NYRB*, 25 April 1968. Ferber, at the time, was a graduate student in the English department at Harvard, and was the youngest member of the Boston Five – Dr Benjamin Spock, Marcus Raskin, Reverend William Sloane Coffin and Mitchell Goodman – who had been indicted for conspiracy to violate the Selective Service Act. Ferber attempted to explain why so many joined what was widely and deliberately called 'the Resistance', with its echoes of World War II and movements resisting the Nazi occupation of most of Europe. In 1968, the decision to resist brought with it the attendant risk of imprisonment:

> Men whose insides were ready for commitment needed only the barest hope of a chance that their gesture would be *more than an act of moral witness*, that with sufficient numbers and organization they just might have a measurable impact. They were willing to pay a high price; all that was needed was the chance that the price *might not be for nothing*.

This formulates the issue beautifully, and the fact that highly intelligent men and women, whose insides may be ready for commitment in 1996, have concluded that society has evolved to the point where any actions in the public sphere would simply be isolated and ignored acts of moral witness, may be the central factor in producing the end of engagement, and hence the end of the intellectual.

If pushed out of my usual role of 'objective' historian, however, I would, if more hesitantly, sustain the prediction I made when *War and the Ivory Tower* went to press. After all, given mass education, the potential recruits to a resurgent intellectual class have grown dramatically in numbers. Obviously, a new generation of leaders and some form of consciousness shift will be needed.

The twin questions of leadership and group consciousness deserve brief commentary by way of conclusion. Regarding the former, except for minuscule extremist fringes, there is widespread scepticism among the educated segments of French and American society, and a clear reluctance to abandon one's critical spirit and follow a single leader, no matter how charismatic. In 1996, it is difficult to imagine the emergence of another Jean-Paul Sartre, who, at the peak of his career, could mobilize a hundred thousand followers. This was well understood by President de Gaulle, who refused to order Sartre's arrest during the Algerian war, despite the philosopher's efforts to provoke the government. Of course, it is always possible that an individual of extreme brilliance and magnetism will appear on the scene and capture the allegiance of a broad segment of the now dormant intellectual class, but one could also imagine a series of smaller, more localized, groupings, temporarily rallying round some larger cause.

This brings me to the question of a consciousness shift. I very explicitly did not suggest that an unswerving commitment to an ideology was a necessary ingredient for a revival of engagement. Indeed, I would agree with Bernard-Henri Lévy that the decline of belief in universals is most likely permanent. It appears doubtful, though not impossible, that a new meta-narrative will emerge, which will have the comparable appeal of, for example, Marxism from approximately 1920–70 and existentialism from 1945–65. But some form of, probably temporary, coalescence of diverse, loosely-held, quasi-ideological groupings around specific issues, which appear to be susceptible to change through concerted intellectual effort, is not inconceivable.

Hence, I submit that it is at least possible that the 'obstructed path' will become clear for the two factors which I have argued to be the necessary preconditions for a resurgent engagement to converge in the United States, and perhaps in France, too. I would not bet, therefore, that Bernard-Henri Levy's definition of the intellectual will be found in dictionaries published in the year 2000, and beyond.

NOTES

1 *War and the Ivory Tower: Algeria and Vietnam*, New York, Oxford University Press, 1991. An abbreviated version of this chapter was given as a lecture at the University of Wales, Swansea, on 30 October 1995. I am grateful to Dr Jeremy Jennings and his former colleagues at Swansea for their invitation and their acute and perceptive criticisms. Some of their suggestions have found their way into the text that follows, though of course I am totally responsible for both the argument and the factual underpinnings of this chapter.

2 S. Vogelgesang, *The Long Dark Night of the Soul: The American Intellectual Left and the Vietnam War*, New York, Harper and Row, 1974, p. 14.

3 B-H. Lévy, *Éloge des Intellectuels*, Paris, Grasset, 1987, p. 48. This, and all subsequent translations, are by DLS.

4 For example, in Bruce Robbins (ed.), *Intellectuals: Aesthetics, Politics, Academics*, Minneapolis, University of Minesota Press, 1990.

5 Published in Paris by Olivier Orban, this fatuous work is in dialogue form and, in this reader's considered judgement, should have embarrassed the participants, even if it did provide them with considerable financial reward.

6 Quoted in Richard Bernstein, 'Those "new" savants: passé or past their prime', *New York Times*, 2 April 1987, p. A4.

7 Lévy, *Éloge*, op. cit., pp. 9–10, 12.

8 The first citation is from Flaubert's *Correspondance*, Vol. II, Jean Brumeau (ed.), Paris, Gallimard, 1980, p. 77; the second from the *Oxford English Dictionary*, 2nd edition, Vol. 8, p. 153.

9   Lévy, *Éloge*, pp. 10–11.

10 *The Spectrum of Political Engagement*, Princeton, Princeton University Press, 1979, p. 116.

11 For anglophone readers, by far the best examination of the French scene, up to date through 1991, is the volume edited by Jeremy Jennings, *Intellectuals in Twentieth-Century France*, Basingstoke, Macmillan, 1993. All the essays are useful and supply a cross-section of French intellectuals' opinions about their own species. Jennings' elegant and judicious introductory essay is especially valuable. See also: G. Ross, 'Where have all the Sartres gone? The French intelligentsia born again', in G. Ross and J. F. Hollifield (eds), *Searching for the New France*, New York and London, Routledge, 1991, pp. 221–49; M. Wievorka, 'French intellectuals: end of an era?', *Dissent*, Spring 1994, pp. 248–52. For the United States, Jacoby's *The Last Intellectuals*, New York, Basic Books, 1987, is a very important work, which generated a lot of discussion and debate, and is certainly the place to turn for a consideration of the intellectual scene in America as it stood in the mid-1980s, and quite probably still stands in 1996. A work which frequently takes issue with Jacoby is B. Robbins (ed.), *Intellectuals: Aesthetics, Politics, Academics*, cited in Note 4 above. Daniel Bell, the inventor of the extraordinarily influential concept of the 'End of Ideology', whom one would have expected to be extremely optimistic about so many intellectual developments in the West, since they appear to follow most accurately his predictions, has in fact written a remarkably intriguing nostalgic piece, 'Into the 21st century, bleakly', *New York Times*, 26 July 1992, p. E.17. A more hopeful perspective is offered by Janny Scott in 'Thinking out loud: the public intellectual is reborn', *New York Times*, 9 August 1994, pp. B1–B4. Finally, see the fascinating article by Robert Boynton, who argues quite convincingly, using Russell Jacoby as his starting point, that public intellectuals have resurfaced in American society, and that they are black: 'The New Intellectuals', *Atlantic Monthly*, March 1995, pp. 53–70.

12 Along with the great majority of my colleagues, I have shared 'That Noble Dream' of historical objectivity, which Peter Novick has shown in a very important and much debated book to have become somewhat of a nightmare for the historical profession in America, *That Noble Dream: The 'Objectivity Question' and the American Historical Profession*, New York and Cambridge, Cambridge University Press, 1988. Novick's book went into paperback almost immediately and was the subject of many debates and symposia. It would not be an exaggeration to say that *That Noble Dream* was among the most influential works of history published in the United States in the last decade.

13 D. A. N. Jones, 'The monstrous thing', *NYRB*, 17 December 1964, pp. 8–9.

14 R. Neustadt, 'The uses of history in public policy', *Humanities*, 2, No. 5, October 1981, p. 1. Letter from Professor Neustadt to the author, 14 May 1982.

15 Letter from Ambassador Malek to the author, 2 April 1991. For fascinating analyses of Redha Malek's remarkable career, see the articles in *Le Monde* from the time of his appointment as prime minister, and when he was obliged to withdraw his presidential candidacy (24 August 1993 and 18 October 1995, respectively).

16 *Why are We in Vietnam?*, a relatively short work, is one of the best from Mailer's massive oeuvre. The novel deals with bear-hunting in Alaska, and American rituals of masculine bonding and initiation into adulthood through violence. Vietnam appears only in the last lines of the novel, when the reader learns that one of the principal characters is about to be drafted.

17 E. Hardwick, 'We are all murderers', *NYRB*, 23 March 1967, pp. 6–7.

18 G. Steiner, 'Letter to Noam Chomsky', *NYRB*, 23 March 1967, p. 28.

19 Noam Chomsky, 'Letter to George Steiner', *NYRB*, 23 March 1967, p. 28.

20 Paul Clay Sorum, *Intellectuals and Decolonization in France*, Chapel Hill, University of North Carolina Press, 1977, p. 244.

21 P. Ory and J-F. Sirinelli, *Les Intellectuels en France, de l'affaire Dreyfus à nos jours*, Paris, Armand Colin, 1986, pp. 47, 113, 189, 223, 242. Ory has turned away from the subject of intellectuals and has been publishing extensively on the history of culture. Sirinelli has gone on to worry the question of the apparent disappearance of engagement and the intellectual class in several later publications which will be reviewed here.

22 Ibid., pp. 237–8.

23 J-F. Sirinelli, *Intellectuels et passions françaises: manifestes et pétitions au XXe siècle*, Paris, Fayard, 1990, p. 245.

24 Ibid., p. 330.

25 Ibid., p. 335.

26 Ory and Sirinelli, *Les Intellectuels en France*, 2nd edition, Paris, Armand Colin, 1992, p. 233.

27 Ibid., p. 241.

28 J-F. Sirinelli, *Deux intellectuels dans le siècle: Sartre and Aron*, Paris, Fayard, 1995, p. 334.

29 Ibid., p. 356.

30 Ibid., p. 383. Sirinelli uses the English word 'trend' in his text.

31 Ibid., p. 384.

32 Vogelgesang, *The Long Dark Night of the Soul*, op. cit., p. 160.

33 Ory and Sirinelli, op. cit., p. 244.

34 Mary McCarthy and Diana Trilling, 'On withdrawing from Vietnam: an exchange', *NYRB*, 18 January 1968, p. 10. McCarthy goes on to say that the war in Vietnam is a case in point, and the intellectuals' problem now is 'to make others smell it, too'.

Epilogue

14 'What truth? For whom and where?'

Martin Hollis

Edward Said calls this '*the* basic question for intellectuals'[1] and it is an apt one to end with. As we shall see, he commits intellectuals to speaking the truth, while leaving them to wonder how local and relative a truth this means. The editors may have hoped for a concluding taxonomy of intellectuals, distilled from the previous chapters. But I cannot improve on their own broad classification into Priests, Jesters and Agnostics, with each tag marking a style of thought and mode of action which allow large variations. On a stage well set by the section of 'Theoretical Considerations', the other contributors have told their divers tales with too much imagination and scholarship for a neater overview. So, presented with intellectuals in all shapes and sizes, from tame to anomic, from rationalist to romantic, from utopian to dyspeptic, I shall continue where the admirable Introduction leaves off. It concluded with what is, arguably, 'the greatest threat to the intellectual', the unsettling question: 'What are the sources of the intellectual's authority and legitimation?'

The threat was that Enlightenment assumptions about the universal character of truth and reason are by now so uncompelling that they may be unsustainable. I shall address it by first recalling the hopes which inspired the Enlightenment project, and then summoning Edward Said and Michael Walzer as shrewd but ambivalent critics, before concluding that intellectuals betray their calling, unless they stick to Reason though thick and thin.

Enlightenment intellectuals were untroubled by the dilemmas of thought and action which spread unease among their modern or postmodern successors. They were critics of an existing social order to which, at least as intellectuals, they were not beholden. If asked whether they were outsiders looking in or insiders looking out, they could have answered readily that they were of course the latter. They looked out in the name of truth, with the help of science and in the knowledge that a time had come for ideas to change the world. The mood was captured memorably by Condorcet in his *Sketch for a Historical Picture of the Progress of the Human Mind*[2], which set out to show 'how nature has joined together indissolubly the progress of knowledge and that of liberty, virtue and respect for the natural rights of man' (p. 10). The Revolution of 1789 would lead to a time 'when the sun will

shine only on free men who know no other master than their reason' (p.
179). The key lay in the nascent moral and political sciences, once they had
learnt how to design perfect institutions to guide the motives animating our
universal, infinitely perfectible human nature. Perfect institutions would
ensure 'the reconciliation, the identification of the interests of each with the
interests of all', thanks to the endowments provided by Nature, which 'has
linked together in an unbreakable chain truth, happiness and virtue' (p. 192).

In this dawn of good hope, the intellectual's task was plain: to identify
error, prejudice and superstition, to unmask the vested interests which rely
on them to keep people in subjection and to set the moral and political
sciences in train. Where the way was already clear, it was to be taken
forthwith, for instance by insisting on greater equality of wealth, education
and opportunity for all. (Condorcet was an early advocate of equality for
women.) Where it was unclear, the new sciences would presently discern it:
'All errors in politics and morals are based on philosophical errors and these
in turn are connected with scientific errors' (p. 163).

This is the Enlightenment project, as conceived by an intellectual
untroubled by doubt, even though in hiding from the authorities who had
unleashed the Terror. Condorcet retained his faith in the Revolution,
however, and it shines from his book, published in 1795, the year after his
arrest and death in prison. It ends with this moving peroration:

> How consoling for the philosopher who laments the errors, the crimes
> and the injustices which still pollute the earth and of which he is often the
> victim is this view of the human race, emancipated from its shackles,
> released from the empire of fate and from that of enemies of its progress,
> advancing with a firm and sure step along the path of truth, virtue and
> happiness.
>
> (p. 204)

How consoling, too, is this view of truth, virtue and happiness, connected
without qualms about the incommensurability of human values or the
contestability of political concepts. Two centuries later, however, Condorcet's
certainties are all in doubt. Enlightenment thinkers issued a licence to
modern states to centralize power and use it for the improvement of their
citizens. How has it been used? Critics note that powerful regimes speak a
language of reason and progress when they organize death camps, *gulags*
and other such improvements. They note that the licence was soon extended
to improving unenlightened societies throughout the world by imposing the
benefits of colonialism. There is no lack of critics who dispute both the
beneficence and the legitimacy of these exercises in truth, virtue and
happiness. This is not to say that the critics are right. As Condorcet remarks,
progress has powerful enemies. They include false friends as well as evident
foes, among them those who usurp the power of reason for benighted
purposes and high-souled fanatics who claim more truth for social policies
than the new sciences have yet achieved. Enlightenment ideas are certainly

dangerous but the persistence of 'the errors, the crimes and the injustices which still pollute the earth' does not prove that they are radically mistaken.

Yet few of today's intellectuals are apologists for the Enlightenment project. Concerns are not confined to the uses to which the vision has been put. Even liberals are prone to doubts about the very idea of a chain linking truth, virtue and happiness. The *Philosophes* tended to assume that truth was universal and seamless, with knowledge in morals and politics all of a piece with knowledge of how the natural world works. Given the truth about the components of human nature, science would presently identify the virtues which make for individual flourishing and social cooperation, and thus be ready to engineer the happiness which everyone in every society has always sought. By now, however, word has spread that facts and values are not linked in this way. It is now widely held that science has no implications for ethics: how we do live is one question; how we should live is altogether another. Nor may we assume that this latter question has any universal answers. Perhaps we should conclude that, as Pascal remarked drily, what is truth on one side of the Pyrenees is error on the other. That would be so, either if each society's values were true relative to its own conditions or if value-systems were incommensurable.

Even liberals who still trust in reason may have doubts due to their belief in toleration. Condorcet himself urged toleration, for instance, when refusing to endorse colonialism. But this was essentially because too little was yet known about distant societies and peoples to warrant interference. Ignorance has always been a liberal motive for tolerance. As noted, however, wherever the new sciences had shown the path, he was ready to take it. His idea of freedom, being bound up with knowledge and progress, cannot easily accommodate the rights-based idea that people are entitled to choose their own way of life, however mistaken. Nor would he countenance the sort of relativism just trailed as a radical reason for toleration. His Enlightenment liberalism was a fighting creed, whereas today's liberals are prone to hold back because they are pluralists in theory as well as in practice.

Edward Said is thus more of an heir of the Enlightenment than one might have guessed from earlier works like *Orientalism*.[3] In *Representations of the Intellectual* he seeks the sources of intellectual authority and legitimation by mixing liberalism, modern and postmodern, with something more local and culturally based. When in universalist mood, he is definite that intellectuals must take their stand 'on the basis of universal principles' (p. 9) in order to advance human freedom and knowledge (p. 13). But he also insists that there is no system or method broad and certain enough to tell us what truth to pursue (p. 65). So he respects the position of the 'yea-sayers', who commit themselves to the values of their own culture and flourish as insiders without dissonance or dissent. But he himself is more in sympathy with the 'nay-sayers', who are critics of their culture's orthodoxies and are among its outsiders when it comes to privileges, power and honours (p. 39), So his favoured and typical intellectual is something of an insider and more of an outsider. Having roots in a particular society but not fully of it, 'the intellectual always stands between loneliness and alignment' (p. 16).

This ambivalence about standpoint is partly cognitive, in that intellectuals must manage somehow to combine universal principles with local commitments, and yet remain aware that each element bids to undermine the other. But the snag is not simply that, as social critics, they get their leverage by speaking in the name of universal and rational principles which, as professional scholars or specialists, they cannot justify. If it were, then this piece of guidance might suffice:

> For the intellectual the task I believe, is explicitly to universalize the crisis, to give greater human scope to what a particular race or nation suffered, to associate that experience with the sufferings of others.
>
> (p. 33)

The ambivalence also stems from elsewhere in the psyche, however, as becomes plain when he insists that intellectuals are, and need to be, 'amateurs'. In forming their views and speaking their minds, they must range more widely and proclaim bolder conclusions than their professional training can endorse. Professionals are not only too cautious or canny to make themselves heard in the public arena, but also lack an amateur's emotional loyalties and passions.

> But what are these amateur forays into the public sphere really about? Is the intellectual galvanized into intellectual action by primordial, local, instinctive loyalties – one's race, or people, or religion – or is there some more universal and rational set of principles that can, and perhaps do, govern how one speaks and writes? In effect I am asking *the* basic question for the intellectual: how does one speak the truth? What truth? For whom and where?
>
> (p. 65)

The basic tension, then, is that the truth sought relates to universal principles, whereas the impulse to seek it is galvanized by loyalties, like one's race, or people, or religion, which it would be treason to betray. Notice that religion is here classed with the primordial, local and instinctual. Said's liberal Enlightenment side prompts him to hold that 'the true intellectual is a secular being' (p. 89). But secular beings are not granted an Enlightened escape from the claims of instinctive loyalties:

> The fundamental problem is therefore how to reconcile one's identity and the actualities of one's own culture, society and history to the reality of other identities, cultures, peoples.
>
> (p. 69)

By juxtaposing scattered quotations, let me confess, I have made the dilemmas of Said's intellectuals starker than in his text. But he poses them squarely enough and I have merely stressed them to suit the present volume.

The reflective intellectual reaches for universal principles to give social criticism an external leverage, but, touched by postmodern doubts, cannot trust their universality. The galvanized intellectual still needs primordial impulses and local loyalties, whose galvanic power is sapped by reflectiveness, modern and postmodern. In sum, both cognitively and emotionally, intellectuals are so squeezed between loneliness and alignment that one wonders how they can function at all. I am reminded of the centipede in the fable, unable to move again after being asked to reflect and say which leg it put forward first. No such agonies troubled an Enlightenment intellectual like Cordorcet, sure that science reveals the guiding principles of nature, and so of human nature, in a form with moral and political implications. But Said speaks for most today in denying that science can thus illuminate a clear path of truth, virtue and happiness.

Has the light of reason indeed failed? Or can intellectuals do without it? Much turns on whether we can disentangle Said's psychological anxieties from his epistemic doubts. This volume has offered little to challenge his acute psychological portrait of intellectuals caught between loneliness and alignment. For, although some essays depict intellectuals who have squarely opted for alignment, especially in the name of nationalism or religion, there has been no suggestion that alignment solves the epistemic problem of 'What truth? For whom and where?' It may seem that yea-sayers are excused this conundrum. Their task as intellectuals is only to raise awkward questions about how best to articulate their favoured cause and translate it into action. One thinks, for instance, of Jesuits in the Catholic church or of the back-room intelligentsia charged with adapting Marxism–Leninism to China. The yea-sayer's task is to expose inconsistencies and so force revisions, which can result in strategies for action disconcerting to the ordinary members of the flock. But a licence to be awkward does not extend to subverting the assumptions root and branch. It is an internal exercise, whose upshot is a refined set of assumptions and a more astute praxis. Yet these excuses do not really suffice. Can yea-sayers honestly avoid asking one question too many in overhauling their own assumptions and thus be forced to justify saying yea? How mind-sets are protected against ultimate questions is fascinating psychologically (and sociologically). But the psychology of alignment does not touch the lonely intellectual's epistemic difficulty in searching for truth amid uncertainty whether there is one truth or many.

'What truth? For whom and where?' Condorcet would reply briskly that there is only one truth. He would grant that we have yet to fill in its details and that it allows variations, rather as the boiling point of water varies with height above sea level. But, these being systematic variations, as in physics, he would reject the deeper relativism suggested by 'For whom and where?'. None the less, once we are clear that the question of 'What truth?' is indeed about truth and not about how the psychology of belief works, Said is still in good company.

There may, of course, be cogent epistemic reasons for pluralism about truth. Philosophically, the strongest known to me belong with a general pragmatism, which argues that there is no way of describing or judging the world independently of a web of concepts and beliefs about it. That can lead swiftly to claims that distinctions between belief and reality, meaning and reference, truth and falsity, are all finally internal to a cognitive scheme or discourse. In Richard Rorty's version:

> For pragmatists, the desire for objectivity is not the desire to escape the limitations of one's community, but simply the desire for as much intersubjective agreement as possible, the desire to extend the reference of 'we' as far as we can.[4]
>
> For a pragmatist, 'knowledge' is, like 'truth', simply a compliment paid to the beliefs which we think so well justified that, for the moment, no further justification is needed.

(ibid.: 38)

Although plenty of pragmatists would disagree with it, this remark does show that not all theories of knowledge are universalist. But, since this is not the moment for a general plunge into philosophy, I shall now turn to Michael Walzer, who shares more of Said's ambivalence about the *locus standi* of the social critic, while offering a more promising escape from a slide into relativism. Since Richard Bellamy has already discussed *The Company of Critics* and *Interpretation and Social Criticism* in his perceptive opening essay, I shall pursue Walzer's thoughts about immanent criticism in *Thick and Thin: Moral Argument at Home and Abroad*.[5]

The title evokes the running dispute between liberalism ('thin') and communitarianism ('thick') and focuses it on the character of morality. The text opens with a vignette of people marching through the streets of Prague in 1989 with one-word placards proclaiming 'Truth' or 'Justice'. Walzer comments that these are moral concepts with universal appeal: everyone can pile in behind them. But they do this universal service not because they are at the eternal core of universal morality but because they say almost nothing. Terms like 'Truth' and 'Justice' have minimal and maximal meanings. 'Justice', for instance, has a minimal, universal meaning of giving everyone their due. It has this meaning in a feudal society or caste system as much as in a meritocracy or commune. But this minimum is too thin to guide action. What matters, therefore, is its local or maximal meaning and that varies from one culture to another. Different cultures, and different subcultures within them, construct their own goods by attaching their own meanings and values to aspects of life. Thus 'distributive justice is relative to social meanings' (p. 26, quoting *Spheres of Justice*, Chapter 1). To demand justice is indeed to join a universal parade but also thereby to voice and reinforce some particular and 'thick' understanding of what it means.

Walzer is here standing traditional moral philosophy on its head. Philosophers like to fancy that moral terms start thin and then thicken locally, as people think them though in their own circumstances. They can thus present the minimal, universal meaning as a core or foundation, with a single correct maximal elaboration by which local variants can be judged. On this view, a caste system simply fails to give everyone their due, whatever its advocates say to the contrary. But the philosophers are radically mistaken, since the universal minimum morality is not free-standing in this way. 'It simply designates some reiterated features of particular thick or maximal moralities' (p. 10). The words on the placards express the thin common element in the many local moralities and thus, epistemically, come not first but last.

The implication beckons that there is no universal standpoint from which to complain about local values and practices: thick trumps thin, both when one asks what can motivate people and when justifications are sought. If so, then not only is cannibalism right for cannibals, but cannibals too can march behind a banner proclaiming the value of human life. Yet this is not quite what Walzer wants to say, since it threatens to leave social critics without a leg to stand on. So he devotes his third chapter, 'Maximalism and the Social Critic', to avoiding having to say it. His line is that thick maximal moralities allow enough scope for internal criticism to bring an oppressive system down. Internal criticism exploits people's need to think well of themselves, and works by confronting them with their own expression of ideals. It exposes 'internal tensions and contradictions', and this is enough. The critic need not try to construct a maximal universal morality, after the manner of the Catholic church or Comintern, not least because no such construct is possible. Admittedly, criticism is often couched in universal terms, as with Amnesty International's campaigns against torture, and is the more effective for that. But this is because it embarrasses rulers to be reminded of their own public pronouncements, not because of a universal truth about the evil of torture. The chapter ends by remarking that 'The work of the critic, when it is maximalist work, is also local and particular in character'.

Walzer's account of social criticism lets us disentangle Said's mix of psychological and epistemic. Although the social critic plays psychologically on people's desire to preserve their self-esteem, there is also an epistemic story to tell about how internal criticism works. It is a 'reiterative activity', which proceeds like the reiterative activity involved in designing buildings (p. 52). Architects improve their designs by taking previous designs as objects of critical reflection and debate. They try to get their next design right, but this is not to say that each new design is a fresh shot at the same ideally and uniquely perfect building. 'Rightness is relative to the architectural occasion: the needs that the building is intended to serve, the materials at hand, the reigning aesthetic idealism (the architectural equivalent of a maximalist morality).' Similarly, critics who aim to get things right aim at a rightness which is relative to their critical occasions, and so objective without being universal.

Does Walzer thus succeed in giving internal criticism leverage without appeal to a universalist standpoint? The answer, I think, is No. To take another Czech example, why exactly could a small band of intellectual dissidents put any pressure on the powerful Czechoslovakian government earlier in the 1980s? As a matter of psychology and politics, the mice in the cat-and-mouse game were helped by the fact that the authorities had given hostages by making idealistic public pronouncements in the name of the liberally-worded Czech constitution. But this bald fact does not explain how a charge of inconsistency works. It stings not just because third parties happen to deplore inconsistency, nor even because the authorities happened to accept that consistency is a virtue. It stings because, objectively speaking, consistency is a universal, if minimal, constraint on any conduct which purports to be moral. Similarly, shame and guilt are not merely instrumental sanctions. They are effective because their logic is universal: both imply that an identified wrong should be repented and remedied not because undoing it will have good consequences (which is not always true) but just because it is a wrong. There are, in short, universal rules of the morality game which no one is free to discard without stepping out of the game altogether. They are, no doubt, more schematic and procedural than substantive. But they stop the authorities saying, 'Ah, but Czech morality does not demand consistency' or 'Czech morality is unconcerned with human rights'; and they do so as a matter of logic rather than of psychology.

Walzer would no doubt comment that this is 'thin' stuff, of no serious value until fleshed out in local and inherently variable ways. But that is because, in my view, he runs together two different sorts of local variation. One is a permissible variation within the universal rules of the game and the other is a proposed interpretation of the rules themselves. Thus, there is dispute of the latter sort between utilitarians and Kantians over whether one could, in theory, liquidate dissidents if doing so would promote the best overall consequences – a dispute about the objective demands of morality itself. This is deeply unlike a dispute about whether to ban, permit or insist upon the ritual slaughter of goats – a matter which different societies may be right to resolve differently.

The difficulty now arises that often it is not obvious which category disputes fall into. Is female circumcision a proper subject of local variation? Does someone executed for blasphemy in a religious society with laws against blasphemy have anything to complain of? Such questions soon put pressure on the very distinction between 'thick' and 'thin'. On the one hand, they make it hard for communitarians to suppose that cultures and traditions are well-defined and self-contained enough to be able to settle moral disputes without external reference. On the other hand, they also make it hard for liberals to fancy that a tenable line can be drawn between procedural and substantive values. There are depths here which I shall not try to plumb. But I do want to insist that the difficulty would simply not exist, if Walzer were right about the relation of minimal to maximal morality. If concepts like Truth and Justice were merely the thin overlap among discrete self-authenticating thick local practices, then games between tyrants and dissidents would be solely power games. The tyrants could simply decree that local values included the wiping out of dissent; and, if successful, would thereby be proved right. Conversely, the fact that what is at stake is their moral authority shows that 'thin' concepts have implications which, once established, supply universal reasons for action and criteria for judging it.

The point may be clearer for Walzer's other placard, 'Truth'. Minimally, it demands only that what authority states to be true shall really be true. It calls for an end to lies and misrepresentations. Perhaps it also objects to carelessness about evidence or to official self-deception. But it is essentially simple. It is not given pause by the thought that often facts are unclear, statistics ambiguous and the effects of policy obscure. Nor does it care about arguments concerning the ultimate character of logic and evidence. Nor does it wait upon philosophical disputes among adherents of the Correspondence, Coherence, Pragmatist and Performative theories of truth. Yet there are deep 'maximalist' disagreements on such matters. They range over the nature of logic, evidence and interpretation. They challenge the very idea of knowledge and rational belief, the possibility of objectivity as standardly conceived. For example, the thesis that all facts involve interpretation is sometimes held to imply that judgements of fact cannot be disentangled from judgements of value.[6] If that were true, and if judgements of value could not be objective, the call to political action in the name of Truth might lose its clarion universality. Indeed, it would lose it, if Walzer were right about the relation of thick to thin. But, short of a radical relativism, thick-seeming concepts of truth are not of merely local validity and do not do merely local work. Rival maximalist ideas compete to offer the uniquely and universally *true* elaboration of truth.

In these terms, the example of architects learning from one another may show that subscribing to Plato's theory of Forms is not compulsory. It certainly shows that the purpose of a building and the needs of the client are relevant and that there are better and worse ways of taking this into account. These complications inject a social perspective. But they do not show that architecture is a wholly local activity or that judgements of merit are subjective, rather than objective. As with arguments about truth, we should not confuse relativities which claim a place in the final objective view with relativism of the virulent sort which would destroy even a local basis for objective argument and learning.

CONCLUSION

I thus agree with Richard Bellamy that Walzer's idea of immanent critique is incoherent. It saws off the crucial branch on which it expects critics to perch. Critique calls for a distance from local practices, which immanence controverts. If Walzer thinks otherwise, it is because he assumes that every viable practice has inbuilt scope for finding discrepancies. This assumption is right in itself, I think; but what it implies is that there are universal constraints on every coherent web of belief and action-guiding scheme of concepts. Indeed, since coherence alone is not enough to settle all questions of truth, meaning and rational action, it implies that every web and scheme have far greater universal resources than relativists care to admit. In short, thin concepts, being implicitly more fertile than Walzer recognizes, give social critics their needed perch.

The critic is thus, in terms of Jeremy Jennings' contrast between Aron and Foucault, at least a *spectateur engagé* rather than a 'specific' intellectual bent on destroying evidence and generalities. In any case, there is something wayward about the latter idea, as can be seen by thinking about collectors. If there is virtue in being a collector, it cannot consist in collecting anything and everything at random. Anyone who did so might be mocking the whole practice of collecting but would have no claim to respect as a 'specific' collector. Irony is parasitic on purpose and loses its virtue once it has destroyed what it ironizes. But a *spectateur engagé* does not thereby escape the original difficulty. Spectators are indeed at a distance, and engaged spectators presumably care about the spectacle. This thought is no advance, however, until we understand how a critical eye for truth can temper the form and purpose of caring. Yet critical spectators still seem too detached to care; and engagement still seems too committed for spectators. The relation of thick and thin remains elusive.

Here we might recall Alan Scott's suggestion that there lies at the heart of Weber a theory of action in which 'ethical' and 'practical' questions cannot be separated, thus entangling *Zweckrationalität* with *Wertrationalität* (despite Weber's seemingly sharp distinction). This strikes me as highly plausible in itself and, although not easily thought through, a suggestive way to end this volume by forcing the issue of 'What truth? For whom and where?'. We are left, I submit, with two possible answers.

One is to accept that ultimately there is nowhere for the intellectual to perch and thus he must return finally to earth. This is Rorty's way, as quoted earlier, when he forgoes the desire to escape the limitations of his community and settles for extending intersubjective agreement as widely as possible. It is also Bauman's way, in declaring that, all disputes being purely local and all truth-claims discredited, we are left only with discourse. The editors, when citing Bauman, commented that this might, of course, be the character of the postmodern world in which we live, and pointed out that, if so, we all lose our power to act. I agree. But this would also leave no way to understand Rorty's desire to extend his own discourse, except as a cosy postmodern form of imperialism. He has remarked that the purpose of conversation is to keep the conversation going. Although mere conversation has some merit when the task is to preserve a fragile peace, intellectuals cannot accept that passing the platitudes is any substitute for seeking a better world. Milton wrote in *Areopagitica*, 'I cannot praise a fugitive and cloistered virtue, unexercised and unbreathed, that never sallies out and seeks her adversary, but slinks out of the race, where that immortal garland is to be run for, not without dust and heat.' That is the intellectual's authentic voice.

The other alternative, then, is to sally out in search of truth. It takes us back to Enlightenment hopes that reason can discern a path of truth, virtue and happiness. Weber sometimes raises these hopes, amid his deep ambivalence about modernity and the spread of its species of rational order. He can be construed without paradox as Alan Scott suggests, if we read him as denying that instrumental rationality, commercial or bureaucratic, is the last word on practical reason. He is hinting at another way of connecting reason and value. Yet can intellectuals still echo Condorcet's belief that Nature has linked truth, virtue and happiness in an unbreakable chain? It may seem too late for that. On the other hand, since they need not suppose it obvious how the links are fashioned, they would at least be able to do as Said bids them: take their stand on the basis of universal principles in order to advance human freedom and knowledge, and so be placed to universalize the crisis and give greater human scope to what a particular race or nation has suffered. I see no other source of a coherent position.

'What truth? For whom and where?' Truth is truth for everyone. Although allowing for human perspectives and diversity, we can only make an Enlightenment reply. Hence the task of intellectuals is still to expose false claims to knowledge and advance true ones. Telling true from false remains a hard task for those who trust in the light of reason; but it is an impossible one for those who do not. Hence the loneliness of intellectuals comes from asking one question too many for comfort in the search for truth. Their consolation, however, is a faith and mutual trust that unwelcome questions have true answers.

NOTES

1 In *Representations of the Intellectual: The 1993 Reith Lectures* London, Vintage, 1994, p. 65.
2 Published in 1795. Quotations are from the translation by June Barraclough for Stuart Hampshire's edition, Westport: Greenwood Press, 1955.
3 New York, Random House, 1978.
4 'Solidarity or objectivity?', in M. Krausz (ed.), *Relativism: Interpretation and Confrontation*, Notre Dame, University of Notre Dame Press, 1989, p. 37. The rest of the article fleshes out his reasons for preferring Solidarity. Although not all pragmatists would agree with him, all would reject Enlightenment ideas of objectivity and of an absolute standpoint from which to discern the truth about reality.
5 Notre Dame, University of Notre Dame Press, 1994.
6 See, for example, Catherine Elgin in 'The relativity of fact and the objectivity of value', in *Relativism: Interpretation and Confrontation*, op. cit., pp. 86–98.

Index

Abbas, F. 92
Addi, L. 101nn11, 12
Adorno, T. 2, 57
Agnon, S. 106, 113
Algeria, E. 12, 72, 80, 87, 91; War in, 272, 273, 274–7
Alterman, N 108, 111, 113
Althusser, L. 73, 82n32, 196–8, 220n7, 221n35
Arendt, H. 77, 252–3, 268nn23, 25
Arnold, M. 2
Aron, R. 12, 75, 77, 90, 279–80, 298
Auden, W.H. 120–3, 126–45

Bahro, R. 219
Baldwin, J. 258
Balibar, E. 80
Barbusse, H. 227, 237
Barzun, J. 264
Baudrillard, J. 17, 78, 81n7
Bauman, Z. 16, 20–1n52, 59, 63n39, 298
Beetham, D. 63n8, 64n45
Begin, M. 114–15
Belhadj, A. 95, 96
Bell, D. 184n11, 255–6, 267n10
Ben-Gurion, D. (David Green) 106, 111, 112, 118n19
Ben-Yehuda, E. 107
Ben-Zvi, Y. 106
Benda, J. 1, 10, 11, 24, 71, 90
Bennett, A. 18
Berlin, I. 66, 77
Berlinguer, E. 185
Bialik, H.N 106, 107–8
Bloch, E. 45
Bobbio, N 15, 23, 27, 38–9
Bonner, E. 152
Boukroh, N 96

Bourdieu, P. 73, 79–80, 83n39, 85nn69, 72, 75, 248, 266n2
Bourne, R. 225, 244n1
Brauman, R. 78, 80
Brenner, J. 106, 107
Brick, H. 256, 269nn38, 47
Brit Shalom Society 109–10
Bromfield, L. 262
Brooks, U.W. 227–8, 239
Brzozowski, S. 5, 8
Buber, M. 109, 112, 118n16
Bukai, R. 117
Bukharin, NI. 171, 219
Burke, K. 238, 246n32
Burke, E. 2, 25, 164
Burns, R. 127
Bush, G. 280–1

Calverton, V.R. 232
Carey, J. 5–6, 19n14, 42n43
Chalasinski, J. 172, 175, 191n18
Charle, C. 70, 73
Chernyshevsky, NG. 151
Chomsky, N 2, 233, 277–8, 281
Cimino, M. 276
Clarté 227, 228, 244n6
Comintern 237
Commentary 249
Condorcet 289–91, 293, 299
Cornford, J. 132, 144n60
Cowley, M. 238
critical theory 50
Croce, B. 27, 35, 38
Crotty, P. 140, 141

Dabrowski, B. 190
Daniel, Y. 151
Daniels, R.V. 152
Davis, T. 122